PLAUSIBLE
DENIAL

Works by Mark Lane

PLAUSIBLE DENIAL

Was the CIA Involved in the Assassination of JFK?

MARK LANE

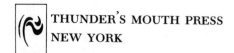

THUNDER'S MOUTH PRESS
NEW YORK

Published by
Thunder's Mouth Press
54 Greene Street, Suite 4S
New York, NY 10013

First paperback edition, 1992

Library of Congress Cataloging in Publication Data

Lane, Mark
    Plausible denial: was the CIA involved in the assassination of JFK /
    by Mark Lane —
        p   cm
    includes bibliographical references and index
    ISBN 1-56025-000-3 (cloth), 1-56025-048-8 (pbk.)
        1. Kennedy, John F. (John Fitzgerald). 1917–1963—Assassination
        2. United States. Central Intelligence Agency.   Title
    F842.9.L296 1991
    973.922'092—dc20   91-30931
                                                                            CIP

Text design by Laura-Ann Robb

Printed in the United States of America

Distributed by
Publishers Group West
4065 Hollis Street
Emeryville, CA 94608
(800) 788-3123

To Patricia Erdner Lane

I began this journey before I met you but together we have resolved to stay the course, whatever the consequences, until the truth about the death of the president is available to all who wish to hear it.

Without your love, patience, friendship, research, editorial suggestions, even criticism, to say nothing of your typing, this work could not have been accomplished.

Together we have cried tears of frustration, and celebrated moments of joy as well, as we wrote these pages. That is as it should be. William Hazlitt perhaps said it best:

"Man is the only animal that laughs and weeps; for he is the only animal that is struck by the differences between what things are and what they ought to be."

—M.L.

In Gratitude

I have not been alone during the past twenty-eight years as I kept the watch. Many people, then strangers to me, some of them now treasured friends, as well as old allies, have provided help, advice, encouragement, support, and evidence.

In this, my last work about the death of the president, I salute you.

Thank you Donald Freed, Dick Gregory, Ann Lane, Bertrand Russell, Lawrence and Pat Lane, Linus Pauling, Arnold Toynbee, Richard Sprague, Hugh Trevor-Roper, Arthur P. Cohen, Ted Gandolfo, Fletcher Prouty, Emile de Antonio, Paul McCartney, Steve Jaffe, Norman Mailer, Graham Hodges, Robert Tannenbaum, Shirley Martin, Cyril Wecht, Penn Jones, Dorothy Kilgallen, Willis Carto, Florence Kennedy, Jim Garrison, Jean Hill.

I especially recognize those persons who served in the United States Congress and there fulfilled their constitutional contribution in reference to this matter. I acknowledge the contribution to this effort: Richard Schweicker, Don Edwards, Henry B. Gonzales, Andrew Young, Bella Abzug, Richardson Preyer, Christopher Dodd, Herman Badillo, Mervyn Dymally, and Mario Biaggi.

Members of the Fourth Estate who served their principles over the years regarding the death of their president comprise a relatively short list, led by Peter Kihss of the *New York Times*, Richard Dudman of the *St. Louis Post Dispatch*, Joseph Trento of the *Wilmington News Journal* and Penn Jones of the *Midlothian Mirror*.

Thank you George O'Toole, John Stockwell, "Paul," Phillip Agee, and Victor Marchetti, all former CIA officers; Arthur Murtagh, William Turner, and Wes S.—all former Special Agents of the FBI and those still active officers of the CIA and FBI who, understandably, have requested that my public recognition of their continuing efforts to serve their nation be postponed.

When all others said no, for reasons I fear unrelated to philosophical contribution or potential profit, Neil Ortenberg and his Thunder's Mouth Press said yes. We are now together in Shakespeare's "thunder's mouth" and will see if our passion shakes the world as he promised.

CONTENTS

CHRONOLOGY

1947	The Central Intelligence Agency (CIA) established by President Truman.
Nov. 1960	John F. Kennedy elected president.
April 1961	The Bay of Pigs invasion of Cuba fails.
1962–63	Angered by CIA incompetence during the Bay of Pigs, JFK establishes several measures limiting the power of the agency.
Sept. 26–Oct. 3, 1963	Lee Harvey Oswald allegedly visits the Cuban and Soviet Embassies in Mexico City.
September	Kennedy asks William Attwood, the American ambassador to Guinea, to investigate the possibility of negotiations with Cuba.
October 2	JFK signs NSAM 263, an order for the immediate withdrawal of 1,000 U.S. "military advisers" from Vietnam. The document also includes a timetable for the withdrawal of all U.S. personnel, including CIA operatives.
November 20	French journalist Jean Daniel, a friend of Attwood acting as Kennedy's unofficial emissary, interviews Fidel Castro in Havana. Daniel tells Castro of Kennedy's willingness to pursue detente.
November 22	JFK assassinated in Dallas. Texas governor John Connally is injured; Dallas police officer J.D. Tippit also killed.
November 24	Oswald, while still in police custody, is shot by Jack Ruby.
November 29	Johnson establishes the President's Commission on the Assassination of President Kennedy, chaired by Chief Justice Earl Warren.
Sept. 27, 1964	Warren Commission releases its report. It ruled out conspiracy, and concluded that Oswald acted alone.
1966	Freedom of Information Act implemented.
Aug. 1966	*Rush to Judgment* published.
1972	Watergate break-in. The ensuing scandal will eventually lead to President Nixon's resignation in August 1974.
1973	Lyndon Johnson admits in an interview that he "never believed that Oswald acted alone."
1974	In response to the growing Watergate scandal, the Freedom of Information Act is amended to provide citizens easier access to government documents while protecting individuals' constitutional right to privacy.

June 1975	Rockefeller Commission, with future President Reagan as a member, uncovers evidence of illegal CIA operations in the U.S.
August 1978	Former CIA operative Victor Marchetti's article "CIA to Admit Hunt Involvement in Kennedy Slaying" appears in Liberty Lobby newspaper the *Spotlight*.
1979	The House Select Committee on Assassinations concludes that there were probably two gunmen who fired at Kennedy. They also stated that conspiracy was "likely."
December 1981	First *Hunt v. Liberty Lobby* trial. Hunt is awarded $650,000 in damages.
January 1985	Second *Hunt v. Liberty Lobby* trial. On February 6, the jury finds Liberty Lobby not guilty of libel.
July–August 1988	The *Nation* publishes two articles charging that George Bush's involvement with the CIA goes back to 1960–61 despite Bush's insistence that he was not involved with the agency before he was appointed its Director in 1976.
September 1991	Clair George, former head of CIA covert operations, is indicted on ten counts of obstructing Federal investigations into the Iran-Contra scandal. Elaine Sciolino, in an article for the *New York Times*, calls George's indictment "the sharpest challenge yet to the culture of the agency . . . a culture of secrecy that for decades has successfully resisted the efforts of Congress and the executive branch to penetrate and change it."

CIA CAST OF CHARACTERS

Allen Dulles: Deputy Director for Plans (1950–51); Deputy Director of Central Intelligence (1951–53); Director of Central Intelligence (1953–61). Member of the Warren Commission (1963–64).

John McCone: Director of Central Intelligence (1961–65).

Richard Helms: Served with OSS (1943–46); CIA, Deputy Director for Plans (1962–65); Deputy Director of Central Intelligence (1965–66); Director (1966–73). Convicted of making false statements to a committee of the U.S. Senate.

William Colby: Served with OSS (1943–45); CIA, Chief of the Far East Division (1962–67); Deputy Director for Operations (1973); Director (1973–76).

Stansfield Turner: Admiral, U.S. Navy (retired 1978); Director of Central Intelligence (1977–81).

James Jesus Angleton: Served with OSS and CIA. Founded the counterintelligence branch of the agency in 1953, and served as counterintelligence chief until 1974 when he was forced from the agency by William Colby.

E. Howard Hunt: CIA operative, Watergate conspirator, and author of spy novels. Fired from the Bay of Pigs operation for refusing to obey orders, he claims to have been in Washington on November 22, 1963. Became key member of Nixon's White House staff after leaving the CIA in 1970.

G. Gordon Liddy: FBI bureau supervisor in the early 1960s. Served as Nixon's Special Assistant to the Secretary of Treasury for Organized Crime and general counsel to the Committee to Re-elect the President (CREEP). Worked with Hunt on several projects for the Nixon White House, including the Watergate break-in.

Victor Marchetti: CIA operative and special assistant to Richard Helms in the late 1960s; co-author, with John D. Marks, of the controversial book *The CIA and the Cult of Intelligence.*

David Atlee Phillips: CIA operative in Havana (1958–61), he blamed Kennedy for the failure of the Bay of Pigs. Very active in Chile, Guatemala, and the Dominican Republic during the 1960s, he eventually became the CIA's head of the Western Hemisphere. Left the agency in 1975 to establish the Association of Former Intelligence Officers.

Frank Sturgis: CIA contract agent working with anti-Castro Cubans in Miami at the time of the assassination. Recruited Marita Lorenz, Castro's ex-lover and mother of his daughter, into the agency with the intention of assassinating the Cuban leader.

Ray Cline: Deputy Director for Intelligence (1962–66). Left CIA in 1969 to become Director of State Department Intelligence.

Newton Scott Miler: One of the founders of the CIA, former head of counter-intelligence.

William Corson: former Marine Corps colonel, with extensive ties to the CIA. Apparently leaked an internal CIA memo, signed by Helms and Angleton, placing Hunt in Dallas on the day of the assassination.

Preface

THE PUBLICATION OF THIS BOOK IN ITS ORIGINAL HARDCOVER edition during November 1991 was followed by the release of the Oliver Stone film *JFK*. Together the two works placed the question of the death of President Kennedy once again on the agenda for the United States and for much of the rest of the world. While *JFK* waffled and averted on the question as to who was complicit in the death (more as the result of pragmatic concerns since Mr. Stone's sponsors were reluctant to place too fine a point upon the evidence, and less as a service to historical fact) *Plausible Denial* presented the facts, the unanswered testimony of relevant witnesses, and the unchallenged documents not previously available, and offered the conclusion that the Central Intelligence Agency had murdered John F. Kennedy.

Thus the winds of change began to stir; before long they would reach tornado velocity with television and radio documentaries and docu-dramas, radio and television non-stop interview programs, more films, additional books, press conferences, and a vast array of news articles comprising new theories and old evidence all set forth in newspapers, magazines, and Sunday supplements. The most barren landscape resembled a littered beach through which a hurricane had passed.

Many nuts had indeed been shaken loose by the storm.

Robert M. Gates himself, director of the Central Intelligence Agency, found his voice; David Belin, a Warren Commission apologist for most of his adult life, continued to whine; and George Lardner, Jr.,the "intelligence writer" for the *Washington Post*, commenced to wince.

Those who had obfuscated the truth for so long were at last on the defensive and constrained to defend their suspect behavior. Issue was joined and the nation would never be the same again, for John Milton was, of course, correct:

> And though all the Winds of Doctrine were let loose to play upon the Earth, so Truth be in the Field, we do injuriously by licensing and prohibiting to mis-doubt her Strength. Let her and Falsehood grapple; who ever knew Truth put to the Worse, in a free and open Encounter?
>
> *Areopagitica*

It is not surprising that there were some agents of the past who still clung to the discredited belief that if the subject was not mentioned it might go away. Both the daily *New York Times* and the Sunday *New York Times Book Review* refuse to review *Plausible Denial*. Yet for more than a quarter of a year *Plausible Denial* appeared on the *New York Times* best-seller list as more Americans bought and read it than did their predecessors a quarter of a century before when *Rush to Judgment* became the nation's number one best-selling book.[1]

It was appropriate for Mr. Gates to speak at last. His predecessor, Allen Dulles, the former director of the CIA who had been fired by President Kennedy for having deceived him so egregiously about the Bay of Pigs and other unnatural disasters, was then appointed by President Kennedy's successor, Lyndon Johnson, to the President's Commission to tell us all the truth about the death of the president. Although it was popularly known as the Warren Commission, the record now reveals the inordinate power wielded by Mr. Dulles in shaping the commission's report, in influencing its conduct, in determining what evidence it might see, and in fashioning its political conclusions. In a real sense, it was indeed the Dulles Commission Report or the CIA's version of history.

It was fit on that account that Mr. Gates be heard; it was disconcerting but not alarming to observe him as he dissembled.

As spring came into America during 1992, almost three decades after the assassination, Mr. Gates said he would release every CIA document bearing upon the matter. Before the month of April had run its course, the press reported that the "Justice Dept. reneges on opening JFK files," by "reversing what Congress thought was a firm promise of support" to "open sealed files on the JFK assassination.[2]

Instead the administration, the FBI, and the Department of Justice suggested that the American people should remain patient and that the files would be made available to them some time during the year 2029.

Lee Hamilton, former chairman of the House of Representatives Intelligence Committee and a member of the House Foreign Affairs Committee, had released some previously concealed data on his own

---

[1] In fact, my perceptive publisher, inspired, or at least encouraged, by the success of *Plausible Denial*, brought out a quality paperback edition of *Rush to Judgment* earlier this year for which I wrote a new essay entitled "Lastword."

[2] USA *Today*, April 29, 1992, p. 1.

in an article which he published in the *Washington Post*.[3] He condemned "excessive government secrecy," stating that it undermines national security, decreases accountability, permits the administration to manipulate the news by withholding relevant information, and because the system established to repress the facts is financially costly. While we heard the same sound arguments made in the past, this time Mr. Hamilton disclosed the cost. "Excessive government secrecy," he said, "[costs] $14 billion per year to meet government requirements for the handling of classified material."

A nation unable to feed its hungry, provide lodging for its growing army of homeless, and unwilling to make available an adequate education for its children because to do so would be expensive, could find $14 billion each year to hide its history and keep its people in ignorance regarding the facts of their heritage.

Outraged by the publication of the evidence presented in this book demonstrating CIA complicity in the assassination of the president, yet committed to the principle that he would not, could not, release the CIA files on the subject, Mr. Gates was in a quandary. On May 13, 1992, George Lardner, Jr., writing for the *Washington Post*, reported:

> CIA Director Robert M. Gates expressed determination yesterday to release "every relevant scrap of paper in the CIA's possession" about the assassination of President John F. Kennedy to dispel the notion that the intelligence agency or other elements of the government were involved in the murder.
>
> Gates made the pledge in an emotional postscript to the testimony before a Senate committee on a bill that could require disclosure of as many as a million pages of still secret records relevant to the 1963 assassination.
>
> The Justice Department has warned that it probably would recommend a veto of the measure if Congress passes it in its current form, but Gates said that "because of high interest in the JFK papers, I am not waiting for legislation."
>
> The CIA director promised a first installment this week. He said he has ordered declassification of all CIA files on Lee Harvey Oswald that were compiled before the assassination and said they will be made public at the National Archives "with quite minimal deletions" in a day or two.

---

[3] *Washington Post*, April 13, 1992.

The defenders of the CIA, led by David Belin, who had assisted Arlen Specter in organizing evidence for the Warren Commission, and G. Robert Blakey, who had declined to subpoena any documents from the CIA or the FBI when he was appointed General Counsel of the House Select Committee on Assassinations, found themselves in conflict with one of their own—the ubiquitious Mr. Lardner. It had been an article of faith for the apologists for the Warren Commission Report that almost all of the evidence had been previously released and that they had personally, so they assured us over and over, seen and studied the few documents not generally available. Gates, attempting simultaneously to clear the air and the CIA, instead muddied the waters. Before his testimony had been concluded it became clear that almost three hundred thousand pages of documents in the files of the CIA had never been released and 499,431 pages of documents had never been released by the FBI. Indeed, more than a quarter of a million of the FBI's documents had never even been processed since the death of the president. Belin and Blakey had not even asked to see the evidence, their repeated public statements to the contrary notwithstanding.

The months have passed. Mr. Gates has not made good his pledge to release the basic material hidden in his files. He did, however, make available 34 documents which he stated comprised the entire CIA file on Lee Harvey Oswald compiled prior to November 22, 1963. Four of the "Top Secret" documents released for the first time after 30 years were clippings from the *Washington Post* and the now-defunct *Washington Evening Star.* One suppressed article was written by Priscilla Johnson,[4] one article was based upon Ms. Johnson's interview of Mr. Oswald, one was illegible, and the fourth was based, at least in part, upon Ms. Johnson's interview.

Many of the pages provided by Mr. Gates are entirely illegible and many others are almost entirely illegible. Others have been subjected to the more routine method of censorship employed by the CIA: names and other data have been redacted.

A few interesting documents did survive. On January 26, 1961, a Department of State "Memorandum of Conversation" reported that Lee Oswald's mother, Marguerite, discussed with the State Department her son's renunciation of his American citizenship at the U.S. Embassy in Moscow. Mrs. Oswald told the government officials that she believed her son might be employed by a U.S. spy agency.

---

[4] References to Ms. Johnson appear in this book on pages 48, 51, 67-71, 312 and 354.

She was told by the government official to "dismiss such an idea."

Yet it is what is missing from the CIA's file that today speaks to us so eloquently across the decades. For the CIA file silently discloses the intelligence legend that the CIA had created for Oswald.

According to the documented CIA account, the first notice that a person named Lee Harvey Oswald existed reached the CIA on October 31, 1959, when a telegram from the U.S. Embassy in Moscow, dispatched at 7:59 A.M., was delivered to the agency. It stated that Oswald had appeared at the embassy that day to renounce his American citizenship and to announce that he had applied "for Soviet citizenship." The telegram stated that Oswald, a former member of the Marine Corps, said that he had already "offered Soviets any information he has acquired as enlisted radar operator."

The second document in the file is a *Washington Post* article which quoted remarks Oswald allegedly made to Ms. Johnson "in his room at Moscow's Metropole Hotel."

A Foreign Service Dispatch, prepared by the State Department on November 2, 1959, was also sent to the CIA. It asserted in pertinent part:

> Oswald offered the information that he had been a radar operator in the Marine Corps and that he had voluntarily stated to unnamed Soviet officials that as a Soviet citizen he would make known to them such information concerning the Marine Corps and his specialty as he possessed. He intimated that he might know something of special interest.

If the file can be credited the CIA expressed no interest in Oswald and his activities during the next two years. It was at this time that the CIA was regularly engaged in illegal actions in violation of its charter with no regard for its geographic jurisdictional limitations. It established houses of prostitution in the United States, spied on American citizens in this country, surreptitiously poisoned its own employees with LSD and other illegal substances, in addition to establishing the Phoenix program in Vietnam responsible for the selective assassination of many thousands of Vietnamese.

Yet the CIA, its files now tell us, learned in the fall of 1959 from the State Department that Oswald planned to share military secrets with the Soviet Union and the agency expressed no interest in the matter and did not even consider a response. It seems likely that the now-public files are less than complete. Oswald was on a mission in the Soviet Union on behalf of the CIA. His mother was correct and no suggestion by the CIA to the American people that we dismiss any such idea need be heeded in the face of the evidence. No file on Oswald was opened by the CIA when it was informed that he was contemplating an act of treason simply because he was playing the role the agency had assigned to him.

Less than two years later, his task was accomplished, Oswald was directed to return to the United States. However, the KGB had learned that Oswald was an employee of the CIA.[5]

Oswald had by then married a Russian citizen and he and his wife were being subjected to close scrutiny by the KGB. The Russians, confused by the events, were reluctant to grant the Oswalds' request for exit visas. The documents recently released by the CIA disclose that Lee Oswald then made several attempts to enlist the United States government in his effort to come in out of the Russian cold. On July 15, 1961, he wrote to the U.S. Embassy in Moscow about his effort to secure a visa, stating that "as per instructions I am writing to inform you of the process and progress of our visas." That one sentence, given the circumstances, tends to place in doubt the CIA portrayal of Oswald, publicly proclaimed after his death as a loner, an anarchist, a man who hated the U.S. government, who betrayed its secrets, and a man constitutionally unable to be part of a conspiracy due to his psychological makeup. Indeed, as Oswald wrote to his CIA control at the embassy in Moscow, he was following their instructions. He wrote again to the embassy on August 8, 1961, asking for funds from the U.S. government to cover the expenses he would incur in traveling to the United States. On October 4, 1961, Oswald wrote to the embassy demanding that the U.S. government intervene with the Soviets to secure his visa. Cryptically he reminded his contacts that it was "in the interest of the United States government and the American Embassy in Moscow" to arrange for his immediate repatriation. Pretty cheeky for a young man who had renounced his American citizenship, condemned the United States in harsh terms, and publically asserted his intentions of providing military secrets to his nation's presumed enemy. Remarkable behavior unless he knew, and he knew that the recipients of his messages knew, that all that had gone before was an elaborate charade.

---

[5] Yuri Nosenko, a former KGB officer, later defected to the United States and tried to inform the Warren Commission that Oswald had been a U.S. spy. See pp. 154 and 311-16.

As the CIA file discloses, the charade continued in New Orleans with Oswald's participation and then without his presence, or even his knowledge, in Mexico City.

There is an additional document in the CIA chronological file before reference to the New Orleans episodes. It is a copy of a letter from Oswald to the United States Marine Corps. Oswald had just been informed that his honorable discharge had been altered to an undesirable discharge because he had attempted to renounce his citizenship and disclose military secrets to the Russians. In the letter, dated March 22, 1962, written from Minsk, Oswald asserts confidently that he will have returned to the United States by the time the letter is received and he demands that the decision to alter the nature of his discharge be reconsidered. He asserts that "I have never taken steps to renounce my U.S. citizenship." He had never really stated that he would provide secrets to the enemy, the newspaper stories did not tell the entire story, and, above all, those who knew the whole story know that there are no "charges or complaints against me whatsoever." He stated that the real story is known to "United States Embassy, Moscow, or the U.S. Department of State, Washington, D.C.," and he urged that the Marine Corps contact officials there "for verification of this fact"— that he never *genuinely* sought to renounce his citizenship or harm the interests of his nation.

The CIA file reveals that Oswald (who had been sent to New Orleans to develop an activist-left background and to claim that he was a Marxist), became a participant in a Fair Play for Cuba Committee action, was arrested while distributing leaflets for that organization, and from his jail cell requested that he meet with special agents of the FBI to explain the circumstances. The FBI report setting forth those facts was prepared on October 25, 1963, by Special Agent Warren C. DeBrueys of the New Orleans FBI office. Although the FBI report was written less than one month before the assassination, it described events that took place on August 9, 1963, when Oswald distributed the leaflets, was arrested, and summoned an FBI agent. A few days later Oswald appeared on a local New Orleans radio program to proclaim that he was a Marxist. The FBI report, now part of the CIA file, reveals that a diligent investigation conducted by the FBI could locate no one who had any knowledge that Oswald had contact with the Fair Play for Cuba Committee, other than his lone and highly publicized act of distributing leaflets for a few minutes one afternoon. According to the FBI report, the literature Oswald gave out was little more than an invitation to write to a Post Office box to secure information. The FBI reported the Post Office box "was determined to be non-existent." What then was Oswald's mission? Clearly his actions could not advance the program of the Fair Play for Cuba Committee.

The CIA was creating a domestic legend for Oswald to complement the international legend already in place. With his crude and false invitation, signed by a local Fair Play for Cuba Committee which did not even exist with reference to a non-existent Post Office box, Oswald became a publicly known activist, Marxist, and troublemaker warranting arrest. His call for the FBI was calculated to subsequently immobilize the bureau and dampen its enthusiasm for full revelation after the events of November 22, 1963.

The documents in the CIA file regarding Mexico City provide further confirmation for the evidence and conclusion in "Book II: Mexico City," published in this work.

A CIA document dated October 9, 1963, and redacted by the agency before its release, falsely asserts that Oswald entered the Soviet Embassy on September 28, 1963. Another "classified message" marked "Secret," dated October 10, 1963, provides information about the background of the man who contacted "SOVEMB," the Soviet Embassy in Mexico City, and added that CIA headquarters knew that Oswald had been given approval by the U.S. government to return to the United States. Another secret message bearing the same date again identified Oswald as the man who had visited the Soviet Embassy.

Six days later the CIA notified the U.S. Ambassador to Mexico that Oswald had visited the Soviet Embassy. On October 24, 1963, the CIA requested that the Department of the Navy send recent photographs of Oswald to the CIA so that they can be forwarded "to our representative in Mexico."

Thus we see in the CIA file the creation of a myth regarding who Lee Harvey Oswald was and what he did in the Soviet Union, Louisiana, and Mexico. The readers of this book will learn that Oswald had never visited the Soviet and Cuban embassies in Mexico City as the CIA was later to insist. The CIA file which discloses the early efforts to falsify the record is remarkable in one other respect as well. What has been identified by Gates as the entire Oswald file prior to November 22, 1963, does not even assert, as the CIA was later to state so unequivocally, that Oswald had been to the Cuban Embassy in Mexico City.

Thus the release of 110 pages, while a million additional pages remain shrouded in secrecy, raises many more questions than it answers, provides further confirmation regarding the complicity of the CIA in the assassination, and constrains reasonable people to wonder what remains hidden from our view, if these few pages were considered by Gates to be benign from his agency's perspective.

Yet for some, further revelations, a jury's verdict, the presentation of evidence with convincing clarity, will not, cannot, alter the conclusions to which they are wedded for life.

Arlen Specter and David Belin, two young assistant lawyers on the staff of the Warren Commission during 1964, had together invented the Magic Bullet Theory, a thoroughly discredited concept,[6] in an effort to shore up the crumbling theory that Oswald had alone fired all of the shots that day in Dallas.

They apparently share also the fear of genuine debate, likely because they understand that their innovative approach to law and evidence cannot prevail when subjected to scrutiny. When Senator Specter, the man who had utilized his manipulation of the facts regarding the death of the president as the foundation for a political career, was asked, during the most recent election campaign, why he refused to debate with me, he responded that he had previously debated the issues with me. That statement was false; Mr. Specter has fled from his city and state with the alacrity of a vampire confronted by a silver cross each time I approached his jurisdiction with an offer to publicly discuss the facts. He never debated the issues. It apparently was more politically convenient for him to make an untrue statement than to explain his irresponsible behavior.

David Belin, on the other hand, has pursued the spotlight on this question. He has demanded the right to debate—Oliver Stone. He has insisted that he has the right to appear on major network television programs, and he has continually whined when his demands have been, on occasion, rejected, giving evidence that he suffers from the spurned-starlet syndrome. When invited to appear, Mr. Belin often devotes much of his time and limited energy to complaining, on air, that he has not been given enough time to speak.

Aware of these circumstances, representatives of various colleges and universities asked Belin to debate with me. I accepted the invitations; invariably Belin declined.

The representatives of Louisiana Tech University in Ruston, Louisiana, were persistent. They invited Belin, Jack Anderson, the

---

[6] See *Rush to Judgment*, pp. 69-80.

columnist, and me to appear. Belin and Anderson declined. They reminded Belin that he had repeatedly complained that he had not been given enough time for his presentation and offered to impose no time limitations. Still he refused.

Finally Belin hit upon the only formula for a debate acceptable to him and to Anderson. I was not to be present at all while Belin spoke. I addressed the group first, then Belin (who had been monitoring my remarks in the audience) was given an unlimited period of time to speak. That evening a forum took place in which Belin and Anderson participated.

When I finished speaking I left—not just the university, but the city. I remained out of the city during the forum as well.

I accepted the terms of the "debate" that Belin and Anderson considered to be a fair exchange of ideas because I had confidence in the students and I believed that when they heard the arguments, even under such bizarre conditions, they would likely reach appropriate conclusions. On April 7, 1992, immediately after I spoke, I left Ruston and Belin addressed the audience. The students made a videotape recording of his words and were kind enough to send it to me. I think it eloquently explains why Belin feared a more conventional format for discussion.

Belin began by stating that he never wanted to make any money from the assassination. Yet he was paid to serve as a junior lawyer for the Warren Commission, was given a promotion by the Rockefeller Commission, has lectured for fees, and has even written a book and a few articles about the case.

He began by speaking about the death of Dallas police officer J.D. Tippit. He stated that there were "three key witnesses" to the murder. Their names, he assured the audience, "You will never see in any" of my books. He then listed the "three witnesses" as follows: "William Scoggins," "Barbara Davis," "Virginia Davis," and "Cab Calloway."

Cab Calloway was a singer and bandleader who lived in New York City. He was not a witness to the murder of Officer Tippit. Ted Callaway was a witness who assisted in placing Tippit's body in the ambulance. In *Rush to Judgment* references to him are found on pages 192 and 201. Scoggins is referred to on pages 177, 191-93, and 201. Barbara Davis appears twice at pages 198 and 201. Virginia L. Davis is referred to on page 334, and Virginia R. Davis is cited on pages 187, 198, and 201.

Thus we see that it is not just in the area of mathematics that Mr. Belin appears to be deficient.

Belin asserted that "the most important conspiracy witness of all" was postal inspector Harry Holmes. Of him, Belin assured the audience, "You will never see his name in Lane's books." Reference to Holmes, and excerpts from his testimony, appear in *Rush to Judgment* from pages 136 to 141. Belin then said that the observations of "Mr. Brennan were covered up by Mr. Lane." There are very likely more references to Howard L. Brennan in *Rush to Judgment* than to any other witness. Many pages of the book are devoted to Brennan's observations and an analysis of his testimony.

Belin told the students that he was present at the first meeting of the lawyers with Earl Warren and that all Warren said is that "truth is our only goal." In this book we cite the memorandum of that meeting in which Warren actually advised the lawyers as to their responsibility to depart from the truth to save the nation from nuclear war.[7]

Belin stated that all references by critics of the Warren Report to suppressed documents were false. He solemnly assured the audience that "98 percent of the documents have been released."

The recent concession that approximately 1 million pages have not been made available, many of them not even processed, would mandate, were one to credit Belin, the conclusion that the universe of documents regarding the assassination totaled approximately 50 million pages. If Belin, Specter, and Blakey, of see no evil, hear no evil, speak no evil fame, were each to expend just one minute reading each page, and worked at the project for eight hours a day, seven days a week, in approximately thirty years they would be able to get through the material. Those figures are interesting to contemplate as the three men regularly assure the American people at press conferences that they have each read all of the documents and that all of the evidence proves that Oswald was the lone assassin.

Belin concluded his remarks by calling for the suspension of reason and logic. He said that citizens' trust of government is necessary. The students by then knew why Belin, who has devoted most of his professional life to supporting the conclusions of the Warren Commission, fears a free, fair, and open encounter.

Following the publication of *Plausible Denial*, G. Robert Blakey, counsel to the House Select Committee on Assassinations, expressed outrage at the analysis published in this book. Yet it was difficult for him

---

[7] See pp. 51-54.

to explain why the committee, under his direction, declined to sub-poena a single document from either the FBI or CIA.

On February 6, 1992, Blakey asserted that he and Rep. Louis Stokes, the former chairman of the House Select Committee on Assassinations, had decided to ask the KGB if Oswald had been a CIA agent. After all, explained Blakey to the press, "the KGB had a bug in his apartment, a wiretap on his phone at the end of the hall and they debriefed all of his neighbors."[8]

Stokes and Blakey, each afraid to subpoena the CIA to find out if Oswald had worked for the agency when they had the power to do so and to demand all of the relevant documents from the agency, decided, several years later, to ask the KGB. That Blakey and Stokes were too craven to speak truth to power or even seek to compel production of relevant evidence is beyond cavil. That they failed to understand the delicious irony of two Americans, leaders of an important American congressional committee, asking the Russians if an American had worked for an American agency, because they were too cowardly to have subpoenaed the CIA themselves, is almost beyond comprehension.

Of course, as we have seen, the KGB, through the efforts of its defector Nosenko, had already provided the answer. Blakey, however, had already assumed his hear-no-evil stance.

If the success of this book and other serious works on the subject measure the commitment of the American people to secure all of the facts, it seems clear that the people of this nation have a different agenda from the politics of suppression, disinformation, perjury, and subornation of perjury readily embraced by their leaders.

—Mark Lane
Washington, D.C.

---

[8] *New York Post*, February 6, 1992.

INTRODUCTION

IT HAS BEEN CLEARLY EVIDENT FOR YEARS THAT THE AMERICAN PUBLIC, AND THE people of the world, do not believe that Lee Harvey Oswald killed John F. Kennedy, president of the United States of America, on November 22, 1963. Their belief is well founded. The evidence is on their side. It is the side of truth.

Despite this fact, newspapers, television and radio networks, and major magazines (with a few rare exceptions) refuse to publish this truth. Herein lies the enormity of the crime. It is not too difficult to arrange for the murder of a man, even a president, especially when much of his routine and expected protection has been removed. On the other hand, it is unbelievably difficult to create and to maintain a massive cover story that will conceal the facts from the public for the best part of three decades. The magnitude of this cover-up alone reveals the power and scope of the conspiracy that brought about the death of the president—and of so many others in directly related instances.

Mark Lane, author of this book and of the bestseller *Rush to Judgment*, is one of the few who have been able to tear aside this curtain of lies to reveal the hidden elements of the true story. On February 6, 1985, in the U.S. District Court for the Southern District in Florida, as lawyer for the defense in the case *Hunt v. Liberty Lobby*, Lane won a verdict from a jury of our peers that upheld, against a claim of libel, a news story that Howard Hunt, a long-time Office of Strategic Services and CIA employee, was in Dallas on the day the president was shot. The testimony at that trial gave more credibility to the notion that the CIA was involved in the assassination.

Did you read about that verdict in your local newspaper? Did you hear about that verdict on your favorite TV or radio network news program? Of course not. They are not allowed to write that. This book tells that story in a way that will make accounts of the historic "Scopes" trial read like the story of "Little Red Riding Hood."

Others have broken the ice of this cover story with similar results. Leo Janos, a writer and friend of President Lyndon B. Johnson, visited the ex-president at his Texas ranch not long before he died. In an article that appeared in *The Atlantic Monthly*, July, 1973, Janos wrote that LBJ had told him:

a. "that the assassination in Dallas had been part of a conspiracy;
b. "I have never believed that Oswald acted alone . . . ;
c. "we had been operating a Murder Inc. in the Caribbean."

These are statements of great importance, coming as they did from the man who succeeded JFK as president, the man who ordered the appointment of the Warren Commission, and a man who was in the Dallas motorcade only three cars behind Kennedy when he was shot. He heard those bullets passing over his car. He heard them the rest of his life. He knew what he was talking about.

The significance of LBJ's reference to "Murder Inc." has never been clarified properly. He understood the nature of that statement. It is of basic importance to an understanding of JFK's murder and to the significance of this book.

In 1956, I was directed to create an office of Special Operations within the structure of the headquarters of the U.S. Air Force. This office operated under the provisions of the National Security Council directive 5412, March 15, 1954, and its purpose was to provide "Air Force support of the clandestine activities of the CIA." This function had never been formalized before.

This is the same NSC directive that defined "covert operations" as "all activities conducted pursuant to this directive that are so planned and executed that any U.S. government responsibility for them is not evident to unauthorized persons and that if uncovered the U.S. government can plausibly disclaim any responsibility for them."

Having written the Air Force policy for this work, and having set up a world-wide system of selected personnel and communications channels, I was sent around the world by the Director, Central Intelligence, Allen W. Dulles, and accompanied by one of his special assistants. I visited many CIA stations and was introduced to their staffs and Station Chiefs.

We happened to be in Europe and in the Middle East during the Hungarian uprising, and the Suez Crisis of late 1956. This may have been the reason that I was taken, at that auspicious time, to a special "village" in the Mediterranean where a highly select group of stateless "mechanics" lived and received their most unusual training. "Mechanics" in the CIA are hit-men, assassins, and other related specialists. They are absolutely anonymous.

President Johnson knew about these men and about their training when he mentioned "Murder Inc." He used the Mafia term for these assassins to disassociate them from the U.S. government. President Johnson's statement is an important detail. When it is illuminated by developments during this trial in Florida, and is related to Dallas, we realize that he believed that a team of these faceless and stateless "mechanics" had been used to kill President Kennedy, while their sinister role was covered by the more or less obvious presence of others brought there under the care of the CIA to shield them. The former committed the crime. The latter provided the covert story, and have been a part of that story ever since. Many of them were paraded through the Florida trial, but none have been charged with the crime.

As I have written above, the crime of assassination is relatively easy to commit, provided normal presidential protection has been relaxed. This is the second major factor in this crime of the century. I had worked on what is called "Presidential Protection." Selected military personnel are trained for this duty in order that they may augment the limited strength of the Secret Service, when necessary. Among the most glaring oversights of the Kennedy visit to Dallas in 1963 were the small number of Secret Service men on duty there, and the total lack of military "Presidential Protection" units. The president had almost no experienced protection that day.

I called a man who I knew was a member of the 112th Military Intelligence Group in the Fourth Army area at Fort Sam Houston, San Antonio, Texas. I have kept the notes I made during that call and shall quote from them here:

a. The 112th "had records on Lee Harvey Oswald before November, 1963."
b. "They knew Dallas was dangerous."
c. They were prepared to go to Dallas, "when you are trained, you do it."
d. The commander of that unit, Lt. Col. Rudolph M. Reich, had offered his unit's services for the entire Texas trip, but "they were point blank refused." He was "categorically refused by the Secret Service." Hot words were exchanged between the agencies.

These are two absolutely important matters: The LBJ statement about the "Murder Inc." or CIA mechanics, and the failure of adequate presidential protection along the streets of Dallas.

Anyone can get a picture of the high buildings that directly overlooked Dealey Plaza where the president was shot, and can see that at the time Kennedy was shot many windows were open. That is against Secret Service regulations. Had the military units been there, those windows would have been shut, and observers would have made sure they remained shut until the president had passed. There could have been no gunman in a sixth floor window.

These are some of the web of facts that Mark Lane created out of the testimony in that trial in Florida. This is the truth and only the truth will eventually demand the official solution of this crime of the century.

The great unresolved question that remains is, "When will the media of this country and the world be permitted to print the truth about this crime? How long is the public going to be fed the lies of the Warren Commission Report and the propaganda that has been developed since 1963 to make those lies appear to be plausible?

The very fact that the media confronts the truth of the Kennedy murder with a story that is implausible proves that what they are trying to hide has got to be the biggest covert operation of the twentieth century.

—L. Fletcher Prouty
August 1991

L. Fletcher Prouty retired from the Air Force as Chief, and Founder, of the Office of Special Operations with the Office of the Joint Chiefs of Staff, 1962–1963. OSO is the military phrase for "Military support of the clandestine operations of the CIA." Prior to that, he had been the Senior Air Force officer with the OSO with the Office of the Secretary of Defense. This office was in charge of the National Security Agency and was responsible for all contacts, except general intelligence, with the CIA and Department of State. He is the author of The Secret Team, Prentice-Hall, 1973.

PLAUSIBLE
DENIAL

PROLOGUE:
Spy Trials

THIS BOOK EXPLORES THE DEFAMATION CASE BROUGHT BY E. HOWARD HUNT, A former high-ranking Central Intelligence Agency official, against a newspaper, the *Spotlight*, and its publisher, an organization named Liberty Lobby, Inc.

The case was unusual in several respects. The basis for the lawsuit was an article asserting that Hunt may have been implicated in the assassination of President John F. Kennedy. Published fifteen years after the murder of the president, it was written by a former officer of the CIA, Victor Marchetti. The newspaper had not previously published anything casting doubt on the official version, offered by the Warren Commission in 1964, which concluded that one man, Lee Harvey Oswald, acting alone, had been responsible for the assassination. The newspaper had not previously been critical of Hunt, though his misdeeds were legion and sufficiently chronicled in the media for an informed public to be well aware of them.

It was only after Hunt had won a judgment in the amount of $650,000, an award that would have forced Liberty Lobby into bankruptcy, that the organization sought my services. The case was then on appeal; Liberty Lobby's officers were hopeful that the verdict would be reversed and the case remanded for a second trial. Despite the fact that Liberty Lobby had, over the years, espoused political positions vastly different from my own, the organization wanted me to act as counsel because I was an experienced trial lawyer who had devoted a great deal of time during the previous two decades to investigating the death of President Kennedy. I was intrigued by the offer, since it might provide me with an opportunity to secure additional information about the assassination—to take sworn statements from men such as Hunt, G. Gordon Liddy, Richard Helms, David Atlee Phillips, and Stansfield Turner. The words that a woman named Marita Lorenz had spoken to me years before might at last resonate in a courtroom. The nation, I believed, would be served if an impartial jury heard her testimony and was obligated to evaluate it.

Hunt v. Liberty Lobby, a case tried in the United States District Court for the Southern District of Florida, was also unlike most other cases in that it was a spy trial. In such a case, two ineluctable themes, each bearing a history of ritualistic obedience to precedent and practice, war with each other.

A trial is, in its simplest form, a search for the truth. Though rules of procedure so surround the trial that they sometimes seem to obscure the facts, their development has been aimed at one paramount objective—letting the jury consider all the relevant facts. In practice, the concept may be flawed, especially in atypical matters, since no set of rules can anticipate every exigency. The prize, however, remains a fair trial secured through the presentation of the truth.

The intelligence community brings its own set of principles to the spy trial. It seeks to mask its most unlawful acts with benign euphemism or blatant deception. Its innocuous, self-chosen name, "the intelligence community," is but a mild example of this technique. It is actually a conglomerate of police and spy organizations, often in conflict with each other; the laws of the state it purports to serve and the rights of the citizens of that state. It operates, as do all police organizations to varying degrees, from an imperial mind-set, but an imperial mind-set paradoxically imprisoned in a fortress mentality. It reserves the right to violate the law and openly asserts the propriety of lying under oath to preserve secrecy regarding its transgressions.

The Central Intelligence Agency, for example, habitually creates a cover story—a plausible denial—before embarking upon a mission that might exceed its authority. The propensity of the agency for deception is both so chronic and so advanced that it more often than not has hired assassins and other operatives in such a manner that it could later deny responsibility for its actions.

One of those operatives, Frank Sturgis, was arrested and convicted with E. Howard Hunt and others for activities carried out at the Watergate complex in Washington, D.C. In the case of *Hunt v. Liberty Lobby*, the relationship between Hunt and Sturgis, and their relationship to the CIA, were issues of substantial significance.

2

Did Sturgis work for the CIA? One would think that the answer to such a simple question might readily be ascertained, since each of the principals was questioned about that matter under oath.

Sturgis testified on February 3, 1978, in a deposition taken in the case of *Hunt v. Third Press et al.*, that while ostensibly working for Fidel Castro in Cuba, before the success of the revolution in January 1959, "I was recruited by the station, CIA station chief in Santiago de Cuba, to spy for the United States government." Sturgis also testified on that occasion that when he was in Cuba, "I would never sign a contract because if I am going to spy for the CIA, I am going to sign nothing." Sturgis also stated under oath that he was involved with the CIA in attempts to assassinate Fidel Castro and the elected president of Guatemala and to overthrow the governments of Guatemala and Panama. He admitted that he had taken a leadership role in Operation 40, a CIA organized and funded association of former "Cuban officers" engaged in assassination actions.

Sturgis affirmed as well that he "was approached by an agent of the Central Intelligence Agency to do a domestic assassination."

When Richard Helms, the former director of the CIA, testified in the *Hunt v. Liberty Lobby* case, he stated that Sturgis was a CIA contract agent, an employee of the agency.

During the same trial, Sturgis *denied* that he was ever an employee of the CIA, directly contradicting his 1978 deposition. Another witness, Newton Scott Miler, the agency's former chief of counterintelligence operations, testified that "to his knowledge," Sturgis had never worked for the CIA. Miler, who had joined the agency at its inception, also testifed that in all his thirty years there he had never heard of Operation 40, although Sturgis had already identified it as a counterintelligence operation.

The Sturgis-CIA connection may serve as a microcosm of the difficulties inherent in a spy trial. What the trial judge and the Federal Rules of Civil Procedure contemplate, and evidence wrested from witnesses obligated to tell the truth demonstrates, is challenged by witnesses guided less by their own more recent oaths to tell the truth, than by their previous solemn and almost sacred pledge to the CIA to lie. Spy trials may enter a new and bizarre dimension in which documents disappear, new originals are created, and testimony is tailored to the agency's desperate demand for self-preservation.

The two most credible witnesses in the discrete area of Sturgis's involvement with the CIA would appear to be Sturgis himself and Helms. Yet Sturgis is a convicted criminal, a man who planned assassinations

(Castro), who participated in the destruction of duly elected governments of foreign nations (Guatemala and Panama), and who sought to subvert the democratic electoral process in the United States (Watergate).

Helms, among his other accomplishments, was indicted for perjury for having made deliberately false statements to a committee of the United States Senate in an effort to prevent the senators from learning about illegal operations of the CIA. He pleaded guilty to withholding the relevant facts and later, after being sentenced for his crimes, stated that he proudly wore the conviction as a badge of honor.

When these gentlemen seem to emerge as the two most credible witnesses in any area, do we begin to hear the familiar strains of "The Twilight Zone" theme?

Despite the agency's special relationship with the truth, there does remain one reliable constant in a jury trial in the United States. The jury is chosen by both parties after considerable investigation and thoughtful examination. Every juror is evaluated by the opposing sides after being probed for obvious and latent prejudice.

The skill of the lawyers is of some consequence. Yet in the final analysis, the good common sense of the jurors is the one factor that predominates. The CIA has not thus far conjured up a method to interfere with the efficacy of the most democratic moment in American society—the trial by jury.

I have studied the facts surrounding the assassination of President Kennedy for more than two decades. I was the only critic of the Warren Commission's work to appear before that body and offer testimony. My first book on the subject, *Rush to Judgment*, was the first analysis of the report of the Warren Commission. Since the book quickly became a bestseller, it helped reshape opinion about the official version of events. I interviewed witnesses to the assassination and its aftermath whom the Warren Commission had ignored; in some cases, the commission denied that the witnesses existed. Those filmed interviews provided little comfort for holders of the official view when they were subsequently assembled by Emile de Antonio and me in an award-winning documentary film.

I then examined more recently discovered evidence in a book, *A Citizen's Dissent*, and in a fiction film, *Executive Action*, for which Donald Freed and I wrote the original screenplay. Each of those works was supported by extensive documentation. *Rush to Judgment* relied on approximately five thousand footnotes and references to the record.

Yet while the Warren Commission, assisted by the FBI, the CIA, and the Dallas Police Department, had the power to subpoena witnesses and thus to constrain them to respond to questions, my more modest efforts were circumscribed by my volunteer status. No witness was obligated to talk to me and those who did so out of their own volition were at liberty to turn away searching questions with a smile or a growl.

This book represents a milestone regarding the body of available evidence and its importance in understanding the forces behind the assassination in Dallas. For the first time, a suspect in the killing voluntarily entered a courtroom and thus exposed himself to questions that he was required to answer. Even less than truthful answers, when explored, may be revelatory.

Of even greater significance is the fact that the plaintiff, E. Howard Hunt, had been employed for many years by the Central Intelligence Agency. The lawsuit thus made vulnerable to legally mandated examination many of Hunt's associates, coworkers, and coconspirators. Before the trial had concluded, G. Gordon Liddy, Stansfield Turner, Richard Helms, E. Howard Hunt, David Atlee Phillips, James Jesus Angleton, Frank Sturgis, Newton Scott Miler, Victor Marchetti, and perhaps most important of all, Marita Lorenz, would be heard. Each would answer relevant and searching questions; each would provide sworn answers.

Therefore, before the trial ended, we learned a great deal about contemporary American history. We heard direct testimony regarding the assassination of President Kennedy, including the names of participants. This testimony was offered reluctantly and in fear by a person who had been involved in the action and who had traveled with the assassins from Miami to Dallas just before the murder.

There is no legal precedent for *Hunt v. Liberty Lobby*. More than two decades after the murder of John F. Kennedy in Dallas, the case against his killers was finally tried in a civil action suit brought in the federal courthouse in Miami.

BOOK I

Suspension
of
Certainty

I Knock at the Door

I FIRST MET JOHN F. KENNEDY DURING 1959. I WAS HELPING TO ORGANIZE THE NEW York City aspect of his campaign to secure the nomination of the Democratic party for president.

At the time, Tammany Hall, a corrupt, racist group with ties to organized crime, dominated the Democratic party in New York City. Its influence extended, as well, into other parts of New York State.

Together with Eleanor Roosevelt, former Governor Herbert H. Lehman, and others, I was a founder of the Reform Democratic Movement, a group determined to return the Democratic Party to the people of the city that year. The liberals in the movement, primarily 1959-style yuppies from the relatively affluent sections of Manhattan's West Side, did not like Kennedy. He was not then considered a liberal icon, he was no Adlai Stevenson, and in addition, he was Catholic. "Not that religion is an issue for me personally," ran the most prevalent disclaimer floated at wine and cheese soirées. "It's how others will perceive him." Later in the evening, after a few more drinks, talk turned to the extraordinary power exercised by the Vatican.

I confronted and defeated the local standard bearer of Tammany Hall, the incumbent representative to the state legislature from the Tenth Assembly District, in a primary election in 1960. The generous endorsements of Mrs. Roosevelt, Governor Lehman, and Senator Eugene McCarthy, and writers and artists, including Norman Mailer and Jack Newfield, were important. Our registration drive was decisive. The district was comprised of Yorkville and East Harlem. The two neighborhoods shared a portion of Manhattan's Upper East Side, divided by Ninety-sixth Street, the local Mason-Dixon line. To its south lived Germans, Irish, and Jews. To its north, blacks, Puerto Ricans, and a few Italians. The blacks were underregistered; the Puerto Ricans, hardly registered at all, due in part to the oppressive literacy test laws. Persons born in Puerto Rico were citizens of the United States. Their mother tongue was Spanish. When they moved to New York City in a desperate search for employment, they were denied the right to vote unless they could pass a test given in English.

From a sound truck in the streets of East Harlem, in an attempt to invalidate a bad law, I passed out the answers to the literacy tests and encouraged the people to become voters. I invited the United States attorney's office and the news media to witness my ongoing attempt to challenge the law. Many hundreds of people were registered. I was not prosecuted for conspiracy to violate the literacy law. Subsequently, the literacy tests were declared to be oppressive and racist and were abolished.

I promised that if elected, I would serve just one term and then become the campaign manager for the candidate chosen to succeed me by the residents of East Harlem. It was time, I argued, for the minorities who comprised the majority in the district to have their own candidate.

Having won the Democratic nomination for president, John Kennedy was having difficulties of his own as he approached the 1960 general election. His problems, of course, covered a much wider canvas. The liberals could not accept him and the regulars thought he was too rich, too spoiled, too young—in short, too unmanageable. Kennedy asked me to help to coordinate the varying, indeed conflicting, elements of the Democratic party in New York for his campaign.

I met with the Reform Democratic leaders and Robert F. Kennedy in an apartment chosen by him. It was a pleasant, well-appointed, but less than luxurious suite on Park Avenue. It was a private place the Kennedy brothers maintained for liaisons. At the meeting a reformer asked Bobby what approach John Kennedy would take toward the internecine warfare then being waged in the Democratic party in New York were he to be elected president. He pushed up his shirt-sleeves and replied, "I just want my brother to be elected president. I want you all here in New York to help. Once he's elected we don't give a damn if blood runs in the streets of New York." The group gasped almost in unison. The reform leaders shifted uncomfortably in their chairs and loveseats. Soon the meeting was adjourned. Later, when we reconvened without the presence of the future attorney general, the reformers allowed how shocked and outraged they had been. I took another view. A renegade movement in an established party can hardly expect the leader of the party to endorse its local revolution. A statement of neutrality, although delivered in violent images, was all that could have been realistically sought. Bobby might be lacking in tact, courtesy, and manners; his honesty was commendable, however, and the substance of his remarks more than acceptable.

Finally, the liberals, moving toward power—the ultimate magnet in their political world—supported Kennedy, albeit with reluctance and reservations. Our efforts to coordinate the two competing Democratic organizations in the campaign were far less successful. Tammany Hall, led by Carmine De Sapio, John Merli, and Frank Rossetti, was fighting for its life. It was committed to the political elimination of its detractors. Locally, Tammany saw my election as a most serious threat. Though I was the party's official candidate, the Tammany Democrats, or "regular organization," as they called themselves, ended up supporting my Republican opponent in the general election.

Mrs. Roosevelt, on the other hand, said she never had greater confidence in any candidate than she had in me. She toured East Harlem with me in an open convertible. A beer can thrown from a tenement roof narrowly missed her and hit me instead, requiring twenty stitches to close a head wound. Death threats against me resulted in an unprecedented twenty-four-hour-a-day massive police escort, which I had not requested and that interfered with the campaign.

On a lighter note, presidential nominee John Kennedy arranged for a meeting with all the local candidates in a New York City hotel, so that each might be photographed shaking hands with him. The pictures, to be distributed on leaflets, newspapers, mailings, and posters, might prove decisive in close contests. The party's regular organization secured the photographers. Within days the scores of pictures were distributed. I was informed that my photograph with the future president was, unfortunately, the only one that did not work out, due to some technical problem.

A week later, when Bobby called to ask about a rally I was organizing, I mentioned the incident to him. He responded, "Those bastards. That's our campaign they're screwing up. John wants you to be elected." He called back later that evening and asked me to meet him at a private gathering a few nights later. "And bring your own photographer along. Or maybe even two of them." I spent part of the appointed evening with John Kennedy—the third time I was to meet the future president—posed for pictures with him, and discussed the campaign. Those pictures, and Kennedy's kind words, were significant factors in my being elected in

November, the same day that John F. Kennedy became the president-elect of the United States.

Two years later, in 1962, I convened a community-wide conference in East Harlem. At it, Rev. Carlos Rios, a fiery Protestant minister from the neighborhood, was chosen to succeed me. I became his campaign manager; he became the first Puerto Rican ever elected to the state legislature from the Tenth Assembly District.

The next year, on November 22, 1963, John F. Kennedy was murdered in the streets of Dallas, Texas.

The question posed to me more often than all others for the past quarter of a century is why I, alone of all Americans, made the Kennedy affair a matter of such active concern from the outset? I have no facile answer, although I have given considerable thought to the matter. Perhaps the circumstances so conspired as to make the result, if not inevitable, at least predictable.

For more than a decade I had appeared as defense counsel in criminal cases. My clients were, far more often than not, African-American or Puerto Rican, and impoverished. In those cases that were very well publicized, the victim was invariably white. It was clear that the right to a fair trial was diminished in many instances by prejudicial pretrial publicity. The source of the information often was the office of the prosecuting attorney or the police department. To these less than impartial agencies, the defendant was always guilty. The crime was almost without exception of the most grievous and unprecedented sort and evidence of a depraved mind. Usually the comments of the police and the prosecutors would be widely published, and on some occasions they were endorsed on the editorial pages or embellished by inventive reporters for competing publications. One had the impression that the judicial system existed only to determine which punishment should be meted out to culprits already tried and convicted by the police and the press.

I also found that if the victim had been popular or portrayed after the crime in a sympathetic fashion, the punitive capacity of the populace could be more easily aroused. A similar response could be secured by painting the alleged perpetrator in unflattering hues. Red was as bad as it got in the early 1960s.

In the case of Oswald and Kennedy, contrast the victim with his presumed murderer. The vital young president, father of infant children, husband of the fashionable First Lady, the man who had created the Peace Corps and who had turned on the charm, the warmth, and the lights at the White House after eight frigid years of the Ike Age, was dead.

Oswald was a pro-Castro, pro-Russian, anti-American defector to Moscow, an ex-Marine married to a Russian woman whose relative may have been an intelligence officer.

From the moment of Oswald's arrest, the federal police and prosecutors utilized the press to develop the concept of instant guilt. Within hours it became an article of faith to believe that Oswald had been the lone assassin. The more respected the journalist and the institution for which he worked, the more firmly the message was delivered. Thus it was Walter Cronkite for CBS and Anthony Lewis and Harrison Salisbury for the New York Times who led the restrained hysteria demanding that the notion of Oswald's lone guilt be accepted as fact and protected from serious inquiry.

It was a Friday morning in New York. I took the Lexington Avenue subway to lower Manhattan and walked to the Criminal Court Building. I visited a prisoner who was in the Tombs awaiting trial. I argued a motion in one court and rushed to a calendar call in another courtroom to see if we were actually going to trial that day. The judge was of the opinion that we were. Before long the prosecution witnesses began to testify. At one o'clock, the court declared a luncheon recess. One of the advantages of the Criminal Court Building is its proximity to the excellent restaurants that comprise the most visible aspect of Chinatown. Following dim sum and chrysanthemum tea, I began the short walk to the courthouse. I saw people on the street clustered around radios listening grimly and intently to news reports. It reminded me of newsreels originating in European cities when news of an imminent war was being broadcast. I asked what had happened and was told that the president had been shot. I ran to the courthouse and then directly to the press room. A number of reporters were there, as were some lawyers, bailiffs, and clerks. The bulletins shot from the radio into the silent, stricken crowd. One assurance was quickly contradicted by another speculation as the nation struggled to find out what had taken place. A voice from Dallas: "It is thought that a Negro was involved in the assassination attempt." A black courtroom attendant shifted from one foot to the other as he tried to look innocent. The others in the room tried not to stare at him. Jack Roth, the New York Times criminal court reporter and an acquaintance of mine, erupted with impatience. He walked past me and said, "Mark, I'll find out what the fuck's going on."

He returned a few minutes later from a telephone booth. There were tears in his eyes. He spoke to me softly. "He's dead."

The radio reports continued to assert that the president had been injured and was alive.

I suddenly realized that for the first time in my life I was late for an appearance in court. The trial was to have been continued five minutes earlier. I rushed to the courtroom not sure of what I would encounter there, but certain that the trial would not go forth that day. I explained to the judge that the president had been shot and that he had died. He was unmoved. He had heard about it; the case would go forward. "Let's move along with this trial," he said.

I hesitated. "Call your next witness, Mr. Lane. We have work to do." My client testified. The jury apparently was satisfied with his explanation, for at the close of the day he was acquitted.

I hurried from the courthouse aware that I was, several hours after the assassination, one of the least knowledgeable persons in the country about the details of the historic event that had transpired earlier that day. I was eager to rush to my office to a television set and telephone.

With a briefcase in one hand and a topcoat in the other, I ran down the massive stone steps, stepping around an elderly gentleman who was walking slowly in the same direction. He turned and said, "Well, Lane, do you think he did it alone?" I recognized a judge of my acquaintance, a distinguished though somewhat irascible jurist for whom I had great respect and at least a modicum of fondness. Identifying with Rip van Winkle as he rose, I responded. "Who, sir? Did what?"

"Do you think this Oswald killed the president?" he asked.

I explained that I had just tried a case and had heard nothing about the details of the assassination. The judge waved away my response, clearly ruling it to be irrelevant. He stopped walking, looked at me and said:

"He couldn't very well shoot him from the back and cause an entrance wound in his throat, could he?"

The rhetorical question required no response. He continued:

"The doctors said the throat wound was an entrance wound. It'll be an interesting trial. I want to see how they answer that question."

More than a quarter of a century later, the question—how could Oswald shoot Kennedy from the back from the front?—remains without adequate response.

There was no trial. In its stead, confident assurances of Oswald's lone guilt were offered at press conferences by federal and local officials and were nicely summarized by the Dallas district attorney, Henry Wade.

At a crowded press conference with Wade, FBI agents, and the local chief of police, a reporter asked if Oswald had given any motive for killing the president. Wade responded negatively, complaining that the murderer was arrogant. He was so arrogant that he wouldn't reveal his motive—in fact, he even said he didn't do it. The reporters dutifully wrote on their slates that Oswald was arrogant. Even though Oswald was proclaiming his innocence, no one asked where Oswald claimed he had been at the time of the assassination.

A reporter asked for the best evidence to prove Oswald did it and eagerly awaited the reply from the chief of police. "We have the rifle. If we can put Oswald's prints on it—that's the case." The leading newspapers reported that tests would reveal Oswald's fingerprints on the murder weapon according to "preliminary reports." Instead, tests revealed that Oswald's fingerprints were not found.

A news conference is at best a less than adequate substitute for a judicial proceeding. Yet reporters who persist in asking difficult questions and who point out apparent contradictions can perform an important public service. A review of the early exchanges between government officials and the news media during the days just after the assassination indicates, however, that the nation was not well served. The reporters—not courtroom veterans, but rather members of the president's traveling entourage—seemed eager to accept and record for history any allegation, no matter how absurd. Inconsistencies were left unchallenged. The reporters had made a fateful decision. They would run with the hounds.

Oswald was sequestered from the public for two days. The government teased the reporters and the nation by permitting glimpses of him as he was led through police corridors from one room to another. When Oswald attempted to answer questions shouted at him by reporters, the police pulled him away before he could complete more than a brief comment.

The disheveled, confused young man, appearing irregularly and always in police custody, was never permitted to make his case. He emphatically denied the charges against him and begged for the authorities to permit him to meet with a lawyer. When told by a reporter that he had been charged with assassinating the president, he seemed stunned, and said he had never even been asked about the Kennedy assassination by the police and FBI agents. When told again that he had been charged, he paused in midstep as he was being led away by police, leaned over to a reporter, and said, "Then I'm the patsy." The police then dragged him away, and he was next seen on Sunday morning, November 24, 1963, in the basement of the Dallas Police and Courts Building.

While Oswald was surrounded by federal and local police officers, who had sealed off the basement so that the well-publicized transfer of the prisoner from one building to another could be accomplished in safety, he was shot to death by Jack Ruby. Ruby, with a long record of service to organized crime in Chicago, had worked for the FBI in Dallas for years before he killed Oswald.

The murder was nationally televised as it occurred, causing some eyebrows to be raised across the land. A few questions were asked even in Dallas. Dallas police captain Will Fritz, who had made the arrangements for the transfer, was asked about the matter. His response was casual.

Q. Captain, what excuse—letting him [Ruby] get that close?

Fritz: What excuse did he use?

Q. No, what excuse do you-all have, you know, that he got that close?

Fritz: I don't have an excuse.

> —Interview recorded by WFAA-TV Dallas Police and Courts Building November 24, 1963.

In light of the murder of the suspect, the questions persisted. To resolve all doubts, Henry Wade called another press conference soon after doctors at the Parkland Hospital had announced that Oswald was dead. Wade had assembled all of the evidence that had been developed by the FBI, the Texas Rangers and the Dallas police authorities. His presentation was the authoritative proffer of the government's case against Lee Harvey Oswald for the murder of President Kennedy, as well as the murder of a Dallas police officer, J.D. Tippit, who had allegedly tried to apprehend him.

Wade began by asserting that he was convinced beyond any doubt that Oswald had murdered both men, that he had acted alone in each crime, and that there had been no conspiracy.

Before the conference had concluded, Wade had made fifteen assertions as to fact that in totality comprised the entire case against Oswald (see Appendix, page 331).[1] Some of the charges were mere conclusions and offered without factual basis. Some were allegedly based upon sources, but the sources were not disclosed for reasons that were unstated. Other allegations were supported by some documentation. While very little of the evidence was then publicly known, it was clear that at least a few of Wade's assertions were contravened by facts then available. Some of the allegations were, in fact, contradicted by other allegations offered by the prosecuting attorney. The press reported the news conference with full solemnity.

---

[1] Wade's statement is published on appendix page 337 along with my contemporaneous analysis of it.

I watched the televised press conference with a concern that grew into alarm. It was clear that the case against Oswald, however internally flawed, had been presented and accepted. What would the defense have been? Oswald was dead and a defense based upon his evaluation of the evidence and his assertions as to the facts could never be assembled.

I picked up the *New York Times* and reread a statement attributed to a Dallas resident named Jean Hill, one of the spectators standing close to the passing presidential limousine when the shots were fired. I called the telephone information service in Dallas and a few minutes later I was talking with Ms. Hill. I told her of my interest. She shared her observations with me. As she began to describe the area, she interrupted herself to ask me if I had ever been to Dealey Plaza. I told her I had never visited Dallas. She then described the geography of the plaza, referring to the area to the right-front of the president when he was shot as "like a grassy knoll." A shot had come from behind the wooden fence at the top of the knoll. Kennedy had been facing in that direction when he was struck. Later I repeated Jean Hill's observations, adopting her phrase when I quoted her. Thus that small piece of land, now part of our history, became for all time the grassy knoll. I doubt that Ms. Hill is aware that she gave it its eternal name.

The doctors who had labored in a futile effort to save Kennedy's life at the Parkland Hospital all had stated in contemporaneous interviews that the wound in his throat had been an entrance wound. Wade and the FBI concluded that Oswald was directly behind the president and that he alone had fired a weapon that day in Dealey Plaza. I thought of the question the judge had posed a short while before. How indeed had Oswald, allegedly behind the president, caused frontal wounds?

When the *New York Times* published the text of the Wade press conference, I studied the allegations carefully. The frailty of the arguments was apparent. The case the prosecutor had presented was weak in some respects, incomplete in other areas, unconvincing throughout, lacking in an adequate evidentiary foundation, and absolutely devoid of proof. Yet it was the official word of the government and it had been accepted without dissent.

In the weeks following the assassination I analyzed the case, setting my analysis alongside what was then known about the case as I had done a hundred times before for clients I had represented. The difference was that here there was no client. I set out to discover what Oswald had said during the many hours he had been questioned by agents of the FBI and others while in custody. I learned that the FBI had refused to record the interviews. No transcript existed that could illuminate his claims of innocence, or document his reference to being a "patsy." The police agents differed as to what he had told them.

When I completed my analysis of the evidence and the charges, I had written a ten-thousand-word evaluation. The work was a plea for the "fair consideration of the evidence." I had not concluded either that Oswald was innocent or that if he were guilty, he could not have acted alone. It began:

"In all likelihood there does not exist a single American community where reside twelve men or women, good and true, who presume that Lee Harvey Oswald did not assassinate President Kennedy. No more savage comment can be made in reference to the breakdown of the Anglo-Saxon system of jurisprudence. At the very foundation of our judicial operation lies a cornerstone which shelters the innocent and guilty alike against group hysteria, manufactured evidence, overzealous law enforcement officials, in short, against those factors which militate for an automated, prejudged, neatly packaged verdict of guilty. It is the sacred right of every citizen accused of committing a crime to the presumption of innocence.

"This presumption, it has been written, is a cloak donned by the accused when the initial charge is made, and worn by him continuously. It is worn throughout the entire case presented against him, and not taken from the defendant until after he has had an opportunity to cross-examine hostile witnesses, to present his own witnesses, and to testify himself.

"Oswald did not testify. Indeed, there will be no case, no trial, and Oswald, murdered while in police custody, still has no lawyer. Under such circumstances the development of a possible defense is difficult, almost impossible. Under such circumstances, the development of such a defense is obligatory.

"There will be an investigation. No investigation, however soundly motivated, can serve as an adequate substitute for trial. Law enforcement officials investigate every criminal case before it is presented to a jury. The investigation in almost all such cases results in the firm conviction by the investigator that the accused is guilty. A jury often finds the defendant innocent, notwithstanding.

"That which intervenes between the zealous investigator and the jury is due process of law, developed at great cost in human life and liberty over the years. It is the right to have irrelevant testimony barred. It is the right to have facts, not hopes or thoughts or wishes or prejudicial opinions, presented. It is the right to test by cross-examination the veracity of every witness and the value of his testimony. It is, perhaps above all, the right to counsel of one's own choice, so that all the other rights may be protected. In this defense, Oswald had forfeited all rights along with his life.

"The reader, inundated at the outset with forty-eight solid television, radio, and newspaper hours devoted to proving the guilt of the accused and much additional 'evidence' since then, cannot now examine this case without bringing to it certain preconceived ideas. We ask, instead, only for a temporary suspension of certainty."

That suspension of certainty as to Oswald's lone guilt was not quickly achieved. Only after the publication of my book, *Rush to Judgment*, during 1966, did national polls reveal a dramatic change in public perception of the case. In the days following the assassination, however, I tried to find a publication that would consider printing the article I had written.

The obvious choice, I thought, was the *Nation*. Its editor, Carey McWilliams, was an acquaintance. He had often asked me to write a piece for him during those sessions when, at his request, he had met with me, and sometimes with young Yorkville activist John Harrington as well, to discuss local politics, my proposal for integrating middle- and low-income public housing in Manhattan, or the white paper I had written for the mayor calling for an enlightened approach to the problem of drug addiction.

McWilliams seemed pleased to hear from me and delighted when I told him I had written something I wished to give to the *Nation*. When he learned of the subject matter, however, his manner approached panic. "We cannot take it. We don't want it. I am sorry but we have decided not to touch that subject." I explained that the burden of the article was not Oswald's innocence nor had I even concluded that others were involved. "All I say, Carey, is that there are serious unanswered questions which should be looked at." He was adamant, as were the editors of *Fact*, the "magazine of controversy"—who said the subject matter was too controversial—*The Reporter, Look, Life, The Saturday Evening Post*, and all the others I approached. *The New Republic*, according to an editor there, was considering a similar piece.

I heard from James Aronson. He was the editor of a publication on the left, the *National Guardian*. He had learned about the article and said he was anxious to see it. I told him that I would send it to him but that I would not authorize him to publish it. He asked why. I said that I was seeking a broader, nonpolitical publisher and that if the piece originated on the left, the subject would likely never receive the debate that it required. He called me the next day. "We consider it to be a very important document and we want to publish it," he said. I told him that I did not wish him to do so. He was disappointed and told me that I was being unfair.

I took the article to James Wechsler, an editor at the then-liberal *New York Post*. He was unable to find anyone who would publish it. He urged me to forget about it. I told him of Aronson's offer. He was furious: "They'll turn it into a political issue," he said. "Don't let them publish it." Having seen the concept of the article rejected by every publication in the United States and by all of my friends with contacts to, and influence with, the media, I was left with the offer of the *National Guardian*. I called Aronson and said the article was his if he wanted it.

On December 19, 1963, the *National Guardian* published the piece. (The piece is reproduced here in the Appendix, page 335.) It covered five pages in the tabloid-sized publication. The *National Guardian* could not keep the newsstands supplied, so great was the demand. Aronson then reprinted it in pamphlet form and distributed many thousands of copies. The *New York Times* published a substantial story regarding the points that I had made, but to my knowledge no other newspaper in the United States published a line about it. The *Guardian*, which owned the rights to the article, later reported that "abroad the reaction was quite different. In Rome, the Lane brief was scheduled to be printed in full in *Paese Sera*, the largest in the evening field, and in *Liberation*, in Paris. *Oggi*, an Italian magazine with a circulation of one million, sought permission to reprint. The Japanese press and news agencies also were on top of the story. Several Mexican papers picked it up, too."

In the United States, the *Guardian* sent the article to the United Press International. A UPI correspondent said his organization "wouldn't touch it."

FBI director J. Edgar Hoover, however, took a different position. He distributed the document prolifically, sending it to his elite contacts in government circles and elsewhere. To make certain that the piece, which had been sold on newsstands, would not fall into the wrong hands, he had it classified "Top Secret." With those words emblazoned in dark ink across the top of the first page, making some of the content difficult to read, he dispatched it to the attorney general of the United States, judges, bar association officials, and police departments.

As it turned out, however, the most important reader of the work was a woman who lived in Hominy, Oklahoma.

Shirley Martin, the resident of Hominy, was deeply moved by the election of John F. Kennedy. She felt that he had willed a new spirit into the nation. His sudden death came as a shock to her, as the end of a great drama that had not as yet unfolded. She was not satisfied by the police stories, which seemed to her to be flawed. She read all that was published on the subject and her doubts were not quieted. She wrote to Marina Oswald, the widow, and to Marguerite Oswald, the mother of the accused.

When she read the article published in the *National Guardian*, she was encouraged. She sent it to Marguerite Oswald. Mrs. Oswald and Shirley Martin were not acquainted; I knew neither of them.

Mrs. Oswald called me. She said that she had read the article and wanted to know if I still stood by it. She said that the Warren Commission wanted to talk to her. President Lyndon B. Johnson, the former United States senator from Texas, had served as vice president under Kennedy. He had, of course, become president upon Kennedy's death. To satisfy all doubts as to the events in Dallas on November 22, 1963, he established, by Executive Order Number 11130, the President's Commission on the Assassination of President Kennedy, chaired by the chief justice of the United States, Earl Warren.

"You are the only lawyer in the whole country who said that my son should not be condemned as a murderer without the evidence at least being looked at," she said. "They are going to try him after his death, when he can't answer. I knew Lee; he was my son. I know he was innocent." She asked me to represent her son's interests before the Warren Commission. "You can find witnesses for Lee, you can cross-examine their witnesses against him," she said.

Of course, the idea intrigued me. However, there were obstacles that I thought to be insurmountable. Most of my law practice consisted of representing defendants who were indigent or nearly so. The one corporate client that made the majority of my *pro bono* work possible had previously told me that the corporation had been embarrassed and had suffered as a result of being identified with me after the publication of my article on the case. I was informed that any further effort on my part regarding the Kennedy assassination investigation would result in the termination of my contract with the corporation. Mrs. Oswald herself was unable to undertake to cover my expenses, much less pay a fee to me for the services she wished me to render. The total income that I realized from the worldwide publication of my article was $100. In fact, I was surprised when a check in that amount arrived from the *National Guardian*.

I believed that I was in no position to accept the brief Mrs. Oswald had offered me. However, she persisted. She reminded me I had written that both Lee Harvey Oswald and the country were entitled to receive a fair and critical evaluation of all the evidence. She said, "He's being tried by the Warren Commission. He has no lawyer. Will you represent his interests, or didn't you mean what you wrote?"

In the end, I agreed to conduct an investigation, providing that Mrs. Oswald, who was, in a sense, my client, agreed that my inquiry would be independent of her as well. I told her that I would not appear as her counsel when she testified before the Warren Commission, and that she must stipulate in writing that if my investigation constrained me to conclude that her son had been the assassin, I would be free to so state publicly. She willingly consented—certain, she said, that evidence would vindicate her son.

With apprehension modified only by my interest in the subject matter, I approached the task that I had never really sought. I began by resigning as counsel for my corporate client. The president of the corporation accepted with alacrity.

Meanwhile, among the members of the press, it soon became clear that the universal lack of interest in the facts was matched only by the hostility towards those who thought the matter relevant and important. I did not know how difficult a journey I had embarked upon until my erstwhile friend James Wechsler attacked me in the New York Post. He demanded to know why I had published my article in a left-wing periodical, rather than in a more responsible journal. He implied that he and his colleagues in the media had been more than willing to publish my dissent. When I called to confront him with the facts, of which he was, of course, well acquainted, he declined to speak with me. We never did speak again. Only a year before he had appeared as a keynote speaker at a dinner held to honor me and urge me to run for an important political office.

My difficult struggle with Mrs. Oswald's offer was rendered almost academic some weeks later. The Warren Commission refused to permit me to appear as counsel for Lee Oswald. It also decided to operate in secrecy. Its hearings were conducted behind closed doors, the minutes of its meetings classified top secret, and the testimony adduced before its members declared unavailable as well. The news media accepted without protest the ruling by the commission that the press would be barred from all proceedings regarding the death of the president.

In an interview published in the New York Times, J. Lee Rankin, the general counsel of the Warren Commission, set forth the modus operandi of the investigation. Six panels were to be established, each directed by a senior lawyer. They would look into, respectively, Oswald's background, his time in the Soviet Union and the Marine Corps, his activities on November 22, Jack Ruby's background, how Ruby had entered the basement unnoticed, and, lastly, the effectiveness of the United States Secret Service on the 22nd. I later explained to the members of the commission when I was called to testify as a witness (not having been present at the scene appeared to be a prerequisite for qualification as a commission witness) that had I established their investigation guidelines, I would have formed a seventh panel. It would have undertaken the assignment of discovering who had killed President Kennedy. Evidence as to that matter could reach the Warren Commission only through the panel charged with exploring Oswald's movements. The lack of a seventh panel demonstrated the authorities' ineluctable commitment to a preconceived notion. The few editorials addressing the Warren Commission's devotion to proving Oswald's lone guilt did so only to praise the commission for its forthright stance.

I formed the Citizens Committee of Inquiry in New York City in a small office on lower Fifth Avenue. A number of young men and women volunteered to help. Together we organized lectures at colleges and law schools and appearances on a few local radio and television programs. Finally we rented a theater at which, each evening for many months, I gave what came to be called "The Speech," about the then-known facts surrounding the death of President Kennedy. This alternative method of dissent was required because not a single network radio or television program permitted the broadcast of a word of divergence from the official view.

Funds were collected and expended to cover the expenses of volunteer investigators who traveled to Dallas in search of the facts. Our small organization, comprised primarily of college students and others of conscience, became the seventh panel the Warren Commission neglected to establish.

We continued to encounter difficulties as we pursued the objective of learning the truth about the death of our president. In Dallas our investigators were harassed and arrested. It almost seemed as if the police had access to our plans as they were being formulated. Fourteen years later, from documents obtained under the Freedom of Information Act, we discovered that the FBI had tapped our telephones and placed listening devices in our office.

In the months after the publication of the *Guardian* article, the federal authorities also prevented me from entering the United States at the John F. Kennedy International Airport in New York until after they had notified "telephonically" the FBI, the Department of Justice, and the office of the United States attorney general that I had come home, presumably to continue my troublesome search for the facts.

Most inconvenient of all, however, was the effort to thwart our investigation by disbarring me.

Foreclosed from reaching the American people directly due to the national news media's endorsement of the official version, I spoke of the case in England, Ireland, Scotland, France, and Italy. The *Rome Daily American* published an account of my remarks on April 9, 1964, under the headline "Lane Condemns Press Silence in Oswald Case."

The editor of the *Richmond Times Dispatch* happened to be in Italy when the article was published. Apparently he took it as a personal affront. He sent it to an influential friend. The friend, utilizing the stationery of the American Bar Association, then enclosed the article in a letter to Rankin at the Warren Commission suggesting that action should be taken against me. In his letter, which began "Dear Lee," and that was signed only "Lewis," he wrote: "There ought to be some way for the bar to discipline people like Lane, as he is certainly bringing serious discredit to the legal processes of his country."

The "Lewis" in question was Lewis F. Powell, Jr., at the time the president-elect of the American Bar Association. He later became a justice of the United States Supreme Court. It will be for history to determine who, between the two of us, brought discredit to the legal profession and who served the best traditions of the American bar.

Powell's suggestion that, in this instance, the First Amendment be abrogated and the independence of the bar be threatened in one fell swoop was eagerly endorsed and advanced by Rankin. Almost immediately thereafter the Association of the Bar of the City of New York, through the efforts of its attorney, John G. Bonomi, commenced a proceeding against me in which the charge was, in my view, attempted freedom of speech. Of course, the specious complaint was never processed, after the intercession on my behalf of a distinguished member of the bar, Edward Ennis, the former solicitor general of the United States. The Bar Association, however, has not yet had the good grace, even now, twenty-seven years later, to notify me that it has finally withdrawn its frivolous charge.

The Warren Commission issued its report during September 1964 finding, as expected, Oswald to have been the lone assassin. After it released the evidence, compiled in twenty-six volumes, upon which it said it had relied, I began to study the record. My analysis, together with interviews of witnesses I had conducted, resulted in a manuscript, *Rush to Judgment*. Virtually every publisher in the United States refused to print it. Years passed before we learned of the pressure that had been exerted by the

FBI and the CIA against those who considered permitting the publication of a dissenting view in this affair.

A British firm with offices in London, The Bodley Head, agreed to publish the book. Subsequently Holt, Rinehart and Winston in the United States agreed as well. That firm was directed by the FBI to cancel its contract with me. It declined to do so due to the courage of its editor-in-chief, Arthur A. Cohen, and the book was published. It quickly became the number-one-selling book in the United States that year in hardcover and the bestselling book the next year in paperback, and enjoyed enormous success in countries throughout the world.

The debate was on. The United States government and its secret teams had been unable to prevent a national discussion. Soon national polls revealed that the conclusions of the Warren Report had been rejected by the overwhelming majority of the American people. In a sense the first major obstacle to the truth, the Warren Commission Report, had been removed. The remaining task was to determine who had killed the president.

During the next decade little progress was made in that regard. CBS and Walter Cronkite offered four hours of prime-time programming to endorse the Warren Report. When New Orleans district attorney Jim Garrison prosecuted Clay Shaw for conspiracy to assassinate the president, a new wave of attacks against the critics of the Warren Commission was launched by the news media.

Shaw was acquitted, Garrison roundly condemned, and the movement for the facts set further back. Later I was able to secure evidence that might have been useful to Garrison in the Shaw case but, of course, the case could not be tried again. That evidence proved that Shaw, who had known Oswald, had worked for the CIA, a fact that Shaw had successfully denied at his trial.

The war in Vietnam and crimes committed by the authorities, including President Nixon and his advisers in the Watergate scandal, convinced the American people that simplistic explanations of past national tragedies might be challenged. Statements by leaders of government or federal police officials were no longer sacrosanct. At lectures, when I quoted Cronkite's earlier assertions that the American people must "have faith" in the Warren Report, the audience laughed in unison. It was a new day. New information might also be made available. The only substantial reform resulting from the Watergate fiasco was an amended Freedom of Information Act, for the first time permitting the American people to have a glimpse of the archives of their national experience.

If the Congress was willing to let us see the record of our heritage, I reasoned, perhaps it would also look into the assassination of the president.

I moved to Washington, D.C., rented an office on Capitol Hill and formed the Citizen's Commission of Inquiry (C.C.I.) in February 1975, a successor to the former Citizen's Committee. Many prominent persons joined the diverse group. For example, Dr. Linus Pauling, twice awarded the Nobel Prize, and George O'Toole, a former CIA official, served on our board. I lectured at schools throughout the country and formed chapters of the national group, 180 of them, in almost every state. I personally briefed more than one hundred members of the Congress and many times that number of congressional aides. I drafted legislation to establish a committee to investigate the assassination of President Kennedy, met with leaders of the Black Caucus in the House of Representatives, and drafted a new proposal to investigate both the Kennedy assassination and the murder of Dr. Martin Luther King, Jr.

I decided to expand the proposed congressional inquiry for two reasons, one based entirely on principle, one pragmatic. Dr. King's death, no less a tragedy and no more easily susceptible to proof than President Kennedy's murder, was equally deserving of scrutiny. The support of members of Congress interested in exploring the assassination of the civil rights leader, when combined with the support of those committed to securing the facts about the death of the president, might be sufficient to bring about the formation of an ad hoc committee on the two assassinations.

Congressmen Don Edwards of California and Henry B. Gonzalez of Texas became early supporters. Representative Thomas P. "Tip" O'Neill of Massachusetts and his friends, Richard Bolling of Missouri, the most influential member of the Rules Committee, Phillip Burton of California, and others who described themselves as "Kennedy Democrats," strongly opposed the effort.

In time the autonomous chapters of the C.C.I. combined to deluge local representatives with a mountain of mail representing a movement that had spread like a grass fire. More than 1.5 million letters, telegrams, and petitions inundated the Congress. The members of Congress knew the facts; we had briefed them and sent documents to them and their aides. It became clear as well that their constituents were educated and determined.

The House Select Committee on Assassinations was established by a vote of Congress.

It is interesting to look back upon that struggle and recall the consistent, almost desperate, efforts by Tip O'Neill to thwart the investigation. He had repeatedly told his colleagues to vote against the proposal, had ordered Bolling to refuse to permit it to be reported out of the Rules Committee in order to prevent the Congress from voting upon it, and had supported his directives with his personal assurances to the members that he *knew* that the Warren Report was accurate and that nothing had been covered up.

O'Neill advised his colleagues that all of the shots had come from the Texas School Book Depository where Oswald had been stationed, and that the Warren Commission's conclusion that there was "no credible evidence" that even supported the rumor that shots had come from behind the fence on the knoll was absolutely accurate. O'Neill made these statements repeatedly during 1976 and 1977.

After he retired from the Congress, he published his political memoirs, *Man of the House*, in 1987. In it O'Neill recounted an event that had occurred in 1968.

"I was never one of those people who had doubts or suspicions about the Warren Commission's report on the president's death. But five years after Jack died, I was having dinner with Kenny O'Donnell and a few other people at Jimmy's Harborside Restaurant in Boston, and we got to talking about the assassination.

"I was surprised to hear O'Donnell say that he was sure he had heard two shots that came from behind the fence.

"'That's not what you told the Warren Commission,' I said.

"'You're right,' he replied. 'I told the FBI what I had heard, but they said it couldn't have happened that way and that I must have been imagining things. So I testified the way they wanted me to. I just didn't want to stir up any more pain and trouble for the family.'

"'I can't believe it,' I said. 'I wouldn't have done that in a million years. I would have told the truth.'

"'Tip, you have to understand. The family—everybody wanted this thing behind them.'

"Dave Powers was with us at dinner that night, and his recollection of the shots was the same as O'Donnell's. Kenny O'Donnell is no longer alive, but during the writing of this book I checked with Dave Powers. As they say in the news business, he stands by his story.

"And so there will always be some skepticism in my mind about the cause of Jack's death. I used to think that the only people who doubted the conclusions of the Warren Commission were crackpots. Now, however, I'm not so sure.

"But I'd rather focus on Jack's life. He really did have the charisma, the glamour, and the talent that has become part of his legend. He had a radiance that made people glow when they were in his company. He brought to all sectors of the American public a new feeling that they were wanted, that there was a place in America for them—regardless of religion or race. And perhaps most important, when Jack Kennedy was president, people had trust in their government. I look forward to the day when that will once again be true."

The trust of the people must be earned by government leaders willing to share the facts with them. Apparently, O'Neill had not yet understood that concept.

Had O'Donnell and Powers, the two most important advisers to President Kennedy, testified truthfully and had the FBI been exposed in its effort to suborn (induce someone to commit) perjury in this instance, the damage inflicted upon the nation by the false Warren Commission Report might have been averted. Since O'Donnell and Powers, two of the most powerful men in the administration, succumbed to the blandishments of the FBI and agreed to lie under oath about the death of their close friend, one can only imagine the effect that the FBI's illegal actions had had upon other witnesses who were less prominent and more vulnerable.

O'Neill's book was widely reviewed, yet not a single review I read even mentioned his disclosures about this matter, although they represent some of the few relevant and newsworthy statements in a book that was little more than a collection of banal anecdotes.

The leadership of the House, still determined to prevent a serious review of the facts, appointed to the House Select Committee on Assassinations members of Congress who would have the minimum impact upon the Congress and the nation. For example, Walter Fauntroy, the nonvoting "delegate" from Washington, D.C., and a man universally considered by his colleagues to be of little influence, was chosen to head the investigation into the King assassination.

Dick Gregory, a man of amazing talent, had traded in his career as a successful comedian and actor to become an advocate for human rights. He and I were old friends and his participation in raising questions about the King and Kennedy assassinations was of great importance in the battle to establish the congressional committee. He called me one day: "Doctor, get Walter over to your house tonight. We'll meet at six P.M. We've got to get this thing going."

He was concerned, as was I, about the failure of the committee to take any steps toward organizing its investigation.

That evening I sat behind my desk as Gregory and Fauntroy sat on the couch in the office of my house. As I glanced out of the window, I saw the Supreme Court across the street and behind it the top of the Capitol building. At that moment, however, history was being created just in front of me, on the Persian rug on the office floor. For Gregory had taken Fauntroy's hand and led him until both men were kneeling. Fauntroy was an ordained minister. Gregory led the prayer.

"Oh Lord, this man [indicating Fauntroy] is the most important man in America. Not the most important black man, the most important man. He is going to tell this nation the truth about how our beloved Martin died. Who killed him. Lord, grant him the wisdom to learn all of the facts. And Lord, grant him the courage to tell the truth to the people."

The men resumed their seats on the couch. Fauntroy spoke:

"Dick, there's a problem. We know who did it."

Gregory answered, "Well, that's fine. That's not a problem."

Fauntroy explained: "Dick, we know the FBI killed Martin. We have the proof. But Dick, the FBI is bugging my home, my congressional office, even my church. We can't report that they did it. It's too dangerous."

Greg persisted, patiently.

"Walter, what did we most love about Martin? He did not hold separate private and public positions. He spoke openly to all of us about what he believed."

Fauntroy responded, "Yes, Dick, and they killed him. I'm not ready to make that sacrifice."

At the end of the evening, over a cup of tea, Greg and I discussed our shared feeling that there would be some serious problems facing the congressional investigation.

The listless and disorganized members of the committee had not taken the first step—retaining a general counsel and staff director to organize the inquiry. When I met with them to urge them to act, the then-chairman of the committee offered me the position. I declined, stating that it could not reasonably be argued that I was neutral and that the inquiry, therefore, would be doomed before it began. He next offered the job to Bernard Fensterwald, a Washington lawyer. Fensterwald was considering the matter when, he later told me, a representative of the CIA called on him and said that the CIA would hand him "his head on a platter" if he took the assignment. Fensterwald declined. I then began an active search to find acceptable counsel.

Richard Sprague, a brilliant attorney with offices in Philadelphia, had served as a prosecuting attorney in that city. In that capacity he had prosecuted and convicted all those involved in the labor union-organized crime conspiracy to murder the Yablonski family. His relentless investigation won for him the almost universal approval of the national news media.

I met with Sprague; he was interested. I met with the members of the committee; they were interested. Later I traveled from Philadelphia with Sprague by train and introduced him to the leaders of the committee, and that day they decided to retain him. The House Select Committee on Assassinations was at last in a position to begin its work.

During the same time frame I had initiated a series of actions in court under the Freedom of Information Act to secure the documents that the Warren Commission and all subsequent administrations had sought to have classified as top secret and thus hidden from the public. As we won our case in the United States district court, many of the documents were made available; however, where the agency had successfully pleaded "national security" as a defense, the court declined to provide the documents. Our rented trucks carried the tens of thousands of pages from the offices of the federal police to our office on Capitol Hill.

Many scholars came from around the country to peruse them with us. They became excited when FBI reports and other documents disclosed evidence that established beyond a doubt that Oswald could not have been the lone assassin. I was basically uninterested in that data. It had been clear for some years that the Warren Report was false and that its authors had little respect for the truth. Further proof was redundant and of little more significance to me than a new scientific study debunking the notion that the earth is flat.

The only question of relevance, I believed, was not whether there had been a conspiracy to murder the president, but who its participants had been. I hoped that documents we might discover could assist Sprague in his inquiries. Before we found all of the crucial data, however, Sprague had been forced out.

The FBI and CIA had made it clear that each organization would decide which documents it would provide to the inquiry. They also decided that they would determine who could be "cleared" to receive classified data. In other words, the organizations would choose their own investigators and determine the scope of the inquiry. Sprague rejected that concept, insisting that he was obligated to conduct a full and honest investigation, follow the evidence wherever it might lead, and publish the truth, whatever it might be.

At his first public appearance as the head of the committee investigating the murders of President John F. Kennedy and Dr. Martin Luther King, Jr., Sprague said that he would call every relevant witness and examine every relevant document. A CBS-TV reporter reminded him that Jacqueline Kennedy and John Connally had been witnesses and that Gerald Ford, at that time president of the United States, had been a member of the Warren Commission.

"Do you intend to call any of them?" he was asked. Sprague answered simply, "All of them." Another national newsman asked Sprague how he could even hope to get classified documents from the FBI and CIA since the House and Senate Intelligence Committee had not been able to. Sprague said, "We are a congressional committee in form, but in substance we are investigating two homicides. We must get every relevant document from the FBI files here in Washington and from the CIA vaults in Langley, Virginia."

The coordinated intelligence attack upon Sprague and the committee began almost at once. Ben Franklin of the Washington bureau of *The New York Times* had in the past written admiringly of Sprague's ability as a prosecuting attorney. When Sprague became the committee's chief investigator, Franklin filed a fair and accurate story from Washington, D.C. He was immediately removed from the assignment to cover the Select Committee. David Burnham was brought in to cover the story. He filed a series of stories containing spurious information about Sprague. The discredited information had been taken from the morgues of two Philadelphia newspapers.

Burnham had covered nuclear energy stories for the *New York Times*. Karen Silkwood, knowing of his specialty, had arranged a secret meeting with him to deliver documents to the *New York Times*. Almost no one knew of the planned trip save Silkwood and Burnham. She never met him; she was apparently murdered on the way to see him and her documents disappeared.

In my view, with Burnham leading the attack, assisted by George Lardner, Jr. of the *Washington Post* and Jeremiah O'Leary of the *Washington Star*, both old hands well-connected with the intelligence agencies, a coordinated campaign against Sprague was under way.

A *New York Times* editorial denounced Sprague and questioned the wisdom of reestablishing the committee as long as Sprague served as counsel. Since the Select Committee was not a standing committee of the House, in effect it was required to be recertified by each new Congress.

Sprague pressed on. He quickly determined that he could not rely upon the CIA, FBI, or Department of Justice for the facts. He decided to secure the services of experienced prosecutors without federal police credentials. He hired a talented, inquisitive, and experienced prosecutor from the district attorney's office in New York, Robert Tannenbaum, who knew about organized crime and criminal conspiracy. He was put in charge of investigating the murder of President Kennedy.

Sprague reached into the New York district attorney's office again. He hired Robert Lehner, an able and experienced prosecutor. Lehner became the counsel in charge of investigating the murder of Dr. King.

Donovan Gay was hired by Sprague as the chief researcher for both the Kennedy and King cases. Gay is a committed scholar. In a short period of time he became the keeper of the most explosive secrets on Capitol Hill.

Sprague also hired Gaeton Fonzi, an outstanding investigator with years of experience in and knowledge of the massive, convoluted evidence surrounding the Kennedy assassination.

With Tannenbaum and Lehner functioning in the office under Sprague's direction, Fonzi uncovering evidence in Florida and elsewhere, and Gay establishing a system to handle the material, the first serious federal inquiry into either murder was finally under way in January, 1977.

The intelligence agencies countered with a desperate effort to remove Sprague before the vote to reestablish the committee in the 95th Congress was taken.

Meanwhile, the *New York Times*, *Washington Post* and *Washington Star* continued their campaign. Harold E. Ford, an African-American congressman from Memphis and a member of the Select Committee, charged that "the FBI has hired former agents to lobby with Congress against the continuation of the Select Committee."

On the eve of the vote, the intelligence lobbying effort and the use of the news media had reached a crescendo. The members of the Select Committee were nervous. Sprague and Tannenbaum were called into an emergency session.

Later, Tannenbaum would describe that meeting for me. "The attacks against Sprague were continuing. It was a very tense time. The Whip of the House had just conducted a poll—a count of the members. The Select Committee members were told that so much hostility against Sprague had been generated that if he remained on as counsel, the committee would be voted out of existence by the House."

At that time Fonzi was in Florida contacting George De Mohrenschildt. De Mohrenschildt was the CIA contract agent who had brought Oswald from New Orleans to Dallas and had arranged a job for Oswald at the Texas School Book Depository.

De Mohrenschildt had previously been charged by the FBI with being a Nazi spy during World War II. He had never been seriously questioned since the assassination. Sprague, Tannenbaum, and Fonzi considered him to be a potential source of crucial data.

Tannenbaum said, "That was some evening. Fonzi was on his way to see De Mohrenschildt; De Mohrenschildt was found dead. A shotgun blast had blown off his head in Florida. At the same time, Sprague was being told that the committee was dead if he remained."

That same day, the eve of the vote, Rep. Yvonne Burke, then the leader of the Black Caucus, called me: "Mark, Sprague must be let go. We have all been counting votes. If he remains on there will be no committee. You understand, don't you?" I said that I neither understood nor approved of firing him. She tried again, "No one has worked harder to form this committee—to learn the truth, all of it—about the assassinations than you. You above all must understand what we must do. None of us want to fire Sprague. We have no choice because of the fury against him in the newspapers. Can I say that you agree?"

"You can say," I replied, "that I trust Dick Sprague because he is a man of honor. You can say that the police agencies want him fired for the same reason. You can say that I beg you, all of you, to tell the truth to the American people from the floor of the Congress—that the CIA and the FBI are trying to destroy the investigation because they fear that the truth will lead to them. And if we lose, if we are shot down, we go down in honor. The alternative is to hire a CIA asset who will close down the inquiry piecemeal."

She sighed and said, "Mark, you just don't know how things work here."

That day Sprague was fired.

The next day Tannenbaum held a secret meeting with the staff. He told them that he too would be leaving soon.

When we spoke later, I asked him why he had wanted to resign. He said, "I didn't want to resign. I gave up a good job to go to Washington to investigate the assassination of President Kennedy. I knew that the threshold question before us in the Kennedy investigation was Oswald's relationship with the intelligence organizations. This was the single most pressing question. It became clear that the intelligence organizations were not going to give us that information, and it became clear that the Congress was not going to take on the FBI and CIA in order to get that information, and so I knew that it was hopeless."

I asked Tannenbaum what information he was able to get from the CIA and FBI. He said, "When I left as counsel in charge of the Kennedy assassination, we had not been able to get a single classified document from either intelligence group." Of course, I had provided to the commit-

33

tee all of the documents I had been able to obtain. The committee was entitled to the essential documents that had been denied to me. Had the committee insisted, it could have secured all relevant documents even if the Agency had raised objections based upon national security conspirations.

After Sprague had been forced out by the actions of the CIA and FBI, and Tannenbaum frustrated by those agencies into resigning, Robert G. Blakey was appointed as the new general counsel. Blakey was a Department of Justice man with interesting ties to a figure in organized crime. In 1975, Moe Dalitz and three of his partners sued *Penthouse* after the magazine asserted that Dalitz had used $57 million of Teamsters' pension funds to set up a country club near San Clemente, California. According to *Penthouse*, Dalitz was a prominent underworld figure who had played "a critical role as the architect in the organization of crime in the country."

Dalitz called upon Blakey for help. In an affidavit, Blakey vouched for the underworld character. Organized crime and the intelligence organizations were coconspirators in the plan to assassinate Fidel Castro. Later they worked together to develop the false thesis that Fidel Castro had murdered President Kennedy. Yet the House Select Committee's new general counsel was willing to vouch for a reputed underworld figure.

At a top-secret meeting in Washington that I attended, Blakey focused on only one theory about the assassination. He tried, almost desperately, to secure some support for the charge that Fidel Castro was behind the murder of JFK.

Blakey abandoned any attempt at a serious investigation. From three sources within the Select Committee I learned that Blakey had not subpoenaed even a single document from the FBI, CIA, or any other intelligence organization although he had been given the power by an act of Congress to do so.

He so thoroughly compromised the serious investigators who remained on staff that they became almost useless and considered resigning. An example of that conduct can be found in the treatment of Gaeton Fonzi. Fonzi unearthed a document of such enormous potential that it was referred to in hushed terms by the very few who knew of its existence only as the "Spanish document." Fonzi gave it personally to Blakey with the provision that it be shown only to a few trusted members of the committee who had a need to see it. Blakey agreed. He had the document photocopied and delivered at once to the CIA.

When hiring new employees, Blakey invariably sought FBI and CIA clearance. Tannenbaum said, "We're supposed to be investigating them.

Instead, they're investigating us." He added, "It looks like a sellout. It's all over."

After Tannenbaum left, Blakey replaced him with a Department of Justice lawyer. The new lawyer had secured FBI and CIA approval.

Donovan Gay, the keeper of the records in both inquiries, was well aware that no classified CIA and FBI files were being acquired. When he asked about that, Blakey fired him. Gay had been the chief researcher for both cases for 16 months. Blakey told Gay that the CIA wanted him out. "It would be easier for the CIA if you left," Blakey told Gay, and then fired him.

With Sprague, Tannenbaum, and Gay gone, and Fonzi compromised, there was not much left of the original top-level staff other than Lehner.

Blakey then fired Lehner, explaining only that he wanted to replace him with someone from the Department of Justice who would secure FBI and CIA approval.

Four of the members of the Select Committee were extremely upset when Lehner came before the full committee in an effort to keep his job. But the committee voted to let him go. It could not muster the requisite courage for an open confrontation with the intelligence groups.

Blakey required each employee to sign a statement of silence. Even lawyers, investigators, and researchers who resigned or who were fired faced a long stretch in a federal penitentiary for telling the truth about what they learned about the Kennedy or King assassinations.

Yet several former employees of the committee, including Robert Tannenbaum, Robert Lehner, Richard Sprague, and other lawyers, researchers and investigators, have confirmed the statements that appear here.

Sprague told me even before the Select Committee had issued its report that he was convinced that "the purpose of the media campaign against me was to prevent a serious investigation. They have succeeded. They got what they wanted. There will be no investigation."

The CIA had effectively captured the House Select Committee on Assassinations. The committee cleared the FBI and the CIA, *while conceding that there had been a conspiracy to murder the president.*

Yet the struggle continued. We pressed for additional documents and the court ordered that they be released. Our knowledge of the details of the conspiracy to murder the president grew to the point where it became clear that the CIA had killed President Kennedy. Unfortunately, the new leadership of the House Select Committee, men such as Fauntroy, were afraid of the facts, and the new counsel and staff director, Blakey, was committed to a political resolution that avoided the unpleasant facts and absolved his friends in the CIA.

The most important documents that we were able to pry out of the vaults of the intelligence agencies focused upon the CIA's story that Oswald had been to Mexico City. As we examined them, we learned of the details of the CIA plan to frame Oswald and to control and limit any potential investigation. The documents told a story that was fascinating and horrifying. Yet, until the Hunt case many years later, it remained as evidence for which there was no available forum. Magazine editors, book publishers, and the news media were either uninterested or fearful. Only when Hunt filed his defamation lawsuit did the body of accumulated and historic evidence become irresistible. Its time had come.

BOOK II

Mexico City

Presumed Guilty

ARL WARREN HAD BEEN CHOSEN TO PRESIDE OVER THE PRESIDENT'S COMMISSION on the Assassination of President Kennedy. From the perspective of those seeking to hide the facts, he was the perfect choice, although at the time it did not seem so. In retrospect, many of those who admired the changes wrought by the Warren court and many of those who opposed them as unwarranted judicial intervention would find themselves in agreement about its methodology. Warren made up his mind about what, in his view, was in the best interest of the country, and then he set about to achieve it. Whether it was the need to protect the *New York Times* and Martin Luther King, Jr., from the abuse of judicial process in a defamation case in Alabama, or to protect a suspect in a criminal case from police excesses, the chief justice first decided what would be best and then sent his law clerks scurrying for some arguably applicable legal precedent. Once Warren decided upon the course of action he would pursue, he was inflexibly determined to see it through and to insist, even when logical arguments to the contrary were subsequently offered, that he had been correct.

Warren was born in 1891 and was raised in Bakersfield, California. The unusual town of 7,000 had more than its share of crime and vice: Five hundred of its residents were prostitutes and gambling houses were abundant, as were saloons replete with outlaws and cowboys. It boasted of its racism. The area in which the houses of prostitution predominated was called "Jap Alley" and Chinese railroad workers were not permitted to have their names listed in the telephone directory. The telephone book instead gave an address and telephone number next to the designation "Oriental."

Warren, to be sure, did not create the scene. He was, however, influenced by it, in spite of his enduring reputation as a leading liberal.

He became an assistant district attorney in Alameda County and was called a "tough prosecutor" by California governor Pat Brown, who remarked that Warren "would really go after people." He was also an active politician in the Republican party; he ran the Alameda portion of Herbert Hoover's campaign for the presidency. He denounced Upton Sinclair and his reform program as "a foreign philosophy of government" that was "half socialistic and half communistic."

Warren harbored a fear and loathing of Asians. He supported Hiram Johnson's decision to prevent Japanese from owning land in California and for years served as an active member of the Native Sons of the Golden West, an organization that demanded that children born in the United States of Japanese ancestry be denied American citizenship.

After the U.S. entered World War II as a combatant, Warren participated in successfully organizing a program to place Japanese-Americans in concentration camps. Soon after Pearl Harbor, Warren stated that "the Japanese situation as it exists in this state today may well be the Achilles' heel of the entire civilian defense effort." Carey McWilliams, the editor of the *Nation*—who was later to preclude in that publication any criticism of the Warren Commission Report, citing his belief in the chief justice as a man of integrity—had earlier observed that "no one person had more to do with bringing about the removal of the West Coast Japanese during World War II—citizens and aliens alike; men, women, and children—than Mr. Warren."

Two months after the United States entered the war, Warren asked to testify before the United States Congress on the question of Japanese-Americans. He said:

"We believe that when we are dealing with the Caucasian race, we have methods that will test the loyalty of them. But when we deal with the Japanese, we are in an entirely different field and we cannot form any opinion that we believe to be sound."

The next year Warren, then governor of California, speaking before a meeting of his fellow governors, said:

"If the Japs are released, no one will be able to tell a saboteur from any other Jap."

Years later, after many had concluded that the internment of innocents in concentration camps and the confiscation of their homes and personal property was one of the most tragic days for justice in the United States, Warren insisted that he had been correct. "I didn't think I had any choice."

Warren ran for vice president of the United States in 1948. Thomas Dewey was the Republican candidate for president that year; they were defeated.[1] In 1952, Warren supported a resolution at the Republican convention that had been drafted by Herbert Brownell, who was running Eisenhower's campaign. The resolution passed, and Dwight D. Eisenhower received the nomination, narrowly defeating Senator Robert Taft.

In return for his help at the convention, Eisenhower promised Warren the first available seat on the Supreme Court and subsequently suggested that he become, in the interim, the solicitor general of the United States as a resume building stepping stone to the higher court. Warren agreed. Eisenhower was elected president. Five days after Warren announced that he would not seek another term as governor of California, Chief Justice Fred Vinson died. Eisenhower explained to Warren through Brownell that the deal had been an appointment to be an associate justice, not the chief justice. Warren was adamant. A deal was a deal and the next vacancy happened to be the chief justice slot. Eisenhower was distressed, but Warren would not yield.

Brownell then told Warren that he could have the chief justice's job only if he accepted an interim appointment to the court and agreed to be in Washington seven days later when the new term was to begin. The hope at the White House was that Warren would not abandon the stewardship of his state on one week's notice after being its chief executive for eleven years. Warren began packing at once.

A week after the assassination of President Kennedy, the new chief executive, Lyndon Johnson, sent his solicitor general, Archibald Cox, and Deputy Attorney General Nicholas Katzenbach to Warren to invite him to chair the commission to conduct an inquiry into the murder. Warren declined. Later that day Warren was summoned to the White House. Johnson told Warren that wild rumors had been circulating that an emergency situation confronted the country, and that only he, the chief justice, with a reputation for integrity and a commitment to principles of law and justice, could ensure both domestic and international tranquility.

Warren agreed to accept the appointment. When he left the White

---

[1] Allen Dulles served in that campaign as the speechwriter for the Dewey-Warren ticket. In exchange he had been promised by Dewey that he would be appointed director of the CIA. When Eisenhower was elected four years later, he honored that commitment.

House, he was brushing tears from his eyes. He had agreed to yield his integrity for what he perceived to be the national interest. He had promised Johnson that he would dispel the rumors and that he would not permit legal niceties or high moral principles to adversely impact upon that commitment.

Warren was a reluctant chairman of the President's Commission on the Assassination of President Kennedy. As Antony said of Caesar, thrice he rejected the crown, before he finally yielded and accepted it. Shakespearean scholars may continue to debate the sincerity of Antony's claim, but no ambiguity was attached to Warren's refusal. He knew he would be compromising the integrity of his office, blurring the constitutional line that separated the three branches of government, and that he would have to confront difficult moral, political, and ethical questions.[2] A commission established by the chief of the executive branch, chaired by the chief of the of the judicial branch, with a majority of its members comprised of representatives of the legislative branch, was an administrative nightmare and might have created a constitutional crisis in other circumstances. But the nation was so overcome by the death of the president and then stunned by the murder of the suspect while he was in police custody, an event broadcast into American living rooms as it was taking place, that any promise of a solution seemed acceptable.

If the CIA had prepared a psychological profile of Earl Warren and made it available to the White House, it would have, of necessity, disclosed that Warren made political deals; that he was willing to sacrifice the innocent if he believed that the nation required it (as thousands of Japanese-Americans could testify); and that he was predisposed to subsequently rationalizing his behavior and maintaining, even when he later discovered that he had made a momentous, historic, and tragic error, that he had been right all along.

In fact, when Johnson, who had appointed the commission, and members of the commission and some of its lawyers began to express doubts many years later about its central finding—that Oswald had acted alone—Warren was immovable. "If I were still a district attorney," he commented, "and the Oswald case came into my jurisdiction, given the same evidence I could have gotten a conviction in two days and never heard about it again."

---

[2] Each of the proposed members of the commission were opposed to the notion that he should serve, with the exception of Allen Dulles. Only General Lauris Norstad, who was the commander of SHAPE, was able to escape from the assignment.

Warren was not alone among the members of the commission with a predisposition to find Oswald, and only Oswald, guilty. Liberals and conservatives alike thought that the best interests of the country would be served by placing the full responsibility upon the man who had already been executed for the crime. The members had been told just enough about Lee Harvey Oswald's resume and travels to think there might be a Communist connection or at least the appearance of one. They had been informed that Oswald had been to Mexico City to talk to the Soviets and the Cubans. The commission asserted that in the weeks preceding the assassination, Lee Harvey Oswald had taken a trip to Mexico City and there had met with Soviet officials in the Soviet Embassy. In addition, the commission said that Oswald, while in Mexico, had called upon contacts in the Cuban Embassy.

Conservatives abounded on the Warren Commission, among them future president Gerald R. Ford.[3] The conservatives took the view that

---

[3] After many years in the House as a representative from Michigan, Gerald Ford had distinguished himself with but one piece of proposed legislation: he had led the effort to impeach Earl Warren. As a member of the Warren Commission, he betrayed the trust invested in him and became the FBI's agent there.

Years after the Warren Report was issued and the commission disbanded, the Freedom of Information Act was amended to make it possible to secure documents that had previously been inaccessible. With the assistance of the American Civil Liberties Union and Morton Halperin, former deputy assistant secretary of defense, and the Center for National Security Studies, I brought various actions to secure documents from the intelligence agencies.

FBI documents not previously available revealed an intimate and furtive relationship between Ford and the FBI. The documents show Ford fed top-secret information to the FBI while he was a member of the Warren Commission.

An internal FBI memo dated December 17, 1963, details the items Ford passed to Cartha D. DeLoach, then the assistant to the FBI director. Ford did not disclose to the other six members of the Warren Commission his course of improper and illegal conduct.

DeLoach reported that Ford agreed to continue to betray his colleagues on the commission. Ford said, DeLoach reported, "I should call him any time his assistance was needed."

Ford, with the approval of Hoover, was given "an FBI agent briefcase containing a lock" so that he could carry top-secret Warren Commission documents with him on a skiing trip.

From his vacation chalet, Ford told the FBI officials which Commission members required additional FBI efforts in order to bring them into line with the FBI view of the assassination. He reported to DeLoach that two commission members said they had serious doubts the president had been shot from the sixth floor window of the Texas School Book Depository. Ford predicted the two dissenters could be brought to the FBI view.

Ford reported to DeLoach that at a top-secret meeting of the commission held on December 16, 1963, the commission's general counsel, J. Lee Rankin, had been empowered to retain two "so-called technicians." The two who were under consideration were Francis W.H. Adams, a former New York City police commissioner, and Albert E. Jenner, Jr., a Chicago lawyer. Ford, the documents disclose, could only remember the last names of the two men. The FBI then began an investigation to determine who "Adams" and "Jenner" were. DeLoach, who was the number-

Oswald, while in Mexico City just a few weeks before the assassination, met with the Russians to work out the details of a murder he was planning. They cited the fact that evidence revealed a continuing relationship between Oswald and the Soviet intelligence apparatus.

During that same trip to Mexico City, according to this scenario, Oswald had carried out a mission at the Cuban Embassy as well. His purpose: to plan his escape after the murder from Dallas to Cuba.

The liberals were also represented on the commission. Led by Warren, they occupied the key positions among the counsel for the Warren Commission. J. Lee Rankin, the commission's general counsel, and Norman Redlich, former counsel for the left-wing Emergency Civil Liberties Committee, were the most influential lawyers in place. A case could be made for the proposition that Redlich, more than any other person associated with the Warren Commission, had betrayed his principles.[4] He later became the dean of the New York University Law School. Rankin became counsel for New York City and a leader of the bar. He sought, unsuccessfully, to have me disbarred for merely having stated that I did not accept

---

three man in the FBI, ranking just under Hoover and his friend Clyde Tolson, reported, "I told Congressman Ford in strict confidence that apparently Chief Justice Warren was quite close to Drew Pearson [a leading syndicated columnist] and obviously used Pearson from time to time to get his thoughts across as to the percentage of the facts in these articles that were absolutely false." [sic]

[4]The first book published in the United States on the question of the assassination and the Warren Commission was *Oswald: Assassin or Fall Guy*. It was written by Joachim Joesten and published in 1964 by Marzani and Munsell. I had met with Carl Marzani, read proofs of the book at his request, and made some few suggestions. It was a very early work, written before the Warren Commission's evidence was released; therefore, while timely, it was of necessity somewhat flawed and incomplete. The Warren Commission was displeased that any criticial view was being circulated. The commission instituted an investigation of the author. Joesten had been born in Germany and was an early and outspoken critic of Adolf Hitler. He left his homeland and traveled to Scandinavia to warn that the emergence of Hitler was a serious threat to Jews and others in Germany and that Hitler harbored plans to attack Germany's neighbors.

The Nazi establishment retaliated. Joesten's citizenship was revoked and his property seized. He was condemned as being "politically unreliable." The Nazi establishment charged that Joesten had been a Communist.

Joesten eventually came to the United States. He saw the assassination of President Kennedy as a political event of great importance. His early investigation led him to conclude, quite correctly, that the Warren Commission was going to publish a political, not a truthful, report.

After the publication of his book, the commission retaliated. Norman Redlich actively sought the cooperation of the CIA to secure for him the Gestapo file about Joesten, which at that time was in the custody of British intelligence. After the CIA secured the Gestapo file for the Warren Commission, Redlich studied it, analyzed it, and then presented it to Earl Warren, with its charge of Joesten's Communist ties, together with a disparaging report about Carl Marzani, who had been a victim of the 1950s witch hunts in the United States.

the conclusions of the Warren Commission. That constituted, he argued, a criticism of the chief justice. Those were indeed wild times, comparable to the Alien and Sedition Law period of the eighteenth century and the witch hunts of the 1950s, in terms of impact on those seeking to establish the truth about the assassination of the president.

The liberals took a different view about the implications of Oswald's visit to Mexico City, although they, too, adopted as fact and without question the Mexico City scenario as related by the CIA. The liberals concluded, from the same body of evidence, that Oswald had acted alone. They assserted that his trip to Mexico City may have been activated by a desire to include the Russians in his murder plot and the Cubans in his escape, but that there was no evidence that he succeeded. More impressed with modern conventional psychiatry than their conservative brethren, they focused upon a psychological profile prepared for review by the CIA that branded Oswald a confirmed loner with delusions of grandeur. Oswald may have dreamed of being center stage in the politics of world intrigue, but at heart he always knew he was alone and he carried out the most momentous action of his life as a solitary figure. He merely had wished to alert the Russians and Cubans in advance so that following his awesome political achievement, he might be properly credited and honored.

President Johnson, who had appointed the commission members, was neither a liberal nor a conservative, just a good, old-fashioned opportunist who knew how to keep his options open. He took a characteristically middle position. In an April, 1975, interview with Walter Cronkite, Johnson said, "I can't honestly say that I've ever been completely relieved of the fact that there might have been international connections." When Cronkite asked if Cuba might have been involved in the assassination, Johnson replied, "Oh, I don't think we ought to discuss suspicions because there's not any hard evidence that would lead me to the conclusion that Oswald was directed by a foreign government." He added, "But he was quite a mysterious fellow, *and he did have a connection that bore examination*, and the extent of the influence of those connections on him I think history will deal with more than we're able to do now." Johnson had also told Leo Janos in an article published in *Atlantic* magazine in 1973, "I never believed that Oswald acted alone."

These, then, were the historic reactions to the evidence presented to the Warren Commission. And the following pages present that evidence. Very little of it is true.

At the outset it should be understood that almost all of the information regarding Oswald's alleged visit to Mexico and his contact with the

Soviets and Cubans while there had been fabricated by the Central Intelligence Agency. In its report, the commission cited the CIA as the primary source for the Mexico City scenario, declining to seek independent corroboration for the CIA's version of events. Nevertheless, the Mexico City scenario constitutes the conventional wisdom as promulgated by the CIA and accepted by the Warren Commission. It remains an article of faith for those who subsequently endorsed the Warren Report, including journalists and official investigating committees. One of the central tenets of the lone assassin theory is Lee Harvey Oswald's presence in Mexico City.

Soon after the commission was created, the CIA informed Earl Warren that Oswald had been in Mexico from September 26 to October 3, 1963, and that he had spent most of that time in Mexico City. According to the CIA, Oswald had visited the Cuban Embassy in Mexico City on September 27 and the Soviet Embassy on October 1. Proof that Oswald had been in the Cuban Embassy, the CIA reported, came from Señora Silvia Duran, a Mexican employed at the Cuban Embassy. Proof that Oswald had been to the Soviet Embassy, the CIA claimed, came from the observations of its own agents.

On October 10, 1963, the CIA sent a teletype to the Department of State, the FBI, the immigration authorities, and the Department of the Navy regarding the "possible presence of Subject [Lee Harvey Oswald] in Mexico City." Two weeks later the CIA asked the Navy to "forward to the office as soon as possible two copies of the most recent photographs you have of Subject. We will forward them to our representative in Mexico who will attempt to determine if the Lee Oswald in Mexico City and Subject are the same individual."

The October 10, 1963, CIA memorandum about Lee Harvey Oswald's visit to Mexico City is the first known documentary evidence developed by the CIA to place the blame for the assassination upon Oswald.

A statement signed by Señora Duran in which she identified Oswald as the person who had visited the Cuban Embassy in Mexico City was presented to the Warren Commission by the CIA. The commission, in its report, concluded: "By far the most important confirmation of Señora Duran's testimony, however, has been supplied by confidential sources of extremely high reliability available to the United States or Mexico. The identities of these sources cannot be disclosed without destroying their future usefulness to the United States." Thus, the Warren Commission was satisfied both with Duran's testimony and with the evidence that provided support for it. The corroboration had come to the commission from the CIA, via secret intelligence sources who had infiltrated the Cuban government.

Oswald had been in the Cuban Embassy in Mexico City. That fact had been established beyond any doubt for the Warren Commission and those who would in the future support its conclusions.

Oswald's visit to the Soviet Embassy was not documented by the testimony of any Soviet national; it did not have to be. Here the CIA had gathered the firsthand evidence itself. The CIA had unchallengeable documentary proof of Oswald's entry into the Soviet Embassy in Mexico City. Not evidence that might be interpreted to demonstrate his association, but absolute proof.

The proof came in two forms, each of which provided corroboration for the other. The CIA maintained a secret hideout near, and overlooking, the Soviet Embassy. Armed with the most technologically advanced photographic equipment, it was able to actually capture clearly on film each visitor to the embassy. The CIA had photographed Lee Harvey Oswald as he entered, and later as he exited from, the Soviet Embassy in Mexico City.

Whom did Oswald meet in the Soviet Embassy? He met, Warren was informed, with a man named Valeriy V. Kostikov. A document was produced, a memorandum to the Warren Commission designated CD928. The document was not published by the commission in its twenty-six volumes of evidence. It confirmed what Warren had been told. "Valeriy Vladimirovich KOSTIKOV, who functioned overtly as a counsel in the Soviet Embassy in Mexico City since September 1961, is also known to be a staff officer of the KGB. He [Kostikov] is connected with the Thirteenth, or liquid affairs' department, whose responsibilities include assassination and sabotage."

Warren was told that assassinations planned by the Russians to take place in the United States were cleared through or initiated by Kostikov. Did Oswald know this man, Warren demanded of the CIA. He knew him, Warren was assured. In fact, Oswald had a continuing relationship with Kostikov and had even been assigned a code name, "Comrade Kostin," to use when he asked for him.

CIA technicians had recorded Oswald's telephonic communications with the Russians in the Soviet Embassy Warren was informed. The conversations they had recorded were most revealing, indeed dispositive, of all the issues. First of all, Oswald identified himself by name, asserting that he was "Lee Oswald." In addition, he specifically asked for an employee of the Soviet Embassy by name, indicating that he was on a mission of some gravity; he knew whom to ask for. He wanted to talk with Kostikov, or as Oswald put it "Comrade Kostin." Finally, the CIA had tape-recorded Oswald's request of the Soviet representative at the embassy: "Are there any messages for me?" That sentence confirmed that Oswald had a continuing relationship with Soviet Intelligence.

The CIA officers then demonstrated how seriously they took this matter. They produced a series of cables that comprised the cable traffic between the CIA's headquarters in Langley, Virginia, and its Mexico City office. The documents revealed that Kostikov had been put under surveillance by CIA agents and that the CIA had met with the United States ambassador to Mexico regarding Kostikov.

The question then became: Did the Soviets plan the execution of John F. Kennedy? The CIA had completed its own assessment of the evidence. Oswald alone had fired all of the shots that had been heard that day in Dealey Plaza. Yes, but was he encouraged by others, did the Russians plan the assassination or aid it in any way? What was Kostikov's role? These thoughts must have terrified Warren as the evidence was presented to him.

Oswald had been to the Soviet Embassy and his covertly monitored and recorded conversations without question betrayed his ongoing relationship with at least one of its employees. The CIA may not have been able to answer all these alarming questions, but it had at least succeeded in raising them.

If the members of the Warren Commission wanted additional evidence, something more tangible than solemn assurances from the CIA, that too was provided to them. On September 6, 1964, three weeks before the members of the commission submitted the report to President Johnson, Marina Oswald, the widow of the presumed assassin, made her final appearance as a witness. She had been called to testify on February 3, 1964. On that occasion she was questioned for four consecutive days. She was called back again and again. It was during her last appearance that she produced the irrefutable documentary evidence that established her deceased husband's presence in Mexico. She had found, just two weeks before, "the stub of this ticket." She offered the portion of a Mexico City bus ticket that could be retained by the passenger. It had been tucked away in "old magazines, Spanish magazines, and there was a television program also in Spanish, and there was the stub of this ticket."

At first she had been confused. She explained: "But this was, you know, a piece of paper and I didn't know this was a ticket." Fortunately, she was not alone at the time. With her was a distinguished journalist, Priscilla Johnson, and Johnson understood its significance at once. Johnson explained to the young, foreign-born woman both that it was a bus ticket and that it was just the physical evidence that the Warren Commission had been seeking. Immediately, the commission was notified. Its busy members, who had thought that their responsibility to take testimony had long since been completed, began to rearrange schedules so that they could meet with Marina Oswald one more time. This newly discovered evidence would demonstrate beyond question that Oswald had been to Mexico City.

It was indicative of the importance the members placed upon this development that they came together. After all, each member had other public and private obligations. The chairman, Earl Warren, was the chief justice of the United States. Richard Russell and John Sherman Cooper were both influential members of the Senate and leaders of important committees there. Gerald Ford and Hale Boggs were leaders in the House of Representatives.

Allen Dulles, on the other hand, was not daily engaged in partisan political encounters. Fired by President Kennedy for deceiving him about CIA operations, including events preceding and related to the Bay of Pigs fiasco in which E. Howard Hunt played such a crucial role, he had been appointed to the commission to tell the new president and the American people the truth about the death of John Kennedy. He had more time to devote to the work of the commission than some of the others. He became its most active member, and its most manipulative and cynical as well.

The commission produced a 26-volume record of testimony and exhibits that the commission stated had formed the basis for the conclusions offered in its one-volume report. The report was released to the media for comment on September 27, 1964. The evidence upon which it was purportedly based was not released until November 23, 1964. Yet when the conclusions, accompanied by a government-prepared news release, but devoid of any evidentiary basis, were published, they were accepted and praised almost universally in the United States. Walter Cronkite, speaking for CBS, urged Americans to "have faith" in the report as if we were undergoing a theological moment, not reading a government document.

Although none of the evidence was available to it, the New York Times, in its editorial published on September 27, 1964, wrote, "The Commission analyzed every issue in exhaustive, almost archaeological detail. . . . The facts, exhaustively gathered, independently checked and cogently set forth, destroy the basis for conspiracy theories that have grown weedlike in this country and abroad."

Clearly there were no serious questions asked at the *New York Times* that day.

In that atmosphere the commission completed its work. At least one question had been resolved beyond cavil. Lee Harvey Oswald had been to Mexico City.

Yet an examination of the commission's paper trail reveals that had Oswald lived, he could not have been convicted. Even after his death he was denied a fair hearing.

The press did its part to create an atmosphere prejudicial to Oswald. When he was murdered by Jack Ruby two days after his arrest, he was still a suspect, nothing more. No evidence against him had been tested, no effort had been made to permit the public to hear his version of the events, and a deliberate and successful effort had been made by the authorities, federal and state, to deny him an opportunity to meet with counsel.

As previously mentioned, Oswald was a suspect who kept crying out, each time he was led from a cell to an interrogation room, that he was innocent, that he wanted to meet with a lawyer, and that he had apparently been set up, since he was a "patsy."

Upon his death, the *New York Times*, on its front page, ran the story of his death under a headline that proclaimed "President's Assassin Shot to Death in Jail Corridor by a Dallas Citizen." (*New York Times*, November 25, 1963.)

Do we perceive any judgments here? Oswald had been found guilty at a meeting held in the *New York Times* editorial room and Jack Ruby, the sleazy, police-connected proprietor of a strip joint, a man who had served as an informant for the FBI, who had been a suspect in a labor union murder done for organized crime in Chicago in 1939, and who had violated the law on numerous occasions since his arrival in Dallas, became "A Dallas Citizen."

While the media was denying Oswald the presumption of innocence, the Warren Commission was doing the same. Years later, following the excesses that marked the Watergate scandal, including but not limited to, the illegal entry of the Democratic party offices, engineered by Hunt, Liddy, Colson, and others, the one positive result was the passage by Congress of amendments to the Freedom of Information Act. As we have seen, that legislation made it possible to procure copies of documents that had been, until that moment, shrouded in official secrecy. Documents issuing from Warren Commission members and the Johnson administration indicate just how much the powers that be had vested in proving that Oswald, and no one but, had killed JFK. As we examine and discuss the documents, it is useful to remember that when they were created, their authors were secure in the belief that not a single memo would ever be exposed to hostile or even questioning review.

On February 17, 1964, Marvin Eisenberg, a lawyer for the Warren Commission, wrote an internal commission memorandum, something never intended for public scrutiny. It was entitled "First Staff Conference—January 20, 1964." The conference, and documents relating to it, had been marked "Top Secret." Warren, having just received his instructions from President Johnson, was issuing marching orders to his staff of attorneys and explaining the reasons for the uncharacteristic directions he was imposing upon them.

He explained, according to the memorandum, that Johnson wanted the commission to squelch "rumors" that "were circulating in this country and overseas." The need to destroy these "rumors" was expressed even before the commission had taken evidence to determine what the facts were, and therefore, whether the despised "rumors" were true.

Warren explained that "some rumors" were so potentially explosive that "if not quenched, [they] could conceivably lead the country to war which could cost 40 million lives." Clearly, the president and the chief justice had something quite specific in mind if a nuclear war might hang in the balance.

What did Johnson expect Warren to do, and what did Warren see as his obligation in order to save his nation and prevent the feared cataclysmic event from occurring?

The memorandum of the meeting provides the answer: "No one could refuse to do something which might help prevent such a possibility." Specifically, Johnson called upon Warren, and Warren explained that he had acceded to the demand, to set aside his belief system and his sense of justice in the face of this national crisis and international emergency. Warren, according to the memorandum, stated: "The President convinced him that this was an occasion on which actual conditions had to override general principles."

What were the "actual conditions" that threatened the peace of the world?

The deputy attorney general, Nicholas Katzenbach, knew. On November 25, 1963, only three days after the assassination, he wrote to Bill Moyers, Johnson's press secretary. The investigation had not yet begun, yet Katzenbach insisted that the "public must be satisfied that Oswald was the assassin; that he did not have confederates who are still at large." He demanded that immediate efforts be made so that "speculation about Oswald's motivation" be "cut off." The incredible effrontery demonstrated by the man soon to run the Department of Justice, upon the resignation of Robert Kennedy, in insisting that there be no public discussion regarding the motives of the presumed assassin, indicates the desperation then rampant among the country's leaders. The concept that the law enforcement officials wanted to prohibit Americans from even thinking about why Oswald allegedly did it, when little else could have been on their minds, is difficult, in more normal times, even to comprehend.

Katzenbach continued, insisting that "we need something to head off public speculation or congressional hearings "of the wrong sort." Public disclosure was an anathema to Katzenbach, as it was to Johnson and Warren. But what would constitute a hearing "of the wrong sort," other than the possibility that it might be conducted in the light of day?

Only many years later were we able to learn the answer to that question and understand what it was that had frightened and paralyzed the nation's leaders and turned the Warren Commission's inquiry into a charade.

On December 4, 1964, when I debated in Southern California with Joseph A. Ball, a lawyer who had served on the Warren Commission's staff. He brought along two lawyers for support, one of them a widely honored and nationally known liberal figure, A.L. Wirin, the longtime leader of the American Civil Liberties Union in California.

Wirin made an impassioned plea for support for the findings of the commission. He begged the members of the packed auditorium at the Beverly Hills High School, many of whom had respected him for many years, to accept the report. Wirin sensed, with some justification, that his message was not being universally received. He then looked directly at those in attendance and made it clear that he was going to confide in them—to offer some information not widely known, not previously published. He said, his voice rising in an earnest plea:

"I say thank God for Earl Warren. He saved us from a pogrom. He saved our nation. God bless him for what he has done in establishing that Oswald was the *lone* assassin."

The audience remained silent. I asked but one question: "If Oswald was innocent, Mr. Wirin, would you still say, 'Thank God for Earl Warren' and bless him for establishing him as the lone murderer?" Wirin thought for but an instant. He responded, "Yes. I still would say so."

He explained that his friend Earl Warren had a greater responsibility than we would ever know or begin to appreciate. And that the reputation, even the life, of one man was of little consequence when compared to the enormous stakes that were involved. I later observed that men had given their lives for their nation in the past, and were in fact sometimes recognized as heroes for having done so, but that the sacrifice was generally voluntary and that the difference was of some importance.

Little of what we said for the next few minutes was heard. The audience had come to life. They condemned Wirin and his willingness to sacrifice an innocent man with a prolonged chorus of boos and catcalls.

Wirin, as was the case with Katzenbach and Eisenberg, was referring obliquely to Oswald in Mexico City. The CIA had concluded that Oswald had acted alone; he had not involved others in his plans and no one had directed him. Warren was respectfully cautioned, however, that if the American people received the facts, surely they would demand, in the existing volatile atmosphere, still heaving with tragedy, and against the backdrop of an escalating cold war, that immediate action be taken against the Soviet Union and Cuba. Warren agreed. Under the circumstances, he was advised that since the fate of the world was now in his hands, it was imperative that the Oswald-Kostikov connection be suppressed.

Warren consented. He told the members of his staff that this was the occasion on which actual conditions had to override his general principles. If not, the matter "could conceivably lead the country into catastrophe."

A few days later, reporters asked Warren when the facts about the assassination would be made known. Warren hesitated, studied the reporters, and said: "You may never get the truth in your lifetime, and I mean that seriously."

In Langley, the celebration was under way. Warren had been encircled and captured. He had agreed to suppress data, distort the record, and issue a false report to the American people. He had been compromised, and now he would never again be a factor with which to contend. The cover-up had succeeded.

Langley had accomplished its goal with the help of its man on the commission. At a meeting of the commission members held on July 9, 1964, former CIA director Allen Dulles advised his colleagues not to be worried that their final report would be closely scrutinized. "But nobody reads. Don't believe people read in this country. There will be a few professors that will read the record ... the public will read very little."

The Facts

Warren was a true believer. He suppressed the essential truth for the worst of all reasons, and through the best of all motives; he alone knew what was right for us. It is difficult, even in retrospect, to know which is more pathetic; his belief that the American people could not be trusted with the truth or his reliance for the truth upon the CIA.

Even if everything Warren had been told by the CIA was true, his response, endorsed by President Johnson, explained by Eisenberg, and apologized away by Wirin, was unsupportable in a democratic society. Warren's primary sin, however, was not venality. It was monumental, mind-numbing stupidity.

Lee Harvey Oswald may never have visited Mexico City. He had not met Señora Duran in the Cuban Embassy there. He had neither plotted with Kostikov nor called him "Comrade Kostin."

In September 1963, the CIA, having planned to assassinate President Kennedy, established a false trail, a charade, that would inexorably lead to Lee Harvey Oswald after the murder in Dallas. The plan was brilliantly conceived. Not only would it implicate an innocent man in the crime and thus spare the CIA from responsibility, but it would focus attention upon Oswald, a man with connections to the FBI. The FBI connection would freeze J. Edgar Hoover into inaction because of fear that his bureau might be terminally embarrassed.

The FBI Connection

One of the first matters of concern to the Warren Commission was the allegation made by the attorney general of Texas, Waggoner Carr, that Oswald was an FBI informant or an FBI contract agent. The information was not offered by the attorney general as a vague rumor. He was, in fact, quite specific. According to Carr, Oswald's FBI number, as assigned to him by the bureau, was S-172 or S-179. Oswald was being paid two hundred dollars per month by the FBI and in return was performing various tasks pursuant to FBI directives.

When the commission was confronted with that evidence from the highest law enforcement officer in Texas, it reacted in alarm. J. Lee Rankin, the commission's general counsel, responded at once: "We do have a dirty rumor that is very bad for the commission."

He said that the evidence that linked Oswald to the FBI "is very damaging to the agencies that are involved in it, and it must be wiped out insofar as it is possible to do so by this commission." The method the commission chose to wipe it out was simply to solicit from Hoover an FBI statement that the assassin had not worked for him.

Orest Pena, an FBI informant, was based in New Orleans after having left Cuba, his native land. He operated a bar and a police-sanctioned house of prostitution in a building he owned on Decatur Street in the French Quarter of New Orleans. Pena provided secret lodging for CIA Cuban recruits who were to undergo training in a camp near Lake Pontchartrain prior to their attempt to invade Cuba.[1] Pena worked closely with, and reported to, FBI special agent Warren deBrueys during that period. Later, when the local police betrayed the arrangement they had entered into with Pena and arrested him, he called upon me to represent him. He told me that if I did so he would tell me all that he knew about Oswald.

Pena told me that Oswald had worked for the FBI. He showed me the

---

[1] The anti-Castro Cubans recruited by the CIA were all closely screened for political acceptability. Those who were rejected were sent to a special camp at Ponchartrain. There they were trained by Marines and others chosen by the CIA. Many of these Cubans were criminals, some were murderers. They were not sent to the Bay of Pigs. The CIA later used them for various projects including the agency's Mongoose program. They were also engaged in propaganda activities, complaining loudly, but falsely, that Kennedy was at fault for the failure at the Bay of Pigs. As Spanish language spokesmen for the CIA, they condemned Kennedy for "vacillating" and refusing, "at the last minute" to provide air cover. However National Security Directive 5412 of March 15, 1954, prevented the president from engaging U.S. troops for the invasion; he had never planned to violate that directive and had said that no U.S. military personnel would take part in the attack.

buildings in New Orleans where deBrueys and Oswald had met, the coffee shop where they had breakfast, and the side entrance to that section of the old post office building where the two men regularly met by prearrangement. He said the CIA was aware of the relationship; deBrueys had introduced Oswald to contacts known by Pena to be CIA through his service to the agency in providing lodging for Cuban defectors.

In 1975, in testimony to a House subcommittee chaired by Rep. Don Edwards, Special Agent James Hosty admitted that the Bureau had contacted Oswald prior to the Kennedy assassination. Three days before the assassination, Oswald visited the Dallas office of the FBI and left a note for his contact, Special Agent Hosty. Hosty had placed it in his work box. It remained there until Oswald was murdered by Ruby, an FBI informant. Hosty testified that two hours after Oswald's death he was ordered by his superior, Gordon Shanklin, special agent in charge, to destroy the note. He complied, tearing it up and flushing it down the toilet. Shanklin had been told by J. Edgar Hoover to get rid of the evidence, according to a *New York Times* report published approximately twelve years after the event had occurred. The note said, according to Hosty: "If you have anything you want to learn from me, come talk to me directly. If you don't cease bothering my wife, I will take appropriate action and report this to the proper authorities."

Because Hosty talked about this incident not long after the assassination, he was suspended by Hoover and later transferred to a less important post. In Oswald's notebook, seized by the authorities after his death, appeared Hosty's name, automobile license plate number, and telephone number. When the FBI submitted the notebook to the Warren Commission, one page was withheld. It was the page that referred to Hosty.

The Warren Commission Becomes Suspicious

The CIA had chosen its candidate with care. His FBI association had been confirmed. Since Oswald had lived in the Soviet Union and returned to the United States with a Russian wife, his connection to International Communism had also been established. Using those facts as the foundation upon which to build its invention, the CIA placed Oswald in Mexico City at the Cuban and Soviet embassies. The CIA story, being an invention, could not bear close scrutiny; some members of the Warren Commission were becoming suspicious when the CIA refused to provide substantiating documents.

Warren and his colleagues had been given more than adequate evidence to alert them to the fact that they were being fed false information. Both deception and self-deception were required under the circumstances. Unhappily for the nation, experts in both commodities abounded on both sides of the table.

Sen. John Sherman Cooper and Sen. Richard Russell were the two members of the Warren Commission who were beginning to become restive about the vague and unconvincing indications offered by the CIA about Oswald's Mexican excursion. They prompted Rankin to conduct an inquiry—to ask a serious question or two.

On March 12, 1964, J. Lee Rankin and other members of the staff met with Richard Helms, then the Deputy Director for Plans (DDP) of the CIA. The DDP is the United States equivalent of the KGB's "liquid affairs" department. It plans and executes covert operations, including assassinations. At the CIA, known to its denizens as "the Company," the DDP is known as "the dirty tricks department." The minutes of that meeting, available neither when the Warren Report was issued nor for years thereafter, reveal that Helms, later indicted for committing perjury while testifying before the United States Senate, told Rankin that "the Commission would have to take his word for the fact that Oswald had not been an agent" of the CIA.

Immediately after Helms offered that light note, the CIA minutes of the meeting disclose, "a considerable part of the meeting from this point forward consisted of a review by Mr. Rankin and his staff of the gaps in the investigation to date. They noted that *the most significant gap appeared in the Mexican phase.*"

The commission also wondered if the CIA had been frank in releasing documents to its members. The commissioners, the minutes disclosed, "questioned the sanitized extracts which they had been shown and wondered if there were not more." Helms admitted that the CIA had "sanitized" or censored the evidence before allowing the President's commission to view it. According to the minutes, "Mr. Helms then explained that as a matter of practice we did not release actual copies of our messages because they contained code words and digraphs which would be unintelligible to a person not familiar with them."

Four months after the Warren Commission had been assured by the CIA that Oswald had been to the Soviet and Cuban embassies in Mexico City, the CIA was still refusing to show the evidence to the commission.

The commission representatives were at last suspicious. They asked why no action had been taken by other agencies of the government after the agencies received CIA information that Oswald had been in contact with the Soviet and Cuban embassies in Mexico City. The minutes reflect that "Mr. Rankin and members of his staff *clearly felt that this was a crucial question* that needed careful review. They appeared to believe that the information on Oswald was unusual enough to have caused recipients to take special measures that might conceivably have led to a closer scrutiny of Lee Harvey Oswald and his movements." The CIA's response was deleted from the minutes before they were released.

This portion of the minutes ended in this fashion:

"At the conclusion of his remarks on the subject, Mr. Helms specified that the information he had given Mr. Rankin was extremely sensitive |CENSORED| |CENSORED|."

The CIA had refused to show its cables, dispatches, and other written documents to the Warren Commission. It offered instead the coerced, prepared statement of Silvia Duran to prove Oswald had visited the Cuban Embassy and assurances that certain unnamed CIA personnel knew that Oswald had been to the Soviet Embassy as well.

The Duran cables contained no code words or digraphs that might confound or confuse the members of the commission. The explanation offered by Helms to Rankin was entirely false. Rankin, Warren, or their colleagues could easily have ascertained that by asking for the cables; instead, they seemed comfortable in accepting what was clearly, at best, a doubtful explanation.

Silencing Silvia Duran

The CIA had good reason not to provide Warren and his associates with the cables. The claim that Oswald had been to the Cuban Embassy rested primarily upon the assertion that Señora Silvia Duran, at the relevant time an employee of the Cuban Embassy, had issued a statement to that effect. Duran was a 26-year-old citizen of Mexico. She was offered a job at the Cuban Embassy during August 1963, just one month before Oswald was said to have visited there. She was a pleasant, honest, inexperienced, and somewhat naive young woman from a family without political or social power or connections in Mexico. Her predecessor at the embassy had been killed in an automobile accident. The Mexican police thought the death was odd, but it was never thoroughly investigated.

Duran was questioned about Oswald's visit to the Cuban Embassy. She then apparently made statements that the CIA did not care for. The agency then directed its assets in the police department of Mexico City to arrest her. The arrest of Duran, necessary so that the CIA could protect its legend about Oswald's visit and permit it maximum maneuverability as it perfected its cover story, was an act that might create difficulties. The director of the CIA sent a cable to the CIA office in Mexico City:

"Arrest of Silvia Duran is extremely serious matter which could prejudice U.S. freedom of action on entire question of Cuban responsibility."

The cable directed that the Mexican police assets isolate Duran and that she be silenced while in the Mexican prison. The police were also ordered to prevent Mexican officials from learning about her arrest, the role of the CIA in the arrest, and the fact that Duran was being placed in vigorously enforced solitary confinement pursuant to the orders of the director of the CIA.

This almost incredible cable reveals the extent of CIA control over Mexican police officials, many of whom had been trained by the CIA, and many of whom were engaged by the CIA while they ostensibly worked for the Mexican government. The CIA's willingness to order Mexican police officials to make false statements to their own superiors and to mislead "circles in the Mexican government" provides insight regarding the CIA's desperation to create evidence to prove to Warren that Oswald had gone to the Cuban Embassy.

The cable sent by the director of the CIA reads: "With full regard for Mexican interest, request you ensure that her [Duran's] arrest is kept absolutely secret, that no information from her is published or leaked, that all such information is cabled to us, and that fact of her arrest and her statements are not spread to leftist or disloyal circles in the Mexican government." It is reasonable to conjecture that the "statements" that so concerned the CIA had to do with Oswald's appearance—or nonappearance—at the Cuban Embassy.

After Duran ultimately yielded and reluctantly signed a statement prepared by the CIA that identified Oswald as the visitor, she was released from prison. She had been ordered never to speak of the subject. She could not understand why the Mexican police would treat her in such a brutal and illegal fashion. She had no idea of the role of the CIA in the affair.

Outraged by the experience, once free she began to speak of her experience and thus to discredit the CIA's fabrication. The CIA was anxious to silence her out of fear that the truth about the agency's role in extracting a statement from her might become known. On November 27,

1963, soon after her release, the CIA directed Mexican authorities to rearrest her. In a cable marked "Priority," the CIA ordered that "to be certain that there is no misunderstanding between us, we want to ensure that Silvia Duran gets no impression that Americans are behind her rearrest. In other words we *want Mexican authorities to take responsibility for whole affair*." (Emphasis in the original.)

The message from the director of the CIA ordered CIA personnel in Mexico City not to confront Duran directly "or to be in contact with her" in order to provide cover for the CIA effort. CIA agents were told they could "provide questions to Mexican interrogators."

She was never called as a witness by the Warren Commission. She was not questioned by anyone associated with the commission. No commission member, lawyer, or staff employee ever talked with Silvia Duran in person or by telephone. No one associated with the commission ever sent a letter to her.

Although Warren and his fellow commissioners had no contact with Duran, they felt sufficiently confident to offer what they presumed would be the definitive words on the subject. Duran's statement had established without question that Oswald had been in the Cuban Embassy.

The commission also concluded in its report: "By far the most important confirmation of Señora Duran's testimony, however, has been supplied by confidential sources of extremely high reliability available to the United States and Mexico. The identities of these sources cannot be disclosed without destroying their future usefulness to the United States."

There was no evidence, except that manufactured by the CIA, which even indicated that Oswald had been in the Cuban Embassy. Thus the story about Oswald's planned escape route, through Cuba to the Soviet Union, which was used as "proof" that Oswald had assassinated President Kennedy, is revealed to have been entirely a CIA fabrication.

The Photograph

The more serious of the Mexico City stories offered by the CIA revolved around Oswald's meeting with Kostikov in the Soviet Embassy, given Kostikov's job description as seen by the CIA. The Soviet Union insisted that Kostikov was not a KGB officer and that it ran no department assigned to assassination and terror in the United States or anywhere else in the Western Hemisphere. Intelligence disclaimers of that nature must be discounted; would the Russians have offered a contrary assertion if Kostikov had in fact run their assassination office?

In order to convince Warren that Oswald had met with Kostikov, the CIA was left to its own internal devices. It could find no recently hired, frightened young woman in the Soviet Embassy who could be terrorized by the Mexico City police. Left to construct a tale entirely on its own, the CIA went to its own agents and its newly developed and improved technology.

Setting aside the fascinating details of how the CIA secured a building opposite the Soviet Embassy, how it placed its photographic equipment in precisely the right location to monitor all entrances and exits at the Soviet and Cuban embassies, and how it cleverly disguised its effort, including the comings and goings of its army of agents, officers, and technicians, and its remarkable achievement in electronically monitoring and recording telephone calls to and from the Soviet Embassy, the evidence of Oswald's visit comprised just what Warren had been told. It consisted of a photograph and a tape recording. The "war stories" amazed and titillated Warren and his staff of officials and lawyers. Yet the evidence, which neither Warren nor his colleagues sought to examine, probe, or inquire about, remained a photograph and a tape recording.

The photograph of the man entering an embassy in Mexico City, which Warren had been assured had depicted Oswald's treasonous act, was not a picture of Oswald.

An error made by Oswald's mother, Marguerite, caused the Warren Commission to focus on the photograph. After the CIA photographed the man who the Agency claimed was Oswald leaving a suspect embassy (the CIA at one time implied it was the Cuban Embassy and at another time asserted it was the Soviet Embassy), the picture was given by the CIA to the FBI on the morning of November 22, 1963, just hours before the assassination. It had been taken, the CIA said, on September 22, 1963, in Mexico City. The day after the assassination, an FBI agent, Bardwell D. Odum, was directed to show the photograph to Oswald's widow, Marina, and Oswald's mother, Marguerite.

Odum later prepared an affidavit in which he described the events: "On November 23, 1963, while acting officially in my capacity as a Special Agent of the Federal Bureau of Investigation, I obtained a photograph of an unknown individual, furnished to the Federal Bureau of Investigation by the Central Intelligence Agency, and proceeded to the Executive Inn, a motel, at Dallas, Texas, where Marina Oswald was staying. In view of the source of this picture, and, in order to remove all background data which might possibly have disclosed the location where the picture was taken, I trimmed off the background."

On the evening of November 23, Odum showed the photograph to

Marguerite Oswald. Initially she told Odum that she did not recognize the man in the photograph. After her son was murdered, Jack Ruby's picture was prominently published in newspapers and on television programs. Oswald's mother then stated that the man in the picture was Jack Ruby. This sensational, yet erroneous, observation caused consternation at the Warren Commission. Why had a picture of Ruby been in the hands of the FBI a day before he killed Oswald and why had it been displayed by the FBI in advance of that murder and to Oswald's future widow and mother?

Both Ruby and the man in the picture appear to be white males who are overweight. The resemblance between the two is not striking. Mrs. Oswald had not seen a picture of Ruby placed alongside the picture in question. In fact, she had seen them a day apart and under the most trying circumstances. Ruby had just murdered her son. Her mistake was understandable, yet terrifying, to the Warren Commission staff, which was anxiously trying to paper over gaping discrepancies in the evidence and displeased about the appearance of new areas of difficulty requiring explanation.

The commission set about to prove that the man in the picture was not Jack Ruby. It asked to see the photograph. James Malley, an FBI inspector, signed an affidavit in which he stated that he had secured a copy of the CIA photograph and that the Warren Commission had requested it. He swore that the CIA refused to permit the evidence to be shown to the Warren Commission unless it had "all background eliminated."

Malley said that the FBI did not show the photograph to the President's Commission on the Assassination of President Kennedy until after it had been altered pursuant to CIA instructions.

The Warren Commission was satisfied by the assurances of the CIA that Jack Ruby was in the United States between July 1, 1963, and November 23, 1963. It accepted an affidavit from a CIA official stating only that the picture was taken "outside the continental United States sometime during the period July 1, 1963 to November 23, 1963." The Warren Commission was content. It was not a picture of Jack Ruby. The commission never sought to discover the identity of the person in the photograph and in a classic display of group selective amnesia, it obliterated any memory of the original intent of the picture—to prove that Oswald had been in Mexico City. It was not a picture of Ruby; Mrs. Oswald had been mistaken. More important, however, is that it was not a picture of Lee Harvey Oswald, as, we shall see, seven FBI agents had already determined for themselves. The CIA had lied to the Warren Commission.

The Tape Recording

The only remaining evidence connecting Oswald to the Soviet Embassy was the CIA's tape recording. If accepted at face value, it did not establish his presence there—only that he had spoken to someone at the embassy, via telephone, had asked if there were any messages for him, and had inquired about "Comrade Kostin." But in those heady moments Warren, Rankin, Redlich, and their associates were willing to settle for any document that established even a tenuous link between Oswald and the Russians.

The CIA was obligated to prove that (1) someone had made the call to the Soviet Embassy; (2) the CIA had monitored the call; (3) the CIA had tape-recorded the call; and (4) the person who had made the call was Lee Harvey Oswald. The first three of the four mandatory objectives were not difficult to achieve, since the CIA had, weeks before the assassination, arranged for the call to be made and recorded. Oswald, however, who apparently was not in Mexico City at the time, had not made the call. The best evidence is, of course, the tape recording. The CIA never offered it to the Warren Commission so that its members might hear it; the commission was content to accept the CIA's word for it.

None of the previously classified documents that I was able to obtain years after the Warren Report's publication was more intriguing to me than a photocopy of a letter sent by Hoover, then the director of the FBI, to James J. Rowley, then the chief of the United States Secret Service. Enclosed with the letter was a five-page document that Hoover referred to as "the results of our inquiry into the assassination of President John F. Kennedy and background information relative to Lee Harvey Oswald."

This first comprehensive FBI report on the Kennedy assassination, completed the day following the murder, was never made available to the Warren Commission. In fact, until I received this crucial document, it had been seen only by employees of spy and police organizations.

The first FBI report reveals that the director of the CIA, the Deputy Director for Plans for the CIA, and the officer in charge of the Western Hemisphere for the CIA had all conspired to lie to the Warren Commission about Oswald's alleged presence in the Soviet Embassy. It reveals that there is no evidence that Oswald had visited the Soviet Embassy.

After Oswald's arrest at 1:51 P.M. on November 22, he was questioned for more than twelve hours between 2:30 P.M. that day and 11:00 A.M. on November 24. Shortly thereafter, he was murdered in the Dallas Police and Courts Building while an army of FBI agents and local police officers watched. Seven FBI agents had participated in interrogating Oswald.

According to the FBI report of November 23, 1963, the FBI agents involved in questioning Oswald were then advised by the Central Intelligence Agency that "an individual identified himself as Lee Oswald [and that that person] contacted the Soviet Embassy inquiring as to any message." This was, of course, the same disinformation later presented by the CIA to Warren.

The FBI report reveals that "special agents of the Bureau" . . . "listened to a recording of his voice." The CIA had given a copy of the tape to the FBI as proof that Oswald had been to the Soviet Embassy. On the tape a man's voice was heard. He identified himself as Lee Oswald and then asked if there were any messages for him.

After the FBI agents had spent two days interrogating Oswald, examining a CIA photograph of a man purported to be Oswald at the Soviet Embassy, and listening to the tape recording, they reported to the bureau. The FBI summarized the matter in a sentence: "*These special agents are of the opinion that the above-referenced-to individual was* NOT *Lee Harvey Oswald.*"

The magnitude of this CIA misconduct can be fully understood only when its conspiracy to cover up is traced to its origin. For the CIA charade, which evidently included employing an imposter for Oswald, began no later than October 1, 1963. One month and twenty-two days *before* President Kennedy was assassinated, the CIA had set into motion a series of events apparently designed to prevent any American institution from ever daring to learn the truth about the assassination, an assassination *that had not yet taken place.* More than seven weeks *before* President Kennedy was murdered, the CIA was dramatically and falsely establishing a link between Lee Harvey Oswald and a Soviet diplomat, whom the CIA would later designate as the KGB authority on assassinations in the United States.

CIA personnel, cooperating with CIA station chiefs and officials operating out of Mexico City, had created a false legend for Oswald. The CIA had established a trail that could be traced with ease from Dealy Plaza, Dallas, just after its assassins had murdered the president, to Mexico City, thus implicating Oswald in the planning stages of the assassination together with a Soviet agent. Prior knowledge of that assassination was requisite to the activation of the CIA developed apocryphal odyssey of Oswald to Mexico City and the dramatic implications of the Oswald-Kostikov meeting that never took place, and the Oswald-Duran meeting that never happened.

What remains then is the frightening, yet I believe inescapable conclusion, that the CIA had planned the murder of the president before October 1, 1963, and that its Mexico City scenario had been established in furtherance of that conspiracy.

The Bus Tickets

Only one body of evidence remained at this point unexplained, yet it is not inexplicable. If Oswald had not been at the two embassies, did not the discovery of the Spanish-language magazine and the Mexico bus ticket stubs by his widow, Marina Oswald, at least indicate that he had been to Mexico?

Here again the fine hand of the CIA may be perceived; intelligence fingerprints are figuratively all over the documents.

As Earl Warren and his colleagues, all leaders in American politics or industry, and their senior legal staff, leaders of the American bar, prepared to put their final stamp of approval on the Oswald-as-lone-assassin theory set forth by the CIA, a major public relations problem emerged. Oswald's widow, the mother of two small children, was an attractive, intelligent, and personable young woman. The problem was, she was sure that her husband was innocent, and she was not reluctant to share her conclusion and the facts that supported it.

Immediately upon her husband's death, she was illegally apprehended by the federal police and held in custody and incommunicado for months. The civil libertarians on the commission, led by Warren, and the lawyers, led by Rankin, endorsed and praised those unlawful acts.

Marina was surrounded by FBI agents and Secret Service agents and through them, and only through them, she was given information about the assassination and the presumed role of her husband.

She persisted in her belief that Lee was innocent; she could not understand the rapidly developing body of evidence, displayed to her by the federal police, that seemed to incriminate him. Many years later, Marina and I met. She told me then that she had learned of my efforts to secure the truth and that she had attempted to contact me to represent her. She was not allowed by her captors to call me; the FBI agents had falsely informed her that I was planning to destroy her by demonstrating that both she and Lee were guilty.

Marina was a Russian citizen, a resident of the United States, who had renounced her ties to the Soviet Union. She was penniless and responsible for supporting her children. The federal police sent agents to her who warned that she could be deported to the Soviet Union, a country where she would not be welcome, and that any child born in the United States was a citizen of the United States. She would be deported, but she would not be allowed to take both children with her.

In an autobiographical sketch, Marina wrote of the FBI agents "who have been tormenting me every day." She wrote that the FBI "should not count on my practically becoming their agent if I desire to stay and live in the United States."

Marina was incredulous when FBI agents informed her that Lee had been in Mexico from September 26 to October 3, 1963. How could that be, she asked, without her having known about it? She said that Lee had never said he had visited Mexico, had never brought anything into the house suggesting he had been there. She said that during the period in question she had been in contact with Lee, and since she had not been in Mexico at all, how, she asked, could he have been there? The agents insisted that Marina was wrong, asked her if she wanted to be deported, and told her to be more cooperative.

FBI agents conducted a thorough search of the motel rooms where Marina and her children were being detained. They reported that they examined every scrap of paper in the rooms—not a difficult task, for Marina had taken very little with her from her home other than a few personal items and clothing for the children and herself. Nevertheless, the rooms were searched again by a different team of agents. Again, no evidence of any kind could be found indicating that Oswald had been to Mexico.

When Rankin and several members of his staff met with Richard Helms in March, Rankin wondered why, according to the CIA minutes, "they had no record of Oswald's daily movements when in Mexico City, nor could they confirm the date of his departure or his mode of travel." While the CIA had stated that Oswald had left Mexico for the United States by bus, it had offered no evidence to support that statement. The commission was worried, Rankin told Helms, because "the original assumption that he [Oswald] had returned by bus could not be proven." From March 12, 1964, until September 1964, when the Warren Report was being written, the CIA was unable to provide the elusive evidence so earnestly sought by the commission—the bus tickets.

Half a year after that meeting with Helms, staff members were engaged in writing the report. Yet neither Senator Cooper nor Senator Russell, who had together instigated the March meeting with Helms, was sanguine about its prospects. The unresolved question still rankled. Oswald was supposed to have been in Mexico for a week; why had no evidence of his presence surfaced other than that meant to place him at the embassies?

Suddenly a special, emergency session of the commission was called. At the very last moment, days before the report was to go to press, the evidence had been located. Bus tickets had been found.

Marina had looked at a Spanish-language magazine and found the ticket stubs. Priscilla Johnson explained to her what they were, their significance, and the need to immediately summon the commission together for an extraordinary session.

The meeting was held, Marina dutifully offered the tickets, and the CIA was sufficiently vindicated for the majority of the commission. With Warren already in on the plan, Dulles functioning at the commission for the CIA, and Ford appearing for the FBI, not a great deal of evidence was required.

However, Russell was not convinced. For him, the remarkable emergence of the bus tickets raised more questions. He demanded to know how it was possible that the documents could possibly have escaped the painstaking, thorough searches conducted by FBI agents. Why did Marina even take the magazine along with her from her home to the motel room months before? Why did Oswald buy and then bring back Spanish-language magazines, since he could not read Spanish? Even if it had been in English, why would anyone save a magazine that was basically a television schedule program for months after it had expired? There was no shortage of incisive questions. There just were no answers.

Apparently off-limits for the commission was a consideration of the credentials of the journalist who was with Marina when the tickets were discovered.

Logically, the journalist, Priscilla Johnson, should have been a suspect in the search for the explanation of the sudden arrival of the bus tickets. Before she had entered the room, it had been thoroughly searched and no tickets could be located. Almost immediately after she appeared, so did the tickets.

This would not have constituted the first occasion that attention of this sort had been focused upon her. The FBI, in its previously top-secret documents, had considered only two persons to be suspects in the assassination of President Kennedy. One, of course, was Lee Harvey Oswald. The other was Priscilla Johnson, probably due to her odd relationship with Lee Oswald. Perhaps when the FBI learned that she also had a close relationship with the CIA, the U.S. Embassy in Moscow, and the State Department, the Bureau decided that discretion required a rapid retreat.

While Marina Oswald was being held incommunicado, many reporters asked for permission from the federal police to interview her. The requests were routinely denied. Her own mother-in-law was not allowed to see her. A lawyer theoretically representing Oswald's interests asked to interview her so that he might fulfill his obligations as counsel. The CIA and the FBI denied his request since he might plant evidence or possibly influence her testimony with his questions, the same reasons that were given as the basis for rejecting interviews by reporters. The CIA made an exception for Johnson, even though she had previously been a suspect.

Johnson publicly stated that she was just a reporter and had no connection with the United States government, either at the time she visited Marina or at any previous time. Warren Commission document number 49 is an FBI report dated November 23, 1963, just one day after the assassination. It is about Johnson, indicating the FBI's interest in her at the very outset. It states that Priscilla Johnson was "an employee of the State Department." Subsequently, when confronted with the FBI report, she admitted that she had been employed by the State Department. Since the State Department is not the KGB or any other organization held in particular disrepute in the United States, it is intriguing to know why Johnson had made false statements about her work there, leading one to wonder if the State Department provided cover for her more furtive enterprises.

Priscilla Johnson had met Oswald in Moscow in 1959, almost as soon as he arrived there. Shortly after Oswald had been killed and questions about the assassination began to surface—particularly in view of Oswald's murder by a friend of the Dallas police and an employee of the FBI, in the Dallas Police and Courts Building—Johnson wrote an article that was published by *Harper's* magazine. In retrospect, it appears to have been a disinformation piece. She wrote:

"I sought him out a few hours earlier on the advice of an American colleague in Moscow. A boy named Oswald was staying at my hotel, the Metropol, the friend casually remarked."

Johnson sought to convince the readers that her encounter with Oswald was hardly prearranged—far more the result of an accident, rather than a plan. They happened to be stopping at the same hotel. Oswald was there, in all probability, as the result of an assignment to appear as a defector; he was the first former Marine to have made that move. Why was Johnson there? CIA document 646-277, a memorandum for the record, was the result of a CIA inquiry as to why the name Priscilla

Johnson appeared in Oswald's personal notebook. The document was almost obliterated by the government censors before we received it. It does state, however, in words still visible, that Priscilla Johnson "has apparently been employed on a part-time basis within the U.S. Embassy during two periods of residence in Russia." "Part-time basis" is a euphemism often employed by the CIA when referring to its contract agents. The assertion that she had been employed "within the U.S. Embassy" rather than "by the U.S. Embassy" may also be revealing.

In seeking to underscore the spontaneous nature of her almost chance meeting with Oswald, Johnson wrote of the "friend" who had "casually remarked" that this "boy" was at the same hotel. She later described her friend as a "colleague," and since she was posing for the American people as a journalist abroad, the illusion she deliberately created was that the colleague too was a journalist.

He may well have been a coworker of hers, as she implied, but he was not a journalist. His name is Richard Snyder. His cover was as an employee of the U.S. Embassy in Moscow. His assignment was Lee Harvey Oswald. And his real title was revealed in a formerly top-secret CIA document. His employment with the CIA began in 1949 as a G-9. The cables he sent from Moscow about Oswald to the State Department and his employers at the CIA headquarters near Washington were based upon intelligence data that had been supplied to him by Priscilla Johnson. Johnson had been assigned by the CIA to meet with Oswald and interview him. There were two possible, but not mutually exclusive, reasons for the interview. The interview would secure information sought by the CIA to be relayed back to the United States to convince the State Department that Oswald had become disloyal. The other purpose may have been to place Johnson in a position to proclaim Oswald's hatred for the United States immediately upon his death when the quotations, that she attributed to Oswald, could not be challenged.

Soon after Oswald was murdered, Johnson wrote: "He [Oswald] was angry at everything American and impatient to become a Russian citizen." Her published words were used by the CIA to demean Oswald and make him appear to be a traitor.

Johnson was married to George McMillan. When the evidence regarding the death of Dr. Martin Luther King, Jr., began to demonstrate the likelihood of intelligence coverup in that crime, and allow for the possibility of intelligence complicity in the murder, the CIA and the FBI were concerned and moved to stifle discussion of the subject. Almost all African-American leaders in the United States, including Rev. Ralph

Abernathy, Coretta Scott King, Andrew Young, Dick Gregory, and Jesse Jackson, publicly stated their doubts about the case and openly speculated about FBI and CIA involvement in the crime.

George McMillan wrote a book attempting to prove that James Earl Ray was the lone assassin of Dr. King and that there had been no intelligence connections. The FBI exclusively fed fabricated information to him which he then published.

Johnson, assisted by the intelligence agencies, entered into a contract with Marina to write a book with her. Marina, desperate for funds, signed the contract, was given a sum, and waited month after month, then year after year, for the book to be published. During that time Johnson prohibited her from speaking to anyone about any of the relevant events. After the book was published, Marina told me that much of it was false and was known by Priscilla Johnson to be false.

Johnson continued to assert that she was an independent journalist without any undercover ties to the government. The Boston law firm that represents her, Davidson and Shattuck, once threatened to sue if a published allegation questioning her disclaimer was not withdrawn. The law firm wrote: "As to the allegations of her being an undercover government employee throughout this period, there exists not even the slightest reasonable foundation for such an allegation." The retraction was not published. Johnson did not sue.

In 1967, Johnson became openly engaged with the CIA, in its most successful public operation. Johnson had interviewed Svetlana Alliluyeva, Josef Stalin's daughter, in Moscow. The CIA was furtively planning to entice Alliluyeva to defect to the United States, offering her large sums of money, some of which would be offered for rights to her life story for a book.

In April of that year, Alliluyeva defected; the CIA had accomplished one of the major coups in its history.

Upon Alliluyeva's arrival in the United States, the CIA formulated and carried out a massive public relations campaign. From its studios in Munich, Radio Free Europe, which described itself as a "private broadcast operation," but that was a proprietary arm of the CIA that provided all of its funding, dispatched the news of the defection of Stalin's daughter throughout Eastern Europe. The Voice of America, the broadcasting service of the United States Information Agency, sent the story of Alliluyeva's arrival in the United States all over the world, including the Soviet Union, where it was broadcast in Russian.

Security concerns and the need to keep hostile, or even genuinely inquisitive, reporters from their prize catch occupied the highest ranking officials of the CIA. Alliluyeva, as in the case of Marina Oswald—who was now just a footnote in a closed history book—needed as a constant companion a person the CIA could absolutely rely upon. She also needed a CIA safe house at which to be placed. Happily for the agency, there appeared an obvious solution.

Stalin's daughter was kept at the home occupied by Priscilla Johnson and Johnson became her companion. The home chosen by the CIA as a safe house was owned by Johnson's parents.

Then there was the question of funding for Alliluyeva. Evan Thomas, who had edited William Manchester's defense of the Warren Commission Report in a book published by Harper & Row, a publishing house the CIA considered friendly and appropriate, decided to edit Alliluyeva's book as well. He assigned Priscilla Johnson to translate the work for Harper & Row.

Marina and Svetlana shared an almost unique experience. Each was cared for, protected, and controlled by Johnson. Lee Oswald and Svetlana also shared one moment at separate times. Each had been interviewed by Johnson, in Moscow, before leaving for the United States. How truly fortunate for the CIA that Johnson happened to be present when the Spanish-language magazine and the devoutly wished-for bus tickets materialized in Marina's room that September day in 1964. With the magic bus tickets, the CIA had virtually silenced the last doubters on the commission, and the report was ready for publication. According to Warren and his associates, Oswald, acting alone, had killed the president, Oswald had been to the Soviet and Cuban embassies in Mexico City, Johnson was an ordinary journalist, and, in the words of Dorothy Parker, "I am Marie of Rumania."

Silencing the Critics

More than a decade after the assassination, when I won a lawsuit against various police and spy organizations in the United States district court in Washington, D.C., pursuant to the order of the court, I received many long-suppressed documents.

Among them was a top-secret CIA report. It stated that the CIA was deeply troubled by my work in questioning the conclusions of the Warren Report and that polls that had been taken revealed that almost half of the American people believed as I did. The report stated, "Doubtless polls abroad would show similar, or possibly more adverse, results." This "trend of opinion," the CIA said, "is a matter of concern" to "our organization." To counter developing opinion within the United States, the CIA suggested that steps be taken. It should be emphasized, the CIA said, that "the members of the Warren Commission were naturally chosen for their integrity, experience, and prominence. They represented both major parties, and they and their staff were deliberately drawn from all sections of the country. *Just because of the standing of the commissioners, efforts to impugn their rectitude and wisdom tend to cast doubt on the whole leadership of American society.* [Emphasis added.]

The purpose of the CIA secret document was apparent. In this instance, there was no need for incisive analysis. The CIA report stated "The aim of this dispatch is to provide material for countering and discrediting the claims of the conspiracy theorists, so as to inhibit the circulation of such claims in other countries. Background information is supplied in a classified section and in a number of unclassified attachments." The commission had been chosen in such a fashion so that it might subsequently be asserted that those who questioned its finding, by comparing the known facts to the false conclusions offered by the commission, might be said to be subversive.

Who were these people who wished to throw suspicion upon the leaders of the land? The CIA report listed them as Mark Lane, Joachim Joesten, as well as a French writer, Leo Sauvage. Most of the criticism was directed at me. The CIA directed that this matter be discussed with "liaison and friendly elite contacts (especially politicians and editors)," instructing these persons "that further speculative discussion only plays into the hands of the opposition." The CIA continued: "Point out also that parts of the conspiracy talk appear to be deliberately generated by Communist propagandists. Urge them to use their influence to discourage unfounded and irresponsible speculation."

The CIA was quite specific about the means that should be employed to prevent criticism of the report:

"Employ propaganda assets to answer and refute the attacks of the critics. Book reviews and feature articles are particularly appropriate for this purpose. The unclassified attachments to this guidance should provide useful background material for passage to assets. Our play should point out, as applicable, that the critics are (i) wedded to theories adopted before the evidence was in, (ii) politically interested, (iii) financially interested, (iv) hasty and inaccurate in their research, or (v) infatuated with their own theories. In the course of discussions of the whole phenomenon of criticism, a useful strategy may be to single out [Edward Jay] Epstein's theory for attack, using the attached Fletcher Knebel article and *Spectator* piece for background." According to the CIA, my book, *Rush to Judgment*, was "much more difficult to answer as a whole." The agency document did not list any errors in the book.

Just in case the book reviewers did not get the point, the CIA offered specific language that they might incorporate into their critiques. "Reviewers" of the books "might be encouraged to add to their account the idea that, checking back with the Report itself, they found it far superior to the work of its critics."

Among those who criticized *Rush to Judgment* and other books along lines similar to those suggested by the CIA were the *New York Times*, the *Washington Post*, the *Los Angeles Times*, and, especially, Walter Cronkite and CBS. Among those who did *not* march in lockstep with the intelligence agencies' effort to destroy the First Amendment were the *Houston Post*; Norman Mailer, who reviewed *Rush to Judgment* in the United States (see Appendix, page 361) and Len Deighton, who reviewed it in London.

The question persists, in view of the elaborate and illegal program undertaken by the CIA to malign American citizens and to discourage publishers from printing dissents from the Warren Commission Report, as to the motivation for these efforts. Again, we turn to the CIA dispatch: "Our organization itself is *directly* involved: among other facts, we contributed information to the investigation." [Emphasis added.] Yes, the CIA *was* directly involved and it did make its contribution to the investigation. What else the CIA did to constitute its "direct" involvement in the assassination was left unsaid by the authors of its report.

Let us focus at this point upon the information that the CIA contributed. Its major contribution was the presentation of the Mexico City story to Earl Warren. The CIA seemed desperately concerned that its Mexico City story might be questioned. Indeed, it was this aberrant behavior by the CIA with this aspect of the case that led me to focus more intently on the case.

The first book review of *Rush to Judgment* was never printed in any newspaper or journal, at least not in the form in which the review originally appeared. The book was published in mid-August 1966. Before I saw the printer's proofs, the CIA had obtained a copy. On August 2, 1966, the CIA published a document entitled "Review of Book—*Rush to Judgment* by Mark Lane." I did not learn the existence of that document for almost a decade. The review centered upon statements I had written about Oswald in Mexico City:

"On pages 351 and 352, Lane discusses the photograph of the unknown individual which was taken by the CIA in Mexico City. The photograph was furnished by this Agency to the FBI after the assassination of President

Kennedy. The FBI then showed it to Mrs. Marguerite Oswald who later claimed the photograph to be that of Jack Ruby. A discussion of the incident, the photograph itself, and related affidavits, all appear in the Commission's Report (Vol. XI, p. 469; Vol. XVI, p. 638). Lane asserts that the photograph was evidently taken in front of the Cuban Embassy in Mexico City on 27 September 1963, and that it was furnished to the FBI on the morning of 22 November."

The concern about my relatively nonincriminating disclosure was surprising to me at the time, however, a decade after the assassination it became apparent that the case that the CIA had so painstakingly constructed, placing Oswald in Mexico City at the two embassies, had fallen apart as if it were a house of cards. Not one material bit of evidence remained. It was a new day. The war in Vietnam and crimes committed by authorities, including President Nixon, were beginning to convince the American people that simplistic explanations of past national tragedies might be challenged. Statements by leaders of government or federal police officials were no longer sacrosanct.

The Confession

DONALD FREED, ONE OF MY OLDEST AND DEAREST FRIENDS, IS A SCREENWRITER, a playwright, and an author. He lives in Los Angeles. During 1977, he decided that it would be useful to the nation if the CIA and its informed critics had a public rendezvous. Donald was in professional contact with the School of Continuing Education at the University of Southern California. He suggested to the director of that institution that a debate be arranged. He said that he knew me, Daniel Ellsberg, and John Gerassi, a former correspondent for the *New York Times* and *Newsweek*. Ellsberg was an authority on the Pentagon, Gerassi was knowledgeable about Latin America, and I had looked into the Kennedy assassination and other CIA excesses.

Freed suggested that the university contact William Colby, the former director of the CIA. Colby agreed to appear and referred Freed to David Atlee Phillips, pointing out that the request came at a most fortuitous moment. Phillips had organized the Association of Former Intelligence Officers, a group 5,000 strong, and was anxious to publicize it. Phillips, and then Ray Cline, former deputy director of the CIA, both accepted invitations.

During September 1977, Donald Freed served as host at a unique event—the only open and public debate between former or present high-ranking CIA officers and those who were critical of their actions.

The first debate was between Cline and Gerassi. While discussing Latin America, Cline professed to be amazed that anyone could be critical of the brutal destruction of the government of the Dominican Republic by the CIA, asserting that it was, after all, "a lousy little country and always has been." After the debate, as Cline was about to leave the hall, I asked him if he really believed that the culture, history, and people of the Dominican Republic could best be summed up as comprising "a lousy little country" and if his view in that regard played any part in the decision by the CIA to destroy the aspirations for democracy among the people of that country. Cline studied me. His face became red. He began to respond, but suddenly he interrupted himself. He then shouted at me, although I was but five feet from him, "I know who you are. You're the Kennedy writer. You're the most disgusting of the lot. I'm going, we're going, to get you."

I suggested that since that was apparently his ambition, he might wish to try to realize it right then. The short and stocky man actually lunged at me, more a figure of amusement than a threat. His security guards quickly surrounded him, leaving the decided impression that they were there less to protect him than to protect others from his temper tantrums.

Later that day I appeared with David Atlee Phillips. Phillips was the first official of the Central Intelligence Agency that I had ever met, or at least the first person I met whom I knew to be a CIA officer. As head of the Western Hemisphere for the CIA, he had been involved in the agency's attempt to malign me and to suppress and discredit *Rush to Judgment*. The organization he had formed after his retirement on behalf of the CIA was committed to combatting criticism of the agency.

Far more important, however, was his central role in the creation, *before* the murder of the president, of the Mexico City scenario while station chief there. The Mexico City card could not have been played at the appropriate time unless the deck had been adroitly stacked. Phillips was the technician, a high-ranking agency official operating under deep cover from Mexico City. It was a brilliant concept, one that both led the investigators inexorably to Oswald and then frightened them into looking no further. Its execution, however, was flawed, as I discovered when it all began to unravel.

I began my confrontation with Phillips by recounting the then-recently published disclosure that the CIA had maintained a house of prostitution. Under its program, code-named "Midnight Climax," the bordello was established at a CIA safe house, equipped with cameras and tape recorders, at which CIA employees, the prostitutes, furtively administered drugs to their own unsuspecting agents, journalists, and diplomats. In referring to Cline, I commented only that I did resent being called "disgusting" by the proprietors of whorehouses.

Then we addressed the question at hand: the role of the CIA in the assassination of President Kennedy.

Not knowing that almost a decade later events would so conspire that I would be able to question Phillips at a deposition, I presumed that my encounter with him at the debate would constitute my only opportunity. The CIA had conducted a series of psychological studies of me and prepared an official document, the Lane Psychological Profile, predicting my reaction to various stimuli, such as how I would respond to false charges that I had investigated the assassination for the sole purpose of reaping financial benefits. I knew Phillips would rely upon the suggestions contained in that file.

In preparation for the debate, I utilized my own limited resources to try to understand Phillips and his mind-set as he emerged into the light of free inquiry after twenty-five years of deception and furtive behavior. A few acquaintances who had been officers or agents with the CIA or FBI provided some clues. I was not about to formally cross-examine Phillips; he could always refuse to answer my questions, pleading his secrecy agreement with the CIA or concerns for that elusive concept, national security. Yet, since he wanted this public exchange to create some indicia of credibility, he would be constrained to say something and to answer some difficult questions. To be effective, I reasoned, my approach to the exchange should be direct, unyielding, and devoid of polite euphemism.

The debate was advertised as an opportunity to hear the expression of differing views by both the defenders and critics of the CIA. I redefined its nomenclature with my opening sentence, in which I thanked Mr. Freed and the officials at the University of Southern California for "bringing about the first serious confrontation between the victims of the excesses of the intelligence organizations over the years and those responsible for the excesses."

The smile on Phillips' face vanished. I continued: "This is not the ultimate step, this is not a trial at Nuremberg; perhaps that will come, probably not, but at least we are now beginning the opening stages of a dialogue." The mention of Nuremberg and the hint of what lay ahead unsettled Phillips. His face became ashen. He knew what he had done over the years; he just did not know how much of it I had discovered.

Phillips had announced before we began that he supported my call for a full-scale investigation by the House Select Committee on Assassinations to discover and report the truth about the assassination of President Kennedy. By this time the CIA had pulled the fangs from the Committee. If he thought that his tardy proclamation would resolve or soften the pending questions, he was soon disabused of that notion. I continued: "We will talk about a thirteen-year continuing effort by the CIA, and Mr. Phillips, to impugn the character and destroy the reputation of anyone in this country who dared to say 'I support an investigation of the assassination' before the official moment, evidently now, when it became permissible to take that position. We will discuss the covert actions of the CIA against every single critic of the Warren Commission Report, while Mr. Phillips was in charge of the Western Hemisphere for the Central Intelligence Agency."

My plan, rather transparent I feared, was to confront Phillips with his past and, by doing so, challenge him to demonstrate his resolve to reform by uttering a few public truths. I went to work. I held up in one hand a book recently written by Phillips in which he wrote on its first page, "I was pleased with the course of my career after twenty-five years in secret operations." He wrote of his quarter of a century with the CIA. In my other hand I held the then current Who's Who in America. I said the material was provided by the subject. According to Who's Who in America, Phillips had never worked for the CIA. "Do you know what he was doing in Havana from 1958 to 1961? This was during the time that Castro came to power and the CIA had entered into a merger with organized crime to assassinate him. According to Phillips, via Who's Who, he was 'proprietor, David A. Phillips, Public Relations, Havana, Cuba.' "

The audience responded with laughter. Phillips wrote furiously on his pad.

Before putting aside Phillips's most recently published work, I observed that in it he had written that Oswald had sent a note to the FBI stating that he would "blow up the FBI and Dallas Police Department."

The note was addressed to FBI special agent James Hosty. As stated earlier, when Hosty appeared before a Congressional committee charged with FBI oversight he testified that the note from Oswald actually said:

"If you have anything you want to learn about me, come talk to me directly. If you don't cease bothering my wife, I will take appropriate action and report this to the proper authorities."

I suggested that Phillips had helped to create and promulgate a fiction for many years. It was comprised of the allegations that he had made in Mexico City in 1964 to investigators for the Warren Commission, when he said he knew that Oswald had been in Mexico City in the fall of 1963. I pointed out that the deception was continued in Phillips's book, just published. Phillips looked up from his notebook, stared at me, and then jotted something down on his pad.

I explained to the audience how Warren and his colleagues, and through them, the nation, were held hostage to the CIA's fabrication about the Oswald-Kostikov meeting. I called upon Phillips, at long last, to make a genuine contribution to his country by telling the truth about the matter. Phillips stared at me.

I said that Phillips had recently testified before the House Select Committee on Assassinations. He seemed startled when I added, "I know what he said there." Phillips had appeared in executive session, having been called by the general counsel and staff director, Richard Sprague. After Sprague was removed from that position through covert actions of the CIA, the new counsel had assured Phillips, in essence, that he had nothing to worry about. Phillips was then under the impression that this testimony was secret and would not be revealed. I recounted Phillips's most recent testimony: "Phillips testified that tape recordings were made when Lee Harvey Oswald called the Soviet Embassy in Mexico City. He explained that the CIA could not give the recordings to the Warren Commission because 'they had been destroyed before the assassination, as a routine matter.' An internal regulation required the destruction of tapes within one week after they had been created, he said. When asked to produce that regulation, he said it too had been destroyed. 'Of course, if we had known how important Oswald was going to be, we would have preserved and guarded those tapes,' he said. 'But this was weeks before the assassination.'"

I told the audience that "Each statement made by Mr. Phillips, is untrue. The CIA, in fact, provided copies of the recordings to the FBI *after* the assassination. Only when the FBI reported that Oswald's voice was not on the tape, that it was the voice of an imposter, did Mr. Phillips and the CIA destroy the evidence. It was not routine; they should be indicted for obstruction of justice and at least as accessories *after* the fact in the murder of the president."

Phillips stared into space as I spoke. I departed from a discussion of the details of the Kennedy assassination and addressed a CIA operation in Vietnam. "The Phoenix Program was established by the United States government under the direction of this evening's guest speaker, William Colby. In his testimony, before a committee of the House, he admitted that his program carried out the selective assassination of twenty thousand Vietnamese. His colleague, the Saigon regime's minister of information, insisted that the figure of forty thousand was more accurate."

I pointed out that Dr. Martin Luther King, Jr., not long before his death, had compared our actions in Vietnam with the excesses of Hitler during World War II. "Dr. King was referring, in large measure, to the Phoenix Program and the CIA-endorsed torture and mutilation of Vietnamese civilians." I cited the recent testimony of Vietnam veteran Bart Osborne before a congressional committee. He had said that in the year and one-half that he had been in Vietnam, he saw numerous people questioned and tortured by CIA-trained interrogators and that "not one of them even survived the interrogation."

I remarked that I had recently read *Spandau*, written by Albert Speer, Hitler's architect. "Speer had, during his twenty years of imprisonment, finally come to grips with what he, and the regime for which he worked, had done in Europe."

I concluded: "Until that moment comes when the leaders of our intelligence agencies, who have participated in similar conduct, demonstrate some understanding of what they have done, and until our nation takes appropriate action, there can be no basic change in the intelligence establishment."

The years in Spandau had been salutary in Speer's case, I observed. "Yet the men who have committed crimes from Langley, to Saigon, to Mexico City—these CIA officials by contrast still travel freely as honored guests of the military, industrial, and academic establishment."

I passed Phillips, who was still seated, his head in his hands, as I walked from the podium to my chair.

In the CIA dispatch to its assets in the news media, the Agency provided specific arguments to be used in condemning me and other dissenters from the Warren Commission Report. It suggested that the critics "have produced no new evidence, no new culprits" and that "conspiracy on a large scale would be impossible to conceal."

The production or creation of evidence is an area that apparently had been preempted by the CIA—I never considered it to be my function. As to a failure to produce a culprit, I believe that such a conspiracy, given the varied nature of the participants, may be subject to gradual exposure, as previously concealed evidence comes into the light.

And so it was in this instance.

Phillips rose slowly, strode to the lectern, and stood there silently for a moment. He pushed his notes aside, as if to demonstrate that he had decided to reject them.

"I think I now realize that my credibility is not now one hundred percent. I want to tell you some things that have happened to me so that they might make some difference in the vital judgments that you and the American public should be making about me and the Central Intelligence Agency."

He appeared to be shaken. His voice had a catch. His eyes glistened as if filled with tears. I looked at him and then at the audience. I felt that his performance was brilliant; that some in the audience were persuaded and were already responding to his plea for understanding. I felt confident that he was a consummate actor; he had been both an actor and a playwright, and I believed that his remarks were entirely insincere and calculated exclusively for effect. I was wrong.

Phillips then discussed the House Select Committee on Assassinations: "As you remember, the House Select Committee started and then self-destructed. They had this terrible problem. Recently, however, I have found it to be very responsible indeed, and I have looked forward to their ultimate report so that we will all know what we are talking about. But now I know that Mr. Lane has been passed information from that committee. I had thought until now that they were assembling the facts and keeping them secret until they could make their judgment."

The audience did not know, but I did, that the "terrible problem" the committee had suffered had been manufactured by the CIA.

Phillips then looked toward me and addressed me:

"About my book, and the statement that Oswald had threatened to blow up the FBI building, I appreciate your clarification on that. I'm glad to get straight on that."

He examined his notes and then said:

"About being in Who's Who in Havana, I mean Who's Who in America, I resigned from the Central Intelligence Agency in 1958. I really resigned. And I went to Cuba to live to start a public relations concern because I was convinced that the dictatorship of Batista was going to be overthrown by Fidel Castro and none of the American companies there had bothered to have public relations there. So I thought I would be on hand. So I really did resign." There was considerable laughter from the audience.

"As it turned out, I went back to work almost immediately for the CIA because there was no public relations for me. That led to the problem in Who's Who in America. It's one of the problems with being a spook; you have to lead a double life. When I signed the paper to become a scoutmaster for my boy's troop, there was a thing that said 'occupation.' What was I supposed to put down—'Spy'? Was I supposed to write to Who's Who and say 'I'm a secret agent'? This is one of the parts of the moral dilemma."

I tried to gauge the audience response to Phillips, but was unable to. At that point, I was not even sure of my own reactions. He did seem to be in some pain as he contemplated his life. Yet I had been too long victimized by him and his associates to be objective, let alone sympathetic.

He then reverted to form. He launched an attack, relatively modest but sufficient under the circumstances, by utilizing the words of others. Covert habits apparently die hard.

"I'm also glad that Mr. Lane and I are not just fighting because I flew in on the red-eye special, and I haven't had much sleep, and I'm a little tired. And I appreciate the fact that there has been some limit to the business of personal attack. So I, in getting into that field, have decided that I won't make a statement like that. But in countering a couple of things that were said I will only refer to published material by others. Mr. Lane has talked about a long period in which the character of certain people was attacked. And I now quote from the *Washington Post* in an article which was written about Mr. Lane, by George Lardner, Jr., quoting George McMillan, author of a book about the killing of Dr. Martin Luther King. And it goes on, it talks about how Mr. Lane has accused Jeremiah O'Leary, of the *Washington Star*, and others. It shows how he has misled the American people and the Congress. At least one of those gentlemen he has implied was an agent of some sort has now written, asking Mr. Lane to please state it in terms that are just a little clearer so he can take legal action."

Having made his point, he looked about and sensed, I believe, that he had lost his audience. A member of the audience grew impatient. He half-shouted: "Mexico City, Mr. Phillips. What is the truth about Mexico City?"

Phillips looked directly at the man and began:

"Mr. Lane has said that what happened in Mexico City, and the report given by the CIA was wrong, wrong, wrong—wrong. He has combined some truth and much misstatement to come up with his conclusions. Now, I am not in a position today to talk to you about the inner workings of the CIA station in Mexico City. I am not in a position to talk to others about the details of my testimony, before Mr. Sprague, in executive session; but I will tell you this, that when the record comes out, we will find that there was never a photograph taken of Lee Harvey Oswald in Mexico City. We will find out that Lee Harvey Oswald never visited, let me put it, that is a categorical statement, there, there, we will find out there is no evidence, first of all there was no proof of that. Second, there is no evidence to show that Lee Harvey Oswald visited the Soviet Embassy."

I sat there stunned. Phillips had confessed.

His statement to the Warren Commission given in Mexico City was, he now admitted, false, as was his recent testimony before the congressional committee and as were his words in his newly published book. I looked at Donald Freed. Had I heard what I thought I had heard? Donald nodded; he had heard the words. The CIA knew that it could not prove that Oswald had visited the Soviet Embassy; the statement had been made by a man who had run the CIA in Mexico City at the time in question.

I looked at the reporter who was tape-recording the meeting, indicating that I wanted a copy of the tape. He, too, nodded in assent.

Phillips realized, I believe, that he had revealed too much. He sought to explain that Oswald might have made a telephone call in which he might have talked to a Soviet intelligence officer.

"If you call on the telephone to any Soviet Embassy in the world, the odds are better than fifty-fifty that the man who picks up the phone will be an intelligence officer and so forth. So I can't make, really make, a big argument about that because I simply am not in a position to go into detail."

Phillips, having started to tell some of the truth, then tried to convince the audience that its worst fears and suspicions might be merited.

"However, I make you this comment. If Mr. Lane turns out to be right, and what he says about Mexico, and what he says about the CIA deliberately giving fake information about all these things, if his story proves to be substantially true, I promise this group that I'll fly back here, at my own expense, for my first public statement calling for the abolishment of the Central Intelligence Agency. I was so sort of taken aback by this, by what Mr. Lane said. If the CIA as an institution proves to have been responsible for these charges, I will do that. If some CIA guy that I never saw did something that I never heard of, I don't want to have to come back here."

The audience was invited to ask questions. Abby Mann, the screenwriter who wrote the classic American film *Judgment at Nuremberg* directed a question to Phillips: "Why did the CIA decide to destroy critics of the Warren Commission? Why don't you address yourself to that instead of reading to us from newspaper articles written by CIA assets? Doesn't that strike you as being unfair?"

Phillips looked at Mann. He suddenly betrayed the impression that he recognized him. He began to speak deliberately, repeating Mann's question:

"Doesn't that strike you as unfair? In twenty-five years as an intelligence officer I have been called on on a number of occasions, to perform actions which were 'dirty tricks'—unfair. To say that one is going to work

83

in the intelligence profession for a quarter of a century and live by the rules of the Boy Scouts, it just doesn't happen.

"There are certainly a number of things that I regret, and I regret the attempts to destroy Mr. Lane. There are a number of things for which intelligence officers should go to jail if they violate the law. Sure, I regret a lot of it."

The next question was directed to me. A student wanted to know how I had learned of the Phillips testimony if it was secret. "Aren't you using the same methods which the CIA used?" he demanded.

I answered that Dick Sprague had been counsel to the committee. After Phillips testified, he talked to the news media. Months later I asked Sprague, when he was no longer counsel, if he was precluded from telling me about Phillips's testimony. He said he was free to discuss it with me; that he had never been asked to sign a document that limited his right to comment. Phillips had made it clear that approximately one week after Oswald had allegedly visited Mexico City during the last days of September and the first days of October 1963, the CIA had destroyed the tape recording.

I pointed out that the only information I ever received from the House Committee was about the Phillips testimony. In all other respects, my relationship with the committee was a one-way street; I provided documents, information, and analysis for the committee and on numerous occasions I briefed both the members and the counsel for the committee.

A student asked Phillips if he had personally approved of plans "to destroy Mr. Lane, to prevent his views from being published, to limit our right to hear another view."

Phillips said: "I was in Caracas, Venezuela, when it arrived there, the CIA dispatch that Mr. Lane has talked about. I had no way of stopping it, of course. Whether I would have stopped it if I were in charge of the CIA, which is the only way I could have since it went for worldwide consumption—well, I think I probably would have sent it. The reason was the institution was under attack by Mr. Lane. And, there were those then, and there are still some, who believe that not all of the things he said were accurate. It is one of those things that happened over the years that I am sorry happened."

I thanked Phillips for being candid. I suggested that now, for the first time, I had proof that the CIA dispatch had actually been circulated. I would now, I said, consider the possibility of bringing a civil action against the CIA.

Phillips closed the debate, pleading with the audience to recognize the anguish of living a double life in the service of one's country. He said:

"You give a dinner party. Four spooks are there and people don't know you're spooks. What can you talk about? Nothing. I remember a dinner party. I was under the cover of being a State Department employee at the time. A woman asked me what did I do all day and I had to say 'Nothing except shuffle papers.' You learn to lie. You have to lie to survive and to do your job. I spent twenty-five years in the netherworld. I tried to answer a question about seeing this document in Caracas. I tried to change. Should I have been a little more careful? Should I not have told the truth?"

After the audience left the meeting hall, Colby, who had not been present at the debate, was spotted by some reporters. He was asked several questions about Oswald, his high-level clearance in the Marine Corps in Japan, and the special courses in the Russian language he was required to take while in the Marines. Colby brushed them all aside. He said, "All I know about Lee Harvey Oswald is that he visited the Soviet Embassy in Mexico City. Ask David Phillips about that. He's the expert. Thank you, gentlemen."

That evening, while I went to Washington to meet with the House Select Committee on Assassinations, Freed was obligated, as host, to take Phillips, Cline, and Colby to dinner. The four men sat around a table of ordinary size for a party of four. "Yet," Freed recalled, "it was as if Phillips were a hundred yards away. Neither Cline nor Colby would talk to him. He sat with us, but alone, morosely isolated. The others would not look at him, would not talk to him. They were livid, as if he had given away a treasured secret."

Freed remembers what apparently passes for polite conversation when men such as Colby and Cline get together. "It was quite bizarre," Freed said, "for the subject they chose was, 'When is it acceptable to assassinate a head of state?'" Colby presented what he said was a theologically and philosophically sound approach. The Catholic church, he said, had long since wrestled with this question and had, to Colby's mind, emerged with a sound concept. "It is acceptable," he said, "to assassinate a tyrant." He had apparently given the matter much thought, because he had decided that it would have been incorrect to assassinate Adolf Hitler before 1937, but appropriate to do so just after that date. "Cline," Freed said, "took the more liberal view." He observed that Catholic church history may be interesting but is quite irrelevant. To put it in its vulgar essence, Cline found it acceptable to kill anyone at any time if it seemed like a good idea at the time, or, as Cline would say, if it was essential and served what he considered to be the national interest.

Years after the debate, Freed began to explore the idea of a book about the murder of former Chilean ambassador Orlando Letelier, which occurred in Washington, D.C. Knowing of Phillips' role in Latin America, and having met, hosted, and dined with him, Freed called him for information. Phillips said that he had nothing to say about the matter. He then asked Freed if he was familiar with an article written by Fred Landis and published in a magazine called Inquiry. Freed said he was not, whereupon Phillips launched into a vehement assault upon the article. It was, he said, "infamous"; it was "vile and vituperative." It not only constituted "the worst smear ever launched" against Phillips, but actually succeeded, he said, "in ruining me." The verbal attack continued. Naturally, after the call was completed, Freed found the article, which dealt with the Letelier killing. It became the premise upon which Freed's book, Death in Washington, was based.

Even now Donald Freed puzzles over Phillips' behavior. "Was it a Dostoyevskian return to the scene of the crime? Did he become an alcoholic because, unlike Colby, he could not turn to the sanctuary of the Church, to confess his sins and be forgiven? Or was it the moral imperative breaking through? Whatever the reason, Phillips put me on his own trail."

Phillips, assisted by his Association of Former Intelligence Officers, then launched a series of actions, in and out of the courtroom, designed to prevent criticism of the CIA and its leaders. Among the first actions was a defamation suit against Donald Freed for having written about Phillips and the events that preceded and resulted in the death of Letelier.

The $220 million lawsuit was, in my opinion, without legal merit. Yet, when it found its way into the courtroom of Thomas Penfield Jackson, who had represented various Watergate criminals, including Nixon's Committee to Re-Elect the President (CREEP), and his own law partner, also an indicted codefendant, the defamation case found new life.

The case was settled ultimately for one dollar.

The lawsuit was most remarkable not for what it alleged, but rather for what was omitted from it. Freed's indictment of Phillips for his alleged actions regarding Chile in the book Death in Washington was more than matched by his charge regarding Phillips's role in the events surrounding the assassination of President Kennedy.

Freed had unambiguously charged that Phillips had committed perjury to prevent the facts about the assassination from being disclosed. Phillips had decided not to base his lawsuit for defamation upon that allegation. While his organization was committed to silencing criticism of CIA officers, he was not prepared to allow a jury to evaluate the CIA's role in the murder of the president. Fortunately, E. Howard Hunt was less reticent.

BOOK III

Motive

"Why Did the CIA Murder the President?"

A S MORE INFORMATION ABOUT THE CIRCUMSTANCES OF JFK'S DEATH BECAME available, the attitude of the American people changed. A pliant willingness to invest faith in the assurances of the leaders of the nation that a lone assassin had been responsible gave way to healthy skepticism about the facts and finally to the near certainty that the truth had been withheld—the essential facts suppressed.

National polls conducted by the leading organizations that do such things, supplemented by numerous surveys conducted by the very newspapers that had hidden the facts, all offered confirmation of this phenomenon. I chronicled the erosion in faith in the national leaders, which in time was transformed into an avalanche of doubt and suspicion, at the lectures I was giving on the subject. At first the most-often asked question was, "How can you doubt the integrity of a man like Earl Warren?" Later, it became "What can we do to learn the truth?" At last it was, "Why did the CIA kill the president?" When, in more recent years, I informed audiences that their predecessors by twenty years most frequently wondered how we could doubt Warren's integrity, it received the biggest laugh of the evening. The times had changed. Americans had become more informed.

The question of motive is not easily resolved because it involves the operation of a mind. In this instance, it requires an understanding of a number of possibly mixed, varying, and even contradictory objectives sought by an unknown number of people.

Primarily because motive is so difficult to ascertain with any degree of certainty, it is not an element that need be proved in order to successfully prosecute a defendant. Each law enacted by a state legislature or the United States Congress proscribing criminal conduct specifically lists a series of elements that constitute the crime. The failure of the prospective defendant to meet each mandatory provision will result in the inability of the state or federal government to prosecute.

For example, in many jurisdictions the crime of robbery requires:

1. The felonious taking of money, personal property, or any article of value,
2. in the possession of another,
3. from his person or immediate presence,
4. against his will,
5. accomplished by means of force or fear.

Aggravated robbery, for which the punishment may be greater, requires six elements. In addition to satsifying the five elements listed above, the perpetrator must use a dangerous weapon or inflict bodily harm in the course of the robbery. If some of the elements are absent, such as the presence of a victim, the defendant may be charged with another crime— burglary, for example, which has its own specific set of requirements.

Motive is not an element in a criminal case.

I have found that jurors and other thoughtful people, nevertheless, in an effort to perfect their understanding of the circumstances surrounding the act and thus place themselves in a better vantage point from which to view the facts, consider it important to evaluate potential motives. At the law, neither the presence of a motive nor its absence are reasons to convict or acquit, given an agreement that the elements of the crime have been established or disproved. Yet jurors have, I suspect from the outset of the jury system, applied their reasoning ability, developed over the years and taken with them into the jury room, in an effort to puzzle through the questions of why a person might act in a certain fashion.

Therefore, with the understanding that, absent a full confession, the search for motive must be a speculative enterprise, we embark upon the question of why the CIA wanted to murder the president. Unfortunately, the usual methods for resolving this question are inapplicable here. Most crimes that are solved—that figure representing a rather low percentage of crimes committed—are unraveled by a simple police technique. In a case involving a conspiracy, the police confront a suspect, either literally or figuratively thrust him up against a wall, and explain the benefits he may realize should he confess and implicate his associates and the decided disadvantages that may befall him, while his colleagues escape punishment, should he fail to cooperate. In a case such as this one, where the government or one of its powerful subdivisions provides both the culprits and the official investigators, no such persuasion is forthcoming. Quite the reverse is true, in fact; the knowledgeable parties are enjoined to remain silent, from the witnesses in Dealey Plaza to Señora Duran in Mexico City.

While motive is not an element in a crime, something akin to it can be an element for the defense. "Self-defense" is a complete defense, that is, the person who genuinely acts in self-defense can never be punished criminally nor even held responsible for damages in a civil action.

A person is justified in the use of force against an aggressor when he reasonably believes that such conduct is necessary to defend himself or another against the aggressor's imminent use of unlawful force. The person may even use deadly force against a deadly attack, defined at law as an attack threatening death or serious bodily harm. What is controlling is not what the fact was, but what the defendant believed at the time he acted and if that belief was reasonably formed.

If the CIA operatives, officers, and former officers believed that the defense of their Agency and their nation required the elimination of President Kennedy because he was about to dismantle their organization, one could comprehend, while neither accepting nor condoning their viewpoint, that their concept of self-defense required them to use deadly force. Most relevant, therefore, is not what Kennedy was or was not about to do vis-à-vis the CIA, but what the leaders of the Agency believed he might do.

John F. Kennedy had made it clear that he planned to destroy the CIA. The *New York Times* reported on April 25, 1966, under a subheadline, "Kennedy's Bitterness," that "as the enormity of the Bay of Pigs disaster came home to him, [Kennedy] said to one of the highest officials of his Administration that he wanted 'to splinter the C.I.A. in a thousand pieces and scatter it to the winds.'" He clearly was not suggesting a modest legislative proposal or executive order to modify or reform the organization. The total destruction of the Agency was his apparent objective.

The antipathy between Kennedy and the Agency reached the point of no return with the failure of the Bay of Pigs operation. Kennedy had said publicly that no segment of the armed forces of the United States would participate in the invasion of Cuba. At the CIA they had heard the words but wanted to believe that he meant them for public consumption only.

The CIA believed that the president had been firm in respect to the Bay of Pigs affair only in taking punitive action against the Agency and its leaders in the aftermath of the failed invasion. At the CIA, unearned suffering was not considered redemptive.

The visceral anguish experienced by the activists in the CIA leadership can be appreciated only by reading the words they used to describe their reaction to Kennedy and his policies. These men were inveterate liars, trained in deception and schooled to disguise their true feelings, lest they be placed at the disadvantage of playing on a level field. Yet more than a decade after the event, they were unable to cloak, even in their own manuscripts, the depth of their emotions and commitment.

Phillips, in a book published in 1977, described his reaction to the failure, which he primarily ascribed to Kennedy, at the Bay of Pigs:

"I went home. I peeled off my socks like dirty layers of skin—I realized I hadn't changed them for a week. Helen [Phillips' wife] tried to feed me, but I couldn't eat. I bathed, then fell into bed to sleep for several hours. On awakening I tried to eat again, but couldn't. Outside, the day was sheer spring beauty. I carried a portable radio to the yard at the rear of the house and listened to the gloomy newscasts about Cuba as I sat on the ground, my back against a tree.

"Helen came out from the house and handed me a martini, a large one. I was half drunk when I finished. I went to the house for the gin bottle, the vermouth, the ice, and sat again with my back to the tree. I could look up and see a clear blue sky above the foliage. Suddenly my stomach churned. I was sick. My body heaved.

"Then I began to cry.

"Helen came out of the house and pleaded with me to come in.

" 'Get the hell away,' I sobbed.

"It was growing dark. Helen came out of the house again with a blanket, which she draped around my shoulders.

"I wept for two hours. I was sick again, then drunk again. I kept thinking of other tears, in another place, of a colonel from St. Cyr whom I had made weep.

" 'Oh shit! Shit!' "

A dozen years after the aborted invasion of Cuba, E. Howard Hunt wrote:

"No event since the communization of China in 1949 has had such a profound effect on the United States and its allies as the defeat of the U.S.-trained Cuban invasion brigade at the Bay of Pigs in April 1961.

"Out of that humiliation grew the Berlin Wall, the missile crisis, guerilla warfare throughout Latin America and Africa, and our Dominican Republic intervention. Castro's beachhead triumph opened a bottomless Pandora's box of difficulties that affected not only the United States, but most of its allies in the Free World.

"These bloody and subversive events would not have taken place had Castro been toppled. Instead of standing firm, our government pyramided crucially wrong decisions and allowed Brigade 2506 to be destroyed. The Kennedy administration yielded Castro all the excuse he needed to gain a tighter grip on the island of Jose Marti, then moved shamefacedly into the shadows and hoped the Cuban issue would simply melt away."

Hunt concluded that Kennedy had deliberately betrayed the "Cuban patriots" and had permitted them to be killed or captured "while U.S. Navy ships and carriers stood offshore" offering no help when it was desperately needed.

Having clearly placed the responsibility for Castro's longevity and all of the cataclysmic historic events that followed upon Kennedy's betrayal, Hunt described his own immediate reaction to the failed attack:

"The invasion was over.

"Wading into the water that afternoon, San Roman sent a final bitter message: I have nothing to fight with. Am taking to the woods. I cannot wait for you.

"Silently we wept. Never before had I seen a room filled with men in tears. I was sure Artime and all the others were dead, and I blamed myself for having been party to their betrayal. I heard Cabell's name go around the room, a curse attached to it with nearly every repetition.

"Our daze lasted until we learned that the White House had ordered task force destroyers to move in and pick up wounded and stragglers, men in boats and on rafts, wounded clinging to bits of wreckage.

"A reconnaissance jet reported seeing a few survivors in the water. But on the beachhead only vultures moved.

"By now the six CRC officials were in a safehouse a few miles from Washington. Bender, his voice breaking, telephoned me for instructions. I told him to report to Bissell's office and said that arrangements were being made for the six Cubans to see the president.

"Someone remembered Niño Diaz and his mutineers. His ship was ordered to the U.S. naval base at Vieques Island where they would be met by armed Marines. We wanted no more trouble from Señor Diaz.

"In Bissell's office Bender told a heartrending story of the six exile officials. Almost all of them had sons, brothers or nephews in the Brigade. I thought of Tony, Miro, and Dr. Maceo and tears rolled down my face. Quietly Bissell said to me, 'Will you escort them to the White House?'

" 'I can't face them,' I confessed. 'They trusted me, and I can't face them.'

"So Bender returned and brought them back to meet President Kennedy.

"Knight and I used one more war communique—our sixth and final one. It denied that there had been an invasion, downplaying the assault as a resupply effort to guerrillas in the Escambray. As we put it, the landing party had reached their comrades—when in fact they were dead, imprisoned or struggling through the Zapata swamps.

"I was sick of lying and deception, heartsick over political compromise and military defeat. When Lem Jones had taken down the final words of the bulletin I went home."

In the months following the invasion at the Bay of Pigs, an uneasy truce existed between the CIA and the presidency.

The CIA had developed a bizarre anti-Castro program named "Operation Mongoose," which consisted of plans to poison Castro, to blow him up with an explosive shaped like a seashell that the CIA believed it could plant near him, and to make him lose face, literally, by making his beard fall out. "Mongoose" also called for a series of small and annoying raids on Cuba.

From the outset Kennedy had insisted that "Operation Mongoose" must be low-key and maintained as a covert program. Kennedy had publicly opposed assassination programs. Yet, in private, he and the attorney general had made it clear that Castro was an obstacle that, as the CIA reasoned, the White House would appreciate having removed. Kennedy saw Mongoose as a vehicle to bring together, keep track of, and control the most virulent Cuban activists. This approach was later adopted and described by Lyndon Johnson in another context. With characteristic grace, he referred to the theory as "the tent-pissing question." Better, he explained, mixing metaphors, to have the loose cannons inside your tent "pissing out" than have them outside "pissing in." If the description was inelegant, its logic was inescapable.

The problem with that approach was that Major General Edward G. Lansdale, the CIA's liaison to Secretary of Defense Robert S. McNamara, became chief of operations for the project and turned it into a small war against Cuba.[1] Lansdale also was the architect of the "strategic hamlet" concept in Vietnam. That program had resulted in the imprisonment of millions of Vietnamese farmers and workers.

During October 1961, the CIA decided to send ten commando teams to Cuba to engage in sabotage there. By the time that Robert Kennedy learned of the effort, three teams had already been dispatched, ostensibly with his approval. He later recalled that "I was furious." The White House reacted immediately and decisively. On October 30, all "sabotage and

---

[1] Operation Mongoose was a major project with an annual budget of $50 million. Lansdale considered his army of Cuban cadre an expendable asset.

militant operations during negotiations with the Soviets" were canceled and shortly thereafter "Operation Mongoose" was abolished. To the CIA activists, detente was again becoming the obstacle to the action they were convinced was crucial. In spite of the White House directives, the CIA continued its military operations against Cuba and its program to assassinate Castro. Robert Kennedy sought to monitor these activities but his domestic responsibilities, the war against organized crime, the continuing racial conflicts in the United States, and other areas that clearly fell within his jurisdiction as attorney general, commanded his attention. He sent Lansdale to Florida to impress the CIA with the solemn nature of the decision to cease its war against Cuba.

The CIA-sponsored military actions continued, leading to FBI raids on Cuban-exile training corps in southern Florida and near Lake Pontchartrain in Louisiana. FBI agents, under the theoretical control and absolute jurisdiction of the attorney general, found themselves in an armed confrontation with the CIA's proteges.

The two opposing groups, the CIA and the White House, bided their time, each confident that a final solution would soon be forthcoming. The 1964 election, the president believed, would resolve the issue. Following his reelection, hopefully with a far greater mandate than conferred upon him by the electorate in 1960, Kennedy would be free to require the resignation of J. Edgar Hoover, and to create a new international intelligence organization as well. In 1963, this fact was widely known within the CIA, where its implications were being assessed.

David Atlee Phillips, writing about this period in his book *The Night Watch* (Atheneum, 1977), described the "few officers remaining" in CIA headquarters as "moving up and down the halls like attendants at a sepulcher." The *American Heritage Dictionary* offers as its first definition of sepulcher, "a burial vault." Phillips completed the scene: "There were long lunches after too many martinis at Napoleon's." The perception among those CIA officers, Phillips reported, was "The Agency is finished." And so it seemed at that moment.

L. Fletcher Prouty is a retired U.S. Air Force colonel who worked closely with intelligence services for more than thirty years. A pilot during World War II, Colonel Prouty rose through the Defense Department chain of command to a point where all CIA military activities were channeled through him.

Between 1955 and 1963, Colonel Prouty served as chief of special operations for the Joint Chiefs of Staff and in a similar capacity with the Office of Special Operations of the Office of the Secretary of Defense, and headed the Special Operations Office for the U.S. Air Force. All of these positions were charged with the military support of the clandestine operations of the CIA.

Today, Prouty offers confirmation that Kennedy had decided to dismantle the CIA. He states that the first steps were "getting rid of Dulles, Cabell, and Bissell." Allen Dulles was the director of the CIA, Charles Cabell was its deputy director (his brother was the mayor of Dallas), and Richard Bissell was the deputy director for plans, the dirty tricks department of the agency. Prouty states that it was known and accepted that "the task of breaking up the CIA was scheduled for 1964, after the foreseen Kennedy reelection."

Kennedy did fire Dulles, Cabell, and Bissell. E. Howard Hunt, in his book *Give Us This Day* (Arlington House, 1973), asserts that Kennedy sought "to whitewash the New Frontier by heaping guilt on the CIA." This guilt, Hunt writes with just a touch of the poetic, was "unearned excrement." During this time, Hunt claims, while Kennedy and his loyal press made false charges "day after day, no one in the Agency, needless to say, was allowed to rebut even the most glaring fabrication." Dulles and Bissell, Hunt wrote, were "scapegoats to expiate administration guilt." Dulles, in Hunt's view, was a "remarkable man whose long career of government service had been destroyed unjustly by men who were laboring unceasingly to preserve their own public images."

Soviet Premier Nikita Khrushchev decided, according to Hunt, to erect the Berlin Wall because he knew that Kennedy would offer no "meaningful opposition" due to Kennedy's "weakness at the Bay of Pigs."

Hunt concluded that Kennedy had abandoned "any serious interest in overthrowing Castro"; indeed, he had even promised Khrushchev that "he would never invade Cuba."

The gentlemen at CIA headquarters saw American foreign policy begin to shift from their control into the hands of the elected leader of the nation. While that concept was sufficiently alarming to them, it was viewed as the precursor of far more frightening events.

Hunt captured the feelings of his colleagues in the CIA at that time: "Under the administration's philosophy, the real enemy became poverty and ignorance; any talk of an international Communist conspiracy was loudly derided. Detente and a positive approach to easing international tensions filled the Washington air, to the wonderment of those of us who still remembered Budapest, the Berlin Wall, and the fate of Brigade 2506 [at the Bay of Pigs]."

At the CIA, "detente" was the despised concept and Kennedy the enemy who had humiliated the Agency and was threatening its very existence. While Kennedy may have been planning the elimination of the Agency after the following presidential election, as Prouty asserts, he was not content to wait that long to muzzle it.

He acted at once to prevent the Agency from further embarrassing his administration and threatening the peace of the world. According to Arthur M. Schlesinger, Jr. (*Robert Kennedy and His Times*, Houghton Mifflin, 1978), Kennedy said to him, "I made a mistake in putting Bobby in the Justice Department. He is wasted there . . . Bobby should be in the CIA." The president acknowledged that "it's a hell of a way to learn things, but I have learned one thing from this business [the Bay of Pigs]—that is, that we will have to deal with CIA."

He dealt with the CIA through the implementation of a three-point emergency program designed to control the agency. He fired its most culpable and powerful leaders, he appointed a high-level committee, the Cuban study group to investigate the misdeeds of the organization so that he might determine what additional short-range limitations were required and, in the interim, he dramatically reduced the powers and jurisdiction of the Agency and established strict limits as to its future actions through National Security Action memoranda.

The members of the Cuban study group were General Maxwell Taylor, the former chief of staff of the United States Army, Robert F. Kennedy, then the attorney general, Allen Dulles, then the director of the CIA, and Admiral Arleigh Burke, Chief of Naval Operations. The investigators, known as the Green committee, were having a decided impact upon the morale of the leaders of the CIA. Hunt recalled the period: "As a member of Dulles' staff I lunched in the Director's mess, seeing him return from each Green committee session more drawn and gray." Hunt was outraged that the inquiry was being held by Kennedy's men, those who "had allowed a Communist dictatorship free sway over an island less than ninety miles from our shores."

Phillips wrote that he had been sent to the Pentagon "to be questioned by General Maxwell Taylor" and that Taylor "shook his head slowly from side to side" as Phillips offered his versions of the events. "Robert Kennedy, in shirtsleeves, delved into the inner workings of the Agency," Phillips complained. It was clear to many in the CIA that the halcyon days were in the past, Phillips concluded.

Kennedy then sought to control the Agency by sharply reducing its ability to act in the future through National Security Action Memoranda 55, 56 and 57. These documents, in theory, eliminated the ability of the

CIA to wage war. The CIA would not be permitted to initiate any operation requiring greater firepower than that generated by handguns.[2]

The intent was clear; so was the CIA's response. Military bases operated by the CIA in south Florida were not closed. The CIA continued to organize, fund, and equip Cuban exiles and send them on military forays to Cuba throughout this period. The raids continued long after the assassination of John Kennedy; they were all in contravention to the newly revised mandate of the CIA.

Robert Kennedy declined his brother's request to head the CIA, for political reasons. He explained that the designation would not go over well since he was "a Democrat and a brother." (Schlesinger, p. 494.) A Republican named John McCone was chosen instead. Clearly, after the 1964 election, political considerations would be less important. Robert Kennedy was assigned, during the interim, the informal responsibility of watching the CIA, according to Schlesinger. (P. 494.)

The CIA had other plans. John Kennedy would not live to face the voters in 1964. He would have to be assassinated during 1963, in a fashion that would diminish neither the image nor the power of the Agency.

At the CIA, Kennedy's every move was closely scrutinized and evaluated. His psychological profile, compiled by CIA experts, provided a basis for determining his future conduct. As they saw it, their guesswork about the future was scientifically grounded, notwithstanding their not infrequent miscalculations in numerous other matters.

From the perspective of the leaders of the CIA, the possibility of a thorough investigation into the shrouded history of the Agency, certainly a prerequisite for a president seeking to justify its elimination, was a risk that could not be taken.

The removal of Hoover following the 1964 elections, if Kennedy were to prevail, was a foregone conclusion. The Kennedys then would be free to operate the Justice Department without interference from the leader

---

[2]The three NSAM were among the most important documents of the thousand days of the Kennedy administration. They were based upon the report of the Cuban study group delivered to President Kennedy by General Taylor on June 13, 1961. Taylor had been asked to recommend a course to prevent future CIA fiascos. Prouty was the officer charged with the responsibility of delivering the documents to the chairman of the joint chiefs of staff and to the other high ranking officers in the U.S. military and to brief them as to their significance. He told me during August, 1991, "Nothing I had ever been involved in in my entire career had created such an uproar. NSAM 55 stripped the CIA of its cherished covert operations role, except for small actions. It was an explosive document. The military-industrial complex was not pleased."

of the department's foot soldiers and investigators. The army of FBI agents would, for the first time in the nation's history, be responsive to the attorney general and the president, not to Hoover. Hoover, during his almost half-century as leader of the secret police, had begun to see himself as the nation's captain. He viewed American presidents as transients who passed through his administration and were soon forgotten. Memoranda addressed to Hoover's offices were directed with respect to "S.O.G." That appellation, created by Hoover, designated the "Seat of Government."

With Hoover gone, all things might be possible for the president in 1964. The alliance between the FBI and the CIA to spare their misdeeds from public scrutiny and judicial accountability would likely be concluded.

The transition from the CIA to a new intelligence organization, responsive to the president and possibly directed by Robert Kennedy, would likely be accompanied by an explanation as to the need for the dramatic change. While it probably would not be show-trial time, Soviet-style, for the major CIA leaders, a public accounting of known trespasses together with a full investigation, the potential of which was fully understood at that time only by the CIA's officers, was the substance of which nightmares are fashioned. More than careers might be ruined by a strong and ambitious president determined to run the nation.

For the CIA, the risks were apparent and too monumental to permit the routine flow of events to be determinative. The officers at the CIA viewed politicians with ill-disguised scorn. The officers not infrequently visited Capitol Hill to appear before committees of the Congress and there dazzled the members and their staffs with lessons in gadgetry. Back in Langley, they laughed about how easy it had been. They viewed any compromise that prevented a full commitment to prosecuting the war against communism as bureaucratic nonsense. They, the officers of the CIA, placed their lives, or at least the lives of their agents, American and foreigners, on the line each day, while the president and his advisers attended security meetings in formal attire as they drifted in from White House dinner parties. If Hoover *thought* he operated from the Seat of Government, the CIA officials *knew* that in reality they did.

Nineteen sixty-four was to bring a sea change to the domestic and foreign policy of the United States unless the hand of the CIA intervened. Before the CIA officials loomed a future marked by disgrace, the shattering of their organization, and the possible prosecution of some of their colleagues. They had the almost unique ability to organize assassinations at a high level, to limit serious inquiry, and to influence a pliant media. They watched and they planned. Almost everything they observed confirmed the need to act.

Kennedy insisted during October 1963 that one thousand U.S. troops in Vietnam, euphemistically referred to as advisers, be recalled at that time. Kenneth O'Donnell has stated that Kennedy planned to withdraw all Americans from Vietnam after the 1964 elections (O'Donnell and Powers, *Johnny, We Hardly Knew Ye*). Arthur Schlesinger, Jr., has also stated that Kennedy was to end the United States adventure in Vietnam: "He was a prudent executive, not inclined to heavy investments in lost causes. His whole presidency was marked precisely by his capacity to *refuse* escalation—as in Laos, the Bay of Pigs, the Berlin Wall, the missile crisis."

Although Schlesinger has a reputation as a respected historian and O'Donnell as a reliable political figure, both men were advisers to Kennedy. Consequently, their retrospective analysis of how the president they admired might have acted, in view of the more recent conventional wisdom that establishes the adventure in Vietnam as a major disaster, should be examined closely and accepted with a degree of caution. The evidence, I believe, supports their evaluation. Colonel Prouty reported that Kennedy had decided to withdraw all personnel from Vietnam. "JFK was going to make the question of peace a major campaign issue in the 1964 elections," he told me. According to Prouty, Kennedy told Major General Victor H. Krulak to go to Vietnam, "get up to date," and determine "who we turn it over to when we leave." Krulak's response, following his investigation, was that General Duong Van Minh, known popularly as Big Minh, was the answer.

In September 1963, Krulak informed Robert Kennedy that the unpopular leader of the Saigon regime, Ngo Dinh Diem, should be flown out of Vietnam. The suggestion was offered that the Pope call Cardinal Diem, the ruler's brother, in an effort to facilitate the amicable transfer of power. Kennedy sent General Maxwell Taylor and Secretary of Defense Robert McNamara to Vietnam in order to prepare a report justifying the withdrawal of all American personnel. The president said their Trip Report would "give some flavor" to the decision to end United States participation in the hostilities. With the two emissaries in Vietnam, Prouty and Krulak prepared the Trip Report to be signed by Taylor and McNamara since its findings and conclusions were preconceived.

The Trip Report was then sent by Prouty to a fine leather boutique in Georgetown, where a cover was added to the completed document. It utilized maps and pictures and presented detailed political and military analysis. It was dispatched to Hawaii to be delivered to Taylor and McNamara, who were then en route to Washington, D.C. The emissaries landed at Andrews Air Force Base near the Capitol, having read and signed the Trip Report on the airplane. It was delivered to President Kennedy, who accepted it and prepared NSAM 263 on October 2, 1963. That memorandum, which incorporated by reference portions of the Trip Report, was the blueprint for the withdrawal of the United States from Vietnam.

"Kennedy dictated the rich parts of 263," Prouty told me. "He was not satisfied with the withdrawal of all U.S. military personnel, he wanted all Americans out of there." He meant, Prouty continued, "all CIA officers and agents." Prouty said that at the CIA there was despair. "They had been there since 1945. They were furious."

Today Prouty reflects upon the importance of NSAM 263 and the Trip Report on which it relied:

"When Kennedy signed it, he signed an order for the almost immediate withdrawal of one thousand men, for all Americans to leave not long after the next presidential election, for the political kickoff for his 1964 campaign and, of course, not known to him, his own death warrant."

Prouty recalls the excitement in the military following the October 2, 1963, release of the memorandum. "*Stars and Stripes* ran headlines, 'President Says—All Americans Out by 1965.' The Pentagon was outraged. JFK was a curse word in the corridors."

Prouty, who had previously undertaken presidential security assignments, met General Lansdale in one of those corridors. "He said to me, 'Fletch, got good news for you. You've been selected to go to the South Pole.'" On November 10, 1963, Colonel Prouty was sent to the South Pole. The strongest military/security supporter for President Kennedy, and a participant in the development of the Trip Report upon which NSAM 263 had been based, consequently was not in Dallas on November 22, 1963.

When Prouty and I had lunch on Capitol Hill during June 1991, he showed me a photograph that had been taken in Dallas that day. It displayed a man striding away from the camera at an angle and therefore provided only a right side-back view. "There is no doubt in my mind," Prouty told me, "that it's Ed Lansdale." When Prouty saw the photograph he knew why he had been sent out of the country during November 1963.

It may not be impossible to find evidence that indicates that Kennedy may not have withdrawn the American presence from Southeast Asia after the 1964 elections. Indeed, it can be argued—relying upon the entire body of available fact, some of it created by military and intelligence sources in retrospect— that either he had not finally made up his mind or he was giving conflicting signals for political purposes. In either event, his public position on the question alarmed the leaders of the Kennedy Watch at the CIA, an Agency devoted to the continuance and escalation of the war—developments that transpired almost immediately after his death.

Kennedy had also embarked upon a program that led the CIA officers to believe that their cherished dream, a free Cuba—that is, one from which Fidel Castro had been eliminated—would never be realized.

During the summer of 1963, the Kennedy administration began to consider a deal with Fidel Castro. Robert Kennedy thought it absurd to prosecute students who, in violation of the law, traveled to Cuba from the United States. He told Schlesinger and Richard Goodwin that he saw nothing wrong with visiting Cuba—that if he were a student himself he would want to travel there.

According to Schlesinger, less than a year later, Robert Kennedy said that the administration had always discussed a deal with Fidel Castro as a possibility.

The winter of discontent had passed. The Cold War was receding. Kennedy had negotiated a test ban treaty with the Russians and then persuaded the American people that it was appropriate. As the summer came to an end, he was able to secure the ratification of the treaty by the Senate.

Kennedy perceived that Castro was interested in exploring rapprochment with the United States. Robert Kennedy later stated that "some tentative feelers that were put out" by Castro were later "accepted by us."

The president chose William Attwood, the American ambassador to Guinea and former editor of Look magazine, to pursue negotiations with Castro. In September, the Cuban ambassador to the United Nations, Carlos Lechuga, met with Attwood and discussed the possibility of meetings about improving relations between the two countries.

On September 18, Attwood delivered his "Memorandum on Cuba" to the State Department. It stated, in pertinent part:

"According to neutral diplomats and others I have talked to at the UN and in Guinea, there is reason to believe that Castro is unhappy about his present dependence on the Soviet bloc; that he does not enjoy in effect being a satellite; that the trade embargo is hurting him—though not enough to endanger his position; and that he would like to establish some official contact with the United States and go to some length to obtain normalization of relations with us—even though this would not be welcomed by most of his hard-core Communist entourage, such as Che Guevara.

"All of this may or may not be true. But it would seem that we have something to gain and nothing to lose by finding out whether in fact Castro does want to talk and what concessions he would be prepared to make. . . ."

Averell Harriman, undersecretary of state for political affairs, Robert Kennedy and McGeorge Bundy, special assistant to President Kennedy for national security, all became involved in discussions about the proposal that Attwood become the unofficial emissary to Castro. Bundy told Attwood that the president favored "pushing toward an opening with Cuba." The purpose was to remove Castro from "the Soviet fold," and perhaps wipe out the Bay of Pigs "and maybe getting back to normal."

Attwood reported to Lechuga, President Kennedy gave the signal to proceed, and Attwood was to be sent to meet and negotiate with Castro during December 1963 or January 1964, according to Robert Kennedy. (RFK *and His Times*.) The purpose, said the attorney general, was to attempt to normalize relations between the two countries.

Not willing to await diplomatic negotiations, President Kennedy sought to make use of the services of Jean Daniel, a French journalist with L'*Express*, who was a friend of Attwood's. When Kennedy learned that Daniel was on his way to Havana to interview Castro, he invited him to the White House.

Kennedy assured Daniel that he had given a great deal of thought to Cuba. He accepted responsibility for the ill-treatment of Cuba by the United States, asserting that the "economic colonization, humiliation and exploitation" visited upon Cuba were at least in part due to policies of the United States during the Batista regime. The president, addressing Castro through the journalist, said:

". . . I will go even further: to some extent it is as though Batista was the incarnation of a number of sins on the part of the United States. Now we shall have to pay for those sins. In the matter of the Batista regime, I am in agreement with the first Cuban revolutionaries. That is perfectly clear."

He added, "I approved the proclamation which Fidel Castro made in the Sierra Maestra." Kennedy then turned to the problem at hand. "The United States can coexist with a nation in the hemisphere that espouses a different economic system, the Monroe Doctrine notwithstanding. It is the subservient relationship with the Soviet Union that creates the problem." Kennedy ended the interview by requesting that Daniel visit him upon his return from Havana stating: "Castro's reactions interest me."

On November 18, 1963, with Daniel in Havana, Kennedy, while addressing the Inter-American Press Associates in Miami, stated clearly and without ambiguity that the United States would "not dictate to any nation how to organize its economic life. Every nation is free to shape its own economic institutions in accordance with its own national needs and will." Once Cuba restores its own sovereignty, the president said, and halts efforts at subversion outside of its borders, "everything is possible" and "we will extend the hand of friendship and assistance."

The following day, Bundy told Attwood that Kennedy wanted to see him immediately after the Attwood-Lechuga meeting took place.

That same evening, Castro and Daniel met in Havana. They spoke for six hours. Daniel said Castro listened to Kennedy's words "with a devouring and passionate interest." Three times Castro told Daniel to repeat Kennedy's analysis of Batista and the responsibility the United States bore in that regard.

Castro was, of course, at least as familiar as Kennedy with the consequences of the sins of the United States upon the Cuban economy and its people. It was that history that led to the Cuban revolution. The United States had controlled Cuba even before the beginning of the twentieth century, had occupied the country for four years following the Spanish-American War, and had withdrawn the Marines only after the Platt Amendment, which permitted the Marines to return almost at will, was imposed upon the Cuban constitution by the military of the United States.

Before Castro began to organize his rebellion, United States corporations owned most of Cuba, including more than ninety percent of its minerals and almost half of its major crop, sugar. People of color and those residing in rural areas existed at near-starvation levels. Fulgencio Batista continued to enter into financial arrangements beneficial to United Fruit and other American corporations, to the decided disadvantage of the Cuban people. Batista, who resided in Havana, then in Florida, and again in Havana, became a multimillionaire in exchange for services.

As Kennedy, through Daniel, appeared to accept some responsibility for that history, Castro paused, thought and then spoke. "I believe Kennedy is sincere," he said. "I also believe that today the expression of sincerity could have political significance." He added he would accept no ultimatum from the United States. Castro said of Kennedy: "He still has the possibility of being, in the eyes of history, the greatest president of the United States, the leader who may at last understand that there can be coexistence between capitalists and socialists."

He urged Daniel to "be an emissary of peace." Castro added, "You can tell him that I'm willing to declare Goldwater my friend if that will guarantee Kennedy's election."

The interview concluded during the early morning hours of November 20, 1963.

On November 22, 1963, two days after their words of peace and coexistence, Castro and Daniel met for lunch at Castro's place on the beach. There they heard that Kennedy had been assassinated. Castro repeated over and over, "Es una mala noticia"—this is bad news. He told Daniel, "Your mission of peace has ended."

Castro asked Daniel a question about the new president, Lyndon B. Johnson:

"What authority does he have over the CIA?"

At that time, the grief-stricken Robert Kennedy was confronting McCone, the director of the CIA, with a single question. He asked, "Did the CIA kill my brother?"

Robert Kennedy, as the president's overseer of the CIA, knew more about the potential, capacity, and inclination of the CIA than any other person in the United States, save the ranking officers of the agency. McCone answered in the negative and the attorney general wanted to believe him. Yet McCone's answer, in view of the evidence, is not credible. It is possible, however, that he believed he was answering truthfully at that time.[3]

The new president began an almost immediate escalation of the war in Vietnam. Years later, after the number of U.S. troops had increased from 16,500 at the time of the assassination to more than 500,000, and after the death of more than 50,000 Americans and more than a million Vietnamese, Laotians, and Cambodians, the war finally ended with the military defeat of the United States. Johnson also directed that all efforts of rapprochment with Castro be ended. During March, 1964, Johnson signed NSAM 288 that repudiated Kennedy's plan to end the U.S. military participation in the war that year. In the months that followed, Johnson

---

[3] Just four days after the death of President Kennedy, Lyndon Johnson signed NSAM 273 that began to reverse the policy of withdrawal from Vietnam and signified the beginning of the escalation of the conflict. The CIA had prevailed. The effort in Southeast Asia was to become a massive land-based war.

increased the military committment from under 20,000 troops approximately a quarter of a million. [See Appendix page 379.] That ruling, made in 1963, still obtains today.

The CIA had been preserved and soon was to be strengthened. The echoes of "Operation Mongoose," with new code names, began to reverberate. The fanatic survivors of the brigade that invaded Cuba were recruited by the CIA. The commando raids against Cuba were resumed.

The CIA prevailed; it did not suffer ignominious abolition at the hand of an independent president. Instead it was the president who died. And today the president of the United States is the former director of the CIA.

The Cuban exiles and their sponsors have prospered and become an integral part of U.S. and world history since the death of John Kennedy. The noted author Georgie Anne Geyer, in her biography of Fidel Castro (*Guerrilla Prince*, Little, Brown, 1991) puts it well in two succinct paragraphs:

"Finally, an entire new Cuban cadre now emerged from the Bay of Pigs. The names Howard Hunt, Bernard Baker, Rolando Martinez, Felix Rodriguez, and Eugenio Martinez would, in the next quarter century, pop up, often decisively, over and over again in the most dangerous American foreign policy crises. There were Cubans flying missions for the CIA in the Congo and even for the Portuguese in Africa; Cubans were the burglars of Watergate; Cubans played key roles in Nicaragua, in Irangate, in the American move into the Persian Gulf. In these ways, too, what Fidel Castro had wrought in Cuba was now governing, through hatred of him, important portions of American foreign policy. And there was one more crucial consequence.

"From Moscow, Nikita Khrushchev watched the Bay of Pigs first with delight, and finally with concern. 'We were quite certain that the ... invasion was only the beginning and that the Americans would not let Cuba alone,' Khrushchev wrote in his memoirs. 'The United States had put its faith in the Cuban emigres once and it would do so again. . . . One thought kept hammering away at my brain: what will happen if we lose Cuba? We had to think up some way of confronting America with more than words. We had to establish a tangible and effective deterrent to American interference in the Caribbean. But what exactly? The logical answer was missiles.' "

From Watergate to Irangate, from the illegal entry into Dr. Fielding's offices to the adventures in Panama, Grenada and the Persian Gulf, up to and including the Reagan-Bush October surprise—this was the history that was. We are left to wonder what events might have unfolded in their stead, absent the fiasco at the Bay of Pigs and the president's concomitant decision to master U.S. intelligence by controlling the CIA and by abolishing it later when he believed himself to be in a political position from which he might safely act. Kennedy thought about his security in political terms, his concerns fixed upon the whims of the voters and their potential reaction to sudden changes that he might initiate. He and his brother ached to remove Hoover and reconstruct U.S. intelligence, yet they would not act decisively; they sought the shelter afforded by a second term. Kennedy's essential and fatal failure was his inability to conceive that a real and deadly threat was close at hand.

The beneficiaries of the CIA's largesse in faraway places celebrated the murder of John F. Kennedy. The former chief of the SAVAK for the United States, the secret police of the shah of Iran, wrote:

"The assassination of President Kennedy on November 22, 1963, made the shah jubilant. Kennedy had put pressure on him for social reforms. The shah, as always, had raised the banner of the fight against communism, saying, 'Our real enemy is communism.'

"I learned later through General [Hassan] Pakravan [then chief of the SAVAK] that the shah had had a kind of celebration.

" 'Can you believe this shah?' General Pakravan said. 'When he received the news of Kennedy's death, he asked for a drink to celebrate.' "

Of course, in the United States, Lyndon Johnson appointed the President's Commission on the Assassination of President Kennedy, known as the Warren Commission, to find and report the facts. The commission said Lee Harvey Oswald had been the lone culprit; Johnson strongly endorsed the report and its conclusions, once even calling me a "scavenger" at a press conference for having raised some questions about its accuracy.

Three years after the report had been issued, President Johnson told his White House staff member and political operative, Marvin Watson, that he "was convinced that there was a plot in connection with the assassination." He added that he felt that the CIA had something to do with this plot." [FBI report of statement by Marvin Watson—released by FBI during December 1977, as reported in the *Washington Post*, December 13, 1977.]

Apparently Johnson was not the only president who believed that the CIA may have been implicated in the assassination of Kennedy. As the evidence about the illegal entry at Watergate began to surface and the White House coverup of those events began to show signs of cracking, Richard Nixon sought help from a reluctant CIA. CIA involvement in

Watergate now seems apparent; at the time, Nixon, in panic, wondered if his administration had been set up by the Agency. (H.R. Haldeman, *The Ends of Power*, Time Books, 1978.) According to H.R. Haldeman, the White House chief of staff, Nixon dispatched him to meet with Richard Helms. Helms had been the deputy director of plans, the master of the illegal operations at the CIA, at the time of the assassination. Nixon told Haldeman to obtain cooperation from the CIA to protect the administration from the then-escalating Watergate scandal. In the absence of voluntary assistance, Haldeman was to confront Helms with Nixon's knowledge about the assassination of President Kennedy in an effort to extort CIA support. Haldeman recounted the events in this fashion:

"So we had failed in our one previous attempt to obtain CIA cooperation, and now in Ehrlichman's office on June 23, 1972, the CIA was stonewalling me again: 'Not connected.' 'No way.' Then I played Nixon's trump card. 'The president asked me to tell you this entire affair may be connected to the Bay of Pigs, and if it blows up, the Bay of Pigs may be blown. . . .

"Turmoil in the room, Helms gripping the arms of his chair leaning forward and shouting, 'The Bay of Pigs had nothing to do with this. I have no concern about the Bay of Pigs.'

"Silence. I just sat there. I was absolutely shocked by Helms' violent reaction. Again I wondered, *what was such dynamite* in the Bay of Pigs story? Finally, I said, 'I'm just following my instructions, Dick. This is what the president told me to relay to you.' "

Haldeman had been speaking in code to Helms. Haldeman explained: "It seems that in all of those Nixon references to the Bay of Pigs he was actually referring to the Kennedy assassination." Judging from the Helms reaction, the message from Nixon was understood.

While Haldeman has his own speculation as to the possible causes of the assassination, the conclusions he reaches, which are based upon fact, are illuminating. Haldeman writes, "After Kennedy was killed, the CIA launched a fantastic coverup." He adds: "In a chilling parallel to their coverup at Watergate, the CIA literally erased any connection between Kennedy's assassination and the CIA."

When Haldeman disclosed that Nixon, in ostensibly communicating with the CIA about "the Bay of Pigs," was actually threatening to reveal information about the CIA's role in the assassination of President Kennedy, he provided the Rosetta stone for the decipherment of the Nixon tapes. With that in mind, Haldeman's recounting of the events at the

White House during the fateful days following the Watergate exposure, becomes fascinating and historically significant reading.

Nixon was hoping that a connection between the Watergate burglars and the Committee to Re-Elect the President might be avoided. Quoting Nixon, Haldeman writes:

" 'Well, we protected Helms from one hell of a lot of things.'

"How to make certain the CIA would cooperate? Nixon suggested the involvement of Hunt as a lever. 'Hunt . . . will uncover a lot of things. You open that scab there's a hell of a lot of things . . . tell them we just feel that it would be very detrimental to have this thing go any further. This involves these Cubans, Hunt, and a lot of hanky-panky that we have nothing to do with ourselves.'

"I didn't know what hanky-panky he was talking about, but Nixon wasn't finished. He gazed out of the window, then turned to me: 'When you get the CIA people in, say, "Look, the problem is that *this will open up the whole Bay of Pigs thing again.*" So they should call the FBI in and for the good of the country don't go any further into this case. Period.'

"Later, in a one o'clock meeting just before I saw Helms and Walters, Nixon expanded on this theme: 'Tell them that if it gets out, it's going to make the CIA look bad, it's going to make Hunt look bad, and it's likely to blow the whole Bay of Pigs, which we think we would be very unfortunate for the CIA.' "

In addition to an attorney general and two presidents, some intelligence officers have informed suspicions of their own about John Kennedy's assassination.

John Stockwell served as the chief of the Angola task force, a subcommittee of the National Security Council. I have never met him. Not long before this book went to press, I heard a Pacifica Radio broadcast in which Stockwell discussed the murder of President Kennedy. He evaluated the facts available to him as an intelligence officer familiar with the CIA's propensities, and came to the conclusion that CIA operatives based in Florida organized the assassination and that anti-Castro Cuban exiles had been involved in carrying it out.

He began his inquiry, as did most of the critics of the Warren Commission, with an examination of the forensic evidence. He concluded that many more than three shots had been fired, thus disputing an essential finding of the Warren Commission. As to motive, Stockwell, viewing his former colleagues with some degree of intimacy, stated:

"President Kennedy had in 1963 antagonized the power structure in the United States. He was pulling out of the Vietnam war. He was curtailing the oil depletion allowance. He was launching a tentative civil rights program."

Stockwell also believed that the fiasco at the Bay of Pigs provided a reason for the CIA to murder the president. "The CIA had bungled the landing at the Bay of Pigs." Yet, he said, the officials at the agency condemned Kennedy for refusing to send in the Marines in order to prevent the CIA from being discredited.

Could Florida-based renegades in the agency, asked Stockwell, have carried out the assassination without the knowledge of their superiors in Langley? He rejected that theory for a number of reasons, including "the almost immediate use by the CIA of its most important CIA operatives acting under "journalist's cover" who focused attention upon Oswald as the assassin with Russian connections. Stockwell concluded that the assassins were "up in the infrastructure of the CIA."

Although Robert Kennedy, then John Kennedy's oldest surviving brother and the attorney general, at the very outset suspected officers of the CIA in the assassination; and although the president who appointed the commission to investigate the crime later stated that he believed the Agency had been involved; and although President Nixon, as we have seen, confronted the CIA on the question, the media has little noted those occurrences. The media seems largely untroubled even by the considered opinion of an intelligence insider like John Stockwell. The result is that most Americans have heard neither of the doubts raised by Robert Kennedy, Lyndon Johnson, and Richard Nixon nor of the evidence in the Hunt case. No major newspaper or television station has ever presented the evidence that comprises the Mexico City scenario, which establishes the CIA's interest both in Oswald and the assassination of President Kennedy in the weeks preceding the murder in Dallas. The media in the United States has failed to report that David Atlee Phillips, the CIA's architect of the Mexico City fabrication, has admitted publicly that he and the CIA knew of no evidence establishing that Oswald had ever been to the Soviet Embassy in Mexico City.

Ritualistically, every few years, the *New York Times* and other lesser publications devote pages of analysis to the recent past of the CIA and conclude, with a banal predictability, that while the agency had committed numerous crimes, including murder, extortion, torture, false imprisonment, drug running, bribery, theft, obstruction of justice, and perjury, to name but a few—indeed all those that comprise the penal code with the possible exception of sodomy—the auspicious news is that the agency is now firmly in good hands and the mistakes of the past were not to be repeated.

Jack Anderson, who enjoys a strange relationship with the CIA far beyond my ken to fathom, has written both critically and glowingly about its activities. In both sets of instances, his articles are based on access to Agency files.

During 1977, he revealed that the CIA "was helping an Asian opium ring smuggle drugs into the United States and then lying to Congress about it." In an October 3, 1977, column published widely and printed that day in the Washington Post, Anderson provided the facts that demonstrated that the director of the CIA, William Colby, had made false statements in an effort to cover up crimes and prevent prosecution. Anderson cited a "Secret House [of Representatives] report," asserting that: "It is ironic that the CIA should be given the responsibility of narcotics intelligence, since they were supporting the prime movers."

The following year Anderson reported that the CIA had·recruited "Mafia hit men" for "international murder missions." The agency, Anderson reported, sought "to create its own branch of 'Murder, Inc.'—a killer squad that would assassinate undesirable foreign leaders for $1 million each." (January 4, 1978, Washington Post.)

Though CIA operatives regularly violate the law, they rarely are called into court to account for their transgressions. Anderson explained why:

"For over twenty years, the Justice Department has been winking at crimes committed by employees of the Central Intelligence Agency. Even serious crimes and felonies unrelated to official duties have been ignored.

"This is the conclusion of a still-secret report compiled by the House Government Rights Subcommittee. The congressional investigators were so shocked by the Justice Department's leniency that they recommended that a 'special prosecutor be appointed to prosecute illegal activities of intelligence agency personnel.'

"An independent prosecutor is needed, the report bluntly states, because the Justice Department has failed to move even in instances where there were 'widespread admissions' of criminal activity and 'the illegalities by the intelligence personnel [were] unrelated to their job activities.'

" 'The Justice Department has assisted in setting the CIA above the law,' the report continues, 'by allowing the CIA to decide which cases would be too sensitive to prosecute, and by allowing the CIA to withhold whatever information it sees fit. . . .'

"The Justice Department's softness on the CIA dates from a 1954 agreement between the two agencies which, in effect, gave the CIA the right to block a prosecution or keep a crime secret in the name of 'national security.'

"A year later, Congress passed a law requiring government agency heads to report the illegal activities of their employees to the Justice Department. The CIA, however, has rarely complied." (*Washington Post,* November 15, 1976.)

From the intimacy of his love-hate relationship with the agency, it was Anderson who could best describe how Watergate and Vietnam and the Kennedy assassination had left the CIA as impervious to challenge as ever. Langley emerged with a heightened resolve to thwart public scrutiny of its questionable activities. Two years after Anderson's article, the agency would come to the defense of one of its own, E. Howard Hunt, when CIA "renegade" Victor Marchetti published the article that resulted in the *Hunt v. Liberty Lobby* court case.

BOOK IV

Discovery

Haviv Schieber

Y OU SHOULD READ BEN HECHT'S *PERFIDY*. IT'S AN IMPORTANT AND PROVOCATIVE work, but since it has been out of print almost since its publication in 1961, a trip to the library might be required. Hecht, best known for the screenplays of such classic Hollywood films as *The Front Page*, wrote an opinionated nonfiction work about a lawsuit in Israel that shook the then newly formed state to its foundation.

Malchiel Greenwald was an impoverished European Jew who settled in Israel and spent his meager life's savings to publish selfpenned articles of a decidedly dissenting political nature, using an antiquated mimeograph machine. (Younger readers should know that the ink-exuding device preceded the widespread use of photocopy machines.) In one article, now known forever in Israeli jurisprudence as "Pamphlet No. 51," he stated that Dr. Rudolf Kastner, then one of Israel's most honored leaders, was a traitor who had cooperated with the Nazi leaders of Germany, including Adolf Eichmann, to deport Jews from Hungary.

Greenwald was charged by the state of Israel with the high crime of having published a criminal libel; in time he was indicted. Before official action could be taken against Kastner, who had embarrassed the state, the good doctor was shot to death in front of his home at 6 Emmanuel Street in Tel Aviv by Zeev Eckstein, who, until a few months before the murder, had been a paid undercover agent of the Mossad, the Israeli intelligence service.

If you had read *Perfidy*, you would immediately recognize Haviv Schieber as the philosophical, spiritual, and political twin of Malchiel Greenwald, the central figure in Hecht's book. They even looked alike.

Haviv left Israel, moved to the United States, became outraged about the conditions imposed upon Palestinians and Jews who were concerned about them, and began to publish Greenwald-like leaflets, mimeographed at first but later photocopied as technology developed.

Until his death in 1988, this Polish Jew, a founder of the state of Israel, became an advocate of another approach for peace in the Middle East. He founded the Holy Land State Committee and urged that Jews and Palestinians together form a secular democratic state on the territory presently comprising Israel, the West Bank, and the Gaza Strip.

During 1980, in the course of my inquiry into Middle East politics, I met Haviv Schieber at a human rights conference in Washington, D.C. We shared neither a political nor philosophical concept and our world views were as divergent as imaginable. Yet he was a witness to history and beyond that so singlemindedly and optimistically committed to his vision for the Middle East that he was irresistible. He made a living, almost, by posing as the world's worst provider of light construction, repair, and painting services. The guise was not to be found in the evaluation of the services as less than adequate but in the claim that they were services at all.

We met for breakfast one day at my house on Capitol Hill in Washington. Remarkably, our friendship had survived his effort to partially remodel and paint the groundfloor apartment of that building.

Without warning or introduction, Haviv exploded, "Too bad about Carter. He's finished."

Haviv's mind worked at great speed, and a casual listener not attuned to his thought processes and cadence might easily be caught off guard. A new acquaintance usually had difficulty with Haviv's version of English, as well. Haviv, who spoke several languages, some of them apparently at the same time, spoke English with a unique Polish, Yiddish, Middle European, and Middle Eastern combination of accents. He once confided to me—perhaps confessed is the better word—that he was most fluent in English.

"Who is Carter?" I asked.

"You don't know Carter, the publisher of *Spotlight* at Liberty Lobby?" he asked.

I offered that I had heard of *Spotlight* and Liberty Lobby. "Isn't that an extremist, anti-Semitic group?" I asked.

Haviv sighed heavily and said, "Not you too, Mark. To be against the policies of Israel, to give Arafat a chance to be heard, it is not anti-Semitic. Arafat is a Semite too."

Haviv then told me of the exclusive interview *Spotlight* had run with

Yassir Arafat when almost no other national publication would permit his words to be read in the United States.

Realizing that we were digressing, a pattern marking all conversation with my guest, I asked who Carter was and why he was finished.

Correcting my pronunciation, Haviv said, "Not Carter, Carto—*Carto*. Hunt is putting him out of business."

The lawyer for Greenwald, as portrayed by Hecht, experienced much the same problems in securing the facts as did I in the talk with my friend Haviv.

I discovered before breakfast was concluded, however, that E. Howard Hunt, the convicted Watergate burglar and official of the Central Intelligence Agency, had filed a lawsuit against Victor Marchetti, a former high-ranking officer with the CIA and against Liberty Lobby, Inc., publisher of *Spotlight*, for an article Marchetti had written and *Spotlight* had published about the assassination of President Kennedy.

Hunt had won the case and had been awarded almost three-quarters of a million dollars for the loss of his good name, a staggering sum and an even more staggering thought when one considered Mr. Hunt's national reputation.

Haviv told me that Mr. Carto, who presides over Liberty Lobby and *Spotlight*, just did not have the funds to satisfy the judgment and needed a good lawyer to look over the case and help him.

Haviv had a new, although limited, mission. He embarked upon a mini-crusade. I would represent the defendants, Marchetti, and the newspaper; we would win, thus establishing the truth about the death of President Kennedy; and a national newspaper that published a dissenting view of Middle Eastern affairs would survive.

In time Haviv's persistence prevailed. Carto and I agreed to meet one afternoon at the offices of Liberty Lobby just a short walk from my home.

Haviv died before his magnificent vision of a peaceful resolution of the conflict in the Middle East could be realized. His more modest dream of taking a step toward the truth in the death of John F. Kennedy and preserving a dissenting voice became a reality as a result of his intervention into my life and the life of Willis A. Carto. Just as it took Malchiel Greenwald and a libel trial to teach the truth about Dr. Rudolf Kastner in Israel, it took Haviv Schieber and a libel trial to teach the truth about E. Howard Hunt and the assassination of President Kennedy in the United States.

Willis Carto

CARTO MET ME IN A VERY SMALL OFFICE, LESS SPACIOUS THAN SOME CAPITOL Hill closets, set in a complex of two substantial buildings. They served, respectively, as the editorial offices and graphics department for *Spotlight* and as offices for Liberty Lobby, which engaged in letter mailing campaigns, direct lobbying, and similar activities.

We talked only about the Hunt case, while I struggled to contain an abiding curiosity about Carto and his beliefs.

The simplicity of his office struck me. It was across the street from the Library of Congress, with a view of the House of Representatives Office Buildings and just a moment from the United States Supreme Court and the U.S. Capitol building. In a city given to symbols—limousines, plush carpets, $500 per hour lawyers, and a coterie of secretaries and receptionists for each minor functionary—Carto sat behind a battered desk in an office with walls adorned only by a framed print of George Washington and a clock.

He looked trim and fit, dressed in a suit clearly purchased off the rack.

He told me that he had never devoted any time to the facts surrounding the assassination of President Kennedy until Victor Marchetti approached him in the summer of 1978 with a proposed article. "We had never written a word concerning the controversy about the Warren Report," he said. "But then Victor came in with this piece."

"You knew Marchetti?" I asked.

"Oh yes. I knew he was an expert on intelligence due to his work with the CIA. So when he called and told me he had written an interesting article about the assassination based upon information he had dug up as the Congressional Committee was getting underway, I told him to bring it in."

Carto had become particularly interested in Marchetti when the former CIA officer's book, *The CIA and the Cult of Intelligence*, was published. At that time, due to the insistence of the CIA and the complicity of the judicial system, the book was subject to pre-publication censorship and was printed and sold with blank spaces where fact and analysis had been. The action by the court was unprecedented in U.S. history and reflected the burgeoning influence of the powerful police and spy organizations in a nation founded upon the free expression embodied in the First Amendment.

The committee of the Congress Carto referred to was the House Select Committee on Assassinations, an ad hoc committee established by the House of Representatives to examine the facts surrounding the deaths of President John F. Kennedy and Dr. Martin Luther King, Jr. Since the Hunt lawsuit was based upon an article written by Marchetti at the time that committee began its work, a full appreciation of the context and contemporary history requires an understanding of the formation and transformation of the Select Committee. I was there as it all transpired and the relevant facts are set forth in Book I of this work.

Carto, a true believer in the Constitution, was appalled by the censorship of Marchetti's work and intrigued as well. "When they suppressed portions of it," he told me, "it was clear that the CIA was vouching for its accuracy. After all, they could not object to fantasy; they could not swear in court that the nation's security was in jeopardy if a paragraph which was untrue was published."

The point of the censorship is not insignificant and clearly it was not lost upon Carto. Thus it was the deliberate act of the CIA in denying full and free expression to Marchetti that convinced Carto that Marchetti's book was an important and historic repository of truthful secrets.

Later, when my wife and I became friends with Victor Marchetti and his family, my curiosity compelled me to ask him about the original revelations that had appeared as blank spaces in the published work. None, as it so often turns out, were secrets which, even by the most absurd stretch of the imagination, could reasonably be said to imperil national security. All, however, contained one ingredient. If revealed, various fools in the leadership of the CIA would be embarrassed. J. Edgar Hoover had coined a slogan for the FBI that was later adopted in principle by its younger sister, the CIA, with which it maintained an incestuous love-hate relationship. The slogan Hoover and his subordinates lived by: "Do not embarrass the Bureau." For Bureau, read bureaucrats.

One example of the material excised from Marchetti's book might suffice. The CIA, having access to extraordinary scientific minds through the promiscuous use of public funds for which it need not account, set a group of geniuses to work on the problem of eavesdropping at cocktail parties. The ordinary tape recorder was next to useless due to background chatter, the clinking of glasses and other sounds not sought by the scientists. This proved to be the case even when skilled surgeons, on loan to the CIA for this secret project, cut open a cat, inserted a transmitter in his abdominal cavity and ran an antenna up through the unfortunate feline's tail. The cat, after having recovered from major surgery, was set free at a cocktail party as otherwise serious experts huddled around a receiver in a nearby room to monitor the results of their innovative enterprise.

Just as we have the ability to focus our vision upon differing objectives at different times, we have the gift of centering in on sounds which interest us and blocking out the rest. The cat at the cocktail party was nothing more than an ambulatory recording device without the ability to discriminate between a diplomatic indiscretion and the proffer of another canapé.

The well-paid experts were neither disappointed nor deterred; they were merely challenged.

Several million dollars and a few major operations later, the scarred and bewildered pussy cat was released at another cocktail party. The scientists had recalled that it was the cochlea that permitted animals, including humans and, hopefully, cats, to focus in on sounds of particular interest. The recording device had been attached to that part of the cat's ear in a series of intricate and innovative, not to mention outrageously expensive, operations.

The cat stalked the diplomats. The decoding experts were poised in headquarters, headsets firmly affixed. The scientists looked on and wondered what they had wrought. The cat, stiff tail in the air, betrayed no interest in the talk of the guests. It looked longingly at the canapés lavishly decorated with caviar, stared at exquisite fish balls, and was suddenly attracted by a sound behind the baseboard, which the listening scientists, upon analysis, concluded might have been made by a mouse.

The experiment had failed. The cat did not share his tormentors' interest in espionage.

The following week, as the finest of scientific minds met to examine this latest challenge, the cat escaped from its safe house, recklessly crossed the street in search of feline female companionship and was run over and killed by an eighteen-wheel truck.

The CIA finally abandoned the project. It is difficult to imagine that the published story would have endangered the security of the nation. Indeed, it may have affected it positively, since the CIA's counterparts throughout the world could well have been temporarily incapacitated by laughing fits.

It would be wrong, however, to conclude that nothing was accomplished by the experiment, or that the unknown cat gave its life, and suffered substantial pain and mutilation, for nought. A friendly nation received an anonymous message that its embassy very likely housed some mice. An examination ordered by the ambassador proved that the intelligence estimate had been accurate, and exterminators were hired at once.

Marchetti struck Carto as a man with a quick mind, an excellent memory, and a gift for analysis. With the CIA's heartfelt, albeit hostile, endorsement, Carto concluded that Marchetti was a reliable source for the proffered article. Carto, the treasurer of Liberty Lobby, Inc., which published the *Spotlight*, carried out many of the functions of a newspaper publisher. He met with Marchetti and the editor of the *Spotlight* and reviewed the article with them. When he was convinced that it was accurate and that Marchetti had written the piece truthfully and submitted it in good faith, he agreed to publish the work.

Carto was a publisher who knew an important story when he saw it. He was also familiar enough with the laws of defamation to know that his good faith reliance upon Marchetti, who was not an employee of the *Spotlight*, made the publication of the piece libel-proof from the viewpoint of the newspaper, since Hunt was without doubt a public figure. What Carto could not know is that the Liberty Lobby Exception, a new and frightening judicial concept, was rapidly developing. Before long, high courts would hold, in essence, that their doors were closed to those with whom they disagreed profoundly about root political matters.

Carto's personal beliefs impact but tangentially upon the substance of this book. Yet, having raised the matter, it seems only fair to comment upon them in a dispositive manner. Since my first interview with Willis Carto half a dozen years ago, I have represented Liberty Lobby in three important political cases. In addition to the Hunt case, I have argued, before the United States Supreme Court, the case against Jack Anderson and for the First Amendment, and I have defeated the arrogant and pompous William F. Buckley, Jr., in a trial in the United States District Court for the District of Columbia.[1]

---

[1]The Anderson case was concluded with Jack Anderson settling the matter by making a financial contribution and by issuing a statement of apology or explanation.

I have heard the allegation, over and over again, that Carto is anti-Semitic and pro-fascist. I have heard the courts solemnly state that since it has been said so often that either each new allegation has lost its sting, or must be true, based upon the "where there is smoke there must be fire" theory. I have also heard the eloquent response by Judge Scalia, then of the United States Court of Appeals for the District of Columbia, now a justice of the United States Supreme Court, in the *Anderson* case:

"We are not yet ready to adopt for the law of libel the principle that 10,000 repetitions are as good as the truth. We see nothing to be said for the rule that a conscious, malicious libel is not actionable so long as it has been preceded by earlier assertions of the same untruth."

Setting aside legal consideration and arguments based upon precedent, I can report my own observation. Carto challenges the power structure, the right of financial institutions, unelected by the people, to rule the nation, whatever their religious or political affiliation may be. No shrinking violet, he speaks openly and without euphemisms. On more than one occasion we have spent the evening sipping Blanton's, a fine Kentucky bourbon, exploring the vagaries of world politics and exchanging world views. I have never heard an anti-Semitic expression from him in all these years. I believe that my own life, marked by a struggle against all forms of racism, has created for me adequately sensitized antennae so that if the offense was present, even in latent form, I would have discerned it.

Contrast Carto with with the more "respectable" William F. Buckley for a moment. At the time of the Buckley case in the United States District Court, it was revealed that Buckley had been opposed to the right of African-Americans to vote in the United States because they outnumbered white voters in certain areas and because, as he put it, the white voters were the superior or master race. In a demonstration of poor taste, to prove that he was not against black people and their various co-minority friends, Buckley testified about lavish parties to which he'd invited Ronald Reagan and other stars, including one Lewis Strauss. "And he's Jewish," Buckley explained to the jurors. The word Jewish was dragged out through six syllables. It has always been my presumption that anyone who takes more than three syllables with the word is an anti-Semite.

Had Carto whispered a fraction of what Buckley had shouted we would have read about it in the *New York Times*. The press, however, has left Buckley's excesses mostly unreported, even his contention that President Eisenhower had been a knowing part of the international communist conspiracy, that Rev. Adam Clayton Powell was a "jig," that Eleanor Roosevelt was probably irrational and perhaps mad, and that blacks in South Africa should not be permitted access to the ballot box any more than should African-Americans. Buckley's America, as it emerged on the witness stand, was a frightening place. When I helped expose it, through Buckley's own words, an article in Buckley's defense appeared in the *Wall Street Journal*, arranged by his attorney, J. Daniel Mahoney, and published by his friend Suzanne Garment.

Buckley's bizarre concepts and extreme expressions are overlooked by a tame media, for he is easily recognized as a defender of established principles and in fact boasts of membership in the ruling elite. He was also a member in good standing of the intelligence community. David Phillips has disclosed in his memoirs that while Hunt ran the CIA station in Mexico City "in the early fifties," he "had handled, among others, an American contract agent named William F. Buckley." Since that time Buckley has sought to pass as an independent iconoclast rather than as an institutional ideologue by devoting little public energy to reminiscing about his CIA days. The biography published with his editorial assistance in *Who's Who in America* does not even disclose the fact that he had ever worked for the CIA.[2] It was in fact in the mid-fifties that Buckley launched his magazine either while he was still with the CIA or, as I presume he might allege if cornered, just after he had left the Agency.

During 1964, however, he was being promoted as the distinguished leader of the activist right. It was the leadership of that group, the CIA had warned Johnson and Warren, which might, by misinterpreting the evidence linking Oswald to the Soviet Union, propel the nation into a catastrophic war.

As Warren spoke privately of the need for suppression of the evidence, Buckley, his ideological enemy, who, in fact, favored the impeachment of the Chief Justice, carried the same story directly from the CIA to his readership.

On April 7, 1964, Buckley wrote an editorial with the headline "Warren's Secret." He asked: "What can Mr. Warren have had in mind when he uttered those resonant words a month ago, that in our lifetime we shall not know some of the things the Commission has learned about the assassination?" Buckley's answer: a friend in the CIA told him that Oswald was a Russian agent, but was probably not given an order to kill Kennedy, and Warren knew this and wanted it kept quiet lest the right-

---

[2]*Who's Who in America*, 39th edition, 1976; *Who's Who in America*, 44th edition, 1986.

the center—the new, liberal Buckley was enrolled in the intelligence effort to help verify the soon-to-be published Warren Report.

Our courtroom confrontation with Buckley came later—at our initial meeting, Carto acquainted me with the facts surrounding the law suit Hunt had filed and won, told me that the jury had awarded Hunt the sum of $650,000 against Liberty Lobby, which, together with costs and interest had reached the three-quarter of a million dollar mark, and asked me to consider taking the case should Liberty Lobby's pending appeal before the court of appeals be granted.

I agreed to read the article Marchetti had written and review the transcript of the trial. I said that the defense offered at the trial, lack of actual malice, was a troubling concept for me philosophically and in my experience a difficult theory for a jury to accept. I told Carto that if I took the case I would be inclined to mount a defense based upon the truth of the central allegations that the CIA had assassinated President Kennedy and that E. Howard Hunt had played a part in that effort. To conduct such a trial, I explained, would be costly and time consuming, since it would be advisable with that defense to take depositions from various potential witnesses including past directors and officers of the CIA and those who had worked with them. Carto seemed almost excited at the prospect. He observed that it seemed possible that the course of the trial and its preparation might have a profound impact upon our understanding of an important event in the nation's history. Before our initial conversation concluded, Carto had assured me that I would have a free hand in deciding who to depose, when to do it and what questions should be asked.

I agreed to read all the relevant material and confer with Victor Marchetti.

Victor Marchetti

VICTOR MARCHETTI WAS, IT SEEMED, THE ESSENTIAL WITNESS. HE HAD REFUSED TO testify at the first trial; his publisher had then been ordered to pay $650,000 to Mr. Hunt.

At a trial, as in a drama, the audience seeks resolution of the questions that have been propounded. Instructions from the court to the jurors to disregard that, to erase this from your mind, or to ignore these matters for they are not within your province, quite properly carry forth the concepts of precedent and regularity and are viewed with favor by appellate courts that may subsequently review the case record. However, they tend to leave the jurors frustrated and less than enlightened, and they do not satisfy the jurors' curiosity as to what it is that lingers in the shadows and why the lawyers for both sides and the judge have apparently combined, in their presumption of infinite wisdom, to allow the corners of the case to remain unilluminated.

I believe that faith between an attorney and the jury is shattered when counsel is seen attempting to suppress relevant, and above all, interesting, evidence. Therefore, such efforts at censorship should be engaged in out of the presence of the jury with the hope that the jurors will not figure out what has happened and who is responsible. A less cynical and more effective approach, which should be utilized wherever it is possible to do so without laying waste to the foundations of the case, is full disclosure. Jurors appreciate candor; often, in spite of instructions from the court to the contrary, they will penalize the party and his lawyer who fail to grasp that fact.

Before I met Marchetti, I knew that he must testify at the trial. The vague but certain principles of the theatre required his appearance.

For our case to prevail, it seemed clear to me that the former CIA officer must emerge as an energetic and knowledgeable witness whom a jury would likely believe and a writer whom Carto could reasonably have relied upon.

In the years I had devoted to studying the assassination of President Kennedy and to examining the clues that led inexorably to the CIA, I had never knowingly interviewed a ranking CIA official. (My confrontation with David Phillips, alas, having taken place in a debate format, did not allow for a cross-examination.) As documents became available under the amended Freedom of Information Act following the fiasco at the Watergate, I began to learn the extent to which the CIA had affected my life.

One press conference, held in Buffalo, New York, in connection with my work in investigating the murder of the president was fairly well attended. Several newspaper reporters, photographers, television crews, and radio journalists apparently were in attendance. Not a word was printed, projected, or heard by the public following the conference. Later, as previously suppressed documents became available, I learned that each "reporter" had been a police agent or spy. Represented had been the FBI, with agents posing as journalists, the CIA, whose agents had the presence of mind to bring a video camera complete with the markings of a local television station, and the local police-intelligence unit in the form of radio interviewers.

I met Marchetti on March 12, 1984, in the offices of Fleming Lee, general counsel for Liberty Lobby. Following Watergate, Marchetti had become a limited hero to those, who anticipated less secret government and more of an open society. Together with John Marks, he had written a book about the CIA, which Marchetti had served for fourteen years, and the government had responded by securing an injunction against the publication of certain revelations. Even more than the contents of the book, the brouhaha created by the government's reaction focused attention on Marchetti, earning him respect from those who, while at a loss to understand why he had been a loyal CIA denizen for so long during the CIA's period of outrageous conduct, were nevertheless pleased by evidence of his reform and his willingness to share some secrets.

The *Spotlight* article that had inspired Hunt's lawsuits purported to contain some of those secrets:

CIA TO ADMIT HUNT INVOLVEMENT IN KENNEDY SLAYING

The Spotlight, August 14, 1978

(Victor Marchetti has been in U.S. intelligence activities for almost 20 years, 14 years of that being with the CIA, the last three years of which he was a staff assistant to Richard Helms. He is the author of *The CIA and the Cult of Intelligence* and *The Rope Dancer*.)

by Victor Marchetti

A few months ago, in March, there was a meeting at CIA headquarters in Langley, Va., the plush home of America's super spooks overlooking the Potomac River. It was attended by several high-level clandestine officers and some former top officials of the agency.

The topic of discussion was: What to do about recent revelations associating President Kennedy's accused assassin, Lee Harvey Oswald, with the spy game played between the U.S. and the USSR? (*Spotlight*, May 8, 1978.) A decision was made, and a course of action determined. They were calculated to both fascinate and confuse the public by staging a clever "limited hangout" when the House Special Committee on Assassinations (HSCA) holds its open hearings, beginning later this month.

A "limited hangout" is spy jargon for a favorite and frequently used gimmick of the clandestine professionals. When their veil of secrecy is shredded and they can no longer rely on a phony cover story to misinform the public, they resort to admitting—sometimes even volunteering— some of the truth while still managing to withhold the key and damaging facts in the case. The public, however, is usually so intrigued by the new information that it never thinks to pursue the matter further.

We will probably never find out who masterminded the assassination of JFK—or why. There are too many powerful special interests connected with the conspiracy for the truth to come out even now, 15 years after the murder.

But during the next two months, according to sensitive sources in the CIA and on HSCA, we are going to learn much more about the crime. The new disclosures will be sensational, but only superficially so. A few of the lesser villains involved in the conspiracy and its subsequent cov-erup will be identified for the first time—and allowed to twist slowly in the wind on live network TV. Most of the others to be fingered are already dead.

But once again the good folks of middle America will be hoodwinked by the government and its allies in the establishment news media. In fact, we are being set up to witness yet another coverup, albeit a sophisticated one, designed by the CIA with the assistance of the FBI and the blessing of the Carter administration.

A classic example of a limited hangout is how the CIA has handled and manipulated the Church Committee's investigation of two years ago. The committee learned nothing more about the assassinations of foreign leaders, illicit drug programs, or the penetration of the news media than the CIA allowed it to discover. And this is precisely what the CIA is out to accomplish through HSCA with regard to JFK's murder.

THEY'LL HANG HUNT

Chief among those to be exposed by the new investigation will be E. Howard Hunt, of Watergate fame. His luck has run out, and the CIA has decided to sacrifice him to protect its clandestine services. The agency is furious with Hunt for having dragged it publicly into the Nixon mess and for having blackmailed it after he was arrested.

Besides, Hunt is vulnerable—an easy target as they say in the spy business. His reputation and integrity have been destroyed. The death of his wife, Dorothy, in a mysterious plane crash in Chicago still disturbs many people, especially since there were rumors from informed sources that she was about to leave him and perhaps even turn on him.

In addition it is well known that Hunt hated JFK and blamed him for the Bay of Pigs disaster. And now, in recent months, his alibi for his whereabouts on the day of the shooting has come unstuck.

In the public hearings, the CIA will "admit" that Hunt was involved in the conspiracy to kill Kennedy. The CIA may go so far as to "admit" that there were three gunmen shooting at Kennedy. The FBI, while publicly embracing the Warren Commission's "one man acting alone" conclusion, has always privately known that there were three gunmen. The conspiracy involved many more people than the ones who actually fired at Kennedy, both agencies may now admit.

POSING AS BUM

A.J. Weberman and Michael Canfield, authors of *Coup d'Etat in America*, published pictures of three apparent bums who were arrested at Dealy Plaza just after President Kennedy's murder, but who were strangely released without any record of the arrest having been made by the

Dallas police. One of the tramps the authors identified as Hunt. Another was Frank Sturgis, a long time agent of Hunt's.

Hunt immediately sued for millions of dollars in damages, claiming he could prove that he had been in Washington D.C. that day—on duty at CIA. It turned out, however, that this was not true. So, he said that he had been on leave and doing household errands, including a shopping trip to a grocery store in Chinatown.

Weberman and Canfield investigated the new alibi and found that the grocery store where Hunt claimed to be shopping never existed. At this point, Hunt offered to drop his suit for a token payment of one dollar. But the authors were determined to vindicate themselves, and they continued to attack Hunt's alibi, ultimately completely shattering it.

Now, the CIA moved to finger Hunt and tie him to the JFK assassination. HSCA unexpectedly received an internal CIA memorandum a few weeks ago that the agency just happened to stumble across in its old files. It was dated 1966 and said in essence: Some day we will have to explain Hunt's presence in Dallas on November 22, 1963—the day President Kennedy was killed. Hunt is going to be hard put to explain this memo, and other things, before the TV cameras at the HSCA hearings.

Hunt's reputation as a strident fanatical anti-communist will count against him. So will his long and close relationship with the anti-Castro Cubans, as well as his penchant for clandestine dirty tricks and his various capers while one of Nixon's plumbers. E. Howard Hunt will be implicated in the conspiracy and he will not dare to speak out—the CIA will see to that. In addition to Hunt and Sturgis, another former CIA agent marked for exposure is Gerry Patrick Hemming, a hulk of a man—six feet eight inches tall and weighing 260 pounds. Like Sturgis, Hemming once worked for Castro as a CIA double agent, then later surfaced with the anti-Castro Cubans in various attempts to rid Cuba of the communist dictator. But there are two things in Hemming's past that the CIA, manipulation HSCA, will be able to use to tie him to the JFK assassination.

First, Castro's former mistress, Marita Lorenz (now an anti-Castroite herself), has identified Hemming, along with Oswald and others as being part of the secret squad assigned to kill President Kennedy. And secondly, Hemming was Oswald's Marine sergeant when he was stationed at CIA's U-2 base in Atsugi, Japan—where Oswald supposedly was recruited as a spy by the Soviets, or was being trained to be a double agent by the CIA.

131

In any event, Hemming's Cuban career and his connection with Oswald make the Lorenz story difficult for him to deny, particularly since the squad allegedly also included Hunt and Sturgis.

Who else will be identified as having been part of the conspiracy and/or coverup remains to be seen. But a disturbing pattern is already beginning to emerge. All the villains have been previously disgraced in one way or another. They all have "right wing" reputations. Or they will have after the hearings.

The fact that some may have had connections with organized crime will prove to be only incidental in the long run. Those with provable ties to the CIA or FBI will be presented as renegades who acted on their own without approval or knowledge of their superiors.

BLAME PAST PRESIDENTS

As for covering up the deed, that will be blamed on past Presidents, either dead or disgraced. Thus, Carter will emerge as a truth seeker, and the CIA and FBI will have neatly covered their institutional behinds.

The timing of the hearings is another clue of what to expect and why. The committee has scheduled its open sessions of network TV to begin after Congress adjourns for the election campaigns. The first order of business will be the Martin Luther King, Jr. hearings—with James Earl Ray and his family as the star witnesses. Then there will be a short break and the JFK hearings will begin.

The committee plans to conclude its work by early October, just a month before the elections, perfect timing to cash in on the publicity the hearings are certain to create. And perfect timing for the Carterites to get the American public to forget about inflation, taxes, foreign affairs, and other White House blunders and elect a Congress more indebted and responsive to the presidency.

Marchetti presented conflicting images to me. He looked genial, balding, with an immense protruding stomach and a willingness, indeed a desire, to make light of the business at hand. He also was furtive and evasive; clearly, whatever he knew he was not going to tell me at our first meeting.

I asked if I might tape-record our interview to save me the trouble and both of us the time of my taking notes. He agreed. My suggestion was probably unsound, as he became even more cautious once the device was activated.

Marchetti emerged in our long interview, which later became a forty-page transcript, as a man still devoted to the principles of the CIA and still enamored of the agency he had left. He was convinced that his article was entirely accurate, although none of the predictions that comprised much of it had come to pass, and was committed to his position not to reveal his sources to the lawyer who was seeking to defend it. Marchetti's internalized contradictions conspired to make an already challenging case an almost impossible task.

Marchetti showed me several pages of notes that he said he had made contemporaneously with the preparation of his article. They contained numerous references to "J.A." and "B.C." As to "B.C.," who appeared from the context in which the initials kept appearing to be Marchetti's main and perhaps sole source, he said, "I know who B.C. is, but I'm not going to tell you at this time."

I asked Marchetti if J.A. was James Angleton, a bizarre and powerful former CIA official. He answered, "I will neither confirm nor deny. Let that be noted for the record." I began to envy the lawyer who had only to deal with Malchiel Greenwald.

A lawsuit that had previously brought an award of $650,000 for the plaintiff was now to be defended through the testimony of an author who would neither confirm nor deny when talking to the *defense* attorney. At least, I thought, things could not get any worse. I was wrong.

Marchetti, his notes revealed, had apparently also relied upon "A.J." Here initials could hardly provide adequate obfuscation; a source for the article had been A.J. Weberman, the less than serious "garbologist" who had become famous in a relatively confined arena for sifting through the waste products of various celebrities and sharing his gems with all willing to attend his press conferences.

Weberman had coauthored a rather fanciful book about the Kennedy assassination that insisted that a photograph taken just after the assassination had captured Hunt and other CIA operatives as they left the grassy knoll. Shots, including the one that shattered President Kennedy's head, had come from that area, as the work done by various serious critics of the Warren Report had demonstrated more than a decade before Weberman wrote his book. I had secured the photograph in question not long after the assassination. It was not a photograph of Hunt. I had often wondered why Weberman had sought to compromise serious evidence of a conspiracy to assassinate the president, evidence that developed painstakingly over a period of years, by adding to it discrediting and transparently inaccurate allegations. Hunt sued Weberman in a trial known as *Hunt v. Third Press* that took place in 1978. Hunt called Marchetti as his witness at a deposition. According to Marchetti, the CIA advised him to "stonewall," that is, to state that he was unable to answer the relevant questions. The CIA, according to Marchetti, stated that it would "back up and support" Marchetti if he refused to provide any evidence against Weberman. The CIA and Marchetti, working in concert, thus provided support for Weberman's efforts.

It has been said that U.S. spy organizations, which prefer to call themselves the "intelligence community," although little of either seems to predominate, comprise a wilderness of mirrors. It is only with that thought in mind that one can begin to comprehend why the CIA wanted to assist Weberman when he had so publicly asserted that a CIA officer had murdered the president. Were there conflicting interests at war within the CIA? Or was the CIA involved in a damage-limitation operation? Had the CIA, after having failed to silence the critics of the Warren Commission, decided to render their evidence less credible by letting Weberman combine it with inaccurate and easily refutable allegations?

In any event, discovering that Weberman had been a source for Marchetti provided disquieting moments for the defense.

Since Marchetti would not reveal all of his sources to me and would not explore with me the intrinsic reasons for his reliance upon them, I inquired about his efforts to secure corroboration. At once he became less reticent. Indeed, he became loquacious. The House Select Committee on Assassinations, Marchetti told me, had confirmed, in his mind, the accuracy of the story.

Marchetti had called an employee of the congressional committee and told him that he had heard about a memorandum linking Hunt to the assassination. According to Marchetti, he told the committee representative that "A.J. swears on a stack of Bibles it's good stuff." Subsequently, representatives of the committee questioned Marchetti at his home. According to him, "Some people on the committee thought I might be working for the CIA and trying to get into their pants, the committee's pants. Their main concern seemed to be that the CIA was using me to try to penetrate the committee."

How had the committee representatives confirmed the accuracy of the story, I asked. "Their demeanor suggested it was real, they came to my house to question me," Marchetti replied. "Anything else?" Marchetti thought and then replied, "Well, they were very skittish, they wouldn't verify it but they wouldn't deny it either." Since Marchetti was the essential witness, our defense, it seemed, relied upon a perilously slender reed.

Marchetti also made it clear that he might decide that it was not in his interest to testify at the trial. He would, he told me, discuss the matter with Carto.

After reading the transcript of the first trial, examining the record of the appeal then pending, and studying the depositions taken in the case, I met with Carto. Before doing so, I had received more disquieting news: Marchetti suffered from a long-standing and serious drinking problem.[1]

I told Carto that Marchetti's presence at the trial would be important. He agreed, but was less than sanguine about the prospect due to Marchetti's erratic behavior. I also explained that Marchetti as a witness would be less than useful unless he was willing to share his sources with me and subsequently disclose them at the trial.

We agreed that I would meet with Marchetti, attempt to gain his confidence, and determine whether I would take the case only after the ruling by the United States Court of Appeals. This approach permitted me to begin preparation for the potential trial and still be spared the necessity of making a traumatic decision that might prove to be academic. If the appellate court sustained the award, there would be no new trial.

As we focused on the published article that formed the basis for the lawsuit, Marchetti at last stated without ambiguity that his sources had been A.J. Weberman and William R. Corson. Corson, known to Marchetti as Bill Corson, had been referred to in Marchetti's notes as "B.C." I also learned that "J.A." did signify James Angleton, but that he had only been an indirect source.

In time Marchetti assured me that it was Corson who had told him about the existence of the alleged memorandum, signed by Helms and Angleton that linked Hunt to the assassination.

"He *told* you about the memo?" I asked incredulously. Marchetti then confirmed my suspicion and deeply held fear that he had never seen the document; he had merely heard that it existed and had been told of its contents. I asked Marchetti if he had any idea what Corson would say if I asked him about the allegation that he had shared his knowledge of the memorandum with him. Marchetti lit a cigarette, leaned back in his chair, and smiled. Finally he advised me against asking that question.

At that point I outlined the essential elements of the defense as I contemplated them. "Victor, I know of no way to successfully defend this case without your testimony. If you are to be a witness, we are required to notify Hunt's lawyers of that fact now. They will, no doubt, seek to take a sworn statement from you—a deposition before trial. At that time you must truthfully reveal your sources. There is no legal basis to shield

---

[1] Subsequent to the second trial, Marchetti overcame that disability and I have been informed by him and others that he no longer drinks alcoholic beverages.

them. A refusal to make full disclosure at the deposition will, in my judgment, doom our efforts to defend this lawsuit." I did not say, but I considered the fact that even if Marchetti was forthcoming, the case would be difficult to defend unless Corson supported his recollection of the events that immediately preceded the publication of the article.

Marchetti shrugged and then said, "Okay. I'll testify." I told Marchetti that after he named Corson as a source, Hunt's lawyers would undoubtedly seek to depose Corson. I asked Marchetti what he thought Corson would say when questioned while under oath. He thought for a moment and said, "He may claim he doesn't recall. I doubt that he will confirm my testimony; he's been around intelligence too long."

Corson had indeed been involved in intelligence activities for most of his life. He had earned a doctorate from American University in economics and finance. He was a retired Marine Corps colonel who had served as the executive secretary of a joint Department of Defense-Central Intelligence Agency committee on counterinsurgency research and development. His book, *Army of Ignorance*, published in 1977, is considered a classic work regarding the rise of the American intelligence empire. During his quarter-century of service in the Marine Corps, Corson worked closely with the CIA and at a very high level. He represented the Department of Defense on committees with the CIA and the State Department, regarding the China project, and on the Interagency Committee, which operated in the Far East. As we neared trial in the Hunt case, Corson was employed by *Penthouse* magazine, ostensibly as its national affairs editor and its Washington, D.C., representative. In reality, he was the resident intelligence authority at the magazine. Corson, for professional and personal reasons, maintained close ties with CIA personnel and with representatives of British intelligence as well. He served as a not-to-be-revealed source on numerous occasions. It was rarely clear to the recipients of his largesse on whose behalf he was providing the data: Two facts did emerge in most instances according to those who received the information; the intelligence was invariably accurate and Corson was apparently not providing it without some specific reason. While it was difficult to ascertain the motive, it was clear that one existed.

Corson enjoyed an excellent reputation in the circumscribed world through which he glided. An outright denial by him that he had heard of the disputed memorandum, which only he and not Marchetti had seen, would be a devastating blow to the defense of the libel case.

After looking into Corson's formidable background, I met with both Carto and Marchetti on several more occasions. Carto told me that when

Hunt, through his attorney, had demanded a retraction and an apology for the publication of the article, he met with Marchetti to fashion a response. Marchetti told Carto at that time that he would recheck his sources.

Subsequently, Marchetti reported to Carto that his sources were standing firm and that no retraction should be offered. The notes revealed that after Hunt had, through counsel, threatened to file a lawsuit for defamation and demanded a retraction, "24 August, VM meets with B.C. who says he discussed matter with JA, who also has to remain anonymous." Accordingly, Carto declined to withdraw the article. The lawsuit then ensued. I asked Marchetti what he had done to confirm the reliability of his original information. "I talked to Corson again. He said that what he had told me about the memorandum was true. He had no doubt about it. He also did not want me to reveal that he was my source. He did not say, 'If you ever quote me, I'll deny it,' but that was the general impression I received."

Marchetti had not tape-recorded the confirmation by Corson, he told me. I hoped that Corson would openly support Marchetti's version or, at the very least, fall short of blatantly refuting it.

As I explored with Marchetti the occasion on which Corson first told him about the memorandum, he began to provide details that made the event seem genuine. They had met at the Hay Adams in Washington, D.C., for lunch. Corson was eager to discuss the British espionage case involving the Soviet moles Philby, Burgess, and McLean. Corson had been in touch with a British author who was soon to assert publicly that there had been a fourth man. At the luncheon, Marchetti expressed skepticism, stating that so much time had passed that it seemed unlikely a fourth person had been involved. Marchetti said Corson then told him that evidence has a way of surfacing long after old cases may seem settled. At that point, according to Marchetti, Corson told him about the memorandum.

I asked Marchetti why Corson had confided in him. He said that he did not know. In spite of the questions that persisted—Why did Marchetti not record the second confirmatory conversation? Why did he not insist upon seeing the memorandum before vouching for its authenticity?—and the fact that not one of Marchetti's predictions so clearly set forth in his article was even remotely realized, I believed Marchetti's version of the events, absent an outright denial by Corson.

Several weeks later, Carto asked to see me. When we met he was elated. The court of appeals had reversed the finding in the original trial.

Holding that the trial judge had given flawed instructions to the jury, the appeals court had remanded the case to the United States district court for trial.

During the request for jury instructions at the first trial, Ellis Rubin, Hunt's attorney, had proposed a clearly erroneous jury charge regarding an element of libel, thereby misleading the court, and counsel for Liberty Lobby had made no objection. The trial judge had then relied on the parameters of defamation set by counsel for Hunt, and had given the jury clearly erroneous instructions.

Carto was not willing to go to trial again with a lawyer who had demonstrated not only that he could lose the case before the jury, but also that he was so unfamiliar with the law of defamation and so feckless that he failed to object to instructions that a law student should have understood to be both erroneous and prejudicial to his client.

Now that it had been established that there really was going to be a second trial, Carto again asked me to take over the defense of the case. Of course, I had for some time been expecting that this moment might arrive. The work I had done to understand the facts surrounding the death of the president and to make them known had not been tested in the crucible of a courtroom. The evidence I had uncovered had not been subjected to cross-examination. While I was anxious for such a test, I was reluctant to gamble on so dubious a case—a case that was in no manner of my making, and one that appeared to rely upon Marchetti's unfulfilled predictions and Corson's as yet untested response to being revealed as a source.

I thought of Jim Garrison's prosecution of Clay Shaw in 1967. As previously recounted, Garrison, the New Orleans district attorney had indicted Shaw for participation in the conspiracy to assassinate President Kennedy. Jim had become a good friend and I tried to assist him in that case. He was opposed by the local and national media, by the attorney general of the United States, and by the FBI, and CIA. Clearly, even with a strong case and a clever presentation of it, Jim was certain to encounter difficulties. But the case was marked with its own intrinsic problems and the presentation of the evidence was far from adequate. Jim experienced almost paralyzing back pain, which hampered his close supervision of the development of the evidence and prevented him from appearing regularly in the courtroom during the trial. His assistants were not able to grasp the complexity of the evidence, with the exception of one young assistant district attorney, Andrew Sciambra. In addition, the CIA withheld important, perhaps crucial, evidence that demonstrated that Shaw had worked for the agency.

The result was the acquittal of Shaw and the concomitant plethora of headlines, editorial comment, feature articles and television newscasts all devoted to the single principle that the Warren Report and each of its conclusions had been certified yet again, this time by a jury. The work of many scholars, investigators, and writers, who together in only the most amorphous sense had formed the critics of the Warren Report, was undone and the effort to discover the truth was set back perhaps a decade.

I was concerned that another unsuccessful challenge in court to the conclusions of the report might be perceived, no matter how unfairly, as the ratification of the findings of the Warren Commission.

The single most compelling argument in favor of undertaking the trial of a case that had already been lost once before a jury was the opportunity to constrain the suspects to answer the questions they had avoided for two decades.

Under the circumstances, I would not have initiated a law suit against Hunt even had conditions existed that would have permitted such an effort. But the case was there. Its trial was imminent. Unlike Jim Garrison, I was not required to consider the wisdom of initiating the legal action and to consider the consequence of defeat. The Hunt case was going to trial. In all likelihood, Hunt would prevail no matter who defended Liberty Lobby. For me, at last, the question was solely whether I might use my knowledge of the underlying events to secure information not previously known.

I explained this to Carto and I told him that I would take the case.

He smiled and said, "Well, it's apparently going to be an education for all of us. Is there any chance we may win?"

I answered, without smiling, "There is always that chance."

Hunt was represented by a large law firm, Ober, Kaler, Grimes and Shriver, which maintained offices in Washington, D.C., and Baltimore, Maryland. William Snyder, Kevin Dunne, and Daniel Dutcher from that law firm participated in the pretrial work.

A paralegal, Brent Whitmore, worked with me. She did legal research, filing, and typing for Liberty Lobby and she became an invaluable asset as the trial approached. The general counsel for Liberty Lobby, Fleming Lee, had sat in during the first trial, making no discernible contribution. He undertook a similar role in the preparation for the second trial.

I notified Snyder that Marchetti would testify at the trial and that he would disclose his sources. I told him that the primary source for the memorandum had been William Corson. I then served a deposition subpoena upon Corson, who worked in Washington, D.C., and lived in

Potomac, Maryland. On May 15, 1984, Corson appeared at my office on Capitol Hill, directly across the street from the United States Supreme Court.

He declined to answer questions about his intelligence assignments for the Marine Corps, stating that the information was classified. He conceded that he had enjoyed a close and continuing relationship with the CIA over a period of many years and that he continued to maintain contact with intelligence officers he had worked with and with other officers as well. He acknowledged knowing Marchetti and recalled that he had met him after *Penthouse* had published an article Marchetti wrote.

It was clear that Corson's view of the relationship between the two men was somewhat different from Marchetti's. "I have not seen Victor, for, I would say, five or six years, at least that. I believe I have talked with him on the telephone, probably in that span of time, but I don't think I have seen him in the last five or six years."

Corson agreed that he probably had met Marchetti every once in a while at his office and then had lunch with him at the Hay Adams. "I believe we probably did, because I usually take lunch there if I'm going to be talking to an author." Corson was obviously being careful to offer no specific information. His answers were punctuated by the use of the words "probably" and "I believe" and "I don't recall." His answer to the most specific question was couched in general terms. The question, "Did you discuss any matter involving the CIA with Mr. Marchetti?" earned the response that "because I'm a student of those matters" and have "written about it in my last book, I can say we probably talked of that."

Had Corson discussed the fourth man in British espionage activity with Victor Marchetti? Corson did not recall, but in general he had known about the matter and could have discussed it with Victor or anyone else.

It was clear to me that Corson was not going to make any specific answer that might serve as a predicate for Marchetti's version of the crucial exchange. While Corson was a poised and almost eloquent witness, the pattern of obfuscation he was establishing with each answer to relatively innocent questions made it apparent that he was not going to confirm Marchetti's account. It was, I felt, time to plunge into the central question. I hoped that Corson might offer vague and ambiguous answers. This would leave Marchetti's account, while uncorroborated, at least unchallenged.

Q. Do you recall Mr. Marchetti coming to you and asking you if you knew anything about the fact that the House Select Committee on Assassinations was investigating the possible relationship of E. Howard Hunt, Jr., to the assassination of John Kennedy?

A. I don't recall that question.

Q. You don't recall him asking about that?

A. No.

Q. Do you recall providing some information to him about that?

A. No.

Q. Do you recall telling Mr. Marchetti that there was a CIA memo which placed Hunt in Dallas on November 22, 1963?

A. No, not at all.

Q. You don't recall discussing that with Mr. Marchetti?

A. No.

Q. Do you recall telling Mr. Marchetti that the CIA was planning some sort of a limited hang-out with the House Select Committee on Assassinations to effect the damage that this memo might cause the agency, the CIA?[2]

A. No.

I persisted.

Q. Did you know Mr. Marchetti wrote a piece about the House Select Committee on Assassinations and E. Howard Hunt?

A. No.

Q. You didn't know he had published a section in *Spotlight*?

A. No. I don't read *Spotlight*.

Q. And you had not heard until now that such a piece was published?

A. If you say it was published, that is as much as I know.

Q. I am just asking you.

A. No. I have no knowledge of such a piece. I did know he was working for *Spotlight* and that he would write for them occasionally.

Q. Do you recall Mr. Marchetti calling you and telling you that he had written a piece about the House Select Committee on Assassinations and E. Howard Hunt, and that Hunt was complaining that the piece was defamatory, and therefore he wanted to check on it, with you, the information you had about the existence of the memo that we have referred to earlier?

A. No. I have no recollection of that.

Q. And then I take it you don't recall that you said to Mr. Marchetti that the original story was accurate, that there was such a memo?

A. No. I am certain of that. Because I have no knowledge of such a memo.

Q. Are you saying now that you never had such a discussion with Mr.

---

[2]Marchetti had defined a limited hang-out as a partial, non-damaging, irrelevant concession used by the CIA to deflect attention from the central question.

Marchetti, any of the discussions I have referred to recently since we began talking about the Kennedy assassination and the House Select Committee on Assassinations, you never had such discussions, or you don't recall?

A. I don't recall.

When Snyder questioned Corson, the answers seemed a bit more dispositive.

Q. Did you ever orally or in writing, or do you believe now that the CIA in general, or Mr. Hunt, as one of its agents in particular, engineered the death of President Kennedy?

A. None, not at all. I don't think that is supportable and I think in fact, to make a conclusion to justify my response, that if there had been evidence to that effect, that Senators Hart and Schweiker would have either unearthed it or established enough leads to pursue it.

Q. And I believe you have already said the subject never came up in discussions you had with Victor Marchetti?

A. To the best of my knowledge, no. We talked of many things, but I can't recall that that was a topic of my real concern.

Snyder's last question made his most telling point.

Q. You said you didn't discuss this alleged memo with Victor Marchetti or with people in the agency. Have you ever heard of the existence of such a memorandum before this deposition today?

A. No, I had not.

Corson had now directly refuted Marchetti's assertion that he had served as the source for the information about the memorandum. Clearly, one of the men had not told the truth. The case, as never before, seemed in jeopardy. That evening, however, when I examined the deposition notes I had made when Corson testified and reflected upon Marchetti's responses, I concluded that Marchetti seemed more credible. Corson had been a brilliant witness; he had been perhaps a shade too brilliant.

Later Snyder deposed Marchetti at the law firm's Washington office. Hunt sat in at the deposition. As a party to the action, he was entitled to be present.

I had recognized that Marchetti's temper often flashed when he was pressed for an answer. I urged him to remain calm and contemplative, to appear to be cooperative, and to respond in a polite fashion. We were in the deposition for just a few minutes when those suggestions were forgotten or ignored. When Snyder asked one not inappropriate question, Marchetti responded, "I'm not going to answer it. I think it's a stupid question." When Snyder asked the next question, also a proper inquiry,

Marchetti bristled and threatened to walk out of the room and thus terminate the deposition. Marchetti then began to interrupt Snyder in order to make caustic remarks. When asked to provide support for an allegation contained in the article he had written, he responded that he was not able to do so since "I'm not a JFK assassination buff." Snyder persisted in an effort to secure the answer. I observed that he had asked the same question several times. Snyder responded, "Well, I still have not gotten a straight answer." Marchetti entered the colloquy to address Snyder: "Well, if you stop screwing around you'd get a straight answer."

During a recess, I urged Marchetti to adopt a different attitude. He resisted the advice, stating that he thought he was doing very well. I told him that I believed a jury would not be favorably impressed with his rude treatment of opposing counsel. Marchetti said he would act differently when he testified at the trial, when a jury was present.

I was not certain that he would be able to carry out that plan. I told him that Snyder could confront him, at trial, with the deposition transcript he was then developing. Marchetti did not respond and the deposition continued at that point. I did notice a slight decrease in the witness's apparent hostility toward Snyder.

Soon, however, I was thinking fondly, almost with nostalgia, of the halcyon moments that comprised the early part of the deposition, when bad form rather than substance had occupied my concern. Since Marchetti had begun to speak frankly to me about his source regarding the memorandum, he had been absolutely consistent. His source had been Corson. A.J. Weberman knew of the memo, and had filled in some details about other allegations that found their way into Marchetti's article, but Corson had told Marchetti of its existence and later reconfirmed that fact for Marchetti with James Angleton.

The article began with the assertion that a high-level meeting had been convened at CIA headquarters in Langley, Virginia, to consider the implications of the newly discovered evidence linking the CIA to the assassination of President Kennedy. The article stated that "an internal CIA memorandum" dated 1966, had just surfaced and it established Hunt's presence in Dallas at the time of the assassination. When asked by Snyder for his source, Marchetti replied, "William Corson. C-O-R-S-O-N." Snyder asked the witness if Corson was the source for the entire paragraph, to which Marchetti replied, "Yes." Marchetti then made it clear that Corson had been his exclusive source, except for allegations he had heard over the years from critics of the Warren Report. For the next several minutes Marchetti continued to offer Corson as the sole source. Snyder then began an inquiry designed to establish that Marchetti could not have had a good faith reliance upon Corson as the source.

Q. Does it make sense to you that someone such as Mr. Corson would be privy to what you regarded as the innermost secret of the Central Intelligence Agency?

A. Yes.

Q. Why?

A. Because he was a good friend of Jim Angleton [James Jesus Angleton had died since the publication of Marchetti's article]. He knows and knew at that time most of the senior officers in the CIA and Pentagon intelligence. He had given me a lot of information upon a lot of the other subjects over the years that was very good. He was a very knowledgeable man. Just one example: He told me about the fourth man in the Philby case and introduced me to some British writer who was working this case, and I thought that was amazing. It later turned out to be absolutely true.

Snyder continued to probe for Marchetti's sources.

Q. Okay. You have a statement in here that "the agency is furious with Hunt for having dragged it publicly into the Nixon mess and for having blackmailed it after he was arrested." What is your source for that statement?

A. Corson, various others—and various CIA contacts. Various reporters around town who have—who followed CIA matters.

Q. Did you attempt to talk to Richard Helms about any of this article before you wrote it?

A. No, I did not.

Q. Did you attempt to talk to Mr. Hunt before writing it?

A. No.

Q. Did you attempt to talk to James J. Angleton?

A. No.

Q. Ray Rocca, R-O-C-C-A?

A. No, I did not.

In the article Marchetti had repeated speculation that Hunt may have been implicated in some way in the death of his own wife. It was a matter that I had looked at in a cursory fashion when it occurred, for I, too, had heard the rumors. I never came across any evidence to support the suspicions. Snyder inquired about the allegations.

Q. Page four of your article, referring to Mr. Hunt, you say, "The death of his wife, Dorothy, in a mysterious plane crash in Chicago, still disturbs many people, especially since there were rumors from informed sources that she was about to leave him and perhaps even turn on him." Who does Mrs. Hunt's death disturb? You say it disturbed "many people."

A. I would say just the general public.

Q. For what reason?

A. Curious. It was a very strange plane crash. There were a lot of theories about what may have happened.

Q. Is it your theory that he blew up the plane?

A. No.

Q. What is your theory? How does a plane crash? How would Mr. Hunt have caused the plane to crash?

A. I didn't say he caused the crash.

Q. What are you saying?

A. Read it. What do you get out of it?

Q. That he caused the plane to crash.

A. Well, then you're an idiot.

Q. Thank you. Who are the "informed sources" that say she was about to leave him?

A. A couple of Washington news reporters highly respected.

Q. Who are they?

A. I'm not going to say their names.

Marchetti gradually began to insert the name of A.J. Weberman into his answers. He testified that he had talked to Weberman before he wrote the article. He testified that Weberman had been the source for the allegation that Hunt had offered various alibis to demonstrate that he had not been in Dallas and that the current alibi "has come unstuck."

Then Snyder moved back into the question of the memorandum.

Q. Did you ever see the memo?

A. No, I did not.

Q. Did Corson ever offer to show you the memo?

A. He did not.

Q. Did Weberman tell you that he knew about any memo?

A. Yes, he did.

Snyder seemed less astonished than I felt. Suddenly Weberman had become a source for the memorandum.

Marchetti then explained that A.J. Weberman had been his original source for the existence of the memorandum and that Corson "felt A.J.'s info was accurate." Marchetti explained that when he rechecked the information after the story had been published and Hunt was demanding a retraction, he sought confirmation from Corson. Corson, at Marchetti's request, contacted James Angleton, and Angleton told Corson that he had written the memorandum. Or so Marchetti testified. Marchetti added that Corson told him that Angleton "seemed very worried about the fact that the committee [the House Select Committee on Assassinations] had the memo."

The newly emerging explanation was intriguing. Weberman was Marchetti's exclusive initial source for the memorandum story. When Hunt threatened a lawsuit, Marchetti asked Corson to check it out. Corson talked to Anglelon, the alleged author of the memorandum, and he authenticated it in a conversation with Corson. There were but two problems with the story. It contradicted Marchetti's previous explanations, including those given to Carto, to me, and under oath at the deposition. In addition, Corson, the essential link, had testified that it was untrue.

I had been practicing law for thirty-five years and I could recall, only with great difficulty, feeling so helpless in the past, when a case began to disintegrate similarly in my presence. I poured myself a cup of coffee, began to sip it, and sought solace in the belief that since we had reached dead bottom in the deposition things could not get worse. They did.

Snyder asked Marchetti if he ever inquired of Weberman as to how he had come across the memorandum. Marchetti explained that at first Weberman told him that a man named Fonzi, a member of the staff of the Select Committee, was the source. Later Weberman told Marchetti that Fonzi had not been his source; his source had been a man named Ed Lopez. Weberman said that Lopez "had seen the memo with his own eyes." However, Weberman later told Marchetti, according to Marchetti, that Lopez "now denies" that he had ever seen the memo. Marchetti identified Lopez as an investigator for the Congressional committee and then he admitted he had never spoken to either Fonzi or Lopez.

It had become increasingly clear in the weeks before the Marchetti deposition that it would not be possible to prepare a successful defense against the defamation action by relying upon the testimony of Victor Marchetti. This was indeed an unfortunate circumstance, given that he was the author of the disputed article that was based upon a memorandum that no one had ever seen—at least no one who would admit it under oath. Marchetti said Corson may have seen it. Corson categorically denied that allegation. Weberman said that Lopez had said he had seen it. Lopez denied that he had seen it and further denied that he had ever said he had seen it.

Marchetti's piece was not capable of being defended intrinsically. Unless I could secure evidence that had not been available to Marchetti when he wrote the article, there seemed to be no defense at all.

I began to doubt that I had made the correct decision when I agreed to represent the newspaper. Before leaving the conference room, I gathered my papers together and placed them in my briefcase. I looked up to see Hunt staring at me. For the first time that day he was smiling. He seemed confident. I resolved that if he had been involved, I was going to prove it. Snyder and I shook hands as I was about to leave. He seemed certain that he had won, that the contest was over. He asked me if I would settle the case for three-quarters of a million dollars. I answered, "Round one."

The Closing
Argument

IN MY MOST SUBJECTIVE ANALYSIS OF THE PROSPECTS FOR A CASE, EACH EVENTUALLY reaches precipice time, or, more grandly, expresses the moment of its continental divide. That is the moment when it becomes clear to me that the evidence is flowing rapidly and perhaps inexorably in one direction or another. It is a time either for restrained jubilation or pretrial depression. The close of the Marchetti deposition was that moment in the Hunt case. It was time to look beyond the gloomy prospect to what might be, indeed what needed to be, for my client to prevail. It was the stage in the case when reason and experience told me I needed to prepare a closing argument for the jury.

I neither mean to suggest that all trial attorneys currently approach the evidence in this manner nor that they should do so. Indeed, I know of no other lawyer who proceeds precisely in this fashion. As I write these words now, more than forty years as a trial lawyer, I know only that this methodology has worked for me.

In the closing argument, the attorney marshals the evidence that has been adduced at trial, including the testimony of the witnesses at trial, the transcripts of those depositions that were taken before trial, and other documentary evidence. He selects and emphasizes the evidence that support of his client's position and seeks to present it, along with the more troublesome evidence, to the jury with an analysis that places it in a context favorable to the client's cause.

Some lawyers make a practice of ignoring contrary evidence. I believe it necessary to focus upon that body of testimony and exhibits and to analyze it from the perspective of my client. Of course, it is important to place each element of the defense before the jury in closing remarks. If the trial is the presentation of bits and pieces of the case, some offered out of context, and some without explanation, the closing argument is counsel's chance, his last opportunity, to assemble the mosaic before the jury with the ardent hope that the jurors will see it, as a completed and whole entity, just as he does.

As a defense lawyer, at the outset of either a civil or criminal case, I find it difficult to create that completed jigsaw puzzle in my mind. At so early a stage there are too many variables that render the case too abstract to contemplate as a whole. At some moment, however, it is apparent to me that I cannot permit the case to develop a life of its own—that I must analyze it, and if need be, to act decisively to change its course. As I contemplated the Marchetti deposition I prepared, in my mind, a potential closing argument that might prevail.

After several meetings with Marchetti, and long before his deposition was taken, I had concluded that it was imperative to secure evidence from other sources to support, where possible, the allegations he had published. Clearly, I could not buttress his printed predictions that the CIA would "nail Hunt" for killing Kennedy and that the CIA would "sacrifice" Hunt by admitting that he was involved in the conspiracy to assassinate the president. These events were all scheduled to take place, according to Marchetti, at sessions to be held by the House Select Committee on Assassinations. The committee had long since ceased to exist and nothing remotely resembling the scenario projected by Marchetti had occurred.

My contemplated closing argument began with the assumption that, where he was not making predictions, but merely reporting what he heard, Marchetti had been truthful. Corson had been his only reliable source. Unfortunately, Corson was apparently a source only after the fact—after the article had been published. I could explain that, I believed. A.J. Weberman, an odd and somewhat hysterical informant, could not, in my view, be offered to a jury as a reliable source. He was further compromised by having given varying, not to say contradictory, stories to Marchetti. No, we would not rely upon Weberman; we would stay with Corson, although he denied that he was a source and even though Marchetti was now stating that Corson offered nothing more than confirmation.

If the story about the memorandum was true, then someone had seen it. If Corson had talked to Marchetti about it, he had possibly talked to others as well.

And so, members of the jury, while Victor Marchetti has not seen the memorandum, it was seen by another responsible person whom we have presented in this case as a witness. Terrific. It had a certain ring to it. Now all I had to do before trial was locate the witness.

Mr. Hunt *has stated that he was not in Dallas on November 22, 1963, and that the article has defamed him by stating he was there. We have offered evidence to establish that he was in Dallas that day and that he has consistently committed perjury to various authorities over the years—and on that witness stand to you—when he denied that he was there.* Yet another stirring sentence or two. All I needed was the proof.

There, then, were two elements of the closing argument I wished to offer. I had several months to gather the evidence regarding events that had taken place twenty years before.

It was not as hopeless as it may seem to you, the reader. I had a lead that I had not previously shared with anyone, including, until this point, you. Years earlier I had met Marita Lorenz. At the time, I tape recorded a long interview with her. The recording would not be admissible under any circumstance that might obtain in the Hunt trial, and with good reason. Marita Lorenz had not been subject to cross-examination by Hunt's counsel. Yet if I could find her and convince her to overcome her fear of being murdered by CIA operatives, her testimony could possibly be dispositive.

Not long before his deposition I had asked Marchetti if he had ever heard that Corson had discussed the memo with anyone else. He had not. I asked him if he had ever heard that an article similar to the one he had written had been published elsewhere. He had no such knowledge.

I discreetly compiled a list of Corson's contacts and cautiously inquired if he had talked about the Kennedy assassination or the work of the House Select Committee on Assassinations with any of them. One or two declined comment; others recalled no such conversation.

An aide checked through the index of leading publications but was unable to locate a published article similar to the one Marchetti had written.

Having almost exhausted the available traditional resources, I turned toward an informal network that had been established years before. In the days following the assassination, I formed an organization based in New York City called the Citizens Committee of Inquiry. Its purpose, from the time it was founded in 1964, was to bring together people interested in securing the facts about the death of the president. It was clear that an extraordinary response was required to meet the effort of the police and spy organizations to offer a sanitized solution to the murder and to discourage serious inquiry. As a result of that early effort, college students, professors, scientists, writers, and others from various professions, as well as homemakers, photographers, dancers, political activists, and high school students exchanged information. They were called the critics of the Warren Commission Report. Probably few, if any, dissenting books or articles of the hundreds published in the years since that time cannot be traced to the Citizens Committee of Inquiry and the early work it accomplished.

It was to the members of this group, and their successors, the second and third generation—some of whom had formed the organization called the Citizens Commission of Inquiry in the '70s—that I turned. One young woman, then residing in Dallas, remembered only that when Stansfield Turner, then the director of the CIA, had visited that city during 1978, he was asked about an article that appeared in "some small newspaper on the East Coast." The original article had made reference to a CIA memorandum placing Hunt in Dallas on November 22, 1963. Turner had addressed the convention of the Veterans of Foreign Wars and had been surprised when asked about the Kennedy assassination.

We were able to determine that the organization had held its convention in Dallas during August 1978. An examination of the files of the Associated Press in Dallas revealed that a dispatch had been sent out by the AP at that time. It was possible the story had not been published. Turner was quoted in the AP story as stating that his agency was unable to locate any such memo. He conceded, however, that it was "always possible" that such a memorandum had been removed from the files in the twelve years that had elapsed from 1966 until the time that Turner authorized a search for it. I immediately secured a copy of the AP story from the Dallas bureau. I read it with more than a modicum of interest. Turner had not been asked to respond to a question based upon the *Spotlight* article written by Victor Marchetti. Apparently the *Sunday News Journal*, published by Gannett in Wilmington, Delaware, was the "small East Coast newspaper" that had caused the Dallas reporter to ask about the CIA memorandum.

Without delay I found the relevant issue, dated August 20, 1978. The story was written by Joe Trento and Jacquie Powers, at that time staff correspondents for the *Wilmington News Journal*. Trento, I discovered, was then employed in Washington, D.C., as a television journalist for the Cable News Network. His name had been on the list I developed of persons who maintained a professional relationship with William Corson. It seemed possible that another journalist had learned of the existence of the CIA memorandum from Corson. Marchetti's version of the events was gaining potential support. Trento and Powers had written this story for the Sunday News Journal:

WAS HOWARD HUNT IN DALLAS THE DAY JFK DIED?

Sunday News Journal, August 20, 1978

By Joe Trento and Jacquie Powers

WASHINGTON—A secret CIA memorandum says that E. Howard Hunt was in Dallas the day President John F. Kennedy was murdered and that top agency officials plotted to cover up Hunt's presence there.

Some CIA sources speculate that Hunt thought he was assigned by higher-ups to arrange the murder of Lee Harvey Oswald.

Sources say Hunt, convicted in the Watergate conspiracy in 1974, was acting chief of the CIA station in Mexico City in the weeks prior to the Kennedy assassination. Oswald was in Mexico City, and met with two Soviet KGB agents at the Russian Embassy there immediately before leaving for Dallas, according to the official Warren Commission report.

The 1966 secret memo, now in the hands of the House assassination committee, places Hunt in Dallas Nov. 22, 1963.

Richard M. Helms, former CIA director, and James J. Angleton, former counterintelligence chief, initialed the memo according to investigators who made the information available to the *Sunday News Journal*.

According to sources close to the Select Committee on Assassination, the document reveals:

• Three years after Kennedy's murder, and shortly after Helms and Angleton were elevated to their highest positions in the CIA, they discussed the fact that Hunt was in Dallas on the day of the assassination and that his presence there had to be kept secret.

• Helms and Angleton thought that news of Hunt's presence in Dallas would be damaging to the agency should it leak out.

• Helms and Angleton felt that a cover story, giving Hunt an alibi for being elsewhere the day of the assassination, "ought to be considered."

Hunt, reached Friday at his Miami, Fla., home, denied that he was in Dallas on Nov. 23, 1963, and denied that he had been in Mexico City any time after 1961.

Hunt said that he was in Washington the day of the Kennedy murder. "I have plenty of witnesses. I took off at noon that day and went shopping and had a Chinese dinner in downtown Washington with my wife."

Hunt said he knew of no reason for such a memo to exist. He said he had he had never heard of the memo's existence.

CIA sources, who have provided the assassination committee with material pertaining to Hunt's alleged presence in Dallas, say that Hunt's story about shopping in downtown Washington was a cover story concocted as a result of the memo. They say all Hunt's witnesses are CIA-arranged and that his wife cannot be questioned because she was killed in a plane crash.

The assassination committee will open hearings this fall on the Kennedy murder.

Dawn Miller, spokeswoman for the committee, said that there would be "no comment on the report of a memo. We will be holding detailed hearings in September. Because of committee rules that is all I am permitted to say."

Committee sources told the *Sunday News Journal* that both Helms and Angleton had been questioned by committee investigators but that the issue of the memo was not raised with either witness. Sources say Helms told the committee he could not answer specific questions on the CIA's involvement because of "an inability to remember dates."

Helms's faulty memory on ITT's involvement in Chile led to his sentencing last year of two counts of withholding information from Congress, a charge reduced from perjury by order of President Carter.

Helms could not be reached for comment. A secretary said that he was out of town and would not be available.

When Angleton was questioned by committee staffers, he was "evasive," according to a source who was present. Angleton could not be reached for comment.

Asked to explain why a potentially damaging cover-up plot would be put out on paper, one high-level CIA source said, "The memo is very odd. It was almost as if Angleton was informing Helms, who had just become director, that there was a skeleton in the family closet that had to be taken care of and this was his response."

One committee source says the memo "shows the CIA involvement in the Kennedy case could run into the CIA hierarchy. We are trying not to get ahead of ourselves but the mind boggles."

As part of its $5-million expenditure on the Kennedy and Martin Luther King assassinations, the committee contracted a Cambridge, Mass., sonics firm to review tape recordings made as shots were fired at the Kennedy motorcade.

The firm has provided the committee's technical staff with new evidence which shows that four shots and not three were fired at the Kennedy car. Sources say this would have made it impossible for Oswald to act alone.

"Combined with the memo covering up Hunt's involvement in Dallas that day, what we have so far puts a real dent in the Warren Commission version," a committee source contends. Helms and Angleton currently are targets of an internal CIA probe and a new Senate Intelligence Committee investigation into the possibility that the Soviet KGB penetrated the CIA with a mole, or a high-level double agent.

Cleveland Cram, the former CIA station chief in Ottawa, Canada, was called out of retirement to investigate Angleton's and Helms' role in the penetration. Cram came across the Hunt memo in his mole study," one investigator suspects.

The urgency of the mole investigation within the agency has reached "a more intense level since the memo was discovered," according to a source close to the internal investigation.

Herbert E. Hetu, public affairs director of the CIA, told the Sunday News Journal, "I had heard rumors of such a memo but had been unable to track them down. I checked with our liaison with the assassination committee and he didn't know about it."

The possibility of a "mole" or double agent in the CIA in connection with Oswald was first brought to light in Edward J. Epstein's book, Legend—The Secret World of Lee Harvey Oswald.

That book details Oswald's ties with U.S., Soviet and Cuban intelligence. According to Epstein's editor at Readers Digest Press, which published the book, Angleton was a main source for the author.

In 1964, a Soviet defector named Yuri Nosenko told the CIA that Oswald did not act as a Russian agent in the Kennedy assassination. For years, according to the book, a battle within the agency ensued as to whether or not Nosenko was telling the truth.

That battle ended in 1976 when Nosenko was accepted as a genuine defector and put on the CIA payroll and given a new identity.

According to the book, Angleton urged that Nosenko not be accepted because he believed the Russian to be a double-agent.

Hunt's appearance on the scene in Dallas and in Mexico City at the time of the murder adds strength to a theory shared by some internal CIA investigators. They believe Oswald was working for U.S. intelligence, that he was ordered to infiltrate the KGB, and that this explains his life in Russia. They also believe that Oswald proved to be so unstable that he was "handled by the KGB into becoming a triple agent, and assigned for the Dallas job."

The same investigators theorize that Hunt was in Dallas that day on the orders of a high-level CIA official who in reality was a KGB mole. Hunt allegedly thought he was to arrange that Oswald be murdered because he had turned traitor. Actually he was to kill Oswald to prevent him from ever testifying and revealing the Russians had ordered him to kill Kennedy, the CIA sources speculate.

CIA investigators are most concerned that either Helms or Angleton might be that mole.

Hunt first detailed the existence of a small CIA assassination team in an interview with the *New York Times* while in prison in December 1975 for his role in Watergate. The assassination squad, allegedly headed by Col. Boris Pash, was ordered to eliminate suspected double agents and low-ranking officials.

Pash's assassination unit was assigned to Angleton, other CIA sources say.

Hunt's fondness for strange plots has been widely reported. He is alleged to have concocted schemes ranging from Watergate to a plot to assassinate columnist Jack Anderson. Hunt is also the author of 45 spy novels.

It was also learned from CIA and committee sources that during the time that the Warren Commission was investigating the Kennedy assassination, Angleton met regularly with a member of the commission—the late Allen Dulles, then head of the CIA and Angleton's boss.

Dulles, on a weekly basis, briefed Angleton about the direction of the investigation. Angleton, according to sources, in turn briefed Raymond Rocca, his closest aide and the CIA's official liaison with the commission.

Rocca, now retired was unavailable for comment. His former wife, who also worked for Angleton, is now working for Cleveland Cram as part of the CIA mole investigation team.

The article was different from the one published by *Spotlight* in many respects. It did not predict events. It clearly did not rely upon A.J. Weberman as a source. It offered an illuminating and relevant historical perspective. Since Trento had contacted Hunt for his response before writing the article, it contained an interesting quotation by Hunt as to where he was on November 22, 1963. Most important of all, from my view, was the article's unequivocal statement that there was a CIA memorandum dated 1966, which placed Hunt in Dallas on November 22, 1963.

I met with Marchetti in order to determine if he and Trento had discussed the subject matter with each other. He was astonished to learn that a story similar to his had been published. He told me that at that time, mid-1984, he knew of Trento, but that they did not know each other, had in fact never even met, in 1978 when the articles were published. Marchetti assured me that they had not coordinated the publication of the two articles. Coincidence seemed too unlikely to be a viable alternative. The memorandum was a dozen years old and the first, and only, stories published about it were published within a week of each other. Both men knew Corson and each of them separately discussed intelligence matters with him before writing their CIA-memorandum stories. I believed both Marchetti and Trento; they had not coordinated the publication of their articles. I also believe that it was probable that someone had. Corson seemed a likely suspect.

I sought to interview Trento. Corson had already testified that he knew nothing about the Helms-Angleton memorandum. I thought it useless to ask him if he had served as Trento's source. If Corson had provided information to both Marchetti and Trento, he obviously was unwilling to take responsibility for having done so. His penchant for secrecy about his own role in the affair was intriguing. It was logical to assume that once having testified that he had not been the source, his resolve not to disclose all of the facts could only have been strengthened. The offer of new and contradictory evidence at that time might have made him vulnerable to penalties.

Trento was the obvious resource to be explored, but for one factor. He was more than reluctant to share his information with me; he refused even to meet with me. Through mutual associates I learned that Trento despised Liberty Lobby and vowed that he would not assist in any way.

He stated that he felt no animosity toward me and none toward Marchetti, with whom he had exchanged information about other stories that had interested the two men. In fact, Trento had written a derogatory article about Liberty Lobby and Carto for *True* magazine some years before and that article became the basis for a defamation action against *True*. Trento remembered the article well. The lawsuit did little to assuage his strong negative feelings about the defendant in this case and all efforts I made to appease the hostility toward my client were unavailing.

My cursory examination of Trento's career as an investigative journalist led me to believe that he was a truthful and competent writer. I thought that under oath he would tell the truth, although I doubted that he would reveal his sources unless ordered to do so by a court.

My obligation was clear, given the circumstances. I decided to take his deposition.

Depositions

T O A CERTAIN EXTENT TRIALS HAVE BECOME THE FINAL PERFORMANCE OF A WELL-rehearsed play. A casual courtroom observer might be impressed with the prognosticative capacity of lawyers who seem to sense the answers to their yet unanswered inquiry. The lawyers, the parties they represent, and to a degree, the witnesses have been through much of it before. The generic term for pretrial preparation is discovery.

Discovery consists primarily of three elements: written interrogations, requests for production of documents, and depositions. Long before trial, written interrogatories are exchanged in which the parties are required to state answers to questions that provide the foundation of their complaint or defense. No system for orderly procedure, however, has yet been devised that an inventive lawyer cannot cheerfully disrupt or destroy. Even requests for the production of documents may be rendered less than effective by dilatory tactics and tangential attack. Full and sound discovery methods before trial being on the side of the angels, that is, favored by the judges, who strongly prefer that the basic work be accomplished well in advance of their own entrance into the fray, have been developed in spite of the legendary recalcitrance of the advocates.

The rules that apply to those who file or defend noncriminal cases in the federal courts are the Federal Rules of Civil Procedure. The courts where the cases are filed are the United States district courts. They are numerous and are scattered throughout the country. A losing party may appeal to the United States court of appeals. These are less numerous, since they process appeals from a host of district courts. The U.S. Supreme Court may, if it chooses to do so, entertain appeals submitted to it from the nonprevailing party in the court of appeals. There is only one U.S. Supreme Court.

The deposition-discovery mechanism established between 1938 and 1970 by Rules 26 through 37 may be the most significant innovation in the Federal Rules of Civil Procedure. The Supreme Court, in an endorsement of the then newly designed approach, said they "make a trial less a game of blind man's bluff and more a fair contest with the basic issues and facts disclosed to the fullest practicable extent."

A deposition is a sworn statement given under oath, usually before the courtroom phase of the trial, by a witness or a party to litigation in response to questions asked of him by an attorney for a party. While geographic considerations that apply to mandatory trial testimony may preclude a party from calling a witness to testify at trial, such considerations do not apply to depositions.

The large law firms and their wealthy clients invariably favor depositions. For the law firms, most of which charge substantial sums for participating at depositions, either conducting them or appearing with witnesses who are questioned, the discovery process is a remarkably lucrative exercise. A firm may assign three lawyers to participate at a session that lasts six hours. If the law firm bills its clients at the rate of $250 per hour, per lawyer—a relatively modest sum compared to some bills I have seen—the client is indebted in the amount of $4,500. No doubt the attorneys discuss the case over lunch, thus adding a possible $1,500 to the day's bill, plus the not inconsiderable cost of the meal. Since a single witness may be deposed for several days and since in some cases numerous witnesses are required to appear at depositions, it is possible for a client to spend tens of thousands, even hundreds of thousands of dollars in legal fees getting ready for trial. Lawyers for wealthy clients are among the strongest advocates of pretrial depositions. Corporate clients use depositions as bludgeons with which to discourage impecunious plaintiffs from proceeding with their claims.

Women seeking to struggle through the courts against sexual harassment by officers of major corporations, members of minorities seeking to challenge discriminatory treatment by large corporate employers, and others in similar circumstances are at a decided disadvantage as a result of the discovery rules, which provide weapons for affluent parties to wield against those without large sums to spend on counsel as they pursue justice in court.

The high courts and the authors of leading legal journals continue to assert that these discovery procedures promote the "just, speedy, and inexpensive determination" of lawsuits, sought by the federal rules.

Depositions *are*, in fact, useful for a number of varied purposes; they may even be essential in certain limited circumstances. As an example of the latter, let us assume that a case has been filed in the United States district court in Sioux Falls, South Dakota, because it involves a federal law and the parties reside there. A reluctant witness with crucial, not to say potentially decisive, testimony to offer has removed himself to the South Bronx in New York City, where he now resides. Without the rule for depositions, the party wishing to present the testimony of the absent witness, absent his willingness to return to South Dakota one winter day to attend the trial, will be precluded from presenting that evidence to the jury. If the witness does not live within the district where the trial is taking place and does not live within one hundred miles of the city, Sioux Falls in this instance, the reach of the trial subpoena is inadequate to compel his attendance at the trial.

Either party, however, may require the witness to appear at an office to be deposed. The office, chosen by the party seeking to conduct the deposition, being located near where the witness resides, leaves the matter of geographic jurisdiction neatly resolved. The subpoena served upon the witness is enforceable. Thus, attendance of a reluctant witness at the deposition is mandated.

In the case of Joseph Trento, the unwilling witness worked in Washington, D.C. The trial was to be held in Miami. Trento could not be compelled to travel to Florida to testify. A properly conducted deposition, however, would result in a transcript that could later be read to the jury in the United States district court in Miami and offered there as evidence.

For the deposition to be admissible at a trial it was essential that the other party, Hunt, and his counsel be given adequate notice of the deposition and an opportunity to attend and participate as fully as they would if the witness were to testify at trial. Hunt's lawyers were entitled to cross-examine Trento after I had completed my inquiries. The witness was obligated to attend and to take an oath to tell the truth. His failure to attend could result in a contempt citation and the imposition of various penalties, including costs and possible imprisonment. His failure to testify truthfully could lead to prosecution by the United States attorney's office for perjury or lesser related offenses.

A deposition differs from trial testimony in a number of respects, chief among them being the scope of the permitted inquiry and the consequences of failure to respond. At trial certain strict rules of evidence govern and may be strictly enforced. Irrelevant information, for example, is excluded. A very different standard exists when a deposition is being conducted.

The Federal Rules of Civil Procedure, which are utilized in trials conducted in federal courts, as opposed to rules that govern actions in state courts, were developed for three purposes[1]:

1. To narrow the issues, so that at trials the parties may offer only evidence that pertains to disputed and relevant questions. The concept is that the pretrial exchanges will eliminate irrelevant issues and expose those areas where no real conflict exists;

2. To obtain evidence for use at trial;

3. To permit each party to learn about testimony that may be offered at the trial and to secure documentary evidence that may be offered at trial.

The operative word is *may*. At trial only relevant information is sought or permitted. The scope of discovery, on the other hand, is very broad, almost unlimited, and the restrictions imposed upon it are primarily directed not at the process of gathering the information but rather upon its use at trial. At trial, one of the standards imposed in order that the evidence qualify as acceptable is whether it is relevant to the issue. During a deposition, the rule governing the propriety of the inquiry is whether the response may lead to relevant information. This is decidedly not a distinction without a difference. In practice, much of the evidence acquired during pretrial discovery is subsequently determined to be inadmissible at trial.

A second distinction between adducing evidence at trial, as opposed to a deposition testimony is the immediacy of the ruling as to the obligation of the witness to respond to a question. At trial, in most instances, summary justice is done. If a witness refuses to answer an appropriate query, the judge will rule; either the witness will be directed to respond or the court will be persuaded that for good reason he need not respond. During a deposition the witness who declines to provide an answer risks much less. The question and the refusal may be certified by the court reporter, and a party may subsequently appeal by making a motion to the judge for a ruling. The process is cumbersome, expensive, and time-consuming. Therefore, unless the question and the potential answer appear to be central to an issue in the case and unless the party asking for a certification is relatively confident of a favorable ruling, the matter is rarely pursued.

Before 1938 there was virtually no discovery, as we now understand

---

[1] Many of the states have now substantially adopted the federal rules of discovery. Almost without exception, alterations in the various state systems were made to create less restricted discovery than that employed in the federal courts.

the term, permitted in the federal courts. There were some limited provisions for depositions, but they were intended only to preserve evidence, not to discover it. A statement taken from a witness who would likely die before trial is one example. Some modifications were made in 1948, 1949, 1963, and 1966, but it was not until 1967 that the scope and mechanics of discovery really began to change. The new rules, now in effect, were adopted by the Supreme Court on March 30, 1970.

Those who drafted the rules "held a utopian combination of hopes about the gains of discovery."[2] They envisioned a free exchange of evidence that would result in pleadings more rooted in fact than conjecture, more rapid settlements, fewer cases going to trial, and trials of reduced length for those cases that were not settled. The academics failed to take into account the vested interest of the lawyers, who would utilize, not to say manipulate, the new rules for themselves and to advance the interests of their clients.

The evidence discovered in depositions led quite naturally to inquiries designed to secure more evidence from newly disclosed sources and, in the adversary system, the information often became an asset convincing each set of lawyers that the scent of victory was beckoning them. Law firms prospered and the courts became more and more a battlefield for the wealthy. Trials did not diminish in number. On balance, it is hard to make a case for the proposition that they have become more orderly, and they certainly did not become shorter. Lawyers became more affluent, persons of limited means were excluded from the court system, and more information became available to litigants.

In the *Hunt* case I sought to utilize the federal rules governing discovery to compel Trento to testify.

---

[2]Glaser, *Pretrial Discovery and the Adversary System*, 1968.

Joseph Trento

CONTACTED JOSEPH TRENTO AT THE OFFICES OF THE CABLE NEWS NETWORK IN Washington, D.C.

If Marchetti had not been the source for Trento, then the *News Journal* article provided more than adequate corroboration for Marchetti. Marchetti told me that he had not been Trento's source and that he suspected that his own source, William Corson, may well have provided similar information to Trento. Trento's recollection was essential. Trento, however, would not speak to me because of the antipathy he felt toward Liberty Lobby.

I served a deposition subpoena *duces tecum* (a command to bring certain documents or evidence) upon him and on June 28, 1984, almost six years after he had written the article for the Wilmington newspaper, Trento appeared in my office for a deposition. He was represented by counsel, one of five lawyers who attended the session. At the outset, it was apparent that Trento, true to his word, was not going to make any effort to assist me.

Q. This is an action brought by E. Howard Hunt against Liberty Lobby in the United States District Court, Southern District of Florida. We are going to be deposing you today about matters relating to that. Did you bring any documents?

A. No, I have no material. I wrote this article six years ago and I since have left the *Sunday News Journal*. And as far as I can tell, all the materials are gone. Most of my files are destroyed after a year or so.

Q. Did you bring the article with you?

A. No. I have not seen the article since I wrote it.

Trento confirmed the fact that he had written the article but was careful not to volunteer any information about how he had done so. I handed him a copy of his work.

Q. If you would look at exhibit one or four, I am going to ask you some questions about it.

A. All right.

Q. The first paragraph of that article states, "A secret CIA memorandum says that E. Howard Hunt was in Dallas the day President John F. Kennedy was murdered and that top agency officials plotted to cover up Hunt's presence there." Is that correct?

A. That's correct.

Q. Can you tell me the basis of that statement?

A. Sources within the agency and outside the agency.

Q. When you say agency, you mean the Central Intelligence Agency?

A. Right.

Q. Will you tell us who in the CIA gave you that information?

A. No, I would not.

Q. What is the reason you are not telling us that?

A. I have an agreement with my sources to protect their identity.

Q. Will you tell us who outside of the CIA gave you that information.

A. I would not.

Q. And the reason?

A. The same, to protect their identity.

Q. Can you tell us how many people within the CIA you relied upon as sources for that first paragraph?

A. No.

Q. And why is that?

A. I feel in order to protect their confidentiality that I agreed with them to protect, that to give numbers or mention numbers would endanger that confidentiality.

Q. Would you tell us how many people outside of the CIA you relied upon as sources for that first paragraph?

A. No.

Q. For the same reason?

A. For the same reason.

Q. I am going to ask you about sources throughout, and I take it that whenever you decline—let's see if we can come to an agreement so you don't have to say this each time, plus confer with counsel—but whenever you decline, it will be for reasons just stated?

A. Protection of my sources, that's correct.

Q. Is that regarding their names, their positions and the number of sources?

A. And any other information which might lead to identification.

It was clear to me that the witness was both recalcitrant and truthful. If he would not provide sources, perhaps he would preclude Marchetti as a source. In addition, since the article was of course not written under oath, I thought I might be able to have Trento swear to its accuracy. I was also hopeful that Trento could be induced to waver a bit from his position to reveal nothing about his sources so that he might assert that those sources were, in his judgment, reliable. With that limited agenda I proceed with the deposition. Two hours later, I was satisfied that the deposition had more than achieved those objectives.

I took Trento through each relevant paragraph of his long and detailed article. He stated under oath that each paragraph was true to his knowledge.

I asked him if he had interviewed Hunt before writing his story. He said he had. I asked him if Hunt had told him about his whereabouts on November 22, 1963. Trento said that Hunt said "he was in Washington the day of the Kennedy murder." Trento testified that Hunt said, "I have plenty of witnesses. I took off that day and went shopping and had a Chinese dinner in downtown Washington with my wife."

I inquired if Trento had asked Hunt to name any of his "plenty of witnesses." Trento said he did make that request but that Hunt refused to provide a single name.

Trento testified that he had interviewed a person associated with the House Select Committee on Assassinations and that his source there stated that the CIA memorandum signed by Helms and Angleton was in the possession of the committee. The source said, Trento testified, that "combined with the memo [concerning] Hunt's involvement in Dallas that day, what we have so far puts a real dent in the Warren Commission version." In response to another of my questions, Trento agreed that Hunt had detailed the existence of a "small assassination team" in the CIA headed by Colonel Boris Pash. The team's assignments included "eliminating" suspected double agents and officials. Trento said he had learned that "Pash's assassination unit was assigned to Angleton." While Trento declined to name his source for that information, he did testify that his sources were persons still with the CIA or persons who were with the CIA at the relevant time.

Angleton, who apparently ran an assassination team, and who later was fired as the chief of counterintelligence for the CIA for conduct that even in the context of CIA excesses was considered outrageous, had been an object of scrutiny by the congressional investigating team, according to Trento. Trento testified that sources at both the CIA and the congressional committee told him that during the time that the Warren Commission was investigating the assassination of President Kennedy, Angleton had met regularly with Allen Dulles. Kennedy's successor, Lyndon Johnson, had appointed Dulles to the Warren Commission. Dulles became its most active member and was primarily responsible for shaping the commission's approach to all matters related even tangentially to intelligence activities in general and the CIA, in particular. As the Warren Commission members sat at the feet of Dulles, who led them through the spy labyrinth at his own pace and in his own fashion, he met with Angleton, who was formulating plans for other assassinations. It certainly could not be asserted that the commission had not been aided by the knowledgeable experts in the field.

I then moved to the question of Trento's presumed relationship with Corson. Trento, holding fast to his commitment not to divulge any information about any possible source, was on guard. When I mentioned Corson's name he seemed concerned. He asked if my questions were about the article he had written. I told him that my questions were simple, not compound, and that they deserved direct answers based upon their own intrinsic merit. He nodded. I asked, "Do you know a man named William Corson?" He responded, "I do." I then asked him if he knew James Jesus Angleton. He testified that he did.

I knew that Trento had written his article during August 1978, during the same time frame when Marchetti had written his. I asked Trento if he had met with Corson during August 1978. He said he had met with him at that time.

I then read to Trento from the sworn statement made by Angleton five years previously, when Hunt had sued A.J. Weberman and others for defamation in the *Third Press* case. The defendants in that case deposed Angleton on May 17, 1979. I knew that we were about to get into the dispositive evidence regarding Trento's source and I suspected Trento would balk. I read into the record the portion of Angleton's testimony that was relevant to the issue before us. No objection was made by either of Hunt's two attorneys. This was a genuine surprise for me since it then seemed likely that a jury in the Hunt case would now be able to learn of Angleton's important testimony by reviewing the Trento deposition taken in this case.

Angleton, who had appeared at his deposition with John Seibert, a Department of Justice lawyer who stated that he was representing both

Angleton and "the U.S. Central Intelligence Agency," had been asked if he had talked with Trento about his authorship of the CIA memorandum. Angleton testified:

A. After publication I had a telephone call from Trento in the office. He said he was calling from the office of one William Corson, who is the *Penthouse* representative ex-Colonel of the Marines—

Q. Oh, yeah.

A. —and he, I think his first question was, "Have you heard from Howard Hunt?" and I said, "No," and his next question, it was a whole series of staccato questions, and I told him that my lunch was getting cold and I was at the Army-Navy Club—

Q. All right.

A. —and that was the end of it.

After hearing Angleton's testimony read back to them, Trento and his attorney looked at each other. As quickly as Trento could respond, "I don't recall," his attorney began to speak sternly to him, on the record, saying, "I direct you not to answer" and "Don't answer that."

I learned more from Trento, the reluctant witness, than I had hoped for before the examination began. I tendered the witness to Hunt's lawyers.

Snyder had made copious notes while Trento testified. He consulted them as he began his cross-examination. It soon became clear that he sought to somewhat lessen the impact of portions of Trento's testimony by suggesting that Trento had little first-hand information, that he had merely repeated what others had told him. These were, after all, unnamed sources, and, he implied, they might be wrong. Snyder told Trento that he could not absolutely vouch for the accuracy of others. Trento tended to agree.

Two principles should guide trial attorneys when questioning a witness. One: Always, if possible, interview the witness in depth before the formal event commences. Two: Do not ask an important and central question unless you are confident that you know what the forthcoming answer will be. Each rule may be abrogated if the fact situation, carefully studied, indicates that another, less orthodox approach might be better. Neither principle, however, should be disregarded out of sloth or recklessness.

I could not interview Trento prior to the deposition as he declined my several attempts to do so. Why Hunt's counsel failed to interview him I never did comprehend. For the deposition, I prepared a scaled-down and modestly ambitious set of goals, due to Trento's almost palpable hostility to the Liberty Lobby and to Mr. Carto. I wanted to know what Trento was specifically told about the CIA memorandum, but I was concerned that any effort to explore the volatile area might jeopardize the important gains we had already achieved at the deposition. My own curiosity was ultimately submerged in consideration of the best interests of my client. Reluctantly I concluded my examination and submitted the witness to counsel for Mr. Hunt.

Snyder rushed in where I feared to tread. In a sarcastic tone through which he clearly implied that Trento, like Marchetti, had written an article based upon a document he had never seen, he sought to impeach Trento's credentials as a serious reporter. He began by laying a foundation. He asked about what he referred to as the "purported memo."

Q. Did you ever see the purported 1966 memo that was supposed to have been initialed by Angleton and Helms saying "We are going to have to explain why Hunt was in Dallas"?

Trento looked right at Snyder and answered the question directly and deliberately. He responded, "Yes."

A stunned silence ensued. Snyder reacted as if he had been struck across the face with a wet fish. His head suddenly pulled back. He was unable to frame another question. The "purported memo" had just secured a life of its own. It was real. It existed. A credible journalist had seen it. The doubts about Marchetti's reliability, carefully constructed by counsel for Hunt, had suddenly become far less important. Snyder had seriously undermined his own case. An oppressive yet expectant silence engulfed the room. Snyder fumbled with his papers. Trento's lawyer looked off into space. Trento stared at Snyder. I wondered who had fashioned the adage, "Never ask a question unless you know the answer," and if he had done so only after having been as grievously wounded as Snyder.

After a pause, Snyder sought to repair the damage by asking detailed questions about the document.

Q. You did see the memo. What did it look like?

A. It looked like a typewritten memo on a plain piece of paper.

Q. What was the size?

A. Standard, I suppose eight-and-a-half by eleven. I didn't measure it. I didn't have a ruler with me.

Q. What was on the paper?

A. Typing.

Q. How many paragraphs, or sentences or lines?

A. I can't recall. It's been a long time.

Q. Your article, I believe, says that Angleton and Helms initialed it.

A. That's correct.

Q. Where were the initials? You have no particular reason to think it's accurate or inaccurate, do you?

A. I trust the source. I have seen the initials of both men from time to time on other documents. It fit in with other documents I had seen. But to answer your question specifically, no. The CIA has some of the best forgers in the world on its payroll, and I'm not a documents expert.

Q. How many lines of typing, to the best of your recollection?

A. Several paragraphs, but I couldn't tell you how many lines. You are going back six years here. I was not permitted to copy it.

Q. Were you told the location of the original memo?

A. No.

Q. Did you ask?

A. I did.

Q. And were you told that it existed or didn't exist?

A. I wasn't told that. That wasn't the question.

Q. What did you ask about the location of the original memo or its existence?

A. I asked if a copy of the memo was at CIA headquarters in the files, and the source would not tell me.

On redirect examination I established that Trento had been a journalist for a decade, that he knew his way around the intelligence minefields in Washington, and that he had regularly been called upon to make value judgments as to the reliability of sources. Then I inquired:

Q. Were those sources within the House Assassination Committee or the CIA?

A. I'm not going to identify the location of the sources.

Q. Were they sources which you felt were sufficiently reliable so you could make the statement which you made in the article?

A. Yes.

Trento, accepting the limitations placed upon his statements by Snyder had testified as to his inability to swear to the accuracy of another's statement. I pursued that matter.

Q. You stated in, I think, answer to earlier questions by Mr. Snyder that when you said in answer to my questions earlier that the paragraphs were truthful and accurate, you meant that the quotations were accurately reported; is that right?

A. Right. It's an accurate reflection of what is said to me.

Q. But I also asked if you stood by this story.

A. I stood by the information as it was—as I reported it, as a reporter can stand by anything he doesn't know firsthand.

Q. I am not asking you, therefore, if you can swear to the accuracy of something someone told you. Of course, you cannot. I understand. But if someone at the CIA believed the moon was made out of green cheese, I take it you would not write a front page story in the *Sunday News Journal* saying the moon is made out of green cheese.

A. That's correct.

Q. So you have to use your own judgment to determine if the information is reasonable?

A. Yes.

I questioned Trento to secure from him the criteria he utilized to determine the publishability of a story. I asked him if he "believed that the sources he had relied upon were sufficiently reliable" to permit him to write the story. He said they were. I then asked him what standards he generally had established in his experience as an investigative reporter to determine the reliability of a source. The question was nonspecific; it bore no direct relationship to the pending case.

He paused for a moment and then decided he would respond. He answered "past dealings, track record or reliability, and access to the information, as best as I can determine it." I then moved from the broad area of his standards to the question at hand, hopeful that given his previous answer he would feel obliged to respond:

"Did you apply those three standards to the sources for each of the points in this article?" Without hesitation, he replied, "Yes." Trento steadfastly refused to provide any information in regard to his sources, including the number of sources he relied upon and their general level in the intelligence world. He even refused to answer questions designed to preclude persons, including Marchetti, as sources, stating perhaps facetiously but entirely insistently that through process of elimination he might reveal too much. I approached that important matter from another direction.

Q. Do you know Victor Marchetti?

A. I do know Victor.

Q. Did you know him during August 1978?

A. '78, no.

Q. You did not?

A. No, not in August of '78.

Q. You met him after August?

A. Yes, I met him specifically at Paul Young's restaurant in a then—then Paul Young's—in a discussion of the Paisley case, and that's the first time I met him, and that was sometime after Paisley disappeared, which was in September of—Paisley disappeared September of '78. So it would have to be sometime in the months following that.

Q. Is it fair to say that, therefore, Mr. Marchetti was not the source of your information?

A. I'm not going to get into sources.

Q. Well, you didn't know him during August of 1978; is that correct?

A. That's correct. Draw your own conclusion.

I completed my examination of Trento by exploring his mind-set at the time of the deposition regarding the article he had written years before that time.

Q. Did you every retract this story?

A. We did not.

Q. Did you ever retract a single word of the story?

A. No.

Q. Why is that?

A. Because we believed the story to be true. We stand on this report.

Q. Do you still believe the story to be true?

A. Yes.

Q. To your knowledge, has Mr. Hunt ever sued your newspaper for the publication of the story?

A. No.

Q. That you would remember?

A. That I would remember, yes.

Each answer given by Trento seemed to provide further basis for the belief that the CIA memorandum existed. Trento's deposition, comprised of the answers of a reluctant and hostile witness committed to protecting his sources, had nonetheless provided the most damaging blow yet to Hunt's case. I left the session with the belief that Trento was the most important witness in the case. But that was before I took a sworn statement from Marita Lorenz.

The First Trial

FOLLOWING THE TRENTO DISCLOSURES, IT SEEMED APPROPRIATE TO QUESTION Hunt. Hunt had testified on numerous occasions and his statements seemed filled with promise. He had testified before Judge John J. Sirica, in the case of *United States v. John Mitchell et al.*, more popularly known as the Watergate trial. Hunt testified, remarkably enough, on Friday, November 22, 1974, just eleven years to the day—after the assassination of President Kennedy.

In an attempt to convince, perhaps to extort, cooperation from the White House, Hunt, facing criminal prosecution for his conduct at the Watergate complex, sent a message to President Nixon. Nixon should be aware, he suggested, that he was privy to many secrets. At the Watergate trial the written message surfaced. Hunt confirmed that the letter he sent contained this message:

"The Watergate bugging is only one of a number of highly illegal conspiracies engaged in by one or more of the defendants at the behest of senior White House officials. These as yet undisclosed crimes can be proved."

Add to that Angleton's bizarre statement, made to the *New York Times* on Christmas Eve 1974, regarding the secrets that he also possessed and might reveal if he was not treated properly: "A mansion has many rooms and there were many things going on during the period [the 1960s] of anti-war bombings. I'm not privy to who struck John." When asked, during his deposition, merely what he had meant by that statement, he volunteered, "It had nothing, the 'John' does not refer to John F. Kennedy." He had not been asked if it did.

Before I concluded that I was sufficiently prepared to question Hunt at a deposition, I immersed myself in the transcript of the first trial of *Hunt v. Liberty Lobby* and the record of Hunt's numerous appearances as a witness in other forums as well. Without some knowledge of the record predating the Hunt deposition, I fear the reader might be less than prepared to place his testimony in perspective. Therefore, we explore the milestones of the first trial.

It took place in the United States courthouse in Miami and was presided over by Judge James W. Kehoe. It began on Tuesday, December 15, 1981, and was completed on Thursday of that week.

To represent its interests at the first trial, Liberty Lobby had retained Miles A. McGrane III, a local Florida attorney who was both unaware and unconcerned about the facts surrounding the death of President Kennedy. McGrane also taught at the University of Miami Law School. The lawyer, without consulting with his client, sought to simplify the case by entering into a stipulation with Ellis Rubin, at that time Hunt's attorney. He agreed that Hunt had not been in Dallas on November 22, 1963, and was genuinely sorry that the article had even implied that Hunt may have been involved in any mischief that day. Hunt and his attorney accepted the stipulation and the judge read it to the jury.

A stipulation is an agreement between counsel for the adversaries that certain allegations are true and that they occurred in fact just as they have been re-created in agreement. The stipulation may then be read to the jury and should be accepted by the jurors as uncontested. The parties are not required, and in fact in most instances are not permitted, to offer evidence in support of or for the purpose of challenging the agreed upon set of circumstances. One of the purposes is to save time. This objective could hardly be served if the stipulation was subject to additional proof. The longevity of the stipulation in the first *Hunt v. Liberty Lobby* trial developed into a central theme before the question of its validity was resolved. Therefore, a word about its ability to survive and prevail. Generally, a stipulation is binding upon both parties for as long as the matter is pending; that is, if a case must be subsequently tried again it will be subject to the same stipulations in force at the first trial and neither party may be permitted to withdraw from them. The law is conservative in nature and tends to venerate precedent. In *Hunt v. Liberty Lobby*, McGrane, the counsel for the defendant, made the first reference to the stipulation in his opening statement to the jury. He could not have been more clear as to his own beliefs:

"We are not going to come forward and try to prove that Mr. Hunt was involved in the Kennedy assassination.

"I will be candid with you, and from what I know about this case, there is no question in my mind that he was not involved. There is no question in the minds of the people at Liberty Lobby."

After having made this major concession to the jury, and thus at least partially undermining the defense of his case, the attorney sought to enter into a formal stipulation with his adversary. He addressed the court:

"Judge, briefly, I wanted to talk to Mr. Rubin to try to enter into stipulations to keep from proving things I don't think are at issue. I suggested to Mr. Rubin certainly there is no dispute in my mind that Mr. Hunt was not in Dallas at the time of the assassination and I think we can eliminate one witness by deposition."

Rubin, who had previously asserted that the trial might last almost a week, responded obliquely, stating only, "I now project a two-day trial."

Later, after Rubin offered evidence designed to prove that Hunt was not in Dallas on the day of the assassination, McGrane stated:

"Your Honor, I think the point we have been trying to make throughout this case, I think Mr. Rubin is trying to prove that Mr. Hunt was not in Dallas, Texas, at the time. I think I stipulated in the opening argument, in my opinion, that he probably was not there. We are not going to prove that he was in Dallas."

Rubin responded:

"The defendants object that we are trying to prove something that they stipulated, that Howard Hunt was not in Dallas on the date Kennedy was killed. I have not accepted the stipulation."

Rubin was quite within his rights to offer evidence since he had not entered into a stipulation. McGrane's concession before the jury was not a stipulation, even though he had later used that word to describe it.

There may be sound tactical reasons to reject a proffered stipulation. Although the agreement has, in theory, the full force of proof, it may be far less dramatic than the presentation of testimony or of documents that make the same point. Thus, its effect upon the jury may be less impressive. Balancing that consideration with the advantage offered by the stipulation, the fact that it will remain uncontroverted, requires a thoughtful value judgment by counsel.

McGrane had surrendered the high ground in this exchange by offering his concession to the jury before working out an agreement with Rubin.

Rubin correctly sought the best of both possibilities provided by his adversary's error: the admission by the defendant that Hunt had not been in Dallas as well as the opportunity to present evidence to buttress that concession. Within moments, however, Rubin, when asked by the judge if he would accept McGrane's offered stipulation, inexplicably responded, "If they want to do that, I will accept that." After a discussion with counsel, Judge Kehoe stated, "I am going to announce the stipulation to the jury." Soon thereafter the judge addressed the jurors:

"I think, ladies and gentlemen, I should explain one thing, because it is going to affect the nature of some evidence that has been admitted and will not now be admitted. But for the purpose of this trial, the defendants have acknowledged and conceded that the plaintiff in this case was not in Dallas, Texas, on the date of the assassination of President Kennedy, which was November 22, 1963."

Almost immediately after the stipulation had been entered into the record, Rubin ignored it and began to question Hunt about his whereabouts on November 22. Although an objection by McGrane was sustained, Rubin returned to the area again and again, all in violation of the stipulation. McGrane failed to object as Rubin focused upon Hunt's latest alibi. This conduct by Rubin was later to cause serious, indeed crucial, difficulties for his client. Rubin's actions were so blatant that at one point, in violation of the terms of the agreement, he tried to offer into evidence documents intended to show that Hunt was in Washington on the 22nd. The court sternly ruled, "I will not admit it. Because of the stipulation, it is no longer relevant."

Before the first trial began, very few depositions were conducted by the parties. McGrane did take Hunt's deposition in preparation for the trial. At that time, Hunt admitted that he had recruited Frank Sturgis to participate in the illegal entry at the Watergate complex. He also revealed that G. Gordon Liddy had called him after the arrests at Watergate, instructing him that "his principals suggested that I join my wife and two children in Europe for the balance of the summer." Hunt testified that he immediately "went home and began packing." At that time, "two gentlemen representing themselves as FBI agents appeared at my door and asked me if they could speak with me." Hunt testified that he refused to speak with the agents. He said he had been "advised" by "a former bureau agent" and by Liddy "to have nothing to do with any law enforcement agency." Later, Liddy called him, just before he was to flee from the country, and withdrew the suggestion that he travel to Europe.

Hunt admitted that in mid-September 1972, his wife and his attorney began to receive substantial sums of money "from unknown sources." The money was in the form of cash. It began to flow just after the Watergate break-in and ended "shortly after the November election, 1972." While the identity of his benefactor may have been unknown to Hunt, as he asserted, he did locate the proper address two years later

(l. to r.) Former governor of New York Herbert H. Lehman, Mark Lane, and Eleanor Roosevelt.

John F. Kennedy with
Lane during the 1960
campaign.

Courtesy of Mark Lane

AP/Wide World Photos

Jacqueline Kennedy (c.), flanked by her brothers-in-law
Robert (l.) and Edward (r.), leads her husband's funeral
procession.

Lane, with a model of the Dealey Plaza assassination
scene.

Jack Ruby murders Lee Harvey Oswald at the Dallas police
station.

President Lyndon Johnson on the day he established the Warren Commission (November 29, 1963).

AP/Wide World Photos

Warren Commission members, from left: Rep. Gerald Ford (R-Mich.), Rep. Hale Boggs (D-La.), Sen. Richard Russell (D-Ga.), Chief Justice Earl Warren, Sen. John Sherman Cooper (R-Ky.), banker John J. McCloy, former CIA head Allen Dulles, and chief counsel J. Leo Rankin.

AP/Wide World Photos

Former CIA director Richard Helms testifies before the House Select Committee on Assassinations (Sept. 1978).

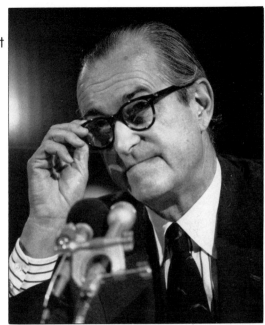

David Atlee Phillips, chief of CIA operations in the Western Hemisphere, announces his retirement (1975).

E. Howard Hunt, CIA operative, plaintiff in *Hunt v. Liberty Lobby*, and alleged assassination conspirator.

UPI/Bettmann

Former CIA counter-intelligence chief James Jesus Angleton.

UPI/Bettmann

New Orleans District Attorney Jim Garrison (r.) announces the arrest of Clay Shaw (March 1967).

Clay Shaw (r.), booked in New Orleans for conspiracy to kill President Kennedy.

Marita Lorenz with her lover Fidel Castro.

N.Y. Daily News Photo

Frank Sturgis, the man who recruited Lorenz into the CIA with the goal of assassinating Castro.

UPI/Bettmann

when he sent his warning about the consequences of not providing him further financial assistance.

As we have seen, Hunt had warned the White House that he might talk about those other "highly illegal conspiracies." At his deposition he claimed that he had been providing information to the government regarding his own role in Watergate, and the role of "higher-ups" as well, "almost continuously for a period of years." Hunt bristled at suggestions that he was involved in any fashion in the death of his wife, Dorothy, who died in an airplane crash in Chicago in December 1972. The original rumors were offered by Sherman Skolnik, an investigator who resided in Chicago. Skolnik claimed that Hunt's wife was leaving him and that she had taken a large sum of money with her. At his deposition, Hunt described Skolnik only as "a crippled paranoid who got a new lease on life as a result of the plane crash in Chicago and proceeded to interest himself in my affairs as a result." Hunt did, however, confirm some of Skolnik's speculations. He admitted that his wife had left with a substantial sum "of our money," which, he said, she was going to invest with her family. In the past I have observed that Skolnik has been given on occasion to hyperbole and I never saw any evidence linking Hunt to the plane crash. I was, in fact, surprised, in reading the deposition, to learn that Skolnik was correct about the sum of cash in Dorothy Hunt's possession at the time of her death.

McGrane questioned Hunt about the financial damages he had purportedly suffered as a result of the publication of the *Spotlight* article. Hunt testified:

"In general, my literary agent, my then literary agent indicated that the Kennedy connection with Hunt loomed insurmountably large in the eyes of and minds of the New York literary community. And this is certainly true of the reprint rights, which is where the money is.

"The liberals we find are willing to overlook Watergate. They are not willing to take a chance on somebody publicly and extensively associated by the media with the Kennedy assassination."

Hunt also stated that at the trial he intended to call as his witnesses Richard Helms, James Angleton and David Phillips, as well as the director of personnel at the Central Intelligence Agency, to establish his presence in Washington, D.C., and at a CIA installation on November 22, 1963.

Perhaps the most moving moment in Hunt's pretrial deposition came when Hunt began to describe the trauma he suffered when his children read the *Spotlight* article. His children, all adults at that time, met with him after the Marchetti article appeared in 1978. They confronted him and demanded to know if he had been in Dallas on November 22, 1963, and if he had been involved in the assassination of President Kennedy. Was the *Spotlight* story true, they asked? Had he been in Dallas that day? If it were not true, then why would the allegation be made? He testified about "strains" in "familial relationships," as he sought to prove that he had not been where his accuser said he was. He wondered how he could prove a negative to his wife. His wife had been "shocked by the appearance of this article." When his children and his wife demanded answers of him, he was exhausted and in pain. He testified:

"Being queried by my adult children, by my wife—'Is there any truth in this? Why would they say this? How can they print this if it's not true?' It's a very heavy psychological burden for me to carry, for any man to carry."

Hunt carried the same theme into the trial, where he told the jurors that he discussed the article with his children and his wife, telling them that he had not been in Dallas that day and if indicted in the Kennedy assassination he would "testify to the truth of the entire matter."

Hunt also testified at the first trial that he suffered greatly as a result of the publication of the story. He suffered, he said, "loss of income." Of far greater consequence was the "eruption of mistrust within my family immediately upon the publication of the article." These doubts, apparently harbored by his adult children even after he explained to them that he had not been in Dallas that day, were, as he put it, "very difficult to quell."

The jurors were sympathetic; how could they not be? The newspaper, through counsel, had admitted that the story was not true and Hunt had explained, in some detail, how he had suffered the loss of the trust of his own children due to the false publication.

In providing background for the jury, Hunt said he had been the "political adviser" for the CIA for the Bay of Pigs invasion, had arranged for the break-in at the Watergate, but only because "he was working for the president and was just carrying out orders," and that he had filed a lawsuit against A.J. Weberman. That suit (the Third Press case) was pending, and he said he would prosecute it vigorously.

As to the alleged CIA memorandum, "nobody has ever seen it," Rubin proclaimed in his opening statement.

Hunt testified that he had been chief of station for the CIA in Mexico City some years ago. Hunt spoke about his financial difficulties, how his children had been injured in an automobile accident, and how he joined a public relations firm in Washington, D.C. The organization, Robert E. Mullen and Company, represented HEW, the Bureau of Rehabilitation for the Handicapped, the Mormon church, and the Howard Hughes Tool

Company, Hunt told the jury. He was the executive vice-president and creative director, he testified.

McGrane's cross-examination was remarkably sparse. The direct examination comprises 137 pages of the trial transcript. The cross-examination was completed in six pages, or in less than ten minutes. While questioned by defense counsel, Hunt admitted that he and Liddy had organized the break-in of the office of Daniel Ellsberg's psychiatrist. He refused to answer questions about other illegal acts, stating only, "I am not prepared to discuss other matters in that context of criminality." McGrane could have appealed to the court for a ruling; instead he abandoned the subject.

Hunt admitted that he had lied under oath in the past. He explained that he had lied during grand jury proceedings in connection with the Watergate case, but that, again, the real responsibility was elsewhere. He did it in an "attempt to shield the people responsible for the entire Watergate fiasco." He summarized that "it was a very poor judgment."

McGrane asked Hunt if he had been invited by the *Spotlight* to visit its offices, make a statement, and be interviewed so that a new story might be written from Hunt's perspective. Hunt testified that it was so, but that he had rejected the request "because the invitation specified I would be able to tell my side of the story, and as far as I am concerned, there is only one side, my side."

On redirect examination of Hunt, Rubin, shamelessly leading his client through a prepared explanation, stated, "You say you did not choose to give the interview that they requested. Was that because of the reputation that Liberty Lobby had and the *Spotlight* and you did not want to be in the paper?"

Hunt dutifully answered "Yes." McGrane did not object to the compound and leading question, permitting the reader to wonder if both he and Rubin were graduates of the Matlock University School of Law.

Rubin offered the testimony of Walter Kuzmuk, Hunt's neighbor and coworker at the CIA, as his next witness. He had taken his deposition just eight days before and had decided to read it to the jury rather than ask Kuzmuk to travel from Maryland to Florida. Rubin could not compel Kuzmuk to attend the trial, but since he was a friendly witness, it seemed likely that Kuzmuk would have testified in person if invited. Various tactical reasons may motivate a lawyer to present a deposition rather than a live witness when he has the option. The record rarely reveals the basis for the determination. It is barren of a clue in this case, as well. Among the possibilities are that Kuzmuk did not like to travel, that he was ill, that the day he was scheduled to testify was inconvenient for him, or, most likely, that Rubin was pleased with Kuzmuk's responses on direct examination and the lack of serious challenge to that testimony during cross-examination.

The direct examination of Kuzmuk was read to the jury. The deposition had been taken on December 7, 1981. Kuzmuk said that he was employed by the CIA and had been for almost twenty-seven years. When he worked with Hunt in Washington, D.C., he saw him "on a daily basis." The men lived just "four or five houses from one another" in a Maryland suburb. They and their families socialized with each other.

For a witness offered solely for the purpose of swearing that he saw Hunt in Washington, D.C., on November 22, 1963, Kuzmuk demonstrated less precision than expected.

Q. Getting back to the month of November of 1963, did anything unusual happen during that month that stands out in your memory?

A. Very much so.

Q. What is that?

A. The assassination of President Kennedy.

Q. Do you know the exact date?

A. Unfortunately no, but it was in the twenties—twenty first or—

Q. Would November twenty-second, would that refresh your recollection?

A. I was thinking the twenty-first or twenty-third, somewhere in there. The twenty-second is fine.

Once the question of the date was more or less settled, Kuzmuk was led into the testimony he had been called upon to offer.

Q. Do you remember that day in your memory, that is, what you did that day? Almost everybody does.

A. Right, of course. I got into the office in the morning and then lunchtime arrived and, as usual, several of us got together and we went to lunch and we went to lunch at Duke Ziebert's right around the corner from where the office was located, and I was with several of my colleagues. I guess it was around one o'clock or 1:30 in the afternoon we came out, and Duke Ziebert's I think is on L Street—used to be on L Street, right around the corner. And coming up Connecticut Avenue, coming back to our office—the Mayflower is across the street, so I don't remember exactly the location—and I saw a car go by and I noticed Howard and Betty—not Betty—

Q. Dorothy?

A. Dorothy, and I waved at them.

Q. What kind of car was it?

178

A. It was a Chevrolet, I thought.

Kuzmuk testified that he went back to work at the CIA that afternoon and he and his colleagues remained there "for quite a while" after learning that the president had been shot. He and Hunt "car-pooled" regularly "almost—well, every day unless I was out of the city and he was out of the city for some reason."

Kuzmuk testified that he had kept to himself the knowledge that he had seen Hunt in Washington on November 22, 1963, until 1976 or 1977" when he was prompted, thirteen or fourteen years later, to write to Rubin and offer himself as a witness.

Fleming Lee had cross-examined Kuzmuk for Liberty Lobby when the deposition had been taken the previous week. After Rubin read the direct examination to the jury, the judge offered Lee the opportunity to read his examination of the witness. As to how effective it had been, Lee's own statement in court, before the jury, provides the most salient analysis. He declined to read it to the jury, explaining, "Your Honor, I don't think much purpose will be served by reading this."

Very soon after it began, the case was over. All that remained were the closing arguments of the counsel and the instructions to the jury given by the judge.

McGrane had little to discuss given the state of the record, except to assure the jurors that Liberty Lobby had relied upon a writer who had impressive credentials in the area of CIA activities, that the corporation harbored no malice toward Hunt, and, in fact, that it had given him an opportunity to assist in correcting any harmful impression that the story may have inadvertently conveyed.

Rubin had more with which to work. E. Howard Hunt was a victim. He did as President Nixon ordered and had ended up in jail. He was so patriotic and so committed to supporting The Presidency that he even violated his own high moral and ethical standards by committing perjury before a grand jury. And, believe it or not, he has been criticized also for that.

He is a good family man; his greatest moment of anguish came when his own children confronted him and, in essence, accused him of killing the president. How could he ever gain their trust again? How could he ever overcome their suspicions created by this false article? How much money would you take to lose the love and respect of your own children?

The answer to that question was apparently $650,000. But before the case could be submitted to the jury for consideration, the judge was obligated to instruct, or charge, the jury as to the applicable law.

The judge requested a meeting with the lawyers in chambers to consider their proposed instructions. Judges are not pleased when a court of appeals determines that they have made an error and that, therefore, the case must be tried again. Appellate courts tend to carefully scrutinize the instructions given by the judge to the jury. While I have found, on occasion, that some portions of the instructions are so esoteric that jurors have substantial difficulty in comprehending them, the courts, as they should, take the matter of the charge quite seriously.

Judges invariably invite opposing counsel to submit proposed instructions in writing several days before the last day of trial. When the evidence is in, and both sides have rested, the court arranges for a charge conference in which the judge discusses the proposed instructions and rules as to which instructions he will give. Often he will explain why he has rejected a proposed instruction. The attorneys may then state their objections on the record. If the court gives an incorrect instruction to the jury or declines to give a correct one, and if the attorney makes a timely objection, an appellate court might determine that reversible error has been committed.

In the first trial of Hunt v. Liberty Lobby, Rubin offered a clearly erroneous instruction as to the law of defamation. Why he did so is not clear to me; the only explanations I can conjure up are ignorance or a deliberate effort to mislead the court to thus secure some advantage for his client and for himself. In my years at the bar I have never sought to mislead a judge and I doubt that any judge before whom I have practiced would offer a contrary opinion. First of all, it is just bad form. In addition, the value of temporary advantage, presuming success rewards the deception, is certain to be overcome as time passes. It is important for a judge to know that when a lawyer argues on behalf of a client, the argument, even if ultimately rejected by the court, was sincerely offered. Judges tend to know which lawyers are serious litigators and which ones freely offer frivolous arguments.

McGrane did not object to Rubin's proposed instruction, even though it bore little resemblance to the existing law. The judge, pleased that the parties agreed about the central instruction in the case, read it to the jury in the same form that it had been given to him. In short, it stated that the standard to be applied by the jury in determining whether or not Liberty Lobby had defamed Hunt was "what would a responsible publisher" print. Since Rubin had conceded that his client was a public figure, the appropriate standard was that of actual malice as established by the United States Supreme Court in New York Times v. Sullivan, and its progeny, more than a decade and a half before the Hunt case was tried.

Following the instructions, the jury found for Hunt and awarded him

$100,000 in compensatory damages and $550,000 in punitive damages. The *Washington Post*, as an example of the news coverage, devoted a substantial story to the Hunt victory.

Liberty Lobby secured new counsel and an appeal from the verdict was taken to the United States Court of Appeals for the Eleventh Circuit, which convenes in Atlanta, Georgia.

The three-judge panel tended to agree that the instructions were erroneous and unrelated to the law. Yet counsel for Liberty Lobby had not made a timely objection; he had, in fact, consented to the incorrect instruction.

There is, however, a concept at the law known as plain error. It holds, in essence, that if a terrible mistake has been made, one so grave that it denies a party to the action of a fair trial, it may provide the basis for reversible error, *even if no objection was made at the time.*

Determining in this rare instance that the Rubin instruction, read to the jury by the court, was so erroneous as to constitute plain error, the court reversed, and remanded the case to the United States district court and Judge Kehoe for a new trial.

Rubin's misplaced zeal had cost his client a small fortune. Since Hunt had agreed to pay Rubin 40 percent of the recovery, it was an expensive error for Rubin as well. Hunt fired Rubin. Another argument for never seeking to mislead the court is that you might succeed in that effort.

Before long, Hunt and Liberty Lobby had each retained new counsel, discovery was well under way and Hunt was about to face his first comprehensive examination in the case.

E. Howard Hunt

SOMETIME BEFORE THE HUNT DEPOSITION WAS TAKEN IN THE SECOND LIBERTY Lobby trial, a serious dispute about the case arose between the adversaries. I revealed to opposing counsel during a telephone conversation that I intended to offer evidence both that Hunt was in Dallas at the time of the assassination and that Hunt, and his employers in the Central Intelligence Agency, had been implicated in the murder. The initial silent response to this disclosure suddenly erupted into a furious and outraged opposition to the concept.

Snyder said that the stipulation entered into by the parties at the first trial was irrevocable and binding during the life of the case. I agreed that this was indeed the general rule. An exception arose, I suggested, where the stipulation carried its own intrinsic limitation as to its longevity. I reminded Snyder that the judge had offered the stipulation to the jury by stating, unambiguously, that it was "for the purpose of this trial." Snyder demanded that I answer what my position would be if the judge had said "for the purpose of this *case*" instead of trial." I said that the stipulation would nevertheless be void, since Rubin, on behalf of Hunt, had violated its terms more regularly than he had observed them. Snyder wanted to know what that had to do with the case. I said that if one party violates an agreement, he can hardly insist that the other party is obliged to adhere to its terms. Snyder's sense of outrage abided for just a moment. He asked if I was interested in settling the case. He said the amount due was more than three-quarters of a million dollars, counting costs and interest from the day of judgment, and that they expected to win a bigger award at the second trial. I told him that my client had not expressed any desire to settle the case but that I would take any offer back to him. Snyder said he would settle for $650,000. I told him I thought it unlikely that my client would seriously consider that offer, but that I would tell Mr. Carto about it. Snyder became angry again, stating that I would never be able to get the facts about the Kennedy assassination before the jury due to the existing stipulation. "The judge," he said, "will not let you turn his courtroom into a Roman circus." I said I was sorry to hear that as I had already lined up some dancing bears and a few clowns, and had been in contact with a high-wire act. Snyder hung up.

He then filed two motions. One was to disqualify me from practice before Judge Kehoe in the case, since I planned, as he said again, to turn the courtroom into a Roman circus. The motion contained a series of highly personal and vituperative attacks upon me, gleaned from newspaper articles written by persons critical of my work. In fact, Snyder distorted the original published remarks through a bit of imaginative zeal. In my years of practice, both before and since the Hunt case, no one has ever filed a motion that had any resemblance to that scurrilous pleading.

He also filed an "emergency motion" requesting an immediate ruling that the stipulation from the first trial was still binding. He hoped to preclude any testimony from being offered to demonstrate that the article was truthful.

Judge Kehoe was a very busy jurist. His courtroom was set in the middle of the drug capital of the United States. As a result, he was required to try drug cases all day, all week, every month. Criminal cases, by law and practice, take precedence over civil cases. Thus, he was unable to find time to respond to the emergency motion for more than a year.

He wasted no time with the Roman circus motion, however. Even before I could send in my opposition to the motion, he wrote DENIED" across the Snyder pleading and dispatched it to all the lawyers in the case.

Unless and until an order was granted precluding any inquiry into the facts surrounding the assassination, I was at liberty to question Hunt and others about that subject.

On July 11, 1984, I met E. Howard Hunt at the Washington offices of his law firm. Snyder was present, as was Brent Whitmore and Fleming Lee. I was determined to be cordial to Hunt and Snyder and I suggested to Whitmore and Lee that they adopt a similar attitude. I had read Hunt's testimony at the trial of former attorney general John Mitchell, deposition transcripts of his testimony in various cases, and the trial record in the first trial. It was, therefore, possible to focus on the one objective I thought might be decisive in the case.

We met at 10:05 A.M. and the deposition was concluded two hours and ten minutes later. The entire deposition was educational for me; however, only one question was of real significance. If I had focused upon that one area, to the exclusion of all others, Snyder and Hunt would have been forewarned as to my strategy and might have taken steps to mitigate what I believe to be the fatal blow struck against their case that morning, one that would be revealed to them only at the trial.

Hunt said that he had cooperated fully with the Rockefeller Commission investigation into aspects of the Kennedy assassination. He told them, he said, that he was in Washington, D.C., on November 22, 1963, and not in Dallas. He said that he had not objected to the effort by the Rockefeller Commission to examine the records maintained by the CIA that would disclose his whereabouts on November 22. He testified that the Rockefeller Commission had accepted his testimony since "they had been able to come up with no credible evidence to dispute my claim." In fact, the Rockefeller Commission had concluded on page 255 of its report: "It cannot be determined with certainty where Hunt and Sturgis were on the day of the assassination." I read that statement to the witness. Hunt then commented, "I don't know how hard they tried. I can only say they failed to dig sufficiently, ask the right questions of the right people."

Hunt denied even having spoken with Joseph Trento. He conceded that he probably told "other reporters" that he had "plenty of witnesses" who could place him in Washington on November 22.

He testified that he had talked to reporters when "Mr. Rubin called a press conference to announce that I was suing the Liberty Lobby."

When asked to give the names of his numerous witnesses, he mentioned "Mary Traynor, a domestic servant," who, he said, was dead. His wife, Dorothy, was, of course, another witness who was dead.

He could think of five live witnesses. Two had worked for the CIA and three were his children. He named and described his children, Howard St. John Hunt, Kevan Totterdale ("She's a member of the California bar") and Lisa Hunt Kyle ("She is my married daughter"). At the time of the assassination, said Hunt, Howard St. John was about nine years old, Kevan was about thirteen, and Lisa about fifteen. He testified that after he picked up his children, the entire family "stayed pinned to the radio and television set for the rest—balance of the afternoon." He added that after "the family was reassembled following the notice of these tragic events, that we stayed in the house pretty much watching television." He remembered that with him, in addition to his wife, now dead, and the three children, was his wife's aunt, now also dead.

Hunt again described the scene. "Once the family had reassembled we all stayed in our house. We had an ample recreation room there, and I believe we had one on the first floor and we, like thousands of other Americans, millions, we stayed there and watched through the burial services which I think was on Monday, and then life resumed for everyone."

Hunt said that he believed that the family never left the house from the time of Kennedy's death on Friday until at least Monday. "I can't recall leaving the house," he said. "There would have been no particular reason to. If you recall the events, there was a pall of mourning cast over the whole nation. People stayed by the television sets in their private grief."

Later, Hunt implied he may not have even left the house on Monday, since "I think government offices were closed" that day due to the "burial services."

Other than his children, who were confined with him to the house for forty-eight or even seventy-two hours—many of them spent in front of a radio and a television set in a recreation room—and the three now-dead witnesses, Hunt again referred to the two CIA witnesses who would testify at trial, Walter Kuzmuk, a CIA officer, and Connie Mazerov, his former secretary at the CIA. Together with his three children, now all adults, and the CIA personnel officer with Hunt's attendance records revealing that he was in Washington on November 22, he had assembled an impressive list of potential witnesses.

While Hunt recalled that he was with Kuzmuk during the morning of November 22 "I probably rode in from Maryland with Mr. Kuzmuk that day and saw him later in the afternoon of that day as well...around twelve-thirty, maybe one o'clock, something like that," his memory, apparently, was selective. He lived very near where Kuzmuk resided in Sumner, Maryland, and occupied an office next to his in the CIA building in downtown Washington. Yet, he did not recall if he saw Kuzmuk at all after 1:00 P.M. on November 22 or at any time November 23, or November 24, or November 25, or November 27.

I inquired about the CIA records:

Q. Are there records maintained by the Central Intelligence Agency, or were there records maintained by the CIA while you were there, which would reveal where you were on any given day while you were employed by the CIA?

A. I presume so. I think there was an attendance clerk, payroll clerk.

Later Hunt seemed to offer a different, even contradictory, answer to a similar question:

Q. Do you recall whether or not there was an attendance record submitted by the CIA to your counsel which showed where you were according to the CIA records on November 22, 1963?

A. I don't believe there was, no, sir. I think that there was a destroy policy after three to five years or something like that, records of that sort were just simply disposed of.

Since Rubin had asserted that he was going to bring an action for Hunt against the *Sunday News Journal* for defamation, I asked Hunt why he had not filed that lawsuit. Hunt replied that he did not "associate myself with those particular remarks." He said, "You must understand that Mr. Rubin is a man who might well be described as a sudden enthusiast. . . .Something attracts his attention and he will summon the media and make a statement, and then he loses interest in it very quickly."

Hunt then asserted that the *News Journal* article "had been based upon the *Spotlight* piece by Marchetti." I then spent the next fifteen minutes comparing one article to the other, relevant paragraph by relevant paragraph. Hunt admitted that a great deal of specific information that was present in the *News Journal* article was absent from the *Spotlight* article.

When he testified at the first trial, Hunt had made reference to the then-pending case against A.J. Weberman, a case he had stated that he would prosecute vigorously. Long before the deposition began, the case had been voluntarily dismissed by the plaintiff. I asked Hunt why he had dropped the case on the literal eve of trial. He responded:

"When I attempted to find out from Mr. Rubin in what courthouse I should appear, what room of the courthouse I should appear for the trial the next morning, I was told by his office that there was not going to be any trial, that he had settled the matter, and, furthermore, that he was not in town. He had previously taken on as a client a Saudi Arabian sheik or princeling named Al Fasi and he was chasing all over the country with him, and as far as I know Mr. Rubin wasn't even in town the eve of the trial.

"In any event, I had assumed that my requirements for the settlement of the case had been met by Mr. Rubin and that a check by Mr. Weberman for five thousand dollars would be forthcoming. I learned the following day Mr. Rubin had told the opposing attorneys who had come to Miami for the trial, that—I forget the term, but it was going to equal out, nobody would charge anyone for anything and they would scrub the case. That was done, I must add reluctantly, without my authorization."

Q. So the case was dismissed on your behalf without your being paid even a penny; is that correct?

A. That's correct.

Q. And there was no apology or retraction from the defendants in that case?

A. None.

The scenario recounted by Hunt was so odd that I asked him if I could explore the matter with Rubin. That could only be accomplished if Hunt was willing to waive his attorney-client privilege so that I could depose Rubin. Hunt said that he did not think he would do that.

Q. So all we have on the question of why the Weberman case was settled for no payment at all, no retraction, is your statement that Mr. Rubin did it without authorization from you and you will not permit us to ask Mr. Rubin those questions?

A. That's correct.

Hunt was quoted in the *Miami Herald* on May 7, 1980, as he announced at a press conference with Rubin that he had filed a $3.5 million law suit against the *Spotlight* and Marchetti, whom he described as a "CIA renegade."

At that conference, he had stated that "it's become an article of faith that I had some role in the Kennedy assassination." He blamed "assassination buffs, Nixon haters, and others," who he said "erected a frame and set me into it." At the deposition, he endorsed those remarks and stated that they certainly represented his sentiments. I asked him to name the persons he was referring to. He blamed Dick Gregory, Weberman and Weberman's co-author, Canfield.

I summarized Trento's testimony regarding the CIA memorandum he had seen and then asked Hunt if Trento was "an assassination buff." He said he probably was. He added that former CIA director Richard Helms previously had "trouble" with articles Trento had written. Hunt added that a person who was not "an assassination buff" would not have written the article Trento wrote, since it was "literally filled with bile and conjecture."

Although Trento had testified that he had not known of the *Spotlight* article when he wrote his piece; that he, unlike Marchetti, had actually seen the CIA memorandum; and that he had not known Marchetti at the time—a statement corroborated by Marchetti—Hunt insisted that Trento's article was based upon the *Spotlight* article. Hunt was willing to disregard the testimony of Trento and Marchetti and to rely upon a vague statement by Helms that he'd had "trouble" with Trento's work because, as he testified, Helms "is a man of integrity." He said he did not know "the substance of that" when I asked him if he was aware of Helms' conviction for making false statements while under oath.

Hunt did agree that he had conspired with Gordon Liddy to kill Jack

Anderson. Hunt said he had contracted with a Dr. Gunn, who had experience "with efforts to discredit foreign leaders or foreign agents through the use of drugs." Gunn was with the CIA at the time, Hunt testified.

While Hunt challenged Liddy's testimony about the plan to commit arson at Brookings Institution, he did concede that Charles Colson, Nixon's counselor, "said at one time to me there is a document being prepared in the Brookings Institution" and that the document was of "interest" to the "administration" or to "Mr. Colson, himself." Colson said that "they would like very much to either have a look at it or to steal the documents from the vault." Hunt added, "I believe Mr. Colson was aware there was an entry capability."

Marita Lorenz a former CIA contract agent, had told me years previously that Hunt used the code name "Eduardo" when working with men he described as Cuban assets." Hunt said he discussed "Cuban assets" with Liddy. I asked him if he had a code name that the Cuban assets used to address him. He answered, "Well, not in the Watergate, no." He paused. I waited for him to continue and then he said, "During the Bay of Pigs operation, I was generally known in the Cuban community as Eduardo."

As we left the conference room, Brent Whitmore and Fleming Lee began to discuss the deposition with me. In the elevator, Lee mildly observed that he thought I was going to make more of Hunt's changing stories. "I thought that in view of the record you would be more confrontational with him," Lee said. He added, "You might have gotten much more." I did not respond.

Brent had worked diligently before the deposition, securing and comparing the numerous and contradictory explanations Hunt had offered at various forums, both while under oath in a courtroom setting or during a deposition and in less formal confrontations with agents of the FBI and the news media. I had studied her splendid research thoroughly days before the deposition and had discussed the matter with Lee.

We left the elevator and began our search for a taxicab. Then, I answered Lee's unspoken question. "It wasn't the right audience." He asked what I meant. I said, "The jurors weren't there."

David Atlee Phillips

SEVEN YEARS AFTER DAVID ATLEE PHILLIPS AND I DEBATED AT THE UNIVERSITY OF Southern California, E. Howard Hunt submitted a list of proposed witnesses for the Liberty Lobby trial. It contained the name David Atlee Phillips. With a number of Hunt's trial witnesses being doubtful starters, in my view, Phillips seemed to be a witness who must be deposed.

If Phillips merely repeated under oath what he had said during the debate, I was satisfied that Hunt could not call upon him to testify at trial. His words would have immeasurably strengthened the defense. I wondered if Hunt's lawyers knew what Phillips had previously said, or even that he had participated in the debate. I could not envision that Phillips would refuse to testify about matters that he had discussed voluntarily at a public event attended by representatives of the news media. He again surprised me and revealed the paucity of my imagination.

I awaited Mr. Phillips and his attorney in the front street-level office of the four-story townhouse I occupy as a home and office on Capitol Hill in Washington, D.C. The building is directly across from the United States Supreme Court and the Supreme Court garden. During proscribed hours, well-posted parking regulations are strictly enforced by efficient, judicially encouraged SWAT teams; no vehicles are permitted to linger on Second Street, Northeast, the roadway separating the Court from my office and residence.

The first caller that afternoon was a tall, relaxed gentleman who looked as though he could have been a college professor. He was Richard D. Sullivan, assistant general counsel for the Central Intelligence Agency.

Of course, knowing the CIA, he really could have been a professor as well.

I asked Sullivan if he was going to represent Mr. Phillips. He replied in a clearly defined Boston accent, "No. No, Mr. Phillips is going to be represented by a leader of the District of Columbia bar, I believe by the president of the bar association, Mr. Bierbower."

Well then, I asked, hopefully not without cordiality but with some concern, "Why are you here?"

Mr. Sullivan answered. "I represent the CIA." He paused and added, ". . .also the United States of America."

I responded, "Really? Don't I discern a conflict of interest?"

Mr. Sullivan laughed. He said, "I heard you were good. . .but that's very good," as he jotted down some words in his English leather-bound notebook.

Turning to a more serious, but no less bemusing, matter, Mr. Sullivan said, somewhat officiously, "Mr. James Smith will be here. He is not with intelligence."

Then adapting a sincere pose, he looked at me and said, "Actually, Smith is not his real name and he works for the CIA."

I asked him if he ever watched the television program "M*A*S*H." He replied that he was a fan and then a moment later he burst into laughter. "Oh yes. 'My name is Colonel Flagg from some outfit, but my name is not Flagg and I'm with the CIA.' Yes, yes. That is very good." I waited for him to make another entry in his notebook, but he disappointed me.

I told the CIA's lawyer that, as he must know, it is customary for all persons at depositions to be identified on the record. He asked if I was going to object to Mr. Smith's presence. I suggested we discuss it on the record when the court reporter arrived. When he asked why, I said that one day I might write a musical comedy about the deposition and I wanted the lyrics to be authentic.

I was rewarded with both a substantial guffaw and a sufficient entry in the notebook.

Before long, Phillips arrived with his lawyer, James Bierbower, Esq., a distinguished member of the D.C. bar, followed by Hunt's two lawyers, Bill Snyder and Kevin Dunne. The court reporter, Rebekah J. Johnson, had just set up her equipment when a stocky man dressed in a brown rumpled suit entered the office. Mr. Sullivan introduced him as Mr. Smith.

The proceedings began.

"Mr. Phillips, my name is Mark Lane. I am one of the attorneys for the defendant in this case, a case brought by Mr. Hunt regarding an article which was published in the *Spotlight*, a publication published by the

Liberty Lobby. We are here today at a deposition to ask you some questions, and I think it would be good if we began by each of us identifying ourselves."

I identified myself, stating my name, address, and telephone number. Snyder, Dunne, and Bierbower did the same. Then Sullivan spoke:

"My name is Richard D. Sullivan. I'm assistant general counsel of the Central Intelligence Agency in Washington, D.C. 20505.[1] I am representing the United States, and I am assisted by James Smith, who is a representative of the directorate of operations of the Central Intelligence Agency. James Smith is not my colleague's true name, but we have all agreed before going on record that he would be present under that name."

I asked: "Mr. Smith, I wonder if you could tell us if you are an attorney?"

He replied, "Negative, I am not an attorney."

I tried to explain the difficulty: "Is there some way we are going to know who you are before we proceed? It is customary, as you probably know, at depositions or other matters related to formal legal proceedings, for each of the persons who participate to be identified, not with a name which is not his real name but with a name which is his real name. Is there some way you could either for the record or off the record tell us who you are?"

Smith remained silent. He looked at Sullivan. Sullivan spoke: "I'm not sure, Mr. Lane, that Mr. Smith is participating in any real sense of that verb, but there might possibly—I don't know, there might be a way in the future that we could clarify that information. But it won't be possible to give Mr. Smith's true name here today."

Since Mr. Smith might not be "participating," according to his counsel, I inquired about his plans. Again Sullivan responded:

"The only role, I would like to state for the record, Mr. Smith is going to play is to inform me if any matters that would be subject to a secrets-of-state privilege are about to be put on the record. That will be the only role he will play."

Likely we would have ultimately prevailed before the court had we declined to proceed with a stranger at the table. However, many months would have been consumed in preparing and arguing motions, thus making our final victory Pyrrhic. I decided to proceed with the unidentified Mr. Smith in attendance.

At that point I looked up from my desk and through the front window.

---

[1]The CIA is one of the few residents in the capital area with no known address, merely a zip code. It is actually situated in Langley, Virginia.

A black stretch limousine was parked in front of my house in clear violation of the law. A chauffeur sat confidently in the driver's seat. He was playing with the radio dials.

Phillips admitted that he had met Hunt during 1954. "I was in Florida at the time with the CIA operation which later became known as the Guatemala Operation."

When asked to describe what Hunt was doing in the operation, Phillips answered, "He was engaged in a secret operation." He would not elaborate.

I asked Phillips what his assignment had been in Mexico City. He refused to answer. I asked him what his title had been in Mexico City. He refused to answer.

I then asked: "Did you have occasion to speak at a debate some time ago at the University of Southern California with me?"

He responded, "Yes, I did."

Smith, Sullivan, and Phillips conferred.

Smith was animated. Answers to questions about the Phillips disclosures at the debate were not to be permitted at the deposition. With his keepers present the "secrets of state" were not going to be revealed by Phillips. I tried in any event. "Do you recall at the debate at USC that I showed you a CIA document which was, in essence, a game plan to destroy my reputation, my credibility, and to prevent my books and views on the assassination of John F. Kennedy from being known?"

Phillips conferred with his associates. Instead of declining to answer, he committed perjury.

"No, I don't remember seeing a document that could be classified that way."

I persisted: "Do you recall stating that you had in fact received that document which I showed to you while you were working for the CIA in Caracas?"

This time Phillips, after again consulting with his colleagues, decided both to make a false reply and plead the privilege.

"Perhaps to help us along with this thing, I would like to say that I was aware and said then that I was aware that the Agency told its people abroad that a number of things had been written about the Kennedy assassination by you and that they were false, and that if anything, anyone were to ask any question, the true facts were these. I recall a document that went along those lines. I am not, however, having been a student of what's going on in the way of legislation since 1977, I simply don't want to put myself in the position of committing a felony by discussing internal documents even though I might have done it previously, not until I know that I have the right to do that."

Phillips seemed genuinely frightened. It was clear that the Mexico City scenario we had discussed at the debate would not be addressed truthfully. I inquired about other, related matters.

I asked Phillips if he had seen Hunt in Mexico City. While the CIA representatives huddled at the table, Phillips replied, "Yes, I did." Having given that answer, he had waived the right to object to questions in that area. I then asked him when he had seen Hunt in Mexico City. He responded:

"It was sometime between September of 1961 and March of 1965." I was astonished by his testimony. The other lawyers did not register concern. I continued:

"Did you see Mr. Hunt anywhere in Mexico prior to November 22, 1963?"

Phillips said that he had seen Hunt in Mexico before November 22, 1963. He added, "I must have seen him once or twice before that occasion."

It had become clear to me that Phillips would not be called as a witness for Hunt at the trial. During March 1974, Hunt had submitted an affidavit to the Rockefeller Commission. On November 3, 1978, Hunt testified before the House Select Committee on Assassinations. On that occasion he adopted the affidavit, and testified that it had been truthful except for the name of the Chinese grocery store where he had allegedly made purchases on November 22, 1963. In sworn statements made before two committees, Hunt had stated:

"I was not in Mexico in 1963. In fact, I was not in Mexico between the years 1961 and 1970, and have not been there since a weekend pleasure trip to Acapulco in July of 1970."

Phillips had run the Mexico City shop. CIA records about his work, contacts, and meetings were unavailable. Hunt had testified that he had "no diaries or other memorabilia prior to 1969," since he had "destroyed" those documents. We were left with the sworn statements of the two men about whether they had met in Mexico City. Clearly, at least one of them had committed perjury.

I turned to the list of Hunt's witnesses and drew a line through the name David Atlee Phillips.

I asked Phillips if CIA officers are required to tell the truth when they testify. I was interested in securing a generic statement that might be useful when Hunt took the stand at the trial. Perhaps I phrased my question too abruptly:

"Isn't it true, Mr. Phillips, in essence, for the last quarter of a century you have been a spy and that spies lie?"

Phillips said that he wanted the record to show that he objected strenuously. As he explained it, it was not that it had been suggested that he might lie that outraged him, it was the notion that he had been a spy. "I have not been a spy," he said. "A spy is a foreigner or a person who sells out his country for money or for some other sordid reason. I was an intelligence officer," he proclaimed. He didn't spy; he paid the spies. When I pressed on, a bit more tactfully, Phillips did concede that "people involved in secret operations find it necessary to engage in duplicity from time to time."

When I inquired of the witness if Hunt might be obligated as the result of some secret CIA oath, which none of the civilians at the table were sufficiently cleared to have been told about, to commit perjury at the trial, Sullivan objected. He said, quite solemnly:

"Section 403(D) of the National Security Act of 1947 requires intelligence sources and methods be protected by the director of Central Intelligence from unauthorized disclosure. Such prevarication could indeed be a method, and to that extent I will object to the question. Now I have no objection to the witness answering the question if you know Mr. Hunt in his nonprofessional life engaged in duplicity."

I asked the CIA's lawyer if it was his position that lying might be a method of communicating so regularly employed by the CIA, its officers, and agents, that Phillips would be precluded from commenting upon the practice because it could be considered a secret "CIA method." Sullivan said he stood by his previous answer and added, "We will be happy to litigate it."

Finally, I put the matter quite bluntly before Phillips, expecting a statement from him in defense of his associate Hunt and their organization:

"If Mr. Hunt was involved in a plan to assassinate John F. Kennedy on behalf of the Central Intelligence Agency, and if he was told prior to that time and subsequent to that time that he should lie about that if asked, do you think Mr. Hunt would lie about that?"

But no ringing denial was forthcoming. Instead, Phillips quietly stated that he preferred not to answer the question. He then offered an explanation which, in my view, merely raised new questions:

"In the course the questions are taking, I respectfully decline to answer. I don't see I can for the record correctly define questions of morality and ethics which apparently is what you are trying to get me to do. I don't feel expert."

Just as we concluded the deposition, I learned that the debate had been a subject of discussion between Phillips and his lawyers. Such colloquy is privileged and may not be inquired into without the permission of the client. Phillips was clearly being less than cooperative; I therefore did not ask him to waive his attorney-client privilege. Instead, I asked if he had a tape recording of our debate. He said he did. I asked, "When was the last time that you heard it?" He answered, "About three years ago. I got it on the advice of my attorney."

When I said the closing words, "I have no further questions," Bierbower responded, "We will waive signature." His direction to the court reporter, through that phrase, meant that her record was complete and that Phillips was not requesting an opportunity to read the manuscript and *change* his answers. Sullivan was alarmed. He quickly said, "We would prefer that you not." The leader of the Washington bar responded with alacrity. He addressed the court reporter: "Withdraw that." If doubt existed until that last moment as to who really represented Phillips, it had been resolved.

As the attorneys mulled about and went through their lawyerly rituals, gathering papers, capping their Mont Blanc pens, exchanging cards, and making quips, James Smith brusquely left the room without a word. He rushed to the limousine, entered the backseat, and was driven away at some speed.

I told Sullivan that I had thought the car was there for him. He modestly observed that his later-model automobile was parked nearby, "just around the corner." He added, with a touch of understandable pride, "at a fire hydrant."

Walter Kuzmuk

ALEGAL SCHOLAR OBSERVED THAT IT IS NOT DUE PROCESS BUT CROSS-EXAMINA-tion that is the engine that runs the judicial process.

Direct examination by counsel is not an art; it is an exercise that invariably improves with rehearsal time. A well-trained parrot, in theory, could make an excellent witness on direct examination.

Cross-examination is another matter; it may reveal another world, one that was barely visible before it began. As in the case of first light, it may disclose details of the landscape, even whole mountain ranges, that were only dimly perceived during the dusk of direct testimony. The Walter Kuzmuk experience provides a classic example of this phenomenon.

Kuzmuk was a CIA officer who had worked with Hunt. To the jurors at the first trial, his testimony may have seemed dispositive of the question of Hunt's whereabouts on November 22, 1963; an experienced, ranking officer of the CIA had seen him in Washington just as the president was being shot in Dallas. According to Kuzmuk, Hunt and his wife had driven by in the early afternoon of November 22 as he exited from a downtown Washington restaurant.

The testimony had not been tested in the crucible of cross-examination and the jurors were obliged to accept it at face value. I read Kuzmuk's brief testimony over and over, more interested in what he had not said than what he said. It was my responsibility to make a preliminary judgment regarding Kuzmuk's credibility before questioning him. Trento had been told, and had written, that all of Hunt's alibi witnesses were to be "CIA-arranged," as per the 1966 memo. My limited contacts at the Agency informed me that there was a growing concern at the CIA about my effort to defend the *Spotlight* article on the basis of truth. They told me that the likely decision would be to send former, rather than present, CIA officers to act as witnesses for Hunt—so that if Hunt lost, the CIA could state that it, as an organization, took no active part in the trial. In addition, the CIA was to focus substantial attention upon its "assets" in the news media, both to plant disparaging ideas about my client and me and to discourage coverage of the case—unless Hunt were to prevail.

Was Kuzmuk a CIA-arranged witness? Hunt had not remembered seeing Kuzmuk on November 22, 1963, until a congressional committee had stated it could not account for Hunt's whereabouts and Kuzmuk sent Hunt a letter "reminding" him that they'd seen each other that day. I concluded that in all probability, Kuzmuk had not seen Hunt on November 22. He worked with him every day, drove to work with him almost every morning and back home with him almost every evening, and their offices were but a few feet from each other. They lived near each other and they socialized with each other regularly during the evening. Yet Kuzmuk never claimed to have seen Hunt in the office or at home during the crucial days. His story of having seen Hunt that day surfaced for the first time many years later, just when Hunt needed a witness. Kuzmuk could, and did, plead ignorance; he didn't know that Hunt needed a loyal witness until he read about allegations against Hunt in a Miami newspaper in 1976 or 1977. Yet Hunt had been questioned many years before by various agencies, bureaus, and reporters about his whereabouts on November 22nd. Was it likely that his coworker, his neighbor, his close friend for more than thirty years, had not heard about the matter when it was apparent, even to a casual reader of newspapers, that Hunt could have used an alibi witness long before 1976?

If Kuzmuk was not knowledgeable, surely the same case could not be made for Hunt. He too, according to the story, was a witness; he saw Kuzmuk wave at him and he waved back. Why didn't Hunt, in need of an alibi witness from 1964 through 1976, call upon his friend Kuzmuk to come forward?

And then there was the story itself. Why did Kuzmuk claim to have sighted Hunt coincidentally and accidentally at some distance, rather than in the office or at home where he saw him regularly? Perhaps because if the men had seen each other in the office, others who they would be called upon to identify would also have been present. The same circumstances might prevail at home. Yet if the story of the accidental meeting was fabricated after Hunt's wife, Dorothy, was dead, it merely required the testimony of the two principals.

If Kuzmuk testified that he saw Hunt at the office, or had driven to work with him that day, he would have been inviting an indictment for perjury if subsequent events revealed conclusively that Hunt was in Dallas, not Washington, D.C. Hunt had, after all, finally admitted his guilt in the Watergate break-in, and then testified for the government against everyone else. By stating only that he had seen Hunt drive by at some distance, Kuzmuk was in a position to later admit that he might have been mistaken since the man was in a Chevrolet and looked like Hunt. Built into the implausible story that Kuzmuk was prepared to tell, under oath, was its easy access to subsequent deniability.

I was ready for the deposition of Walter Kuzmuk.

Kuzmuk had received the transcript of his 1981 deposition. He had read it, verified its accuracy, and signed it. He knew that it would be read to a jury and that his statement had been given under oath.

Kuzmuk testified that the office he had occupied in November 1963, was just "two doors away" from the office occupied by Hunt. He admitted that he had routinely attended meetings with Hunt and the other CIA officers every Wednesday and Friday at "0700." He could recall having seen Hunt neither on Wednesday, November 20, 1963, nor on Friday, November 22, 1963, at the regularly scheduled meetings.

Although he had previously testified that he and Hunt drove together to the CIA almost every morning, alternating automobiles, he could not testify that he had seen Hunt on any day of the week beginning Monday, November 18th, and ending Friday, November 22nd, except for the time Hunt drove past the restaurant that Kuzmuk was leaving after lunch. Finally, Kuzmuk asserted that he had not driven to work with Hunt on November 22.

Before Kuzmuk's testimony was completed, he admitted that he had not seen Hunt from November 18, 1963, until December 1963, with the exception of the moment he had seen him in the automobile. However, he was unable to describe the car Hunt was in, even though he had previously testified that he had been in Hunt's car on numerous occasions.

The witness, originally offered by the plaintiff to establish beyond question that Hunt had not been in Dallas on November 22, had been converted into a witness who had closely associated with Hunt at home, in the office, and in the drives back and forth, but who could not account for Hunt's whereabouts for almost the entire second half of November 1963.

Mr. Snyder sought to salvage what he might from the encounter. He elicited from Kuzmuk that Hunt would never conspire to do an illegal act.

This irrelevant inquiry permitted me to ask the witness, on redirect, if he had learned that Hunt had been convicted for conspiracy to do illegal acts, and, in addition, that he was convicted for executing the illegal conspiracy. He admitted that he had heard something about that.

The testimony concluded with questions about Kuzmuk's willingness to commit perjury.

Q. In your almost quarter of a century working for the Central Intelligence Agency, Mr. Kuzmuk, did you ever make a statement on behalf of the CIA which was not true?

A. No, I would never make a statement one way or another so long as they were paying my salary.

Q. You would never make a statement one way or another?

A. Pro or con. If I didn't like it, I wouldn't get their salary. I'd quit. Is that what you are asking?

Q. No, I am not asking you if you like the CIA. I am asking if you ever made—

A. Derogatory?

Q. No, not derogatory, a statement while you worked for the CIA which statement was not true? Did you ever lie or cover or tell anybody something that was not true because it was going to help the whole agency?

A. I don't see how it has any bearing.

Q. I think it goes to the heart of your testimony, and if you do not answer we are going to get the court to instruct you to answer this. If you refuse to answer, you may do that at this stage, and I would like to know your reason for refusing to answer.

A. Well, I think maybe the IG [Inspector General] from the department would have to answer that, my friend.

Q. Well, he's not here and he's not under oath. So I am asking this question.

A. I know.

Q. Just listen to the question, Mr. Kuzmuk. In the 25 years you worked for the Central Intelligence Agency, did you ever make a statement on behalf of the CIA which was not true? You can answer yes or no or you can refuse to answer.

A. I am not going to answer because I think it comes under the IG and I can't do that.

I never did request that Kuzmuk be ordered by the court to answer the question.

Before I could prepare a motion to compel Kuzmuk to respond to the proper inquiry and submit it to the court, Snyder said he was going to withdraw Kuzmuk as a witness. Now the only potential witnesses for the plaintiff, other that Hunt himself, were his three children, David Phillips, Connie Maserov, and the keeper of the records at the CIA.

If Hunt had not been sighted by Kuzmuk from mid-November 1963 until early December of that year, where had he been? How could Kuzmuk explain his absence from the regularly scheduled meetings of CIA officers at the downtown Washington CIA office?

I considered calling Kuzmuk as a witness for the defense. He had been the one person, other than Dorothy Hunt, who had seen Hunt daily, and he, unlike Mrs. Hunt, saw Hunt not only at home but in the office. I decided not to call Kuzmuk because I did not believe him to be a truthful witness. Clearly, he was an adverse witness and I would, therefore, have been permitted to cross-examine rather than conduct a direct examination of him even if I presented him as my own witness.

That distinction is of some importance. In the ordinary instance, a lawyer may neither ask leading questions of his own witness nor confront him with contradictory evidence. The lawyer may utilize those techniques during cross-examination only. I was confident that I would have been able to utilize the transcript of the deposition I had conducted, or, with Kuzmuk's cooperation, present him in person at the trial as a witness I would be free to question.

There were no ethical considerations that precluded me from presenting Kuzmuk's testimony regarding his close association with Hunt in general, or Hunt's mysterious disappearance during the crucial days. I was not concerned that a thoughtful jury, having been exposed to Kuzmuk's futile attempt to deal with probing questions, would believe his story about seeing Hunt as he drove through a street in downtown Washington.

I just did not believe Kuzmuk, and I thought it would be breaking faith with the jurors to place his doubtful testimony before them as if I did.

G. Gordon Liddy

THE APPEARANCE OF G. GORDON LIDDY IN MY OFFICE ONE FINE JUNE AFTERNOON during 1984 was unique in several respects. He was not accompanied by a coterie of lawyers furnished by the CIA or the United States government or drawn from the leadership of the local and prestigious bar association. Liddy arrived alone.

He was willing to answer all questions put to him.

My associate, Fleming Lee,had developed an interest in the deponent. Lee, a lawyer who had never tried a case on his own, had authored several mystery novels, including works in the Ellery Queen series. He was fascinated by Liddy, had read his books, and asked if he might ask some of the questions at the deposition. I agreed to his proposal.

Since Liddy did not much admire or respect Hunt, his statements should be carefully evaluated. In a deposition taken in another case some four years before his testimony in my office, Liddy was asked if any agency of the United States government had ordered him to kill Hunt. He responded that there came a time "when I felt I might well receive such instructions." He then volunteered that "with respect to Hunt, I was prepared, should I receive those orders, to carry them out immediately."

Liddy arrived wearing a natty blue blazer that sported a substantial metallic emblem. He explained, when asked, that it signified his membership in an elite organization of former intelligence officers. Liddy testified that he had been a "bureau supervisor" in "J. Edgar Hoover's inspection division," an assistant district attorney in Dutchess County, New York, the chairman of Richard Nixon's presidential campaign for that geographical area and, after Nixon's election, the "Special Assistant to the Secretary of the Treasury for Organized Crime." Later, he said, he was appointed enforcement legislative counsel for Treasury, then staff assistant to the president. During December 1971, he became general counsel to the Committee to Re-Elect the President and then general counsel to the Finance Committee to Re-Elect the President.

His criminal record was also lengthy and illustrious. He was indicted, he testified, for "wire tapping, breaking and entering, things of that sort, and I think I ended up with around eight or nine felonies, a sentence of twenty-one-and-a-half years in prison." His sentence was commuted and he was relaesed from prison during September 1977.

Liddy had been assigned to a group later called "the Plumbers." This special investigation unit in the White House was a delegate body with each player, including John Mitchéll, Henry Kissinger, John Ehrlichman, and Charles Colson, sending a representative. Liddy represented Attorney General Mitchell; Hunt represented Colson.

Liddy worked with Hunt on a number of projects for the Nixon White House. During this period Hunt claimed to be a retired officer of the CIA. Liddy said that Hunt maintained a working relationship with the CIA, securing disguises from the Agency—such things as voice-altering mechanisms and gait-altering devices—as well as photographic equipment. Hunt was also trained by CIA personnel in the use of this equipment during the same period.

Liddy testified that Hunt introduced him to CIA operators who provided him with disguises and photographic equipment and another person "who delivered to me the cartoons that had been prepared in the Central Intelligence Agency, political cartoons attacking Senator [Edward] Kennedy, for use should Senator Kennedy at that time run for president of the United States." It was through Hunt, Liddy testified, that the cartoons were obtained.

This discrediting program was carried out through Operation Gemstone, which, Liddy explained, "was a political intelligence and disruption operation planned to be directed against the Democratic party and its candidates in the 1972 presidential election." He testified that he and Hunt jointly developed a number of concepts "which I believe could be considered illegal."

They had planned, he said, "to sabotage the air conditioner in the convention center in Miami" during the Democratic convention. He testified that the two had organized an attack on Senator Ed Muskie's wife, since Muskie was a potential candidate. Hunt and Liddy believed that in defending his wife, Muskie would act in an emotional manner and thus appear weak to the voters. They were right; the resulting incident contributed to Muskie's decision to drop out of the race.

Hunt and Liddy also planned, according to Liddy, "to intercept the radio communications of the Democratic campaign aircraft."

Liddy testified that the White House approved several plans that were then implemented, including "break-ins and enterings" as well as "wiretap and oral communication interception through room microphones" and placing spies in the Democratic party offices. Hunt, Liddy said, was the controller for those operations—"Mr. Hunt would pay him [the agent] his stipend and then Mr. Hunt would give me the product."

Hunt had thus been established as a paymaster for illegal activities approved by his supervisors. That testimony might echo loudly in the courtroom at a later moment in the trial.

The two men also contrived to secure information about what the Democratic party members might be considering at their convention center—in addition, that is, to complaining about the heat.

In this matter, however, they discovered that they were on philosophically divergent paths. While they both agreed that it was appropriate to "take some very good-looking prostitutes," and "dress them with finesse," then use them to "get [mid-level Democratic staffers] into bed" to secure "pillow talk of a political nature," Hunt and Liddy could not overcome their differences as to what constituted an attractive woman. Liddy complained that while "Hunt was attempting to get the appropriate prostitutes," his "particular taste was toward very dark, sort of Cuban women." Liddy observed that "they didn't particularly attract me" since "I like the more blonde types." Liddy also testified that "the Cuban women they came up with couldn't speak English."

They were at an impasse until "finally we compromised and the task was given to Mr. Frank Sturgis, and Mr. Sturgis produced two very beautiful Anglo-Saxon women who were school teachers." Apparently the appearance of a third procurer ensured the safety of the republic, at least as Hunt and Liddy saw it.

I asked Liddy if he and Hunt had ever discussed the rather odious aspects of their aberrant behavior. Were they concerned that they were interfering with the democratic process and adversely impacting upon the right of the American people to make decisions without the secret intercession of government-paid agents acting in secrecy?

Liddy was pleased to respond:

"No. Because the position I took, and I believe he agreed with it, was what we were trying to do was get information, not false information, but accurate information about other candidates and then expose them to the American people so they could make their decision intelligently. An example would be, we knew of the weakness of Senator Muskie in that he had difficulty controlling his emotions, could break down. We believed that it would be a disaster for the United States of America for Muskie to break before Brezhnev, better he break on the snows of New Hampshire, and we conducted our activities to bring something like that about. Eventually we were successful. Muskie was eliminated as the candidate. I would take the position that would not harm the democratic process, with a small 'd.' It's an advantage. It's my belief Mr. Hunt agreed with that position."

One of the most bizarre activities planned by Hunt and Liddy, at the suggestion of Colson, was an elaborate scheme to enter the Brookings Institution in Washington. Liddy described the concept:

"There came a time during the summer of 1971 when Mr. Hunt approached me and said that Mr. Colson, his principal, was concerned with what might be in the holdings of the Brookings Institution. And to gain access to those he proposed a special operation. Mr. Hunt and I sat down and devised one. The operation that we planned was to purchase several used fire engines from the market where they are available, have them painted and decaled in the colors of the Washington, D.C. fire department, to have our Cuban assets dressed in firemen's uniforms and attending the engines, to have a penetration which would then—during the period of time there would be no one there, so no one would be hurt—start a fire in the Brookings Institution. The first engines to respond would be ours. It would be our people who would enter and in the guise of putting out the fire they would take whatever it was that Mr. Colson wanted out of the Brookings Institution and we would have it.

"This plan was turned down when Mr. Hunt's principals refused to pay for the fire engines. They thought it would be excessively expensive."

I was interested in Liddy's reference to "our Cuban assets." I asked about it. Liddy obliged:

"Mr. Hunt informed me he had played a major role in the aborted attempt to overthrow Fidel Castro that has come to be known historically as the Bay of Pigs episode. He told me that there were still many very well-trained, trained by the Central Intelligence Agency, very pro-American, anti-Castro Cubans in Miami, and that he knew them well, that he believed that they would be available, indeed eager, to engage in special operations, special missions on behalf of the special group of which Mr.

Hunt and I were members. And the first time they were recruited for that purpose was for the Fielding operation [breaking into the office of Daniel Ellsberg's psychiatrist], and we referred to them as our Cuban assets."

Lee asked Liddy if Hunt had contact with members of organized crime. Liddy testified:

"I would say yes, based upon what Mr. Hunt told me. There was a meeting which I attended in Miami in which we were seeking to recruit personnel for clandestine operations for a plan which we designated by the code word Gemstone, which was for the purpose of political intelligence-gathering and a clandestine operation to disrupt as best we could the successful operation of the Democratic party campaign for the presidency in 1972. In the course of that I met numbers of people in Miami who were of Cuban extraction."

Liddy explained that Hunt had introduced the Cuban assets to him. He elaborated:

"And we interviewed them and decided some were suitable to take on board and some not. Amongst those we decided to recruit, Mr. Hunt told me afterwards, were some who had been involved in organized crime and who had among them killed, I believe the figure was twenty-wo men, including two who were hanged from a beam in a garage. Mr. Hunt was explaining this to me not gratuitously but by means of impressing on me that we were dealing with competent individuals with that."

Since a jury would subsequently be required to evaluate all of the evidence to determine if Hunt possessed the character traits requisite to plan the murder of the president, we inquired if Hunt had ever, to the knowledge of the witness, planned the murder of an American in time of peace. Liddy testified that he had met with Hunt and "Mr. Gunn" from the CIA for luncheon at the Hay Adams Hotel in Washington for the purpose of conspiring to murder Jack Anderson. According to Liddy:

"We discussed with Dr. Gunn aspirin roulette, in which one takes a single tablet of a deadly poison, packs it in a Bayer aspirin jar, we place it in the man's medicine chest, and one day he gets that tablet and that's that."

Liddy said that Hunt seemed familiar with that approach since "it was he who referred to it as aspirin roulette."

Hunt and Liddy then considered an alternate method of murdering Mr. Anderson, according to Liddy:

"We discussed Dr. Gunn's suggestion, which was the use of an automobile to hit Mr. Anderson's automobile when it was in a turn in the circle up near Chevy Chase. There is a way that apparently had been known by the Central Intelligence Agency that if you hit a car at just the right speed and angle, it will flip and burn and kill the occupant."

The men decided to use neither poison nor an automobile as the weapon of choice. Liddy testified:

"And finally I used an elaboration from an FBI technique when the FBI goes in to, say an embassy to crack the safe and extract information therefrom. Everybody who would potentially be going in there was under surveillance, and if somebody would come back too soon, the way the agents inside would be protected is there would be a bogus mugging of this individual, a watch would be stolen, wallet taken, et cetera, and that would eliminate that individual. They wouldn't kill him. But what I suggested is we just kill him. And they both agreed that that would be the way to go about it, and the task would be assigned to the Cuban assets. And the luncheon broke up. And Mr. Hunt said, 'Suppose my principals say that this is too sensitive a matter to be assigned to the Cuban assets, who should do it?' I said, because I am probably best at that, I will do it."

However, neither Colson nor Nixon approved the recommendation and the plan was not executed, Liddy said.

Having established that Hunt was willing to recommend or endorse a full menu of illegal acts, I wanted Liddy's opinion on Hunt's truthfulness. If Hunt had committed a serious crime under orders and on behalf of his superiors, would he subsequently lie about it? That question, it seemed to me, bore a special relevance to the matter at hand. I asked Liddy if he had ever had a discussion with Hunt about the need to lie. Liddy responded:

"We both remembered Winston Churchill's maxim that in severe situations, time of war, what have you, 'Truth is so precious she must be surrounded by a bodyguard of lies.' Any time you take an alias and give an alias, that is a lie. So yes, we discussed that sort of thing all the time."

I then posed a hypothetical question to Liddy. "If you did go forward with the program to kill Jack Anderson and for some reason you were picked up and able to escape jurisdiction, if Mr. Hunt were called before a congressional committee and he had taken an oath to tell the truth, and if he were asked, 'Did you meet with G. Gordon Liddy and plan the murder of Jack Anderson?' what would you expect him to say?"

He answered: "I would have at the time expected Hunt to say no."

I pursued the matter: "That he was not involved in such a plan even though he were under oath when he made such a statement?"

Liddy explained why Hunt would be expected to commit perjury. "Yes, I would have expected that of him out of loyalty to me and to the organization, institutional loyalty."

Liddy completed his testimony perfectly, stating that while he no longer associated with Hunt, he did see him last, he recalled, when both men demonstrated their support for another former CIA officer, William F. Buckley, as Buckley celebrated the anniversary of his television show at the New York Yacht Club.

Stansfield Turner

STANSFIELD TURNER, THE FORMER DIRECTOR OF THE CIA, WAS THE ONE WITNESS who was going to establish beyond cavil that the Marchetti article was a fabrication, according to Bill Snyder, Hunt's lead counsel. The former admiral, who prefers to be addressed with that title, consented to be questioned on the condition that the deposition be conducted at his home.

When Brent Whitmore and I drove up to a dwelling in the upscale Washington suburb of McLean, Virginia, we looked for Snyder's little sports car with its memorable license plate, FUN CAR, to be sure we were at the right house. Instead we saw what must have been Snyder's other car, a large sedan with the license plate BIG CAR.

Turner had been replaced at the CIA more than three years earlier, yet he was represented by Lee Strickland and Page Moffett, two lawyers who declined to provide a telephone number or office address beyond, "Assistant General Counsel, Central Intelligence Agency, Washington, D.C. 20505."

We met in what would have been designated a parlor in former years; Turner on a sofa, his two attorneys poised on either side of him and almost trembling in anticipation, in the manner of high- strung Dobermans.

Turner had been appointed by Jimmy Carter, a classmate at the U.S. Naval Academy. He was director from March 1977 until January 1981. The Marchetti article was rich with allegations of CIA plans and decisions all related to Hunt and all made during that period.

If the man who directed the agency during the relevant time period disclaimed knowledge of those events, meetings, concerns and decisions about Hunt that were purportedly shaking the CIA at that time, Marchetti's article would suffer a serious, perhaps fatal blow.

Turner did not keep us in suspense very long. When asked, he said he had read the article in question. Snyder said he planned to take Turner through the piece "paragraph by paragraph" so that Turner might brand each allegation false. Turner made a suggestion:

"I would like to make a statement first that might help shorten the proceedings. I have no recollection of ever discussing E. Howard Hunt at the CIA during my four years as director of Central Intelligence. If my memory is inaccurate, a casual reference to Hunt is the most that there would have been. I can even be more categoric in stating that I know that during these four years I never had any discussion involving—and I'll insert a word here—my making a decision about E. Howard Hunt. I just want to make it clear that I have no connection with Mr. Hunt in an official capacity."

It would not have been inappropriate for Snyder, at that moment, to announce that he had no further questions. What was one to make of an article describing, in exquisite detail, CIA meetings attended by ranking officers all addressed to the traumatic question posed by the actions of E. Howard Hunt, when the director had sworn that, to his knowledge, the subject had never even been discussed?

Lawyers, due to training, temperament and financial considerations, are generally not driven by concerns for judicial economy. Snyder spent the next hour methodically reading each relevant sentence of the Marchetti article and asking Turner if the sentence was true or false.

Turner had never heard of any meeting at the CIA to discuss Hunt; "to the best of my knowledge," he testified, there was no cover-up of the Kennedy assassination "designed by the CIA; the CIA decision to "sacrifice Hunt" referred to by Marchetti had not taken place, to his knowledge; the CIA had not "moved to finger Hunt," so far as he knew; the CIA was not involved in the assassination of President Kennedy, to his knowledge; he had never heard of the "alleged internal CIA memorandum" that the Marchetti article was based upon.

By late afternoon, when the Turner-Snyder dialogue had been completed, a reasonable juror, having read the Marchetti article and having heard Turner's testimony, would be constrained to come to one of three conclusions. Either the article was false, Turner had committed perjury, or he was uncommonly ignorant regarding important events about which he should have been knowledgeable.

The first option was unacceptable from my client's viewpoint. The second would have been difficult to demonstrate. The third seemed most promising—Turner was an outsider, a latecomer to the intelligence "community" and not a member of the Hunt Club. I began my examination with questions designed to explore the limits of Turner's knowledge about the central issues in the case:

Q. Do you know of every memorandum and document which the Central Intelligence Agency made available to the House Select Committee on Assassinations?

A. No.

Q. Were there some memoranda which the House Select Committee on Assassinations secured from the CIA about which you do not have specific knowledge?

A. My answer is I don't know.

Q. Do you know where E. Howard Hunt, Jr., was on November 22, 1963?

A. No.

Since Turner had already testified that to his knowledge the CIA had never tried to hide any facts from the Warren Commission, I wanted to find out how much he actually knew about the Commission. As a preliminary question I asked Turner if he agreed that the Warren Commission "actually was called the President's Commission on the Assassination of President Kennedy, was appointed by Lyndon Johnson, and there were seven members of that commission; is that right?"

He answered, "I don't know."

Since Allen Dulles, the former director of the CIA, had been one of the members of the Warren Commission, indeed its most active member, I raised that matter indirectly:

Q. Was there anyone associated with the Central Intelligence Agency who served on that commission?

A. I don't know.

Q. Was there anyone who had been associated with the CIA who served on that commission?

A. I don't know.

Q. Do you know the name Allen Dulles?

A. Yes.

Q. Who was Allen Dulles?

A. Former director of Central Intelligence.

Q. Do you know that Allen Dulles was not only a member of the Warren Commission but the single most active member of the Warren Commission?

A. No.

At that moment an aide arrived, whispered to Turner, and the two of them left the room without a word of explanation. A few minutes later Turner returned, carrying a cordless telephone pressed against his ear. During 1984 those remote telephones with long aerials were far less common that their technological descendants are today. The instrument remained clasped to Turner's head throughout most of my cross examination of him. I suspected at first that he might be receiving assistance, but the nature of his answers soon belied that theory.

I asked Turner if the CIA, to his knowledge, had ever in its entire history violated any law of the United States. That question could have been answered in the affirmative by any casual reader of a daily newspaper or any person who had on occasion watched a television news program. One didn't need to be a student of the reports issued by the various committees of the Congress that had catalogued CIA misconduct.

Turner replied, "Yes, I think it has, possibly. I think there is a fine line as to whether it was breaking the law or not."

Q. Do you know if the Central Intelligence Agency was ever involved in a plan to cover up any of its questionable practices?

A. No.

Q. You don't.

A. No.

Perhaps Turner could provide information about CIA procedures that were in effect while he ran the ship. I asked him if the CIA maintained attendance records for its employees while he was director. He answered, "I don't know." I asked if the CIA maintained records of vacation days taken by employees. He said that he did not know. I asked if the CIA kept records regarding sick leave for employees. He assumed that there might be such records, but he did not know.

Thus we moved from the general to the specific.

Q. You said Mr. Hunt worked for the CIA; is that correct?

A. I understand that he did.

Q. In what capacity?

A. I understand he was an officer in the Directorate of Operations.

Q. Are there records which would be maintained to show where an officer in the Directorate of Operations would be on any given day?

A. I don't know that.

Q. You don't know.

A. No.

Turner testified that while he had been Director he could recall no employee of the CIA ever using a pseudonym or alias. He did not even know that any CIA employee had ever used a pseudonym or alias before he was director, although he did concede that "one reads about it in the press." I asked him if he had examined the CIA files for the period preceding his directorship. He said he had. When asked if he had ever come across any indication that any CIA employee had ever used an alias or a pseudonym, he responded, "Not to my knowledge, no."

Increasingly, I believed, Turner was becoming a witness of fragile credibility. The two CIA lawyers, having stirred about uneasily during my questioning of Turner, suddenly rose, excused themselves and escorted the witness to another room for a conference.

They returned several minutes later. Turner announced that he had decided to "amplify" his statements. This he did by repudiating his previous testimony and asserting that pseudonyms were used and false statements had been made by various CIA employees.

While Turner had stated on direct examination that he knew of no CIA effort to hide the facts from the Warren Commission, he admitted during cross-examination that he really knew almost nothing about the subject. I asked him, "If you did not even know that the former director of the CIA was one of the seven members of the Warren Commission, you have not made an in-depth study, isn't that correct, of the relationship between the CIA and the Warren Commission?"

He replied, "Oh, that is correct. I did not make an in-depth study."

Having exhausted Turner's scant knowledge of the Warren Commission's efforts, I was interested in learning of his efforts to determine Hunt's whereabouts on November 22, 1963.

I asked if he had personally searched the CIA files to discover where Hunt was that day. He said he had not. I asked if he had ever caused a search of the CIA records to be made by anyone to secure that answer. He said he had not. I asked if he had ever personally searched the CIA files for the Angleton/Helms memorandum in question. His answer was no. He also stated that he had never caused a search to be made for that document, nor had anyone requested that he make such a search for any documents relating to Hunt.

On August 21, 1978, the Associated Press reported that when Turner was asked about the Angleton/Helms memorandum he had said, We have searched, and there is no memorandum." He added, according to the wire service, that it was "always possible" that the memorandum might have been removed from the files. Turner had been in Dallas when questioned about the matter, the Associated Press had reported.

Since Turner had now stated under oath that he had neither made nor directed a search for the memorandum, the previous statement allegedly made contemporaneously was of interest. I asked him if he knew where he had been on August 21, 1978. He believed he was in Dallas at that time "making a trip to the American Bar Association." I pointed out that the AP story said he had visited Dallas to address the Veterans of Foreign Wars convention. He responded:

"I've confused the two. I thought it was the American Legion, but maybe it was the Veterans of Foreign Wars. They gave an award to the CIA, which I accepted and didn't make a speech. I just received an award for the Agency."

I asked him if he recalled telling a reporter for the wire service that "we," meaning the CIA, had searched for the memo. He said no, but added that it was entirely possible that he had made that statement. Had he told the reporter that it was possible the memorandum had been removed from all CIA files? He did not recall having said that. However, he agreed it was entirely possible he had said that as well.

As the deposition was concluding, Turner addressed me. Although Turner had been called as a witness for Hunt, had been talking with Snyder for months about his proposed testimony and had just met me for the first time less than 90 minutes before, he said, "Mr. Lane, this is an imposition on me. I shouldn't have been called in the first place. I'm not a public servant anymore."

I was confident as we left Turner's home that his testimony would not persuade the jury that the article was fallacious. In my judgment, he had displayed an almost incomprehensible lack of familiarity with relevant events.

Only by placing Turner in context was his testimony explicable. The outsider, appointed by an outsider president, was not part of the Agency's old boy network; he had been isolated from its crucial actions and even its decision-making process. He seemed to know or care little about the Kennedy assassination, and anyone seeking to cover up the agency's role in the murder hardly need involve the oblivious Stansfield Turner. Just how much transpired at the CIA without Turner's knowledge should become clearer as we learn more about the apparent efforts of the Reagan-Bush campaign to delay the release of the American hostages in Iran.

Richard Helms

IT WAS IMPORTANT FOR ME TO ATTEMPT TO COMPREHEND THE CIA'S PERCEPTION of the evidence and its approach to the case. Based upon remarks made by the attorneys for the plaintiff, the response of the former CIA officers who testified, and the attitude and objections proffered by counsel for the CIA, I concluded that the CIA, at that point, wanted the case to go away.

Since that seemed unlikely, the Agency strongly preferred that the second trial closely resemble the first and that the question of the assassination and those responsible for it be barred from the proceedings. Snyder and Dunne exuded confidence in that regard, and it appeared to me that the CIA had been persuaded that evidence about the events in Dallas during November 1963 would not find its way into the trial record.

Since the question of whether or not information about Hunt's whereabouts would be permitted at trial was not yet resolved, I was free during depositions to inquire about the matter. Though they still hoped that the judge would uphold the stipulation barring testimony about Hunt activities on November 22, Snyder and his associates attempting to prove that Hunt had not been involved in the JFK assassination by eliciting the testimony of former high-ranking officials of the CIA.

While counsel for Hunt had been hopeful, even sanguine, about Turner's testimony before it had been offered, they had wisely determined that they could not rely upon it exclusively. They had arranged in advance for the deposition of Richard M. Helms to be taken forty-eight hours after Turner was to testify. Turner's performance rendered the Helms deposition important to the plaintiff's case.

Surely counsel for Hunt, at the outset, would have preferred that Turner and Helms appear before the jury rather than have their words, taken at a deposition, be read at trial. Yet the presence of two former CIA directors in Miami would have focused media attention on the trial, and that was a circumstance the agency so avidly sought to avoid.

Thus, in this instance, the interests of Hunt and the CIA diverged. Snyder was therefore obliged to secure statements via deposition from important witnesses who adamantly refused to appear at the trial and were less than eager to testify in any public forum. They could not avoid the subpoena requiring them to testify, but they could rely in their answers upon ambiguity. In the case of Helms, the amorphous response almost invariably replaced the anticipated precise assertion.

It was a Friday afternoon in June 1984 when I met Helms in the posh downtown Washington law office where his deposition was to be taken. A plush red carpet was not unfurled. Excepting that, and the absence of a drumroll, his appearance was quite royal. He was preceded by the ubiquitous duo Moffett and Strickland. Accompanying them was a man introduced as "John Smith," presumably related to the mysterious James Smith, who had served as the "advisor-censor" for David Phillips. Moffett sought to explain:

"With me is a gentleman from the agency whose identity is protected pursuant to statute, but whose name is John Smith, obviously a fictitious name. He is here solely for the purpose of a complex matter, advising us if a question calls for classified information and solely in that capacity, and will not be stating anything for the record whatsoever. But I wanted everybody to know that."

Of course, Mr. Smith, who was not a party to the proceedings, had no right to be present at the deposition. I pointed that out:

"I object to proceeding at this time with Mr. John Smith, who apparently has refused to tell us his real name, being present unless he identifies himself. This is not Madison Square Garden. It is not a public event. This is a solemn proceeding. The record of this deposition should reveal who is present, the real names of people who are present. And I ask Mr. Smith to identify himself or to leave."

Moffett responded, raising questions of national security. I replied:

"If there is a reason why Mr. Smith feels that the security of this nation would be imperiled were we to know who he actually is, then I think the nation's security should be saved by Mr. Smith's exodus from the room at this point rather than revealing his identity. I do not believe he should be present at this proceeding unless he can identify himself."

I was as intrigued as was Hunt's counsel to question Helms, though I harbored no illusion that I would secure complete and truthful answers to my inquiries. I anticipated responses that might be revelatory in their very deceptiveness. Weighing the advantage of going forward versus seeking to halt the deposition, in view of the CIA's apparent contempt for the rules of procedure, I pressed no further for the removal of Mr. Smith. The deposition commenced.

Snyder, Moffett, and Strickland—and presumably Smith, when he whispered conspiratorially into his ear—always addressed Helms as Mr. Ambassador, Ambassador Helms, or even more obsequiously on occasion, "Mr. Ambassador, sir." A substantial portion of the early testimony was taken up by Snyder playing the role of a court sycophant, presenting accolades to Helms, who was eager to accept, evaluate and then enhance them. Counsel began:

"I am reading from a citation awarded you by the president of the United States, apparently a few months ago, that is part of the Central Intelligence Retirees Association newsletter, and I'm going to offer that as plaintiff's exhibit number one. According to the newsletter, a part of which has been introduced as plaintiff's exhibit number one, you were recently awarded the National Security Medal by the president, is that correct?"

A. That's correct.

Q. Do you remember when that was?

A. It was in October of last year, 1983. Reference to it is also in the wire services and in the *New York Times*. That's not the only reference to it.

Q. Is that the country's highest medal for work in the national security field?

A. I believe so.

Q. Were you awarded anything else in prior years for your services in the CIA?

A. I was awarded the Distinguished Intelligence Medal when I left the CIA in February 1973.

Q. Did you also receive the William J. Donovan Medal?

A. Yes, I did. I received that in, I think it was, May 1983, last year.

The CIA attorneys and operatives in the room nodded sagely and with approval as each medal and citation was commented upon. In that time capsule, as we sat in deep leather chairs around a burnished conference table, Nixon and Helms were honorable men and the CIA a responsible organization. That moment is one which no doubt continues even now and into the foreseeable future in the minds of the CIA's officers, advocates, and apologist. That room and that mind-set seemed impervious to the winds of reality. Helms was a convicted criminal who had committed perjury before a committee of the United States Senate and had been sentenced for his crimes. Richard Nixon was the only president forced to resign in order to escape impeachment. The CIA had been established as an international Murder Incorporated that had planned and carried out the murders of heads of state who held political positions at a variance with those shared by the leaders of the CIA. It had also been responsible for the Phoenix program in Southeast Asia, which comprised the most extensive mass assassination operation in the history of the United States; many thousands of village leaders, elder statesmen, and leaders of women's organizations had been selectively murdered as part of that CIA plan and action.

Helms demonstrated no reluctance to confirm the existence of the CIA awards ceremony, although details of the ritual remain a zealously guarded secret. Some years ago, a fairly high-ranking CIA officer, had, just following the cocktail hour, entertained me with an anecdote or two.

A CIA awards ceremony is a most convoluted affair, an animated oxymoron. It almost has to be. The award is generally for a clandestine activity that must remain shrouded in secrecy. A medal is meant to be worn conspicuously, to be observed and commented upon. It has no other function. The CIA attempts to combine these two mutually exclusive concepts through a new abstraction—an invisible medal.

A place is chosen with care for the awards dinner. Various exits and entrances, some shielded from public view, are a prerequisite. The chosen area is not frequented by reporters or other potentially inquisitive folks. The background of such potential guest is sanitized. The final list is thoroughly vented and contains only those with adequate security clearance.

At the appropriate moment, dinner service is halted, and a CIA officer of rank makes a speech about the heroism of the guest of honor, not infrequently a man who has never left his desk in Langley. After the usual words about honor and love of country are spoken, the medal is removed from its box and presented to the recipient.

At that moment, the CIA's obsession with secrecy makes one of its habitual excursions into the absurd. The recipient, after basking in the glow of applause and briefly fondling his award, ruefully returns it to his benefactor, who places it back in a box where it will remain in eternal storage. Given the Ivy League backgrounds of the CIA's first generation, the echoes of a fraternity or secret society ritual seem only natural.

Exhibit two, offered by counsel for Hunt, was a letter from Helms to Hunt dated May 6, 1970, upon Hunt's retirement from the CIA. The director had praised Hunt and stated that he had "every reason to feel great pride and satisfaction in your accomplishments." Thus one ex-convict was called upon to vouch for the integrity of another.

Having completed the preliminaries, Snyder turned to the question at issue in the case. He asked Helms if the CIA had "anything to do with the engineering of the killing of President John Kennedy." We all expected, I believe, a ringing denial and the assertion that the notion was absurd and not worthy of serious consideration.

Helms paused, considered the question, looked toward Mr. Smith, and then testified that "to the best of my knowledge," the CIA had not executed the president.

Snyder also asked if the CIA had made "any attempt to cover up the true identity of the killers of President Kennedy." Helms considered that query and then, speaking slowly, as if measuring each word, he said that "to the best of my knowledge," the Agency had not sought to cover up the facts.

The memorandum about which a portion of the case revolved was allegedly signed by Angleton and Helms. Snyder asked Helms if it was "reasonably possible that Mr. Angleton could have either engineered the Kennedy assassination or set the wheels in motion to cover it up or withhold information as a vest-pocket operation, that is without the knowledge of you as director or his immediate superior?" Snyder had asked three basic and important questions. Helms decided to answer two. He was silent as to whether Angleton could have covered up the facts. Helms began:

"Well, sir, I regard it as such a speculative question that I don't know how to answer it," then he added, "I don't believe it is likely that Mr. Angleton (a) would have wanted to assassinate President Kennedy, or (b) that he would have taken off from the agency and done this without anybody's being aware of it." All the former director was prepared to state on the question was that he did not *believe* that it was *likely*. Ringing denials were absent that day.

Snyder then moved to the question of the memorandum allegedly signed by Helms and Angleton regarding Hunt's role in Dallas on November 22, 1963. Surely he was entitled to an absolute assertion that the witness had neither seen nor signed such a document. Snyder put the question to Helms unambiguously. "The allegation of Mr. Marchetti, as I understand it, is that there was a memorandum, either written by you to Mr. Angleton or by Mr. Angleton to you, and either signed or initialed by one or both of you, that said in effect, 'Someday we will have to explain what Hunt was doing in Dallas on November 22, 1963.' Have you ever seen or heard of such a memorandum?"

Helms paused, sighed, and looked from Smith to his two lawyers. He then answered: "Not to the best of my knowledge."

Snyder, seeking a more definitive response from Helms that would clear the CIA from all culpability, at least according to the CIA's former director, stated that a committee of the Congress had found the CIA blameless. "And my question to you is: Is that conclusion, that the Agency was free of any blame in the arranging of the killing or the covering it up, an accurate conclusion as far as you know?"

A. This is with respect to President Kennedy's assassination?

Q. Exactly right.

A. It sounds all right to me.

I understood Snyder's plight. If the former director of the CIA could not assert that he knew the CIA was not implicated in the assassination of the president, that his former associate, Angleton, was not a murderer, and that he, Helms, had certainly not signed the memorandum, the testimony of the witness would be of doubtful value to Hunt. As a result of his frustration, I believe, Snyder lost his composure. He could not lash out at his witness or his counsel. Instead, he sought to conjure up in his witness the same sense of outrage he himself felt about Marchetti and the article. He blurted to Helms, "We are dealing with an asinine article." When I suggested that the jury would decide that question, he responded, "I remain of the opinion that the article is a fabrication almost from start to finish." Snyder also informed his witness, "I don't believe there's a shred of truth in it."

With that preface Snyder asked Helms if the article was false when it claimed that the CIA had decided to expose Hunt:

"Have you ever heard from any personnel, past or present, that the Agency had decided to sacrifice Hunt to protect its interest?"

Helms answered, "I don't recall."

Snyder told Helms that the remainder of the article described a theory that Frank Sturgis was among the assassins of President Kennedy. He then asked Helms if Sturgis had ever been an employee of the CIA, "if you are at liberty to say." That caveat indicated to me that Snyder and Helms had not previously plowed this ground. It was clear that the CIA's reluctance to proffer Helms as a deposition witness had severely circumscribed Snyder's ability to prepare for the deposition. Under those circumstances I awaited the response with great interest. Helms equivocated: "Sturgis I have heard of." Snyder, unwilling to accept the inconclusive answer, restated the question.

"Do you know if Sturgis was ever an employee of the Agency?" Helms paused, then looked directly at Snyder and said:

"To the best of my recollection, Frank Sturgis was an agent, an outside agent, a contract agent, of the Agency. He was not a staff member of the Agency."

Snyder was stunned. He moved quickly to another subject, asking a question that seemed to be of doubtful relevance. "Do you know of any conspiracy or any attempt by the Agency to pin the Kennedy killing on Lyndon Johnson or Richard Nixon?"

I did not object, since it appeared to me that Snyder was primarily seeking to distance himself from the response to the Sturgis inquiry. I expected, at last, a strong disclaimer from Helms to the notion that the CIA had schemed to falsely charge a president with murder.

Helms responded merely that he did not recall that plan.

In spite of that unexpected reply, or perhaps because of it, Snyder relentlessly continued:

"If there were such a thing, would you have been in a position to hear about it as either deputy director or director of Central Intelligence?"

Helms did little to assist the lawyer. He said that the question was speculative and I don't know how to answer it." When Snyder continued to pursue the matter with yet another inquiry, Helms said that he could not respond with "any assurance," but that if the CIA was planning to secure an indictment against a president for having murdered a predecessor, he was "relatively certain" that he would have known about it, "if it was an Agency policy."

When Snyder had exhausted his list of questions, I began to cross-examine Helms. I asked him about Sturgis and he replied that Sturgis was a contract agent for the CIA who carried out CIA actions in Florida "having to do with Cuba." Since Hunt had run that operation for the CIA, Helms had offered evidence potentially linking the two men and thus materially damaging the plaintiff's case. I confronted Helms with a statement he had made in a deposition in another case during May 1979. At that time, when asked about Sturgis, he had responded, "Who is Mr. Sturgis?" When I asked him if he had known Sturgis before 1979, he admitted that he had known Sturgis before 1979, he admitted that he had known him previously and sought to explain away his earlier testimony by stating, "I had obviously forgotten who he was." I asked Helms if he had ever, through others, directed Sturgis in an operation. He said that he was not certain, since Sturgis "might have been the instrument of carrying out something that I asked somebody else to do."

During March 1967, Jim Garrison, the district attorney of New Orleans, ordered the arrest of Clay Shaw on charges of conspiracy to murder John F. Kennedy. Garrison contended that Shaw had acted on behalf of the CIA.

The CIA did not acknowledge any relationship with Shaw, Shaw denied that he had ever been associated with the CIA, and Garrison had been unable to discover evidence linking Shaw to the agency. Later Garrison explained that given those circumstances, "I could not even introduce this possible motivation" at the trial.[1]

Two years later, during the early morning hours of March 1, 1969, the jury acquitted Shaw after a long and contentious trial. I was present in New Orleans during this period, meeting with Garrison and the members of his staff. When the trial had concluded, I learned that the laws of Louisiana did not preclude persons from interviewing former jurors. I questioned a number of those who had served at the Shaw trial. Each juror agreed that the prosecution had established that Kennedy had been killed as the result of a conspiracy. Each juror also told me that absent from the case had been any explanation of why Shaw would have been part of the plan. As one former juror put it, "Garrison had said in the newspaper and on television that Shaw was with the CIA, but at the trial he didn't offer any evidence about that. Hell, we couldn't convict because of press conferences."

In a book about the trial, Garrison later wrote:

"While the jury accepted my argument that there had been a conspiracy, it was not then aware of Shaw's role as a clandestine CIA operative. Unconvinced of his motivation, the jury acquitted him of the charges."—It would certainly have helped our case against Shaw to have been able to link him definitively with the CIA."[2]

It seems likely that the CIA took an active part in an effort to retroactively sever its relationship with Shaw as the trial appeared imminent. In an article published in True magazine during 1975, Victor Marchetti referred to the mood at the CIA during the trial:

"I used to attend, among other things, the Director's morning meeting, his morning staff meeting. This was Richard Helms at the time and he held a meeting every morning at nine, which was attended by 12 or 14

---

[1] On the Trail of Assassins, Sheridan Square Press, 1988.
[2] Ibid.

of his leading deputies plus three or four staffers—the executive assistants to the number one, two and three men in the Agency and also the Press Officer. I also used to take the minutes of this meeting."

Marchetti said that while the Shaw trial was taking place, it was the subject of discussion at the CIA staff meeting. According to Marchetti, "During the Clay Shaw trial I remember the director on several occasions asking questions like, you know, 'Are we giving them all the help they need?'"

Marchetti said that since those present had expressed their dislike for Garrison, he presumed that the "help" was being provided for Shaw's defense. When Helms asked about the matter at the meetings, the conversation deteriorated into half-sentences such as, "Is everything going all right down there?" or "Yeah, but talk with me about it after the meeting." Later Marchetti was told, he said, that Shaw had been associated with the CIA and the Agency was afraid that Garrison would "misconstrue" the meaning of that relationship.

As I sat across the table from Richard Helms, I believed that the two of us were well aware of the importance of the evidence unavailable to Garrison back in 1969. I asked, "Do you know the name Clay Shaw?"

Had I rolled an armed grenade down the polished surface of the conference table, it would not have caused a more dramatic response. The CIA lawyers froze, then quickly huddled together. Snyder talked to his associate. Helms stared at me and I at him. Finally he said softly, "Clay Shaw?" He seemed puzzled. I did not respond; since although the two words were uttered with the inflection generally reserved for a question, no question, in any genuine sense, had been asked by Helms. The frantic conferences swirled about Helms. He continued to stare at me. Finally he spoke again:

"Can you help me a little out as to who Clay Shaw was?"

Shaw had died on August 14, 1974. It was therefore quite appropriate for Helms to speak of him in the past tense even though I had not done so. Yet if he did not recollect anything about Shaw, how did he know he had died? I did not explore that matter. Instead I replied:

"Yes, I can. Clay Shaw is the person about whom you swore when you testified on May 17, 1979, in Alexandria, Virginia, in the case of E. Howard Hunt, Jr., against Alan J. Weberman et. al. And during your testimony on that occasion, you stated that Claw Shaw—I'll read the answer:

"'The only recollection I have of Clay Shaw and the Agency is that I believe that at one time as a businessman he was one of the part-time contacts of the domestic contact division, the people that talked to businessmen, professors, and so forth, and who travelled in and out of the country.'

"Do you recall making that statement under oath on May 17, 1979?"

Helms appeared to be startled that he had, five years previously, identified Shaw as a CIA contact. He then conceded that "if it says here I did make it under oath, I guess I did." He said his previous testimony did not refresh his recollection even "a bit." He added that "it simply indicates that I guess I had heard of him." He both guessed he had made the statement and that he had heard of Shaw? I pressed him for a more definitive response:

"Well, it indicates if you were telling the truth that you knew he worked for the CIA; isn't that correct?"

Helms never answered that question. His CIA counsel erupted in anger, loudly stating, "Mr. Lane, please refrain from making those insinuations." He later addressed the court reporter as well, stating, with less visible fury, "Madam Reporter, I wish to note for the record that we consider that last comment to be insulting, and that's one." I never discovered what he meant by "one." And I never knew what the attorney was complaining about, except perhaps that I was asking questions in an area he wished to proscribe.

During this colloquy Helms took out a sheet of paper. It was, so far as I could see, the only document in his possession except for copies of his citation and other awards for distinguished service to the nation. I asked him if Shaw had been a CIA contact. Helms began to study the single sheet. With that question still pending I asked Helms, indicating the document he was reading, "Do you have the testimony in front of you?" He said that he did. He then read aloud from the answer about Shaw that he had given during 1979, in which he had sworn that Shaw was a CIA contact of the Domestic Contact Division.

I was astonished. Helms had, while under oath, told me but a few minutes ago that he needed help from me to remind him who Shaw was, yet apparently he had had a copy of the relevant page of his 1979 deposition with him. I inquired, "Now, where did you get that document that you just read from?" He responded only, "I beg your pardon?" I repeated the question. Helms remained silent. One of his two CIA lawyers spoke instead. Strickland said, "His counsel provided it for the ambassador's perusal."

Since in my view the credibility of the witness was no longer a matter seriously in contention, I moved to another, although related, area. I asked Helms if he knew the name Jim Garrison. I had assured myself that no response Helms might make at that point could surprise me. His response demonstrated that I was in error. He asked me, "Is this the Garrison who was at one time the mayor of New Orleans?"

I set forth the facts for Helms. I then asked him if he knew that Shaw was a defendant in a trial in New Orleans in which District Attorney Garrison had charged him with the crime of conspiracy to assassinate President Kennedy. His answer was vintage Helms, as I was beginning to comprehend it.

"Now that you link Clay Shaw and Jim Garrison, I do recall that there was a lot of—there were newspaper stories many years ago about allegations of some sort. The specific one that you mention I don't recall."

I asked Helms if he recalled that at the time Shaw had been very publicly insisting that he had never been in contact with the CIA. Helms responded, "Well, it may have been widely publicized at the time, but I don't recall it."

Helms had previously testified that he would never advocate a policy of withholding information concerning President Kennedy's assassination from any constituted authority. I asked him if he had informed the district attorney's office in New Orleans that Shaw had been associated with the CIA. He said, "I don't remember." I also asked Helms if the CIA did anything at all to assist Shaw during his trial. He said that he did not remember. Did the CIA assist Shaw's lawyer? Helms testified that he did not know.

I asked the witness about the CIA's briefing of the Warren Commission regarding allegations that Oswald had been in Mexico City:

"Did the Central Intelligence Agency inform Earl Warren, the chairman of the President's Commission on the Assassination of President Kennedy, that Oswald had been in Mexico from September 26 to October 3, 1963, and he spent most of that time in Mexico City?"

While I had inquired about Oswald, Helms was apparently focusing on Hunt. He answered:

"Well, I don't know. You have some very specific dates in there, and my memory doesn't go to recalling dates like that. I do recall having submitted information that indicated that Hunt was in Mexico City before the assassination."

Thereafter, each time I asked about the role of the CIA as it related to the legend that Oswald had been in Mexico City, the CIA counsel directed Helms not to answer the query on the grounds that "any answer could lead to the discovery or not of classified information."

All that Helms was permitted to disclose were facts regarding the general responsibilities he had undertaken on behalf of the Warren Commission. He testified:

"My role at the time was to take leads from the Warren Commission or areas of investigation or inquiries which applied overseas, in other words, outside the United States, and attempt to run down these inquiries as best we could and reply to the commission in response to the inquiries. That was the relationship that I had with the commission."

I asked a question about the memorandum that the witness and Angleton had allegedly signed, according to Marchetti's sources and Trento. Helms interrupted me to ask a question. He said, "I'd like to ask a question, if I may. Did the House Assassinations Committee ever produce the memorandum?" He spoke with obvious sincerity.

Here was a conundrum with which to reckon. If Helms knew that there had never been such a memorandum and that he had never signed off on any document asserting that Hunt may have been implicated in the Kennedy assassination, why was he asking me about the production of the memorandum? Of course, Helms had not denied the existence of the memorandum; he had merely testified that he did not recall seeing it.

Had Helms participated in a series of telephone conversations with Hunt? He said he "may have" and that he did not recall.

Did he tape record his telephone conversations, I asked him. He said that he had done so. He could not now produce those recordings, he said. He then testified that he had "destroyed" the tapes, including recordings of conversations with Hunt, if he had had such conversations.

Two former directors of the Central Intelligence Agency had testified at the request of E. Howard Hunt, including one of the signatories to a memo Hunt insisted did not exist. In my view, neither Admiral Turner nor Ambassador Helms had offered a single sentence that could provide any solace to the plaintiff.

Book V

The Issue Is Joined

Defamation

BEFORE EXAMINING THE DETAILS OF A DEFAMATION CASE, EXPOSURE TO THE rudimentary elements of the prevailing law might prove useful. An objective analysis of the law is difficult to come by; most experts who publish law review articles on the subject tend to favor the abolition of defamation law or at the very least such a drastic curtailment of the process that no potential plaintiff may likely prevail. The relevant literature is filled with testimony by experts and advocates from myriad seemingly dissimilar perspectives, legislative history, speeches by judges and of course, most important of all, the decisions of the United States Supreme Court.

Remarkably enough, the powerful law firms with branches in many cities, all meticulously set forth on their high rag-content letterhead, that invariably appear as counsel to such media giants as the Los Angeles Times, CBS, and NBC and its parent company General Electric share the same point of view as witnesses who testify before the Judiciary Committee of the United States House of Representatives on behalf of the ACLU. To each of them, to all of them, defamation law is an anathema. The ACLU brandishes the First Amendment; those who make a very substantial living from the manipulation and sale of sports, entertainment, and news cower behind it. Thus, having demonstrated my own detachment, we begin to turn to the subject of defamation. First, the *law*.

In a high school civics class given long ago, I memorized a lesson as to how an idea becomes a law. If a similar educational experience has been imposed on you, it might be useful to exorcise it from your consciousness. When I served as a member of the New York state legislature and before that as an executive assistant to a United States Congressman, I saw the actual process of lawmaking in operation. Long before then I had begun to suspect that the civics teacher had it all wrong.

In a capitalist society, laws are enacted for the most part to serve the interests of that class which prevails. Therefore, the laws enacted by city, state, and national legislative bodies generally favor and advance business interests. For example, in a rural area where farm business dominates, if a motorist strikes a cow on the highway, the law may presume negligence by the driver. Lengthy and pretentious law review articles will contend that the cow, after all was walking at a normal pace, the automobile, driven by a thinking human being, was projected at many times that speed and should have slowed, swerved, or stopped. This logic, which may fill thousands of pages of legislative history, seems impeccable. Judgment for the cow.

In a more urban setting, in an industrial state where busy executives must hurry to and fro to accomplish their important missions, the same motorist striking the same ubiquitous bovine is presumed to be a victim of the cow's lack of comprehension and discretion. Judgment for the driver.

The metamorphosis of libel law in the United States is a microcosm of the development of our nation—from early revolutionary commitment, a zeal to oppose and denounce royalty and tyranny, to abject surrender to business interests even when those concerns are inapposite to the interests of the nation.

In England during the 18th century, it was well-settled law that evidence of the truth of the statement was not a defense to the charge of libel. No defendant in a criminal libel case could even offer evidence that his statement was truthful. A great legal thinker of the time, Lord Mansfield, authored the maxim, "The greater the truth, the greater the libel." His statement was premised upon the belief that a truthful publication would be more likely to gain public acceptance than a false allegation, which might be vulnerable to proof of its untruthfulness. While the reasoning seems sound enough, the conclusion that flows from it represents a manifest and perhaps terminal blow to free speech and free inquiry. Robert Burns, a poet given to free thought, immortalized the pompous lord in "The Reproof":

> Dost not know that old Mansfield
> Who writes like the Bible
> Says the more 'tis the truth, sir,
> The more 'tis a libel?

While Mansfield was hardly an advocate of what we now know as First Amendment rights, neither was he much of an innovator. At the start of the 17th century, the Court of the Star Chamber in the case of *De Libellis Famosus* asserted without equivocation that "It is not material whether the libel be true or false." That rule also applied in the thirteen colonies, and even after 1776 the English rule was adopted in various states.

It was finally tested, indeed confronted, when Andrew Hamilton defended John Peter Zenger in New York during August 1735. Since November 1733, Zenger had been publishing the *Weekly Journal*, in which he strongly criticized William Cosby, the Colonial Governor of New York. Cosby ordered Zenger arrested and charged with Seditious Libel for having published comments deemed to be offensive to the Crown. Zenger remained in prison for almost a year before his case came to trial. From his cell he continued to publish the *Weekly Journal*. From their barracks soldiers of the Crown continued to burn it.

At the trial Chief Justice de Lancey instructed the jury that the truth was no defense to the serious charge lodged against Zenger. Truth, as we have seen, was believed by the Crown to be more potentially incendiary and therefore more grievous an offense than mere falsehood. Hamilton had another view. Only with difficulty may one encounter a more stirring and eloquent plea for truth and liberty than in Hamilton's argument to the jury. Hamilton was rewarded as no other lawyer in a criminal case has been since. The jury understood his plea for license to speak the truth and motivated by their hopes and dreams, not bound by their fears and doubts, they found Zenger innocent of the charges. In spite of the strict injunction of the Court and the Law the jury established freedom of the press and speech in the Colonies. Zenger continued to publish.

Hamilton's argument that men must be given the right to speak and publish the truth proved to be so powerful and pervasive that it was reprinted and widely published throughout the colonies as well as in England.

Later, on December 15, 1791, Hamilton's words led to the promulgation of the First Amendment as part of the new nation's Bill of Rights. Legal scholars agree that the First Amendment was written for the purpose of eliminating forever the common law of sedition and to make further prosecution for criticism of the government forever impossible in the United States. During the four months required to draft the Constitution, concerns for states' rights were expressed by some. Others voiced the fear that the listing of certain basic rights might be counterproductive, since the inadvertent omission of any right might later be construed as evidence that the nation's founders did not wish to ensure such right. Patrick Henry, who urged Virginia not to ratify the Constitution until the basic rights were added to it, was joined by Thomas Jefferson and others and the proposed first twelve amendments were considered. Ten survived the process, the most important being the First. James Madison drafted it as a commitment that the people:

> "shall not be deprived or abridged of their right to speak, write, or to publish their sentiments; and the freedom of the press, as one of the great bulwarks of liberty, shall be inviolable."

It emerged as:

> "Congress shall make no law respecting the establishment of religion, or prohibiting the free exercise thereof; or abridging the freedom of speech or of the press or the right of the people peaceably to assemble, and to petition the government for a redress of grievances."

The question seemed at last to have been settled.

However, international events—a treaty with Great Britain, which angered France, then at war with England, and resulted in American ships being commandeered by the French—had impact domestically. The Federalists enacted the Alien and Sedition Act, which read:

> That if any person shall write, print, utter, or publish, or shall cause or procure to be written, printed, or uttered or published, or shall knowingly and willingly assist or aid in writing, printing, uttering or publishing any false, scandalous and malicious writing or writings against the United States, or either house of the Congress of the United States, or the President of the United States, with intent to defame the said Government, or either house of the said Congress, or the said President, or to bring them, or to excited against them ... the hatred of the good people of the United States ... [that person] shall be punished by a fine not exceeding $2,000 and by imprisonment not exceeding two years.

It was anticipated by its supporters that the Alien and Sedition Act could be employed against supporters of the French in the United States. Thomas Jefferson and the members of his party, confronted by the extreme scope of the act, were driven to originate a broad theory of freedom of expression so that the concept of seditious libel was directly repudiated.

Although the Alien and Sedition Act appeared to contravene the First Amendment, convenient legal scholars, as available then as now, were found who could nicely reconcile the two.

Ten persons were convicted under the act. When Jefferson was elected president he pardoned those who were still imprisoned and Congress subsequently voted restitution of the fines. The Supreme Court did not hear arguments as to the act's constitutionality; theoretically, therefore, the issue was never resolved.

As the case of Zenger had initiated the debate, it appeared that another New York case, this one involving Harry Croswell, editor of a newspaper called *The Wasp*, might end it. In 1804, charged with being a "malicious and seditious man" for having vilified Jefferson, Washington, and others, Croswell sought to prove that his accusations were truthful.

Old and venerated concepts die hard, however, and the chief justice of the state court wrote in response that "*Truth* may be as dangerous to society as falsehood" and that *truth* may be destructive to government. Thus he upheld the ruling of the trial judge that the truth of the printed declaration was irrelevant. On appeal Alexander Hamilton became counsel for the defendant. In an eloquent plea for respect for the sanctity of the truth, reminiscent of the impassioned oratory offered by Andrew Hamilton 70 years before, Alexander Hamilton argued that liberty of the press "consisted of publishing with impunity, *truth* with good motives and for justifiable ends, whether it related to men or to measures." Hamilton also argued that the question of truth and of intent must be decided by a jury rather than a judge. Hamilton feared, he said, that a judge might be swayed by allegiance to the government.

While Croswell was ultimately convicted and an order for a new trial never carried out (likely because Hamilton was killed by Aaron Burr in a duel soon after the argument), Hamilton's twin concepts—that truth is the absolute test in a libel case and that the jury, not the judge, must make the relevant determinations, became the basic law of libel in the United States.

After a long and difficult path, by the first quarter of the nineteenth century truth and the jury system were vindicated and a sensible and fair test of defamation had evolved. Elected officials, governmental institutions, large financial interests and all others could be tested, questioned, even vilified, so long as the allegations were truthful. The truth speaker was immune from prosecution and insured against a successful lawsuit. The test was a simple one; had the litigant spoken or written the truth? The method for determining whether the allegations were truthful was equally straight-forward; a jury would hear the facts and decide. These standards survived and served the nation with honor for more than a century.

During the last quarter of a century jury trials in defamation cases have become rare, almost extinct, and the matter of truth again made irrelevant. The courts have so effectively legislated in the area that the people's right to speak and write the truth, and its corollary, the right to have the truth spoken and written about them, has been taken from them. The United States Supreme Court has returned to the concepts—the judge, not the jury, decides, and truth is irrelevant—favored by the Crown and imposed on the Colonies.

A recent law review study disclosed that media defendants in defamation cases have been successful in having the judge dismiss cases against them before trial in seventy-five percent of the cases. When the cases do go to trial, the media defendants have lost eighty-five percent of the time. Thus the disparity between the actions of the judge, with allegiance to the power structure, and the actions of the jurors, who are non-aligned, is readily discernible. However, after the jurors found for the plaintiff in those relatively few instances where the case was presented to them, the judges granted judgments notwithstanding the verdict to the media corporations in twenty percent of the cases. That is, the judge has over-ruled the jury's conclusions and found for the defendant—thus abrogating the jury trial.

In virtually all cases where the media defendant has lost it has filed an appeal. A notable and perhaps unique exception was Handelman against Hustler Magazine, in which the judgment was for but one dollar. In two-thirds of those few cases submitted to them, the appellate courts have found for the media defendant and the plaintiff has lost his judgment, often after years of litigation costing him tens or hundreds of thousands of dollars. In only six percent of all cases where plaintiffs sue media businesses for defamation do they get to keep at least part of an award. Almost all of those judgments are small dollar awards and some have been reduced still further by the trial or appellate courts.

The case that began the abolition of truth as the relevant standard was *New York Times v. Sullivan*. It also ushered in the era of federal involvement in defamation law. There is an ancient saying at the law—"hard cases make bad law." No better example may be found than in the *New York Times* case. Until 1964, for nearly 200 years the States had exercised exclusive domain over libel law based upon the theory that the First

Amendment did not protect false and defamatory speech. As we have seen, that amendment and the cases preceding and following it had in common the determination that truthful speech should in no fashion be prohibited.

It was a time of confrontation and change in the United States. Civil rights demonstrations, often led by Dr. Martin Luther King, Jr., were taking place across the South. On March 29, 1960 a full-page advertisement was published in *The New York Times*. It was signed by sixty-four persons of prominence and it listed grievances against the defenders of segregation in Montgomery, Alabama, including the police. Several of the allegations contained in the advertisement were false. L.B. Sullivan filed a lawsuit against *The New York Times* and others associated with the advertisement. Since he was not mentioned in the advertisement, his case appeared to have little merit. Sullivan, one of Montgomery's three commissioners, contended that false statements about the city police defamed him, since he had supervisory power over them.

For the most part, Montgomery's white residents were neither admirers of Dr. King and his movement nor of the big Eastern newspaper. A representative jury awarded Sullivan $500,000 and the Alabama Supreme Court, with views not radically dissimilar from the residents of Montgomery, upheld the verdict and the award. While the *Times* could afford, but not happily, the half million dollars, its very existence was threatened by the subsequent $2,500,000 lawsuit brought against it by the other two city commissioners and the Governor of Alabama and an unlimited potential of additional similar lawsuits.

The Sullivan case reached the United States Supreme Court in 1964. It was a civil suit between private parties and no federal issue or law was involved. The tradition and precedent regarding defamation law was until that moment in opposition to federal intervention. Yet a major business institution was in jeopardy.

A unanimous Supreme Court decision struck down Sullivan's attempt to collect from the *Times* for having published false statements.

In doing so, the Court had offered the First Amendment, for the first time, as a safe harbor for *false* statements. The Court fashioned a new formula, impelled by its desire to save the Times and its duty to offer at least lip service to precedent. *Actual malice* must now be present for a public figure to bring a lawsuit. Yet *actual malice* as defined by the Court is neither. A public official may succeed only if he shows that the false statement was made with knowledge that it was false or with reckless disregard of whether it was false or not.

In time the courts expanded the protection to those who lied not only about public officials but any "public figure," who, as it turned out were, by and large, merely plain folks who commented upon any question that might be in controversy. This was all done under the banner of increasing the ability of the establishment media to participate freely in public inquiries without fear of being hampered by lawsuits brought by those destroyed in the process. This odd concept has been championed by the American Civil Liberties Union, which fears that without it, independent journalists will be made excessively cautious, the press will be chilled and the public denied the facts.

Recent disclosures made possible under the Freedom of Information Act have revealed how U.S. intelligence agencies, particularly but not exclusively the CIA and the FBI, have utilized a willing and eager establishment media including, ironically, the *New York Times*, to plant false and defamatory stories about those they wished to discredit. Invariably, those targeted for such treatment are seeking to uncover some matter of public interest which the government wishes to suppress. When the target discovers the underlying facts and seeks to clear his name and be made whole for the losses he has suffered through the lawful process of filing a defamation suit, he discovers that in the name of free and uninhibited inquiry defamation suits have been all but abolished. He may not clear his name; the courts will strike down his efforts in most cases. He risks even greater financial loss should he seek to be compensated for what has been taken from him.

Law firms, propagandists and law review contributors for conglomerates in the media business are now circling sharklike, seeking to find and destroy the last vestige of procedural rights left to those who their masters defame. Do I exaggerate?

Let us examine the case of *Herbert v. Lando*. Colonel Anthony Herbert witnessed war crimes and atrocities while in Vietnam. He reported those excesses to the proper authorities. Subsequently he was relieved of his duties in Vietnam and the U.S. Army placed a poor efficiency report in his military record. CBS, through its continuing reports by Walter Cronkite, was at that time a major supporter of the war, which it chronicled inaccurately, deceptively and inhumanly, the stentorian voice proudly read off an enemy body count that later turned out to be mostly a tally of dead farmers, children, and old people.

CBS was not pleased when Col. Herbert demeaned the war, admittedly a dirty little one, but the only one going at the time. "Sixty Minutes" aired an attack on Herbert entitled "The Selling of Colonel Herbert." Barry Lando produced and Mike Wallace narrated the diatribe. Lando then published an article in *Atlantic Monthly* based upon information that had been gathered for the show.

Herbert filed a defamation action against Lando, Wallace, CBS, and *Atlantic Monthly* for damages to his reputation, asserting that "the program and the article maliciously portrayed him as a liar, one who had committed acts of brutality and atrocities in Viet Nam and an opportunist seeking to use the war crimes issue to cover his own alleged failure in the Army."

He was considered to be a public figure for defamation purposes and thus was required to examine the thought processes of the defendants inorder to establish that they knew what they said was false or that they had recklessly disregarded the truth. Proving that the statements were false, even outrageous, and that he had been caused to suffer financial and emotional loss was not enough to satisfy the newly developed standards. Herbert's lawyer asked Lando a number of questions relating to his intent and conclusions in preparing the false and defamatory program. Lando refused to answer; he sought both to designate Herbert as a public figure and thus require him to probe Lando's state of mind and then to refuse to answer questions about that state of mind.

When the United States Supreme Court in a six to three decision asserted that logic required Lando to answer the few questions, the media erupted in fury. Reflective of that anger was the sanguinary lead editorial in the *Los Angeles Times* condemning the Supreme Court, entitled "Blood on the First Amendment."

It has become scoundrel time in the executive suites that control what Americans see and hear about the world and their fellow citizens. The chilling effect apparently not contemplated by the courts, has been felt by those who wished to dissent, to protest, to uncover unpleasant facts and to probe into those areas which the government wishes to keep secret. They do so now, as in the past, at their own peril. However, they do so now knowing for the first time that if a segment of the media acting on its own or on behalf of a government agency wishes to publish false and discrediting allegations about them, they will likely never have their day in court to respond.

The courts, bowing to the industrialists who control the newspapers, television and radio networks and stations, have converted the First Amendment from a refuge for the truth speaker into a refuge for the liar.

The case of *Hunt v. Liberty Lobby* is an anachronism; a dinosaur living in another age.When I entered the case it was clear that Hunt was a public figure, indeed a former high-ranking officer at the CIA. I did not, however, seek dismissal of the complaint solely on the grounds of *actual malice.* My client and I were both willing to submit the case to impartial jurors and to have the truth of the matter determined by them. That is, I believe, how it should be in all such cases.

The law permits a defendant in a civil or criminal case to offer alternate, indeed, contradictory theories of defense. Thus a defendant may offer evidence which asserts that he was in Chicago, when the assault took place in San Diego, and that he had acted only in the interest of self defense.

Quite naturally, the defendant risks loss of faith with the jury in such a matter. Some attorneys made a routine practice of proffering inconsistent concepts to the jury in the hope that at least one will be accepted by them. I abjure that notion. I believe that it is essential for the attorney to develop a bond with the jury and to make every reasonable effort not to harm that necessarily fragile one-sided relationship. The jurors watch and listen. They do not participate except through body language, a nod of agreement or encouragement, a look of disbelief or disdain and an occasional laugh which often is open to interpretation. Providing inconsistent explanations for one event does have the advantage that a responsive chord may be struck that might otherwise be ignored. The disadvantage, however, is insurmountable in my view; the lawyer has informed the jurors that he does not know what really happened and that it is up to them to sort it all out.

In the Hunt case, it would have been irresponsible to waive any defense available to my client, including absence of malice, since its corporate future was to be decided. But that future rested, I believed, upon my ability to demonstrate that the article was truthful and, in fact, understated, except as to its predictions which were, in any event, non-actionable.

The primary defense was truth. When the case was submitted to the jury, a verdict would be rendered based upon my ability to demonstrate that the Central Intelligence Agency, with the assistance of Hunt, among others, had assassinated President Kennedy. Comments by the jurors, after they had rendered their unanimous verdict, disclosed that the issue they decided was the matter of whether the allegations were true, not whether actual malice was present.

Thus, with both parties committed to the presentation of evidence that would test, for the first time in a trial, the claim that the CIA had murdered the president, we settled into a rare, old-fashioned defamation trial.

The Trial

SINCE THE ORIGINS OF SAXON AND OLD ENGLISH LAW, THERE HAVE BEEN CERtain refinements in the authorized process for securing the truth. The most ancient species of trial was "judicium Dei"—judgment of God, the prevalent theory being that at the propitious moment supernatural intervention would prevent the innocent person, the one who had spoken the truth, from suffering physical harm. The learned jurist, as respected then by the populace as are their black-robed successors today, would preside over an ordeal designed to catch God's attention, hopefully in a timely fashion.

The class structure of society required, of course, separate tests for the ruling elite and for working folk. In this respect there has been little change over the centuries. To the casual and distant observer, however, the two tests seem to have celebrated a distinction without a difference. The lords and ladies and their entourage, indeed all those of higher rank, were required to submit to an ordeal by fire. This method required the defendant to take up in his hand a piece of red-hot iron weighing one, two or three pounds, depending upon the exquisite exercise of judicial discretion, and to emerge from the experience unscathed. Or the judges might decree that the suspect walk, while blindfolded, over nine red-hot plowshares placed lengthwise at irregular intervals.

The water ordeal was utilized for the those who were not of the propertied class and devoid as well of political connections. During plowing season, presumably, the standards were flexible enough to accommodate the demands of a burgeoning agricultural economy. The presumed miscreant was obliged either to plunge his arm up to the elbow into boiling water and escape from the experience unhurt or to be cast into a river or pond. If he sank to the bottom, he was acquitted, one suspects posthumously. If he floated without participating in any action that might be deemed voluntary, he was guilty.

The modern methodology usually requires a trial by a jury of one's peers. This process is not without tribulations of its own sort. The defendant in either a civil or criminal case is rarely pleased about the events which are to unfold. The plaintiffs in civil cases, and the prosecutors in criminal cases, have brought the moment about. Yet they too experience doubts regarding the uncertain outcome that looms ahead. All of the participants, the parties, their supporters, and their lawyers, approach the day of trial with more than a modicum of apprehension. The lawyers, the only ones paid to be there of the contesting forces, being therefore professionals who have been through it before, don their first-day-of-trial countenances. The theatrics begin before the judge arrives.

It was a January day in Miami when the combatants first saw each other's full complement approaching the assigned location.

E. Howard Hunt, Jr., was flanked by his wife and two other persons who were never introduced or identified. His two lawyers, William Snyder and Kevin Dunne, were also there, leading the way. With them was a paralegal from their law firm.

Everyone was properly dressed for the occasion, but Hunt's attire was different from that sported by his associates. It was just a soupçon more modest, more worn, yet substantially this side of threadbare. If it made any fashion statement, it was, "I am not a rich man; I could use a favorable verdict and a tidy monetary award."

The Hunt phalanx had been stalled at the electronic scanner in the lobby of the courthouse, where, one by one, its members had been required to remove pocket change, keys, even belts with buckles, in order to enter. This was the courthouse for the drug capital of the nation.

The party of the defense converged upon the scanner from two directions. Brent Whitmore, the paralegal on our side; Willis Carto, the chief executive officer of Liberty Lobby, Inc., the defendant corporation; Victor Marchetti, and I walked into the lobby together from one entrance, while Fleming Lee, the corporation's general counsel, arrived from another entrance a bit later with his wife due to a previous breakfast commitment. We too were dressed for the occasion, all in suits of dark hues, the men with conservative ties. The plaintiff and his entourage reached the elevator as we began to divest ourselves of metallic objects.

Several minutes later the first real encounter took place. As we entered the modern courtroom, staggering under the burden of the huge leather carrying cases containing the weapons with which we would soon do battle, the lawyers, affecting an air of bravado, greeted each other with a pretense of joviality and warmth. Each team seemed to exude confidence and poise. In reality, nobody was fooling anybody, but certain time-honored rituals must be observed. It is what makes us professionals and sets us apart from our clients, who are unable to disguise that they have entered a terminal stage of worry and anguish.

The introductions were made. Hunt nodded, his wife looked away, Carto returned the nod, Brent offered her hand as did all of the lawyers. Marchetti walked around the courtroom as if inspecting it for cameras or hidden listening devices.

It became a courtroom when the bailiff warned us, with a half-shouted proclamation, that the judge was to make an entrance immediately and that we were all required to stand in anticipation of that event. We did. He did. And we were under way.

Judge James W. Kehoe was all business. He gave the decided impression that he expected the parties to work long hours to complete the case in an appropriate length of time and that he was not pleased to be there. He was more than content to preside in his courtroom; he was not happy that he was required to try this case again. He later explained to counsel in a conference at the bench:

"For me, trying a case the second time around is like going to the theatre to see a movie twice—a movie you didn't even want to see the first time."

The message was received by counsel. Unnecessary delays were to be avoided. In spite of the concerns I expressed that first day about the possibility of a truncated trial, in retrospect it is clear that Judge Kehoe was fair, patient, and knowledgeable as to the relevant law. He gave the parties not only the adequate trial mandated by the appellate courts—which constantly remind the appellants that they are not entitled to a perfect trial, only a fair one—but as close to a perfect trial as I have experienced now in forty years of practice. The highest praise I can bestow upon a judge, in addition to concluding that he had made no substantial errors as to law, is that after the trial I could not discern which side he had himself favored. The jurors judge the facts. The judge applies the law. The dichotomy could not be more clearly established. Yet the judge, being human, reaches conclusions as well. It is important that he not communicate those judgments to the jurors. In most cases the bias of the court is readily apparent to counsel, and in many cases the judge is not unwilling to indicate his feelings to the jury in one subtle form or another.

When the Hunt case concluded and we took our leave of Judge Kehoe for the last time, I was still unable to discover his personal feelings about the merits of the lawsuit he had tried. Bravo, Judge Kehoe.

The first matter on the agenda for the court was the question of the stipulation that had been entered into at the first trial. In the event that the judge ruled against us, I had a fallback position that might prove serviceable. Nevertheless, this ruling might prove decisive; it could determine whether there would be a trial on the merits or merely a replay of the first contest.

At the first trial Liberty Lobby's lawyer had agreed that Hunt had not been in Dallas on November 22, 1963, and the court had read the stipulation to that effect to the jury. It was Hunt's contention that the stipulation extended to any subsequent proceeding and that the defendants were obliged to honor it at the present trial. I had, many months before, sent a letter to the plaintiff's attorneys stating that the stipulation was no longer binding and asserting that at trial our primary defense would focus on Hunt's role in the assassination, including his presence in Dallas at the decisive time. Snyder and Dunne had filed motions designed to prevent the defendants from offering a defense at the second trial that was different from the one that had failed at the first trial.

I understood their position. They hoped that the first trial would prove to be merely a rehearsal for the present encounter and that this time around the rewards might be even greater. I wanted to prove to the satisfaction of an impartial jury that the CIA had murdered President Kennedy.

Realizing that the judge had a calendar with waiting cases, the attorneys for Hunt stressed not only the law, which they said favored their position, but the hideous practical results of permitting us to try the case as we wished. Permitting the question of the CIA's alleged participation in the murder of President Kennedy would result in a complex, lengthy, and time-consuming exercise. The judge considered the suggestions.

If there is one constant point of contention between attorneys and judges, it is the pace of the trial. Many trial lawyers are strangers to the concept of persuasion through understatement and tact; they tend to overtry the case. Juries are more often alienated by redundant evidence than bemused by omission of necessary data. I routinely seek to acquaint the court at the outset, generally in response to questions as to the estimated length of the trial, with my philosophy of trial. The most serious offense is to bore the jurors; they will not forgive the trial lawyer and can respond in a punitive fashion only against the client. It really is, in my view, a question of respect. Having made a point adequately the matter will be pursued, presented again and dwelled upon only by an attorney who is so insecure that he fears the jurors were unable to comprehend the issue and his view of it. If jurors are treated as if they are intelligent and interested beings, not blank slates with names, they invariably respond at a sufficiently high level.

Since Judge Kehoe suspected that I did not intend to dally with the case, Hunt's argument as to time consumption lost much of its sting.

Hunt's motion to preclude my client from withdrawing the stipulation entered into at the first trial had been pending since June 1984. It had been filed almost on the eve of the originally scheduled date for the second trial. It was considered by the court during oral argument seven months later. The long delay was occasioned by a problem I had encountered just before the scheduled trial date. On July 12, 1984, I underwent emergency open-heart surgery at the George Washington University Hospital in Washington, D.C. It was a quintuple bypass operation performed by Dr. Benjamin Aarons, the same skilled surgeon who had saved President Reagan's life by removing the bullet fired by would-be assassin John Hinckley. The court was notified of my illness and immediately removed the case from the trial calendar. Two months later I notified the court that I was ready for trial. The surgery, from which I quickly recovered, had saved my life, although since it did not address itself to the causes of the illness, it provided only temporary relief. I was able to complete the trial and then undertake the arduous posttrial work of appeals, depositions, and argument as the result of chelation therapy, an alternative medical approach administered by Dr. E.W. McDonagh in Kansas City, Missouri. His revolutionary and cautious work actually cured me of my longstanding illness, as it had thousands of others.

On the opening day of trial, Judge Kehoe considered the question of the longevity of the stipulation. The attorneys for the plaintiff offered four basic arguments:

1. The mere fact that a case is to be retried is insufficient reason to allow a litigant to withdraw a stipulation made at the first trial. In support of that contention Hunt's attorneys offered a standard reference work, American Law Reports, which summarized the general principles that prevailed in courts in the United States:

"Where a stipulation is distinctly and formally made for the express purpose of relieving the opposing party from proving some fact or facts, or where a formal admission of facts is made by counsel and becomes a part of the record, such a stipulation or admission, provided it is not by its terms limited to a particular occasion, or a temporary object, can be introduced in evidence and is available as proof of the facts admitted upon a subsequent trial of the same action, unless the court permits its withdrawal upon proper application therefor."

2. The proposed withdrawal of the stipulation by the defendants was "too untimely to be sustained." Here Hunt's attorneys cited several cases that held that "as litigation proceeds from the pretrial phase into trial and beyond, the burden on one seeking to alter or withdraw stipulations of fact necessarily increases in order to protect the integrity of the process to date. Thus, 'if a party fails to seek relief from a stipulation until after trial has begun, that factor does not preclude relief, but it must be considered.'"

3. Neither the language of the stipulation nor the original intention of the parties suggests that the stipulation entered into at the first trial should not also be conclusive at the new trial.

4. New counsel is bound by a stipulation entered into by prior counsel.

I responded by conceding the propriety of the citation from the *American Law Reports* and the cases cited by that review, all of which held that a stipulation is considered to be binding at a subsequent trial "provided it is not by its terms limited to a particular occasion." Here, I suggested, the limitation was apparent. At the first trial, the judge had recited the stipulation to the jury, stating:

"But *for the purpose of this trial*, the defendants have acknowledged and conceded that the plaintiff in this cause was not in Dallas, Texas, on the date of the assassination of President Kennedy, which was November 22, 1963." [Emphasis added.]

A more interesting challenge was posed by the assertion that I had waited too long to attempt to withdraw the stipulation. I had made a deliberate decision soon after having been retained to wait before I filed a pleading seeking to withdraw the stipulation. An early adverse ruling at that stage would have prevented me from taking the depositions and compiling the evidence that I hoped to use at trial. I also reasoned that if my understanding of the law was correct, there was no need to make a motion. I argued that the stipulation was, on its face, self-limiting and that it had expired at the conclusion of the first trial. In order not to unfairly inconvenience my adversaries I had, at an early stage, notified them in writing that the stipulation, in my view, no longer existed. If my position was sound, there was no need to burden the court with the necessity of considering a moot point. It was for that reason that Hunt's attorneys felt constrained to file a motion. If its filing was untimely, the responsibility for the delay could not attach to my client.

I agreed that a valid and lasting stipulation, made by Liberty Lobby's previous counsel, even if entered into unwisely, would be binding upon subsequent counsel.

One of the weaknesses I perceived in Hunt's motion was that it relied for its authority upon decisions by appellate courts in other regions. The nation is organized into various geographic divisions, or judicial circuits. The United States District Court for the Southern District of Florida is governed by decisions of the Eleventh Circuit Court of Appeals, sitting in Atlanta.

The Fifth Circuit, based in New Orleans, previously had that responsibility, but that circuit was too large and burdened by an almost impossible caseload. Therefore, the new Eleventh Circuit was established and Florida assigned to it. District court judges are of necessity most responsive to rulings by the circuit court that review their rulings. For that reason, I stressed the most recent relevant decisions of the Eleventh Circuit and relied for early precedent upon its ancestor, the Fifth Circuit.

The judge did not rule at once. After the argument but before the court's decision, Carto asked me if it was likely that we would be precluded from offering evidence of Hunt's involvement in the assassination. I was sanguine about the impending adjudication, but ready to proceed with the central defense—Hunt's participation in the murder of Kennedy—even if the ruling was adverse. I told Carto that if the stipulation was to govern the trial, it was limited to preventing us from offering evidence that Hunt had been in Dallas on November 22, 1963. The other evidence that might demonstrate Hunt's involvement in the crime should not be obscured. That was, in any event, the next argument I was prepared to proffer. It was not necessary. The court ruled that the stipulation, by its language, was confined to the first trial, and, that being so, I had not been obliged to bring the matter to the court's attention by making a motion.

Various other pre-trial motions of less consequence were argued and ruled upon. In each instance, whether our position prevailed or was defeated, Judge Kehoe gave evidence of being a thoughtful arbiter who was governed only by the rule of law.

Since the parties had not waived a trial by jury in favor of permitting the judge to render the verdict, it was necessary to select a jury. I had given some thought to advocating a trial by judge alone. The numerous concerted attacks in the media over the years upon my client, alleging that Liberty Lobby, Inc., was racist and anti-Semitic, had created an atmosphere less than conducive to a fair trial.

The theory is that a judge, unlike jurors, may rise above an acrimonious sea of prejudice and render a calm and dispassionate judgment. Two arguments tend to vitiate that concept. I have met a few judges who were so biased that they would be ineligible to serve as jurors but cannot, nevertheless, be prevented from presiding over trials. In addition, I believe that the democratic nature of the jury system should be supported and preserved. I have not once waived the right to a jury. I have, on several occasions, seriously considered the possibility, but in each case declined to do so.

The panel of potential jurors arrived and filled the courtroom. They represented a true cross section of the population. Some were just old enough to cast their first vote, others had been retired for a decade or more. At least half of the candidates were women. The panel included African-Americans from Miami's ghettos, recently arrived immigrants from Cuba, white men and women, unemployed workers, members of affluent families, and corporate executives. In addition, there was an abundance of former residents of the New York area and the Northeast. These citizens were generally older white men and women who had established residence in or near Miami to spend their retirement years in a more mild and less stressful climate.

I wanted fair and impartial jurors. Therefore, in the *voir dire*[1] examination of the prospective jurors, I asked questions designed to probe a conscious or subconscious commitment to the Warren Commission Report or to any other official decree of the government in this area.

I was also constrained to discover any hostility toward my client, whether it was apparent or latent. This task was fraught with difficulty, since I did not know if the members of the panel were acquainted with the politics of Liberty Lobby, Inc., or if the judge was going to permit the introduction of evidence at trial that would expose my client's political views.

I asked questions that I hoped did not betray my concern. For example: "Do you agree that if you are chosen to serve on this jury in this case, you will set aside all nonrelevant considerations, such as the fact that the plaintiff, E. Howard Hunt, has been convicted of serious crimes

---

[1] From the French, meaning literally to speak the truth, but in practice denoting a preliminary examination of a witness or juror to determine his competency or prejudice.

or that the defendant, Liberty Lobby, Inc., being a national lobbying organization, may espouse various political positions with which you may or may not agree?"

Before the case began, I asked Carto what kind of jury he would like. He surprised me by responding, "I'd like blacks and Jews to be on the jury." When I asked for his thinking, he said, "I'm tired of being called racist and anti-Semitic. I want all the facts to come out so that a jury can rule on all of it." I suggested that those issues might better be left for another occasion since our present trial agenda, proving that Hunt and the CIA were responsible for the assassination of President Kennedy, was sufficiently complex. Later, the question of racism and anti-Semitism became factors in a case I have previously mentioned, a case that found Liberty Lobby, Inc., and William F. Buckley, Jr., as adversaries in a defamation trial in the United States District Court for the District of Columbia. The jury for that trial, at which Liberty Lobby prevailed, was composed entirely of African-American men and women.

The jury chosen to try the Hunt case was considerably more representative of the nation. One retired man from New York City, a prospective juror named Goldstein, told the court that his son was a high school teacher in Brooklyn, New York. I asked the name of the school and when he replied "Erasmus Hall," I recoiled with mock horror. I confided in him that I had graduated from James Madison High in Brooklyn and asked if he would penalize my client as a result. He laughed. We explained to the others present that the two schools were, or had been almost half a century ago, archrivals.

When the selection process was completed we had offered a jury comprised of blacks, Cubans, Jews, Southern whites, rich and poor, men and women. For a considerable period of time, Hunt's two lawyers carefully scrutinized the list and asked incisive questions. Finally, both sides certified that the jury was satisfactory to them. The two parties agreed that an impartial jury of intelligent and open-minded citizens had been chosen. The judge swore in the jurors, gave them preliminary instructions, and the trial began.

Counsel for each side made an opening statement. In essence, Snyder said that Hunt had been in Washington, D.C., on November 22, 1963, was a patriotic and loyal citizen who had served his country well, if not always wisely, and that everything in the article Marchetti had written about him was false. He said that Marchetti had even lied about the position he had held in the CIA; he was in fact little more than a "gofer," a person who does odd errands and carries his superiors' briefcases. I responded that the statements in the article that were offered as facts were true and that we would present witnesses to verify its most serious allegations.

The first witness to testify was E. Howard Hunt. His testimony might prove to be dispositive of all of the issues in the case. If the jury believed him, then the allegations published against him were untrue. He appeared to be open and frank and righteously indignant that so grave and so false an assertion might have been published against him. I studied his demeanor; it could not be faulted. If I were a film director casting the role of an aggrieved public servant, I would have hired him on the spot. He seemed sincere, but perhaps a trifle too contentious to be likable.

Snyder carefully and cleverly led Hunt through the early stages of his direct examination. The attempt was obviously to demystify the Hunt aura; to explain to the jury that this man who had been branded as a criminal by his government was, in fact, a decent, patriotic, and brave American who had served his nation at great personal risk. He was, in fact, a war hero and then some. The effort seemed to me to be entirely successful. I watched the jurors as Hunt testified. They seemed impressed, even moved, by the understated fashion in which Hunt told the story of his pre-CIA years. His entry into that organization had been wonderfully and simply presented. The jury admired Hunt. I admired the classical selection and presentation organized by Snyder, who had begun:

Q. When were you born, Mr. Hunt?

A. October 9, 1918.

Q. Where were you born?

A. In Hamburg, New York.

Q. Could you describe your educational background for us briefly?

A. I attended public school in western New York, and my father had a winter law practice down here and I spent some winters going to school in Hollywood, Fort Lauderdale, Miami Beach. But generally, the balance of the school year was up north. Eventually, in 1936, I graduated from high school, and I was fortunate enough to win a partial scholarship at Brown University in Providence, Rhode Island.

Q. Did you graduate from Brown?

A. I did. I graduated in 1940.

Q. What subjects did you major in?

A. My degree was in English literature.

Q. Did you receive any kind of recognition or awards of any sort?

A. Yes, I did. Phi Beta Kappa.

Q. All right. When you graduated from Brown, what happened then?

A. Within six weeks, I enlisted in a Naval Officers Training Program, went to sea qualified as a midshipman by the Naval Academy, and was commissioned in the Naval Academy in May of 1941.

Q. Did you see duty at sea?

A. I did. I was a destroyer gunnery officer. I was at sea on the North Atlantic convoy run to Iceland and Russia. Until the time of Pearl Harbor, I was at sea with the Atlantic Fleet. After that, I was injured at sea, hospitalized, and received an honorable medical discharge the fall of 1942.

Q. Did you reenter the war, so to speak?

A. I did by—first by means of becoming a war correspondent for *Life* magazine in the South Pacific, flying out of Guadalcanal. And down in the New Guinea fighting, I contracted malaria fever, more or less bedridden; came back to the United States, recuperated and enlisted in the Army Air Force as a private in the fall of 1944. I guess it was, 1944.

Q. Where were you at that time?

A. I was—my basic training was up in New Jersey, Fort Lee, and then I qualified for Officer Candidate School, came down here to Miami. I went through OCS and was commissioned in the spring of 1944 as a second lieutenant in the Army Air Corps.

Q. Did you serve any time in the Air Corps?

A. Yes, I did. I went up—I was sent up to the Army Air Force Intelligence School in Orlando. After a while, they made me an instructor. At that time, I was losing a lot of friends and classmates, and I wanted to get back overseas again, and I did so through the medium of the Officers Strategic Services which had sent a recruiting team to my Air Force base in Orlando.

Q. Officers Strategic Service is OSS?

A. That's the OSS, yes, sir.

Q. You joined the OSS?

A. I did.

Q. What was the nature of your activity with them?

A. Well, after training, I was sent to the Far East to the—over the hump to the China area of command, and I was part-time working behind Japanese lines. We were cutting Japanese lines of communications, sabotaging vehicles, blowing POL dumps, that sort of thing. And rescuing American fliers who were down in that area.

Q. When you speak, just for the jury's benefit, to clarify this mysterious term "intelligence," you talk about intelligence activities, what does it mean?

A. Well, the acquisition of information really. And whether it is covert or not depends upon two things: upon the classification that the original possessor of the information places on it and the means that you use or that our government uses to acquire by "covert."

Q. You use the word "covert," what do you mean by covert?"

A. I mean clandestine.

Q. What does that mean?

A. Not—our government does not own up to it. It does not admit that this is going on.

Q. It is not out in the open?

A. It is not overt. No, it is not out in the open.

Q. When did you cease working in China for OSS behind Japanese lines?

A. I was there until the bomb dropped in August of '45.

Q. You are speaking of the atomic bomb?

A. I am, yes.

Q. —over Japan?

A. After—right after the Japanese surrender, I brought my people back over the hump and in due course we were repatriated in the United States.

Q. When you say "back over the hump," what does that mean?

A. That was the Himalaya mountains between China and India. We flew over there and took a boat back to the United States and an Army transport, arriving in the port of Hoboken on Thanksgiving Day of 1945.

Q. Did you get out of the military at that point?

A. I did. I was demobilized honorably as a first lieutenant and—

Q. Discharged?

A. —discharged, yes. And at that point, I was free to take up the Guggenheim Foundation Fellowship in creative writing that I had won.

Q. What did you do with the fellowship?

A. I spent a year in Mexico doing a book that I had proposed to do when I applied for the fellowship.

Q. Did you publish that book?

A. Yes, I did.

Q. What is the name?

A. That book was called *Stranger in Town*, published by Random House.

Q. Did you then go to California?

A. I did. On my—after leaving the—at the end of the Guggenheim year, I made my way back to the States via California and stayed with a fellow OSS officer at his home. He was then actively involved in writing motion pictures, and I helped with him, got into the screenwriting business with him for a while. And then the television business began picking up on the East Coast and screenwriters were forming long unemployment lines on the West Coast, so I came east and got a job with the Marshall Plan.

Q. What was the Marshall Plan?

A. That was the plan conceived by General George C. Marshall and approved by then-President Truman, to reestablish the European economy that was destroyed or semidestroyed by the war as a means of withstanding the Soviet encroachment from the east.

Q. Was it a humanitarian gesture?

A. It was.

Q. Where were you?

A. I was press aide to Averell Harriman in Paris.

Q. What was Harriman's job with the Marshall Plan?

A. He was the European director of it.

Q. Did there come a time you were recruited to join the new Central Intelligence Agency?

A. There did. That was fall of—late part of 1948 that I was approached by a gentleman named Frank Wizner.

Q. Did the CIA exist at that time?

A. It had been signed into law by President Truman in 1947. They were still really reestablishing themselves or establishing themselves, I should say. Recruiting personnel by then, by 1949.

Q. I told the jury, Mr. Hunt, that you served in the agency from 1949 to 1970. I would like to have you recount the early part of that service from 1949 up until the Cuba project.

A. 1949, I was in headquarters. 1950, I went down—

Q. Excuse me. Where is headquarters?

A. In Washington, D.C.

Q. Okay.

A. Went down to Mexico City as chief of station, Mexico City, in 1950.

Q. What is the chief of station?

A. Head of the unit, at that time.

Q. Would it be fair to say the FBI then became responsible for security—national security within the borders of the United States and the CIA aspects outside the United States?

A. That is absolutely correct.

MR. LANE: I object to the question as leading. Many of the questions have been leading. I haven't objected but I will object now. I ask Mr. Snyder not to lead the witness.

THE COURT: Objection sustained. Don't lead the witness on a crucial matter.

The judge's ruling was correct. A leading question is one that instructs the witness how to answer or puts words into his mouth. Leading questions may not be used during direct examination, but are permitted during cross-examination. In preliminary matters it is good form for counsel to refrain from objecting to leading questions, but when the subject matter becomes germane, such allegations should be made and sustained.

Snyder had already established that Hunt was hardly a thug. He had won a scholarship, earned membership in Phi Beta Kappa, secured a Guggenheim Fellowship, was persistent and lionhearted, and was a published author. His employment with the CIA seemed to flow quite naturally from his patriotic commitment. Hunt testified that in 1950 the CIA assigned him to its Mexico City operation. Later he was given another job:

"I was assigned to what became the Guatemala project, which was the removal of the Marxist dictatorship from Guatemala. I was chief of psychological warfare in that operation."

Q. What did your duties involve?

A. Well, it largely involved morale operations for the Guatemalan population. I worked on that with a fellow named Dave Phillips, whose name may come up in this later on, preparing pamphlets and brochures, airdrops of leaflets over the area, cooperating with certain Catholic church functionaries and officials to bring the word of the real face of Communism to the Guatemalan people so that when the day came they could make an informed choice.

Q. Did the day come?

A. That day came.

Q. When was that?

A. That was in June. I believe June of 1954, if I am not mistaken. It was a near bloodless revolt. The Communists were thrown out and a temporary dictatorship took place, which was supplanted by a democratic election.

Hunt's facile description of the violent overthrow of a democratically elected government by the CIA was at variance with the facts. The jury, however, seemed impressed.

Later, when he answered a question about his family, he volunteered the information that he married "Marquise De Courtier," who was then "in the process of being divorced from the Marquis De Courtier." The jurors did not seem to me to be favorably impressed by what appeared to be an inappropriate boast about his wife's title and how she had earned it.

Hunt described in detail his leadership role in the Bay of Pigs operation

252

designed to overthrow the Cuban government. When asked the outcome of the invasion, his anger, obviously directed against President Kennedy for not providing what Hunt and his colleagues considered sufficient air support, was apparent. He said:

"The outcome was that the force landed where they were either killed or captured and the landing craft and support boats were sunk or scattered. It was a fiasco."

Q. What happened to the people who were captured?

A. Many of them were killed en route to Havana. They were put in steel trucks. They died of heat and exhaustion on the way to Havana. Those who survived were put on public trial, mock trial, so typical of the Commmunist world. And then sent to the dungeons where they spent anywhere from a year, two years, eighteen months.

Q. What happened to Manuel Artime?

A. He was one of the fortunate ones. He had a great deal of spiritual fortitude and he survived. He ate flies and cockroaches, things of that nature, to get protein enough to survive.

Later Hunt seemed unable, when asked about his initial meeting with Allen Dulles, then the director of the CIA, to disguise his enmity toward the man who had "summarily discharged" Dulles. That man was, of course, President Kennedy. Hunt added that Dulles "had been cast to the wolves," as had others in the CIA after the failure of the Bay of Pigs.

The questioning then turned to the matter at hand. His attorney asked the witness where he had been on November 22, 1963. Hunt said he had been in Washington, D.C. When asked what he had been doing that day, Hunt testified:

"That morning, I went to my office as usual. And midday, my wife drove down from our home in suburban Maryland with our two-month-old child, picked me up at the office, and we were going to have Chinese food that night, so we drove down to Eighth Street, between Eighth and Ninth, where the majority of the Chinese restaurants are located, and I sat in the car with our infant son while she went into a couple of Chinese grocery stores and made purchases. This was midday, I couldn't be exact. But I was seated in the car when the first news flash came that Mr. Kennedy had been killed, and so when my wife came back a few minutes later, I told her.

"As we pulled away from the curb, I heard that government employees were not to return to their office, that the government was closing down for the rest of the afternoon, so we drove out Connecticut Avenue for a ways and then saw Walt Kuzmuk, a colleague of mine, on the way out; veered over to Wisconsin Avenue, picked up my younger daughter Kevan who was at the Sidwell Friends School, and it was no surprise to her because some of her classmates were children of the Robert Kennedys' and Secret Service people had come to pick them up immediately, including the attorney general."

"And by the time we got to our home out just beyond the District line, my elder daughter who had been bussed in from Ursaline Academy, a girls' parochial school, and my son, who was about nine or ten then, St. John, just walked home the two or three blocks from the Brookmont Elementary School. So by two o'clock, three o'clock—three o'clock at the latest, the entire family was assembled in the house.

"Well, we stayed pinned to the television sets watching the events. The shocking redepictions of what went on, on-the-spot tales from reporters of what had happened and all the speculation. And I remember at one point, there was some thought that maybe it was going to be an invasion, the Russians were coming, or right-wing kooks had done it and so forth.

"But it was a very bad day for the entire nation, and like I suppose many other families, we spent the entire weekend at our television sets until after the services on Monday, at which time the nation began to breathe again and we with it."

The jurors looked at Hunt as he told this story, anxious to determine if he was speaking truthfully. He testified firmly and without hesitation. This speech, I concluded, had been well rehearsed, an observation that contains no innuendo. Counsel was obligated to review the expected testimony with the witness before trial and to concentrate upon the pertinent aspect of the attestation until it was molded into a form that would have the appropriate impact on the jury.

As Hunt described the moment when his family could breathe freely again, Snyder heaved a not-insubstantial sigh of relief. He exchanged glances with Dunne. The testimony had gone perfectly. I watched the scene closely, confident that we had, in all likelihood, just won the case.

In my opening statement, I had asserted that Hunt had committed perjury after his arrest in the Watergate episode. I urged the jurors to bear in mind, as he testified under oath in this case, that he had previously taken an identical oath and then proceeded to make a series of false statements. I had also made reference to Hunt's apparent effort to extort funds from the White House in payment for his silence. Snyder tried to undo the damage he thought might have been done to his client by asking his client about the matter in a rather ingenious and oblique fashion:

Q. We heard a lot in opening statements about your repeated lies. I want you to, first of all, tell us: What was the clandestine tradition if a CIA agent were captured on foreign soil?

A. Well, he is supposed to keep his mouth shut until those who are responsible for him have a chance to get away or secure their own person. That is just standard. It's the same in peace as in war. And I felt a particular responsibility to my superiors in the White House, and I felt a particular responsibility to the four Miami men that I had recruited.

Q. Was there anything in the clandestine tradition about supporting a captured agent's family or providing them with legal assistance?

A. Absolutely. And we have many records—we have many examples on the record, Gary Powers' family, for example, is maintained.

Q. Who was Gary Powers?

A. He was the U-2—

MR. LANE: I object, Your Honor, to any discussion about what takes place in a foreign country. This is Washington, D.C. [where the perjury was committed]. It is part of the United States. The total discussion is quite irrelevant.

THE COURT: Objection sustained.

Snyder then inquired about the matter directly.

Q. Mr. Hunt, what were you asked to testify to and what did you lie about?

A. In 1973, after my guilty plea, I began testifying before a wide variety of investigative bodies: the Senate, the House, the Watergate special prosecutor, the U.S. attorney, the Los Angeles County district attorney, and so forth. Basically, my position was that I did not know anything about higher-up involvement. I wanted to keep—give these people, certainly through the election period, to give Mr. Nixon an opportunity to be reelected.

Hunt's explanation, that he had committed perjury to prevent the American people from learning the truth about Nixon's role in the Watergate crimes, it seemed to me, was not appreciated by the jurors. Of the menu of explanations available to him, he may have chosen the least injurious. In my view, however, it was not a truthful answer. Hunt, I believed the evidence demonstrated, had committed perjury for financial motives.

Snyder explored that matter. Hunt testified that after Nixon had been reelected, the funds from the White House stopped flowing to him and to the other convicts. His attorney then asked a question that surprised me, for it was an inquiry that the rules of evidence would not have permitted me to make:

Q. Have you ever been accused of blackmailing the president?

255

A. Yes, I think John Dean did that on one occasion. Mr. Dean was a rather young and inexperienced fellow, and when the budgetary requirements for the maintenance of the Watergate conspirators' families came to him, he, not knowing the clandestine tradition, and being unaccustomed to large numbers, went to Mr. Nixon, as I recall it, and said, "They are blackmailing us for a million dollars." It was not a question of blackmail at all. It was simply a question of another element to having requested a budget, a maintenance budget about which perhaps Mr. Dean did not know.

John Dean had been counsel to the president of the United States. He was neither inexperienced nor ignorant of budgets with large numbers.

Hunt testified that he had been sentenced to serve a maximum of thirty-five years in prison. When Nixon refused to pay any additional sums to Hunt, in spite of Hunt's efforts to induce the president to be forthcoming at the risk of the release of incriminating information, Hunt decided to assist the prosecutors in preparing "a case against the president's top advisers," as he put it.

After Hunt testified against the president's men, his sentence was reduced to "two-and-a-half years to eight years," he asserted.

During his appearance on the witness stand Hunt had made it clear that he admired President Kennedy, shared common concerns with him, and would never seek to harm him physically or in any other fashion. He liked the man and felt an empathy for him. The suggestion that he would conspire to assassinate him was absurd.

When the direct examination was completed, Dunne, Snyder, and Hunt shook hands. They all seemed to agree that the plaintiff had been a formidable witness who had favorably impressed the jury. Lee and Whitmore, the other two members of my team, shared that belief. We all agreed that the only obvious flaw in his testimony was the expression of anger regarding the treatment of his CIA colleagues by President Kennedy. It raised questions about the extent and genuineness of his stated admiration for the late president.

Cross-examination is to direct examination as night is to day, however, and the test of Hunt as a witness was still ahead. The attributes required to be a compelling witness on direct examination are very different from the dexterity necessary to survive during cross-questioning. A well-prepared actor may be a brilliant spokesperson when presented by friendly counsel. A practiced smile of warmth at the appropriate time, eyes that fill with tears on another occasion, a straightforward look to the jury box to underscore an answer of significance can be learned and mastered through practice. Think of Ronald Reagan as a witness. One could hardly imagine anyone better able to forge a covenant with the jurors. However, if the former president were to be submitted to the probing of a skilled attorney who has mastered the facts of a complex situation and who is prepared to formulate challenging questions, one would have difficulty conjuring up a more vulnerable witness.

Manuals have been written about the art of cross-examination; this is not one of them. Perhaps one sentence will suffice. While it is useful for the attorney to think quickly during the process, even a mediocre questioner may appear to be superb if there has been adequate preparation. Due in large measure to the long hours of research that Brent Whitmore had devoted to the case, we were prepared. As I reviewed the record, I concluded that it might be possible to demonstrate that almost every relevant statement made by Hunt during his direct testimony was either questionable or false.

To the courtroom spectators, including some representatives of the press, Hunt had been a credible witness. A less casual observer might have noted his tendency to dissemble in moments of crisis. He had sought to conceal his own effort to extort funds from the White House by accusing John Dean, a practiced and deceitful young lawyer, of terminal innocence. He tried to disguise his own almost pathological hatred of John Kennedy with vague and banal phrases, not easily disprovable, regarding his respect and esteem for the office of the president—an office that he would never seek to undermine or subvert—and the allegation that the young president possessed certain admirable traits not dissimilar from his own.

I introduced myself to Hunt again and went to work. If the jurors believed that the plaintiff liked the president and had been frank with them throughout his testimony he would prevail. I sought to explore those areas.

Hunt had made it clear, both in the complaint he had prepared with his lawyers—the document that initiated the lawsuit—and in his testimony, that every statement in the article was untrue and defamatory. He had taken particular umbrage about the allegation that he had tried to blackmail the Nixon administration. Had John Dean used the right verb to describe Hunt's actions?

I knew that Hunt had made a demand for funds from the Committee to Re-Elect the President, referred to in the media as CREEP. I asked him if he had spoken with any member of that organization. He responded that he had met with "Mr. O'Brian, who was a member of the Committee to Re-Elect the President. He was assistant counsel for it." I asked Hunt if he demanded that O'Brian provide substantial sums for him. He responded, "Yes, I did." He said he could not recall how much money he had ordered CREEP to pay him on that occasion. I asked Hunt if, in essence, he had told the CREEP attorney that "I want that money. If I don't get it, I will reveal certain seamy things." He admitted that he had made that statement. He also admitted that when he testified before a federal grand jury about that confrontation with O'Brian, he had committed perjury by denying that it had taken place. The evidence revealed that Hunt had directed Nixon's committee to pay him fifty thousand dollars, and then sixty thousand, and then seventy-two thousand. If the White House did not provide the demanded funds, Hunt had threatened to expose their illegal conspiracies in other, more serious, affairs.

I showed Hunt a document he had written while he was attempting to extort money from the White House. I asked him about it.

Q. Do you recall having written, at any time, documents which contained the statement: "The Watergate bugging is only one of a number of highly illegal conspiracies engaged in by one or more of the defendants at the behest of senior White House officials. These as yet undisclosed crimes can be proved." Do you recall ever writing that?

A. I have a recollection of it. I think it was a reminder I sent to Mr. Colson, possibly.

Q. When did you send that to Mr. Colson, if you recall?

A. After the death of my wife—probably before I entered prison.

Q. Was that in reference to a request by you for sums of money?

A. Yes, definitely.

Q. Were you saying to the White House that you had information about highly illegal conspiracies engaged in by one or more of the Watergate defendants at the behest of senior White House officials and these undisclosed crimes could be proved, and they better pay you the money you asked?

A. And they were proved.

Q. Is that what you were saying, these could be proved; you had the information; they were undisclosed and they had better give you the money?

A. They had better keep their promise. That's right. My last gasp trying to keep my family intact before I went to prison.

Q. Is that blackmail?

A. No.

Hunt denied that he had engaged in blackmail; since what he had done had been established beyond cavil, the only remaining question appeared to be the definition of the relevant term.

Q. What is blackmail?

A. Blackmail is extortion, as I understand it, which is trying illegally to obtain that which is not your due. That is the operative word. All these sums described had been promised at the outset of Watergate, and the principals had fallen by the wayside, and we had—we were the ones who were left exposed and in prison.

Q. Are you an attorney?

A. No, I am not.

Q. Would you accept that it is the rule of law in this country that extortion, which, you are quite correct, is the technical and correct term for blackmail, is an effort to secure something which, whether it is due to you or not, you try to secure through extralegal methods?

A. I never heard that definition of it until now.

Q. Have you ever read any law book where the crime extortion is defined?

A. I looked it up in the Webster dictionary, in the large one, yes.

Q. How about Black's Law Dictionary?

A. No, I don't have access; Webster's.

THE COURT: I have another matter I have to take up.

[Recess taken.]

[Jury left.]

[Jury entered.]

BY MR. LANE:

Q. During the recess, I went to the library on the second floor of this building and I got from it *Webster's Third International Dictionary*, unabridged, which has 2,662 pages. Perhaps that is the one you were referring to. I have copied page 806, which has the definition of extortion. I think you said you read it in here. It is defendant's exhibit eight for identification. I ask you if you can read that and see if that is what you read in the big Webster dictionary? [pause] Have you finished reading that definition of the word extortion, to extort?

A. Extort is what I am starting to read.

Q. Tell me when you finish reading.

A. I shall. [lengthy pause] I am with you.

Q. Is that what you read?

A. Can't have been this, because the distinctive phrase I recall was something which is not once due you. That does not appear here.

Q. It does not appear?

A. It does not appear here, no.

Black's Law Dictionary, compiled by Henry Campbell Black, M.A., and published by West Publishing Co. is the standard accepted text. It defines extortion as follows:

"Extortion: The obtaining of property from another induced by wrongful use of actual or threatened force, violence, or fear, or under color of official right."

The pertinent federal statute, Title 18, United States Code, Section 871 *et seq.*, Section 1951, defines extortion:

"A person is guilty of theft by extortion if he purposely obtains property of another by threatening to: (1) inflict bodily injury on anyone or commit any criminal offenses; or (2) accuse anyone of a criminal offense; or (3) expose any secret tending to subject any person to hatred, contempt or ridicule, or to impair his credit or business repute; or (4) take or withhold action as an official, or cause an official to take or withhold action; or (5) bring about or continue a strike, boycott or other collective unofficial action, if the property is not demanded or received for the benefit of the group in whose interest the actor purports to act; or (6) testify or provide information or withhold testimony or information with respect to another's legal claim or defense; or (7) inflict any other harm which would not benefit the actor."

By any authoritative standard, Hunt had repeatedly committed the crime of extortion. He was not prosecuted for those crimes, no doubt, due to the reluctance of federal authorities who feared that the highly illegal conspiracies engineered by the administration to which Hunt had continually made reference would be exposed.

What was perplexing to me was why counsel for Hunt would allege that their client, so notorious a blackmailer, was offended and defamed when a publication observed that he had engaged in extortion.

I asked Hunt to tell us about the conspiracies that were so serious that he had expected the White House to provide, in the final analysis, hundreds of thousands of dollars to purchase his silence. He replied, "Now, I am not sure what I had in mind at the time. I was on the verge of going to prison, and my thinking was very, very disturbed at that point."

The jurors stared at Hunt. Hunt had based his entire post-Watergate behavior upon the fact that he had the proof about the highly illegal conspiracies that had been initiated by the White House. On innumerable occasions he confronted Nixon, through his counsel, Charles Colson, or through officials of his reelection committee, CREEP, to make more funds available to him or risk the consequence of disclosure. Hunt had made it perfectly clear that he had squirreled away the evidence—that he was in a position to deal a serious, perhaps fatal, blow to the administration. After Nixon was reelected, he refused to submit any longer to Hunt's extortion. He called Hunt's bluff and Hunt flinched, no doubt after considering the not inconsiderable risks to himself inherent in publicly confessing that in addition to being guilty of the crimes with which he had already been charged, he was also a self-confessed black-mailer at the highest level.

Hunt discovered what his colleagues among professional extortionists had long known: It's a difficult business replete with uncertainties. It has much in common with kidnapping, another hazardous occupation. Unlike bank robbery or insider trading, crimes that may be committed in one fell swoop, kidnapping requires a second stage of criminal exposure—the criminal has to seek to ransom the fruit of his first crime. Likewise, the blackmailer, who may have obtained his evidence through illegal means, must expose himself each time he requests payment. It is for that reason that the quality criminal shuns extortion and kidnapping as too chancy.

Perhaps the jurors could understand why Hunt had exercised discretion and had not sought to bring down the administration in a Samson-like act of revenge; after all, it hadn't worked out too well for Samson. Yet they could hardly believe that Hunt just did not remember the cataclysmic events he had in mind while he was so persistently making demands on the White House in person and in writing. Hunt looked away and shifted uncomfortably in the witness chair. I sensed that a sea change had occurred. The jurors, I believed, had decided that Hunt was telling monumental untruths.

I began another line of questioning.

Q. What is a plausible denial?

A. Denial that is believable.

Q. Is that a term of art within the CIA?

A. In the intelligence community it means a story that is plausible, it could be believed by a substantial number of people. Plausibly denying, a denial that is believable, that is credible.

Q. Do you recall testifying on June 28, 1974, in the case of *United States versus Ehrlichman*? Page 761, were you asked these questions, and did you make these answers?

> "Question. What was the reason or was any reason given, why you and Mr. Liddy couldn't perform this operation?
>
> "Answer. Because of our connection with the White House and the fact that plausible denial would have to be maintained.
>
> "Question. You said plausible denial would have to be maintained?
>
> "Answer. Yes.
>
> "Question. Would you explain what you mean by that?

"Answer. The principle of plausible denial is simply if an operation or action is later disclosed, for example, as an action by the United States government, the government can plausibly deny it, deny any involvement or connection with the action."

Do you recall those questions and answers?
A. Yes.
Q. Would you accept as a fair definition which you gave, when you testified as to what a plausible denial is?
A. Yes.

Hunt had established his *modus operandi*, the approved and premeditated methodology for CIA covert activity. It not only contemplated the necessity of lying about the operation, but it also concocted the fabrication, and the "facts" and the evidence," to support the lie, even before the commencement of the action. The jury realized, I believe, that we had entered into the big leagues of calculated prevarication. The case would never be the same.

Having established the methods employed by Hunt and his colleagues, I thought it appropriate to acquaint the jurors with their proposed victims. Hunt had implied that these questionable tactics were employed only on foreign soil, due to the CIA's specific mandate precluding activity in the United States, and that draconian measures were utilized solely against foreigners.

I never did accept the birthplace of the intended victim as a valid distinction, and, as it turned out, neither did the CIA. The press handouts containing that disinformation were designed primarily to provide comfort for the population and to allay the fears of a Congress already predisposed to self-deception. In reality, all those who seek the truth about matters of significance, whatever their nationality or residence, may be at risk from the illegal actions of the Central Intelligence Agency. It was important, I thought, for the jurors to understand that. After all, John Kennedy was an American and he was murdered in the United States.

We began with Dr. Daniel Ellsberg and Leonard Boudin. I count it as a privilege that I know both men. Dr. Ellsberg graduated *summa cum laude* from Harvard, served with the State Department in Vietnam, and was the assistant to the United States Ambassador to South Vietnam. During the war against the people of Vietnam, Laos, and Cambodia, Ellsberg secured secret documents, which if published would then acquaint the American people with the facts about the war, facts that had been withheld from them by the CIA and the administration. The release of the information would provide the people and their congressional representatives with an opportunity to assess the wisdom of continuing the conflict. Informed judgment, Ellsberg reasoned, might well lead the United States to disengage from the conflict.

Understanding the personal risk he was taking, Ellsberg made the papers available to the Senate Foreign Relations Committee and to the New York Times. The newspaper published the documents and an aroused and growing antiwar movement, led at least in part by active-duty members of the military as well as by veterans of the war, became better informed and in time ended the war. A less than grateful administration directed that Ellsberg be indicted for criminal conspiracy, theft, and violation of the Espionage Act. Ellsberg retained Boudin, a distinguished and brilliant member of the New York bar, to represent him. The duplicitous charges were dismissed. The judicial system had worked and there the matter should have rested. Ellsberg had saved the lives of countless members of the United States military and residents of Southeast Asia and his talented lawyer, who had acted in the highest tradition of the American bar, as he had done over the decades, had secured his client's vindication.

Enter the Nixon administration, Charles Colson, E. Howard Hunt and the CIA. It was decided at "the highest level of government," as revealed by documents now available, to destroy the reputations of Ellsberg and Boudin through the use of criminal activity. All that is not clear is whether the august reference was to President Nixon or the director of the CIA, since each apparently claimed supremacy over the other. I asked Hunt about the operation.

Q. Did you write a memorandum in which you suggested that an operation should be mounted for the purpose of destroying the public image and the credibility of Dr. Ellsberg?

A. I did.

Q. Was that your proposal that that be done?

A. It was my proposal and I referred it to Mr. Colson who recommended it be done.

Q. Did you write this paragraph? "I am proposing a skeletal operations plan aimed at building a file on Ellsberg that will contain all available overt/covert and derogatory information. This basic tool is essential in determining how to destroy his public image and credibility." Did you write that?

A. I did.

Q. Are you complaining in essence that Spotlight did a kind of similar thing to you in this case?

A. I don't think it is an act of comparison. I think you are asking for a legal conclusion that I am not prepared to make.

Q. As part of your plan to destroy Dr. Ellsberg's reputation, did you suggest that his first wife be interviewed?

A. Yes.

Q. Did you suggest a request be made to the FBI, to the CIA, and CIC for their full holdings on Dr. Ellsberg?

A. Yes.

Q. What is the CIC?

A. Counterintelligence Corps of the United States Army.

Q. Did you suggest Ellsberg's files from his psychiatrist be obtained?

A. I did.

Q. Did you request the CIA perform a covert psychological assessment evaluation on Ellsberg?

A. I certainly was in favor of it.

Q. I will show you page 753 of your testimony and ask if you requested the assessment?

A. Okay, psychological examination, yes. Request CIA to perform a covert psychological examination. It is a memorandum to Charles Colson. In the end it was done. No argument about it.

Q. Do you think that is right?

A. Do I think what is right?

Q. To try to destroy a person's reputation utilizing the armed forces of the United States government in its secret operations, to destroy the credibility of an American citizen. Do you think that is right?

A. If he were the individual that we believed him to be at that time, absolutely.

Q. If he was a traitor, he should have been tried for treason, is that correct?

A. That's correct.

Q. He then could have defended himself against the charge in court, is that correct?

A. That's correct. That is the way our judicial system works. We like to think so.

Q. But he was not given that opportunity, was he, Mr. Hunt, because you were mounting a covert operation to secretly destroy his reputation and his credibility; is that correct?

A. It had begun, yes.

Q. Is that right? Do you support that activity?

A. Do I support that activity?

Q. Yes.

A. I wish I never heard of Watergate. I wish I never had been employed in the White House.

Q. It did not work out too well for you. That is not what I am asking. Do you support the use of secret weapons by the U.S. government to destroy the credibility of American citizens?

A. I would have to say it depends upon who those American citizens are.

Q. If they are criminals, should they not be prosecuted for their crimes? But should people be hiding in dark shadows to destroy their reputations in such a fashion that they cannot defend themselves?

A. You are asking me for a legal conclusion?

Q. I am asking you what you believe. Do you believe that is proper?

A. If what is proper?

Q. To try to destroy the credibility and reputation of American citizens in a secret fashion?

A. Under the circumstances then obtaining, I had no problem with it at the time. Today, I obviously would.

Q. Why? What is different?

A. A lot is different.

Q. What is different?

A. I have matured a good deal since then. I have seen how insubstantial Mr. Colson's frame of reference was.

Q. Have you sent a letter of apology to Dr. Ellsberg?

A. No.

The plan to destroy Dr. Ellsberg included breaking into the offices of his psychiatrist, Dr. Lewis Fielding, in whom Hunt believed Ellsberg had confided. Illegal activities of this nature are described by the CIA and FBI as "black bag jobs."

Q. Did you conclude at the very least a black bag job was in order regarding Dr. Fielding?

A. If by that time the FBI declined to do it, yes.

Q. Was that your recommendation?

A. Could well have been. It is a black bag job. Type that the FBI performs in this country, as you well know, and the CIA overseas to obtain materials that are not conveniently made available to it.

Q. Did you testify, "It seemed to me at least that a black bag job was in order?" Do you recall testifying to that?

A. Yes.

Thus Hunt, who in fact had recommended and organized the illegal entry into Fielding's Los Angeles office, continued to dissemble regarding the jurisdictional limitations of the CIA and FBI when he testified about the crime. Hunt and his associates had decided to plant false information about

Ellsberg in the press. At first Hunt was less than certain about the matter, but his memory improved when he was shown the relevant documents.

Q. Did you state at a meeting that it would be a fine idea to try Ellsberg in the press if he could not be tried in the courtroom?

A. I may have.

Q. Page 766 of your testimony, defendant's exhibit J, your testimony in the *Ehrlichman-Liddy* case:

> "Mr. Hunt, was there any discussion during this meeting with Dr. Malloy concerning trying Dr. Ellsberg in the press?
> "Answer. I recall an allusion to it.
> "Question. What would your allusion have been?
> "Answer. That if he could not be tried in court, it was a fine idea to try him in the press.
> "Question. Do you recall who made that statement?
> "Answer. Offhand, I would say it was myself."

Does that refresh your recollection?

A. Yes.

Q. Was there a discussion that you had with Mr. Colson about not just Dr. Ellsberg, but his lawyer?

A. You have to refresh my recollection on that.

I paused here and looked at Hunt incredulously. I was asking, without words, if Hunt had formulated and carried out a program designed to destroy the reputation of a noted attorney and had since then forgotten about it.

Q. Page 767 of your testimony:

> "Question. Do you have a recollection, Mr. Hunt, of discussing with Mr. Colson the preparation of material on an individual by the name of Leonard Boudin?
> "Answer. I do.
> "Question. Who was Mr. Boudin?
> "Answer. Mr. Boudin at that time was the chief legal counsel for Dr. Daniel Ellsberg and Dr. Ellsberg's difficulties with the United States government."

Does that refresh your recollection?

A. It does.

Q. Did you suggest, as you testified at that time, that there should be material prepared about Leonard Boudin?

A. I did.

Q. Leonard Boudin was not a Marxist dictator?

A. No.

Q. Is Mr. Boudin considered by the bar to be an extremely competent, fine, talented, and distinguished member of the New York bar?

A. I, not being a member of any bar, I would not be able to assert an opinion.

Q. Did you do some research on Mr. Boudin?

A. Yes, indeed.

Q. Did you discover what I asked you, whether that was true?

A. That was not a part of our guy's discovery.

When I asked Hunt about the research he had authorized, he responded by attacking Boudin's other clients and his daughter.

Q. You think it is relevant now, when I ask you what research you did at that time, for you to tell the jury about his daughter? You do know what guilt by association means?

A. Very definitely.

Q. I am asking you about a distinguished member of the New York bar and you are telling me about his daughter. Is that guilt by association?

A. You are characterizing him as a distinguished member of the New York bar, and I say I have no idea what he is.

Q. Is guilt by association the kind of thing that you used to do years ago, but now that you are more mature, you don't engage in anymore?

Hunt was not in the business of securing pure research to develop a file. He was an activist determined to destroy his opponent. I asked him about the result of his work.

Q. Did you write a memorandum about Mr. Boudin?

A. I believe I gathered some file material on Mr. Boudin in the form of a memorandum.

Q. Anything else happen?

A. That was passed to a person in the presence of Mr. Colson's confidence.

Q. What happened?

A. I think a portion of it was published in the press. I think the *New York Times*.

Q. In fact, you wrote an article about Mr. Boudin. You did not pull together some file material; is that not correct? You wrote the article; is that true?

A. I did not write the article that finally appeared.

Q. Did you write an article?

A. I wrote a long memorandum that was transposed into an article formed by the man who published it under his name.

I then confronted Hunt with his previous testimony.

Q. Page 768:

267

"Question. Did you do some research on Mr. Boudin?
"Answer. I did.
"Question. Did you prepare a memorandum about him?
"Answer. I *prepared more than that. I prepared an article—a journalist article on* Mr. Boudin."

Were those the answers that you gave when you were questioned under oath on that occasion?

A. Yes.

Q. Were they truthful?

A. They were.

Q. Under what name was the article published?

A. I don't recall.

Q. Do you know the name Jerry terHorst?

A. Yes.

Q. Does that refresh your recollection?

A. Yes.

Q. Was that published under Mr. Jerry terHorst's name?

A. It was.

Jerry terHorst, the putative author of the article in question, headed the Washington bureau of the Detroit News from 1961 until 1974, when he became press secretary to Gerald Ford in the early days of his administration.

Q. Do you think that is right?

A. Do I think what is right? That was the purpose of the operation.

Q. I know that was the purpose. Do you think it is proper for public funds to be used in a surreptitious fashion to write an article in a newspaper, so that when the American people read the newspaper they think it was written by a journalist, not by someone being paid by the White House?

A. I thought so; that it was proper under the circumstances prevailing at the time. I no longer think so.

Hunt had taken all available positions on the question. He justified his actions, he denied doing what he had done, and finally, when the evidence was undeniable, he asserted that he had reformed. Moments before the reformation, however, he had made disparaging and irrelevant remarks about Leonard Boudin's family. The jurors watched. They knew that the plaintiff, in spite of his protestation, had been engaged in criminal conduct and had utilized deception within the United States for the purpose of destroying the reputation of American citizens. But would he have acted similarly if the assigned target had been President Kennedy? Absolutely not, he proclaimed. He liked John Kennedy. I asked him what his attitude had been about the late president.

"Well, he was a young man of my generation. I had met him socially in Boston. Thought well of him. I served in the South Pacific the same time he did. We were both naval officers. At one time, I felt a great deal of empathy for him."

Q. Were you ever involved in any kind of disinformation to embarass him?

A. President Kennedy?

Q. Yes.

A. No.

The problem with Hunt's response, although it was presented without hesitation and with apparent sincerity and feeling, was that it was entirely untruthful.

I continued:

Q. Did you ever have discussions with Mr. Colson about forging some cables in order to blame John F. Kennedy for the death of the leader of South Vietnam?

Hunt paused. He looked at his attorneys for help. There was nothing they could do. The question was proper. Finally, Hunt spoke, slowly and quietly.

A. Yes, that is a matter of public record. I can't remember whether Kennedy himself was to be blamed. But certainly the Nixon administration—the Kennedy administration, by the Nixon administration.

Q. Did you ever have discussions with Mr. Colson in which you agreed to falsify State Department cables to show that President John F. Kennedy's administration ordered the assassination of South Vietnamese President Diem?

A. I did.

Q. And, in fact, did you falsify and forge those cables?

A. Did I? [lengthy pause] Yes, I did.

I then asked Hunt to explain how he had forged the documents in order to charge John F. Kennedy, after his death, with a murder for which he was not responsible.

Q. How did you do that?

A. Well, I did that by this means: I checked all of the cable material relating to the death of President Diem of South Vietnam that was available in State Department files, and those available in other agencies of the Government; such as NSA. I found that there was a series of them that had been taken out. They were not in the files. They were marked "at Kennedy Library," which meant they had been taken up to the J.F.K.

Library in Boston. Those files were not there. Those cables were not there. Using that particular time frame, I thought, knowing what little I did about the background of the assassination, I went ahead and provided cables that could logically have been, in the sequential flow between Washington and Vietnam, concerning the death of President Diem.

Q. What do you mean you provided cables? What did you do?

A. Did I say provided?

Q. I thought you did.

A. Well, I fabricated them.

Q. You—

A. Fabricated, right.

I wondered how one would go about fabricating official cables after the fact to make them appear authentic. I asked Hunt to explain to the jury how he had accomplished the task:

A. How did I do it? You mean, mechanically?

Q. Yes.

A. I had them typed up on a typewriter, and they were Xeroxed, and the Xeroxes were eventually shown to a person of Mr. Colson's confidence, and in *Time* and *Life*.

Q. Is that Mr. Lambert?

A. Bill Lambert, yes.

Q. And were they shown to Mr. Lambert for the purpose of publishing them?

A. Yes.

Q. And were they shown to him with the assurance they were genuine?

A. [pause] I have to think about that. It seems to me that he was shown the cables in Mr. Colson's office, rather than in mine. I don't recall that I showed them to him. I may have given them to him. [pause] Whether I said they were genuine or not is another matter. I may have. It would have been tough for me to say that, but I could have.

Q. Did you say, "These are forgeries. I just fabricated them. I'd like you to put these forgeries in your publication?"

A. Of course not. Of course not.

Q. So, when you offered them to Mr. Lambert, you offered them—

A. The implication is that they were the real thing, which they were not.

Hunt, after swearing that he had never been involved in a disinformation effort to embarrass Kennedy, had now testified that he had merely sought to doctor and create evidence to prove that Kennedy was a murderer. Hunt offered a rationale for his aberrant behavior that I found no less astonishing than the fact that he had fabricated the evidence.

Q. In essence, then, you forged documents in order to make it seem that John F. Kennedy and his administration were involved in assassinating the head of state; is that correct?

A. Which I believed to be the case.

Q. And so you forged evidence to show that your theory about the matter was accurate; is that correct?

A. That is correct, yes.

Q. Was that proper?

A. No, it was not proper.

We had learned a great deal about Hunt in the hours of cross-examination. I think we had demonstrated to the jury that he disliked John Kennedy; had used deception to frame him after his death; was willing to violate the law to complete his assignments; had no respect for the basic institutions of this nation or any other nation; found the judicial system to be an inadequate method for settling disputes; had regularly and persistently committed perjury; and favored, as he testified, the murder of a head of state who pursued a foreign and domestic policy that contrasted with the CIA's worldview. Hunt had testified that he certainly hoped the CIA was attempting to kill Castro, and had no objection based on morality to the assassination of the leaders of the Soviet Union.

Kennedy had betrayed Hunt's operation to destroy the Cuban revolution and assassinate Castro. He was also about to wind down the CIA's adventure in Vietnam.

The jurors believed, I think for the first time, that Hunt and his colleagues in the CIA may have had the motive, inclination, and ability to kill the president. That certainly was far short of proof that they had done so. The next step was establishing opportunity. Where had Hunt been on November 22, 1963?

It is a characteristic of all Americans of a certain age that they can fix with certainty where they were, what they were doing, and whom they were with when they learned, on November 22, 1963, that President Kennedy had been shot. This is a trait shared with millions of people through the world. I have lectured extensively in the United States and Europe on the subject of the assassination. After each lecture scores of people from the audience told me of how the tragic news reached them. They would invariably recount, years after the event, each detail, whom they talked with, what was said, where they were, and what they did. I have no doubt that each of them, if required to do so, could round up numerous witnesses to demonstrate the accuracy of their account.

The only person I have encountered in almost three decades who

271

appears to be uncertain in this matter is E. Howard Hunt. It is not that he is unwilling to hazard a guess as to where he was; it is that he has offered, over the years, too many contradictory stories, each replete with phantom witnesses.

He was at the time an employee of the CIA. Surely records there would reveal his presence in Washington that day. They do not. Before the trial Hunt had answered the question as to his whereabouts that day on numerous occasions, generally under oath.

During March 1974, Hunt appeared before the Rockefeller Commission. He later said that he had answered all of the questions put to him. He also provided an affidavit to the commission. The affidavit reads:

> I, E. Howard Hunt, affirm the following to be my recollections of my whereabouts on November 22, 1963:
>
> 1. On that date I was an employee of the Central Intelligence Agency assigned to the Domestic Operations Division, located in a commercial building in Washington, D.C.
>
> 2. I was driving with my late wife on H Street near 8th or 9th Street where we first heard of the Kennedy shooting on our car radio. We had been purchasing Chinese groceries at a store named, as well as I can recall it, 'Wah Ling.' I do not know how long after the initial radio reports were made that my wife and I first heard the news. Brinkley was the commentator I remember because of his having theorized a 'right-wing plot': i.e., Dallas citizens had abused Adlai Stevenson and the climate of Dallas extremism had caused Kennedy's shooting.
>
> 3. From the Chinese grocery store we drove out Wisconsin Avenue to pick up our daughter, Kevan, from Sidwell Friends School. On joining us my daughter told us what we already knew: that President Kennedy had been shot. She had learned this because two of Robert Kennedy's children had been taken from Sidwell Friends School, presumably by Secret Service agents.
>
> 4. From Kevan's school we drove directly to our home on Baltan Road in Sumner, Maryland (off Massachusetts Avenue extended). At home was my newly born son, David (DOB 9/1/63), a maid, Mary Trayner and my wife's aunt, the late Leona Drexler of Chicago. Our elder son, St. John, a student at nearby Brookmont Elementary School, was probably already at home. As I recall, our eldest child, Lisa, arrived soon afterward by bus from Ursuline Academy and joined us at the television set in our basement recreation room, where we stayed long hours watching the unfolding of events: the swearing-in of LBJ, the arrival at Andrews Field of the presidential coffin, et cetera.

5. As to why I was not at my office that entire afternoon, I can only presume that I had left early to help my wife shop for a planned Chinese dinner, in the preparation of which I normally assisted.

6. I was never in Dallas, Texas, until late 1971, when, at the request of Charles Colson, I flew there to interview General Paul Harkins, former U.S. military commander in Vietnam.

7. I did not meet Frank Sturgis until the spring of 1972, the introduction being performed by and at the office of Bernard L. Barker.

8. I never at any time met or knew Lee Harvey Oswald, Jack Ruby, or any other person involved in the Dallas slayings.

9. I was not in Mexico in 1963. In fact, I was not in Mexico between the years 1961 and 1970, and have not been there since a weekend pleasure trip to Acapulco in July of 1970.

10. I have no diaries or other memorabilia prior to 1969, having destroyed as many outdated files and records as possible to save weight in the move to my Florida home in July, 1974. I retained only such records, bank statements, etcetera, as are required by the 5-year Internal Revenue Service for income tax purposes.

A search of the records revealed that there was no grocery store named "Wah Ling" in Washington, D.C. during 1963, though there would be one later. The only living witnesses listed by Hunt who could verify his presence in the Washington area were his children. And as we have seen, Hunt, according to the testimony of David Phillips, had been in Mexico between 1961 and 1970. According to Joseph Trento's article and to author Tad Szulc, in his book *Compulsive Spy: The Strange Career of E. Howard Hunt*, Hunt was temporary station chief of Mexico City in August and September of 1963.

When Hunt was deposed in the case he had filed and later abandoned against the Third Press, A.J. Weberman, and others, he testified that he had been in his basement recreation room with the "neighbors, Mr. and Mrs. Raymond Thomas," in addition to his children.

He also said at that time that he "had no idea" if he had been to his CIA office the morning of the assassination. He was certain, however, that during the afternoon of November 22, 1963, after he had learned of the death of the president, he had gone to his office.

When asked for the name of the grocery store he had visited that day, he replied without qualification, "Wah Ling," and added that the store was located in downtown Washington, quite a distance from his home in Maryland. He testified that he had been away from his home that day only "about two hours" before the assassination. He had driven from his home in Maryland to the Chinese grocery store. He did not recall the name of a single person to whom he had spoken by telephone that day.

Another deposition was taken in that case on April 14, 1978. Hunt had learned that Wah Ling, his alibi store, had not existed in 1963. He had apparently learned by then that his adversaries were aware of that fact as well. When asked where Wah Ling is located in Washington, he responded that the grocery store may not have existed at the time. He then sought to withdraw from his previous sworn statements:

"In fact, in the testimony that I gave to the Church committee [sic], if you recall, I said to the best of my recollection the name of the grocery store was Wah Ling.

"Having revisited the site—in fact, by chance having dinner in Chinatown fairly recently—I determined the name of the grocery store was probably Tuck Cheong, T-U-C-K C-H-E-O-N-G."

He was then asked if he had changed his alibi for the day of the assassination from one store to another. He answered:

"Well, I am saying now that in attempting to recollect a couple of years ago, the name of the Chinese grocery store, one of several on H Street, that my wife visited on that afternoon certainly is subject to reexamination and refreshment, which I have done."

Hunt had previously identified Wah Ling as the store in the most recent testimony that he had offered before the April 1978 deposition. He had even offered at that time an estimate as to the distance between Wah Ling and his home.

During December 1981, when being deposed before the first trial of the Liberty Lobby case, Hunt said that he recalled November 22, 1963, "very well." He then proceeded to offer a new version of the events. He testified:

"My wife had given birth to our second son on the first of September of that year and on that particular date she had driven downtown with our infant son, who was only about three months old, to pick me up.

"She wanted to buy ingredients for Chinese dinners, and we proceeded from my office downtown over to H Street where there are several Chinese restaurants and a number of grocery stores.

"I should say that before I met my wife, she had lived in Shanghai, China, and was an excellent Chinese cook. And I also had served in China and was fond of Chinese food, and it was our custom to eat it frequently and she prepared it in our home.

"She needed me in the car to sit in the car while she went into the grocery store and made her purchases of fresh ginger and things of that nature which are peculiar to Chinese cookery.

"While I waited with the radio on, I heard the first news flash from Dallas that the president had been shot."

When asked if he had seen anybody that day who could verify his new account, he answered:

"The people who were under me, a lady who has since remarried—I can't think of her name—and there was Connie Mazerov, who was a file typist.

"And after my wife rejoined me in the car, we drove up Connecticut Avenue in the direction of our home in suburban Maryland and I saw an individual accompanied by Mr. Walter Kuzmuk, who was a neighbor of mine, and he was coming out of Duke Ziebert's restaurant with one or two companions.

"He was familiar with the vehicle I was driving because we formed a car pool from time to time, and I would drive one week and he would drive the next, to hold down expenses and also as a matter of just genuine efficiency because we only lived really a few houses from each other.

"He waved at me and I waved at him, and I proceeded north knowing that the president was dead and having heard that all government offices were being closed for the rest of the day, and rather than return to my office, my wife and I decided to pick up our children on the way out to Maryland, which we did, and we went home and like many millions of other Americans stayed glued to our television set for the rest of that period of time."

Thus two new witnesses had materialized. Both had been employees of the CIA. Trento's article, published three-and-one-half years before Hunt offered his final story, had cited CIA sources who predicted that all of Hunt's witnesses would eventually be "CIA-arranged." However, in order to accommodate the testimony of the CIA witnesses, Hunt was required to repudiate substantial portions of his previous testimony. How could he have seen Connie Mazerov at the CIA offices during the morning of the assassination if he had not been to the CIA offices that day until after the death of the president had been announced, as he had previously testified? How could he have been at the CIA offices that morning if he had been away from his home only two hours, as he had previously testified? The automobile trip from his home in suburban Maryland to Chinatown in downtown Washington, allowing for a few moments to shop, and the return home after picking up his children, might be accomplished in two hours. However, that would certainly preclude Hunt's appearance at the CIA office that morning. The entire alibi story had to be revamped to account for the newly developed testimony of the CIA-arranged witnesses.

There was an additional problem as well. Hunt had, on several previous occasions, presented the names of all of the potential witnesses regarding his whereabouts on November 22, 1963. He had done so, he claimed at the time, to prove that he had not been in Dallas that day. Yet many years later, when each of his previous stories had collapsed, he presented the names of two CIA witnesses *for the first time*.

As we have seen when I took Kuzmuk's deposition, he testified that he had not seen Hunt from November 18, 1963, until December 1963, with the exception of the chance encounter when Hunt drove past a restaurant from which Kuzmuk was exiting. This was so, he said, even though Hunt and Kuzmuk were neighbors, they usually drove to work together and they worked in the same building in offices in close proximity to each other. Specifically, Kuzmuk testified that he had not driven to work with Hunt on November 22. Hunt had originally testified that he and his wife drove from their Maryland home that morning directly to the Chinese grocery store. However, when the predicted CIA witnesses came forward, and one of them, Mazerov, was going to place Hunt at the CIA building on the morning of the assassination, Hunt was presented with a new problem. How did he get to his CIA office that morning? If he had driven his own automobile to the CIA building that morning, how did his wife get from Maryland to downtown Washington? The only possible solution was for Hunt to claim that he had been driven to work by Kuzmuk. How else could Hunt and his wife end up in one automobile and see, and be seen by, Kuzmuk later that day?

Hunt was flexible enough to adjust to the new situation. He had previously sworn that he had not been to the CIA building on the morning of the assassination, and had testified regarding his itinerary and time schedule, which at that time had been coordinated to complement each other—that is, he described a two-hour trip that he swore took approximately two hours. Now he swore that he had been at his CIA office in the morning to accommodate both the Mazerov testimony and the Kuzmuk story.

Even though Kuzmuk had sworn in his deposition that he had not driven to work with Hunt on November 22, that being the one fact that both Hunt and Kuzmuk had agreed upon, Hunt now was required to repudiate his own earlier testimony as well as the current testimony of his alibi witness. At the trial, Hunt testified that "I saw Walter Kuzmuk, with whom I shared driving chores to and from our nearby homes in the suburbs of Sumner, Maryland." I asked Hunt when he had first seen Kuzmuk on November 22, 1963. He responded, "On the first time, in the morning when we drove to work."

Hunt had by then contradicted almost every detail he had previously offered under oath over a period of several years, regarding what he did on November 22, 1963, and who had seen him do it. He was now contesting the essential testimony of Kuzmuk, one of his two remaining witnesses. I asked him about that.

Q. Do you know Mr. Kuzmuk testified he did not drive with you to Washington, D.C., on November 22, 1963?

A. No, I don't know that.

MR. SNYDER: Objection.

THE COURT: Grounds.

MR. SNYDER: Mischaracterization of Mr. Kuzmuk's testimony.

THE COURT: Overruled. The answer is, he does not know that.

BY MR. LANE:

Q. I am going to show you the transcription of a sworn statement, deposition, given by Mr. Kuzmuk in this case on Thursday, June 28, 1984, in the presence of your attorney, and ask you if that is what this document purports to be. It is exhibit M for identification.

A. That is what it purports to be.

Q. Do you have a copy, Mr. Snyder?

MR. SNYDER: Yes.

BY MR. LANE:

Q. Question, page 11. Question by me, to Mr. Kuzmuk:

> "Question: During the week ending November 22, 1963, did you come to Washington in a car?
> "Answer: Well, the only car pool I had was with Mr. Hunt, and I think that is what we are pointing at is the twenty-second of November, correct?
> "Question: That is the date we are pointing to, that is correct.
> "Answer: So on that date, I drove because Mr. Hunt was not with me that day until I met him on the avenue, as I stated in here. Now, on the twenty-first, I don't know."

Did you know Mr. Kuzmuk so testified?

A. No.

Hunt, when confronted with the evidence, admitted that when he had testified during a deposition in July 1977 in the *Third Press* case, he had sought to prove that he had been in Washington, D.C. on November 22, 1963, and that he did not mention Kuzmuk as a witness. He explained only that "I had not remembered him." I then asked him if he had mentioned Connie Mazerov's name as an alibi witness during the 1977 deposition. He said he had not.

I then began to question Hunt in an effort to sum up the conflicting aspects of his changing stories.

Q. You said several times in your testimony that you have been entirely consistent in each of your appearances. In 1977, when under oath in a lawsuit which you had brought against Weberman and others, when asked to give the names of the persons you had seen on November 22, 1963, you did not mention Kuzmuk and you did not mention Mazerov, is that correct?

A. That has been established.

Q. And they will be your two alibi witnesses at this trial?

A. They will be two alibi witnesses at this trial, that is correct.

Q. Today did you mention Mr. and Mrs. Raymond Thomas when I asked you to list every single person you would recall seeing on November 22, 1963?

A. No, I did not.

Q. But in 1977, did you mention Mr. and Mrs. Raymond Thomas as two alibi witnesses?

A. I did.

Q. Today when I asked you to list every single person who you saw on November 22, 1963, did you mention any neighbors?

A. I did not mention any neighbors.

Q. In 1977 when you were asked the same question, did you say they were neighbors?

A. I did.

Q. A year after you testified at a deposition in the case which you had brought against Weberman, a year after that, you testified before the House Select Committee on Assassinations, is that correct?

A. Well, a year means what year?

Q. November 3, 1978.

A. I forced my way on the committee.

Q. You wanted them to know you could prove through alibi witnesses and other witnesses that you were in Washington, D.C., on November 22, 1963?

A. That is correct.

Q. You gave this matter serious thought as to how you could most effectively convince them you were there in Washington, is that correct?

A. That is a fair characterization, yes.

Q. You did not mention Kuzmuk on that day, did you? You did not tell the House Select Committee on Assassinations you had ever seen Mr. Kuzmuk on November 22, 1963, did you?

A. No, because I do not think that he had revealed his presence to me. At that time, I was unaware he would write a letter to me.

Q. He was in the car with you on the morning of November 22, 1963, according to your sworn statement, is that correct?

A. That is correct.

Q. You saw him later in the day, just after you were leaving Chinatown in Washington, D.C., is that correct?

A. That is correct. These are matters he reminded me of when he resumed the contact with me.

Q. It was not a question of his revealing his presence. It was a question of refreshing your recollection. Is that correct?

A. Fair characterization, yes.

Q. When you went before the House Select Committee on Assassinations, desperate to convince them that you were in Washington, not in Dallas, you never mentioned your other alibi witness, Miss Mazerov?

A. I thought I did.

Q. Maybe I am wrong. Let us take a look at the testimony. This is dated November 3, 1978, and purports to be a deposition which was taken of you by the House Select Committee on Assassinations on that date, is that correct?

A. Yes.

Q. Were you asked by the House Select Committee on Assassinations for the names of your alibi witnesses?

A. I do not know. I imagine I volunteered them.

Q. The subject was addressed by you, was it not, page 6?

A. Addressed by me in my initial statement to the committee, yes.

Q. Did you mention Connie Mazerov?

A. Not in my statement, no.

Q. Did you begin your appearance before the House Select Committee on Assassinations by reading an opening statement?

A. I did.

Q. Who prepared that statement?

A. I did.

Q. Was it several pages long?

A. It was.

Q. Had you given some thought to it before you prepared it?

A. Yes.

Q. Was it a very serious matter for you?

A. Extremely.

Q. In preparing paragraph number four, which appears on page 6 of that deposition, where you presented the names of the alibi witnesses, did you mention that you drove to the CIA building with Kuzmuk?

A. The CIA office, no.

Q. Did you mention that you saw Kuzmuk outside the restaurant?

A. Counselor, I was not aware. I forgot about the Kuzmuk connection until he wrote the letter to me some months later.

Q. Did you mention that you had spent part of November 22, 1963, with Connie Mazerov in your prepared statement?

A. No.

Q. Is it true that the only two alibi witnesses you will present at this trial are those persons who you did not tell the House Select Committee on Assassinations about when you testified there?

A. That is correct.

I looked at the jurors. They seemed to be very interested in the exchange, yet I believed that I was dangerously close to overproving this aspect of the case. It occurred to me that I may have, in fact, already crossed the fine line that separates the presentation of compelling evidence from tedious overemphasis. Although there was considerably more potential testimony on this point, I abandoned the area.

Since both Hunt, during his direct testimony, and his counsel, in statements to the jury, had asserted that the Rockefeller Commission had exonerated Hunt, I explored that matter briefly. The plaintiff had also made it clear by then that he would not present payroll records or other CIA documents to establish that he had been in Washington when the president was murdered. Those documents were unavailable to me. The Rockefeller Commission had examined some records pertaining to Hunt and had reached certain conclusions. I sought to ask questions that might illuminate both areas.

Q. When Mr. Kuzmuk drove you to work was that because you were on duty that day at the CIA?

A. Duty every day, yes, sir.

Q. Do you know that the Rockefeller Commission concluded, "Hunt could not recall whether he was on duty on the morning of that day," and by that day, they are referring quite clearly from the context to November 22, 1963. Did you know that the Rockefeller Commission published that conclusion?

A. Yes. I do know that.

Q. Do you know why the Rockefeller Commission—

A. I think because they didn't ask me where I was.

Q. Of course, the conclusion is not that they did not ask you, the conclusion is that "Hunt could not recall whether he was on duty" with the CIA on the morning of that day. Do you know why they reached that conclusion?

A. I would have no idea.

Q. You know they reached that conclusion?

A. It is published, that's correct. Whether I was on annual leave, on sick leave, or reporting in is of little consequence.

Q. Did you use any sick leave in the two-week period ending November 23, 1963?

A. It is possible, I have no recollection of it.

Q. Did the Rockefeller Commission conclude that you used eleven hours of sick leave in the two-week period ending November 23, 1963?

A. If that is what they found, they had access to agency records. I did not.

Q. I am asking you if you know whether or not they concluded that?

A. If you say so, yes. I will accept that.

Q. I don't want you to rely upon me. If there is any question in your mind, I am asking you if you know that they said it.

A. You have it in your hand, why don't you show it to me.

Q. I will show it to your lawyer, then I will show it to you. It is defendant's exhibit L for identification, page 254 and 255 of the Rockefeller Commission. Your attorneys have compared this to the entire volume. It is two pages. I ask you to read this paragraph.

A. Read it aloud.

Q. To yourself, please.

A. If the agency said that I took eleven hours of sick leave in the two-week period prior to November 23, 1963, it is fine with me.

Q. First question about this is: Is it true that the Rockefeller Commission concluded that you took eleven hours of sick leave in the two-week pay period ending November 23, 1963?

A. How many hours?

Q. Eleven hours of sick leave.

A. Yes.

Q. In the two-week pay period ending November 23, 1963.

A. That is exactly what it says.

Q. Is that true, to the best of your knowledge?

A. I have no independent recollection, Counselor. They had access to the agency records and I did not.

Hunt had apparently testified that he could not recall whether he had visited his office on the day in question, in addition to having testified both that he had been there that morning and that he had not been there that morning.

In spite of the record, Hunt insisted that he had been "exculpated by the Rockefeller Commission." I continued by asking Hunt if the Rockefeller Commission also concluded that:

"Contacts with relatives, friends, neighbors or fellow employees, who might have known of the whereabouts of Hunt and Sturgis on that particular day could not be recalled."

He admitted that the Rockefeller Commission had reached that conclusion.

I then asked Hunt if the final conclusion of the Rockefeller Commission was that "it cannot be determined with certainty, where Hunt and Sturgis were on the day of the assassination." He agreed that the report did make that statement. The jurors stared intently; some sat at the edge of their seats and leaned forward. I refrained from asking Hunt how he was able to derive any comfort, let alone exculpation, from the report. That question was placed in abeyance; it was one that I believed the jurors would raise and ponder when the case was submitted to them.

The jury had been given a more than adequate opportunity to evaluate Hunt's character.

I now set out to close the trap I had set many months before when I had taken Hunt's deposition. On that occasion, Hunt had described in great detail how his entire family had huddled together in his Maryland home from Friday, November 22, 1963, until either Monday or Tuesday of the next week. He could not recall leaving the home for forty-eight or possibly seventy-two hours. "There would have been no particular reason to," he testified. Hunt, his wife, and his children, "like thousands of other Americans, millions," remained together. They all "stayed there and watched [via television] the burial services."

At this trial he acknowledged the accuracy of that deposition transcript and asserted that his statements were truthful. I then asked him about the testimony he had offered at the first trial of the Liberty Lobby case, on December 16, 1981.

Q. Do you recall testifying back on December 16, 1981, that when the allegation was made that you were in Dallas, Texas, on November 22, 1963, your children were really upset? Do you recall testifying to that?

A. Yes.

Q. Do you recall testifying that you had to reassure them that you were not in Texas that day?

A. Yes.

Q. That you had nothing to do with the Kennedy assassination?

A. That's right.

Q. And that you were being persecuted for reasons that were unknown to you?

A. Yes.

Q. Did you say that the allegation that you were in Dallas, Texas, on November 22, 1963, was the focus of a great deal of interfamily friction, and tended to exacerbate difficulties in the family?

A. I did.

Although neither Hunt nor his attorneys seemed to sense what danger was about to befall them, it appeared that the jurors were anticipating the next question, confident that they knew what it would be.

I put down the dog-eared 1981 trial transcript. I looked at Hunt and softly asked the most difficult question he was going to face at this trial:

"Mr. Hunt, why did you have to convince your children that you were not in Dallas, Texas, on November 22, 1963, if, in fact, as you say, a fourteen-year-old daughter, a thirteen-year-old daughter, and a ten-year-old son were with you in the Washington, D.C., area on November 22, 1963, and were with you at least for the next forty-eight hours, as you all stayed glued to the T.V. set?"

If someone had struck Hunt in the face his reaction would not have been more physical. His head jerked back. He stared at his attorneys. Snyder and Dunne, apparently thunderstruck, began to speak to each other in whispers. The delay before Hunt responded seemed interminable. In absolute time it probably was not more than half a minute. Finally, Hunt spoke, looking away from the jurors:

"May I reply?

I answered, "Please. It is a question."

He spoke quickly, as if he hoped the subject would soon be forgotten.

"These were unformed minds, and I felt that it was absolutely imperative that I remind them of the circumstances attendant upon our family that day.

"Yet, my other son, Howard St. John, had read in the Berkeley Barb and in other papers these constant reiterations of my involvement in the Kennedy assassination.

"So, it was less a question of my convincing them that I was in Washington, D.C., with them—rather, reminding them that I was—than it was to assure them that none of the charges and allegations that had been made, particularly those of the tramp in Dealey Plaza, had any substance to them at all."

Q. How could they believe, Mr. Hunt, that the tramp photographs, as

283

they have been called, which purport to show you in Dealey Plaza, Dallas, Texas, on November 22, 1963, could be authentic, when they were with you at that time in the Washington, D.C., area and were with you for forty-eight hours, in front of a TV set?

A. Because of the constant reiteration of the charges. The appearance of people like Dick Gregory at news conferences, Dick Gregory call-in radio shows. The prevalence of the theories that Hunt or the CIA somehow had something to do with it. Of course, they were well aware that I worked for the CIA. My name was linked with it, and usually linked in connection with the Kennedy assassination. It was a very difficult problem that I had with my children.

Q. One can see where they might be disturbed that you were being charged with this. But weren't they of the opinion that there were three people who could prove to the whole world that these charges were a tissue of lies, that "I was with my father during that whole time period?" What I want to know is since they knew how outrageous the lies were, why did they have to be convinced by you that you weren't in Texas?

A. Reminded, reminded.

Q. They didn't remember that themselves?

Hunt paused again. He wiped his forehead with a handkerchief.

A. The constant reiteration of these charges, in one form or another, had an extremely deleterious effect on my children. I conferred with them, I answered their questions. I gave them every assurance that I was never in Dealey Plaza at any time in my life—not only on the fatal day, but the day before, the day after. In short, never. That was the type of assurance I was forced to give to my family.

Q. Were all of these children with you on the day after the assassination of President Kennedy?

The witness reached for a glass of water and drank it slowly. Then he spoke:

A. They were, as during the day of the assassination; that is correct.

Q. You testified, Mr. Hunt, that your adult children came to you after it was alleged that you were in Dealey Plaza on November 22, 1963, and said to you, "Is there any truth in this?" Have you testified that was what they said?

A. I have. That is correct.

Hunt's explanations only exacerbated the matter. If the three children had been exposed to the false allegations over a period of time, does it not seem likely that they would remember somewhere along the line where they had spent one of the most traumatic moments of their lives and who had been with them? Why had they not shouted out that their father was innocent? Failing that, how could they require constant reminders from their father that they had all been together that day? The record revealed that as each new allegation was made, asserting that E. Howard Hunt had been in Dallas on November 22, 1963, the children, then adults, demanded to know if the charges were true.

Rarely does a witness testify that he had to remind his alibi witnesses where they were at the crucial moment. In this case, the time frame was considerably prolonged and the event nationally significant, thereby substantially diminishing the possibility that it could have been so easily forgotten.

These three witnesses were to offer the essential testimony placing Hunt hundreds of miles from the crime. They, not the two CIA-arranged witnesses, held in their hands the alibi their father so desperately required.

Hunt had told so many stories, and given so many differing versions of his actions and whereabouts on November 22, 1963, that he had apparently failed to realize that two sets of stories—that he had been with his children the whole time and that his children did not know where he had been at the time— were mutually exclusive explanations.

The jurors understood, however, and in my view before Hunt's cross-examination had concluded his cause had been lost. Yet ours had just begun.

Hunt may have had the motive, ability, and opportunity to participate in the CIA plan to assassinate President Kennedy, but we had not as yet offered direct evidence to demonstrate his involvement.

When Hunt finally left the witness stand, we were deep into the case. The jurors had been listening attentively for days.

Hunt was about to offer the testimony of other witnesses, but before he did so, I had to make an irrevocable decision as to how to proceed.

I was fairly confident about the outcome of the case at that time; my inclination was largely to abandon the defense of the defamation suit and to focus almost exclusively upon evidence linking Hunt and the CIA to the assassination of the president.

In practical terms, this meant I wanted to put little emphasis upon the testimony of Victor Marchetti, the author of the article. I did not intend to present Willis Carto as a witness to demonstrate the lack of actual malice of the defendant, or to engage in further substantial cross-examination of Hunt's witnesses on the questions of malice by the defendant or damages suffered by the plaintiff. Instead, my approach would concentrate the jury's attention on one central question—had the CIA murdered President Kennedy?

The risks were apparent. If the jurors ignored the defense of actual malice and determined that Hunt had suffered serious financial loss, a finding that neither Hunt nor his organization were involved in the Kennedy murder could result in an award that would force my client into bankruptcy, close down the newspaper, and threaten his reputation.

I met with Carto to discuss my proposal. He listened carefully and then asked one question. "Have you ever been this confident about a jury's verdict in advance and been wrong?" I laughed and said that I had made a number of mistakes at trial over the years, including misreading a jury's reactions.

His sense of history apparently overcame his instinct for survival. He said only, "Go for it!" I suggested that since he would not be needed as a witness, he might leave Miami and go home to his work. He was on the next flight to California, confident that he had made the correct call. I returned to the courtroom, grateful that I had a courageous client, but concerned for a moment that my assessment of the case might have been erroneous.

The plaintiff then called Edward J. Dunne, Jr., a retired FBI agent. He testified that he had been Hunt's friend since 1939. He said that when Hunt saw the *Spotlight* article, "he was very upset." On cross-examination, I asked Dunne if he remembered what time of the year during 1978 he and Hunt had discussed the *Spotlight* article. He did not remember. His testimony had been, in my judgment, of no value to Hunt. Yet a portion of it had been so bizarre that I was anxious to see if I had misunderstood it.

Snyder had asked Dunne where he was at the time of the assassination. Dunne said he had been an agent in Providence, Rhode Island. He also testified that he had graduated from Brown, as had Hunt. He said that FBI inquiries regarding Brown graduates were often assigned to him and that the FBI had not asked him to investigate Hunt after the assassination of President Kennedy.

I asked: "Is it your testimony, Mr. Dunne, that if there was any investigation of anyone who had ever attended Brown University—if the investigation was in relationship to the assassination of President Kennedy, or any part in that assassination, that that investigation would be referred to you, in Providence, Rhode Island?"

Dunne responded: "Probably would, sir, yes."

If Dunne can be credited, the notion of old school ties had reached its zenith in the FBI.

Snyder then decided to have Kuzmuk's deposition read to the jury. He chose the December 7, 1981, deposition that had been taken in connection with the first trial, rather than the more recent deposition I conducted just before the trial in progress. Either one was confusing to the listener, since Kuzmuk was a poor witness. He could not remember, he said, if Kennedy had been assassinated on November 20 or November 21. Snyder reminded him that the correct date was November 22, to which Kuzmuk replied, "I was thinking twenty-first or twenty-third, somewhere in there. The twenty-second is fine."

Once Snyder and Kuzmuk had settled on a date for the Kennedy assassination, Kuzmuk testified that on November 22, he'd had lunch "as usual, several of us got together and had lunch." He was with "several colleagues" and as they left the restaurant, "Howard and Betty" drove by. Hunt was married to Dorothy, not Betty. As I listened to the deposition being read, I wondered if the jurors were interested in the nonappearance of the other CIA employees who allegedly had been with Kuzmuk and therefore might have corroborated his account.

Kuzmuk also testified that he did not believe that he drove to work with Hunt on November 22, 1963, and was not even certain if Hunt was in the office at all that day. When Kuzmuk was asked who might have seen Hunt that day if he had been in the office, he replied Betty McDonald. He did not mention Mazerov.

The plaintiff did not call McDonald; Hunt explained that she had been absent that day. No reference was made by the plaintiff or his counsel to Kuzmuk's colleagues at the restaurant, who were also Hunt's colleagues.

Although Kuzmuk had given a somewhat different version of events when I took his deposition during June 1984, I did not press that question and did not move to have the later deposition read at this time. I could not believe that anyone would take Kuzmuk's testimony seriously.

Hunt's other witnesses were of little consequence. His testimony about alleged financial loss due to the publication of the article was contradicted by his own income tax records and the testimony of his literary agent. Hunt's income had decreased before the publication of the article; his books had been rejected by publishers before that date as well.

Connie Mazerov offered the most pathetic testimony I had encountered in some time. It was a sad rendition of the stand-by-your-man theme, later employed with equal credibility by Mrs. Gary Hart. She had seen Hunt early that morning. As to the meetings he was supposed to have attended later that morning (according to one of Hunt's versions of events), she couldn't recall seeing him there. She never saw anyone else that morning who could have seen him. She was apparently willing to help Hunt out, but not if she had to name a single other person who might come forward to dispute her account.

The plaintiff rested. The gasp from the audience was more modestly replicated by the jury. Hunt had refused to call as a witness even one of his children; the children had been the only alibi witnesses about whom he had been consistent from the outset. The record had previously disclosed that all of the children were alive, in good health, and available. Apparently, unlike the CIA-arranged witnesses, none of them was willing to offer testimony of a questionable nature.

During our side's presentation of the case, Marchetti, who at the outset of the proceedings appeared to be an important witness, merely recounted how he had written the article and what his sources had been. I could not defend the odd predictions he'd made, which had, in fact, both comprised and compromised much of the force of the story. I ignored the predictions and errors and focused instead upon the implication that Hunt and the CIA may have been involved in the assassination. I was no longer defending the defamation case; I was prosecuting a murder case within a civil action.

In accordance with that trial strategy, I set aside other evidence we had prepared designed to demonstrate that Liberty Lobby had acted in good faith and had reasonably relied upon Marchetti's expertise in the area. We called no editor, researcher, or publisher's representative to establish those points. Instead, I presented the testimony of Marita Lorenz.

On January 1, 1959, Fidel Castro's revolution in Cuba achieved its victory. Many observers were surprised by the spectacular suddenness of the event. Among those unprepared for the dramatic change was the captain of a West German luxury liner docked in the Havana harbor. His beautiful eighteen-year-old daughter, Marita Lorenz, was caught up in the excitement of the revolution. She was even more pleased when Fidel Castro paid a visit to the ship a short time later. The leader of the revolution and the captain's daughter began a romance. She remained in Cuba when her father sailed away. Later, a child was born.

The CIA, having badly miscalculated Castro's potential for prevailing as well as his commitment to Marxism, was determined to destroy his revolution by destroying his nation's economy, launching military strikes against Cuba and setting into motion long-range plans to assassinate him. This panoply of options was justified by the belief in Langley that any attempt by a nation ninety miles from Florida to pursue a foreign policy different from that current at CIA headquarters was punishable by death.

American-born Francisco Fiorini was chief of security for the Cuban air force under Castro. If the size of the air force during the days following the revolution characterized the importance of the position, Fiorini could not be considered a major leader. It was not an insignificant military post, however, and it was made more significant by the fact that Fiorini was simultaneously employed by the Central Intelligence Agency.

One evening Fiorini furtively informed Marita Lorenz that he must meet with her immediately and secretly. When they met, he informed her that Castro was going to murder her and her child. She was dubious at first, yet frightened. She had seen nothing in Castro's manner or character that permitted her to accept such an assertion. Yet she knew Fiorini to be Castro's trusted aide. She did not know of his association with the CIA. Fear overcame her judgment and she agreed to flee, pursuant to Fiorini's well-thought-out plans. She was expected, he said, at the United States Embassy. Personnel there would protect her and her child and arrange for immediate and secret passage to the United States.

The CIA analysis of Marita disclosed that she would be vulnerable to the agency's recruiting effort. When she arrived in the United States, she was recruited by the CIA for a series of low-profile actions designed to provide weapons to Castro's enemies in Cuba. She was assured that the CIA had saved her life and the life of her child. She was grateful to the CIA and convinced that Castro was deranged and wanted to kill her and her child. She was furious at him and this feeling, added to her sense of personal betrayal, so prejudiced and motivated her that she was willing to work to destroy Castro.

Years later she was to discover that Fidel Castro never intended to harm her or her child. The elaborate scheme had been developed by the CIA to recruit her so that she might agree to use her association with Castro to murder him.

Fiorini left Cuba and worked with Hunt and other CIA operatives based in Miami in the clandestine program to overthrow the government of Fidel Castro. Marita Lorenz was an active participant in that effort. Together they secured weapons from various United States arsenals and arranged for transportation of the weapons to Cuba.

Finally the CIA determined that Lorenz was sufficiently committed and trained for the operation for which she had been recruited. She was given the assignment to assassinate Fidel Castro.

The scenario, she was told, was foolproof. She would return to Cuba, embrace Castro, and seek to resume her previous relationship with him. She was given poisoned capsules to place in Castro's drink. The escape plan seemed less than feasible, but the CIA experts had assured her that she would be easily whisked away in the confusion that followed. The CIA was certain that the death of Castro would signal the revolt of the masses against his government. A similar CIA misunderstanding led the agency to predict an uprising following the invasion of Cuba at the Bay of Pigs, one of many failures of intelligence that doomed that ill-fated adventure. The clandestine section of the CIA rarely makes the same mistake just once.

Marita agreed to the proposal. She notified the Cuban authorities that she wished to return and boarded a jet for Havana. As the flight approached Cuba, she began to experience conflicting feelings. She now stated that she was not sure that she wanted to murder the man who at one time had been so kind and so close to her. She also feared that if her belongings were searched, the CIA's poisoned capsules would be detected. Although the CIA had assured her that her luggage would not be searched, she was less than certain, since in her experience the CIA's percentage for accurately predicting events was remarkably low. She took her makeup kit and large pocketbook to a restroom on the plane. She placed the poisoned capsules into a jar of cold cream and buried them there so that they were no longer visible.

This time the CIA had been correct. Her belongings were not searched as she was warmly greeted and driven directly to a hotel. Before she met Castro that evening, she sought to retrieve the capsules. She discovered that they had been dissolved in the cold cream. She was relieved and immediately disposed of the poisoned cream in the commode. Much later Castro, having learned of the plot, said to Lorenz, "You couldn't kill me. You would never do that, would you?" She told him that she could not have carried out the plan.

After Lorenz returned to Miami, Francisco Fiorini, now operating under the name Frank Sturgis, recruited her for one more operation. Frank Sturgis is the name under which he was later convicted along with Hunt, Liddy, and various other Miami-based anti-Castro Cubans recruited by Hunt for the Watergate crimes.

During 1977, according to Lorenz, who was then living in New York City, Sturgis threatened to kill her. She called the local police and Sturgis was arrested. At that time, I contacted Lorenz to discuss evidence tying her to the initial stages of the plan to assassinate President Kennedy. She was then working for a United States spy organization at a particularly low-level job. She resided in a huge apartment building on the East Side of Manhattan in which several Russian families, minor and mid-level diplomatic employees, also lived. Her assignment was to pore through the garbage each day and sift it for letters, notes, or other objects discarded by the Russians that might prove useful upon close examination.

Marita Lorenz spent hours talking with me. She had known of my work in the area and she told me in some detail of her knowledge of the plan to assassinate President Kennedy and of the roles played by Sturgis and Hunt. The information was startling and impressive, but I was unable to locate anyone who would publish her account.

Years later, when the matter was being considered by a United States district court for the first time since the shots had been fired, I located her and asked her if she would testify at the trial in Miami. She seemed genuinely frightened and said, "You don't know these people. They have killed and would not hesitate to kill again." She said she was terrified at the prospect of returning to Miami.

I asked her if she would consider testifying at a neutral site, a hotel suite in Manhattan, if I agreed not to require her to state her home address or telephone number and place of employment and if I agreed not to inform Hunt's counsel, who of course would be present, of her home address. She considered my suggestion and in time acceded to it.

The deposition began with Hunt's counsel, Kevin Dunne, in attendance. I offered a stipulation into the record in which I stated that the witness's location would not be provided but that I would arrange for any subsequent deposition that Hunt wished to take of Lorenz. Dunne agreed.

There are various methods for communicating the contents of a deposition to a jury. Snyder had chosen to read the Kuzmuk deposition, punctuating it regularly with the word "question," followed by the inquiry, and the word "answer," followed by the response. Unless the testimony is riveting, its recitation in that fashion almost invariably diminishes its impact. Another approach is to offer a transcript of the deposition into evidence and provide copies for the jurors so that they may each read it individually. This method permits the jurors to study the document closely, but it is utterly lacking in drama.

To present Marita Lorenz's testimony, I arranged for Julia Lee, the wife of Liberty Lobby general counsel Fleming Lee, to study the deposition transcript. At the trial she took the witness chair and answered questions by reading from the transcript. The jury was informed, of course, that the witness was not Lorenz but that the testimony was authentic.

The testimony began:

Q. What is your present employment?

A. I do undercover work for an intelligence agency.

Q. Are you permitted to discuss the nature of that work, or where you work?

A. No, I am not.

291

Q. Is it also true that, as I have stipulated, you do not wish to give your home address?

A. No, I do not.

Q. Have you been employed by the Central Intelligence Agency?

A. Yes.

Q. Are you at liberty to discuss the details of that employment?

A. No.

Q. Have you been employed by the Federal Bureau of Investigation?

A. Yes.

Q. Are you at liberty to discuss that?

A. No.

Q. Have you been employed by the New York Police Department?

A. Yes.

Q. Was that intelligence work?

A. Yes.

Q. Are you at liberty to discuss the details of that work?

A. No.

Q. During 1978, did you appear as a witness before the United States House of Representatives Select Committee on Assassinations?

A. Yes.

Q. Was that in relation to the assassination of President John F. Kennedy?

A. Yes.

Q. Did you appear as a witness after the chief judge of the United States district court of Washington had signed an offer conferring immunity upon you and compelling you to testify?

A. Yes.

My questions and her answers established the foundation for the relationship that existed among Lorenz, Hunt, and Sturgis. I then moved toward the matter at hand.

Q. During and prior to November 1963, did you live in Miami, Florida?

A. Yes, I did.

Q. I want you to understand, if I ask you any question which you are not permitted to answer, you may of course say that, but I will try, based on my previous interview with you, to just ask you questions which you can answer.

A. Yes.

Q. During and before November of 1963, did you work on behalf of the Central Intelligence Agency in the Miami area?

A. Yes.

Q. Did you work with a man named Frank Sturgis, while you were working for the CIA?

A. Yes, I did.

Q. Was that in Miami, during and prior to November 1963?

A. Yes.

Q. What other names, to your knowledge, is Frank Sturgis known by?

A. Frank Fiorini, Hamilton; the last name, Hamilton. F-I-O-R-I-N-I-.

Q. Was Mr. Fiorini or Mr. Sturgis, while you worked with him, also employed by the Central Intelligence Agency?

A. Yes.

Q. During that time were payments made to Mr. Sturgis for the work he was doing for the CIA?

A. Yes.

Q. Did you ever witness anyone make payments to him for the CIA work which you and Mr. Sturgis were both involved in?

A. Yes.

Hunt had testified that Sturgis had never worked for the CIA and that he and Sturgis had never met until the Bay of Pigs episode. Yet Hunt had run the anti-Castro organizations from Miami for the CIA for years preceding the invasion and Sturgis had been an important contract agent for the CIA in those operations. Sturgis, too, was based in the Miami area.

When Richard Helms, the former director of the CIA, testified in this case, he said, "Sturgis I have heard of." He described the relationship between the CIA and Sturgis: "Frank Sturgis was an agent, an outside agent, a contract agent, of the Agency."

In the Third Press case, Sturgis himself testified that "while I was in Cuba, I was recruited by the station, CIA station chief in Santiago de Cuba, to spy for the United States government."

Hunt had written a novel, Bimini Run, published years before the CIA-coordinated invasion at the Bay of Pigs. In it a character who was a soldier-of-fortune and a former bartender was named "Hank Sturgis." Sturgis had testified, on February 8, 1978, that he had worked as a bartender. Obviously, a good portion of his life had been devoted to the role of soldier-of-fortune. He was asked about the "Hank Sturgis" in the Hunt book. "This character in that book, known as Hank Sturgis, seems to follow your own history to a great extent." Sturgis responded, "Right. My wife thinks that too. She said, 'It could be you.' "

When Hunt was asked to explain "Hank Sturgis' relationship to the historical jobs held by Frank Sturgis," he answered only "I wouldn't attempt to answer that."

Hunt's sworn denial that Sturgis had a CIA connection was repudiated by the testimony of all of the relevant witnesses and even challenged by the words he had himself written in his novel.

On the other hand, Lorenz, who had testified that Sturgis worked for the CIA, received corroboration from Helms, Sturgis himself, and possibly *Bimini Run*.

It was clear that Lorenz was about to reveal the name of the paymaster and control for Sturgis' secret operations. The courtroom was hushed. Even the miscellaneous spectator background sounds, coughing, clearing of throats, rustling of papers, and moving about, came to a sudden, almost eerie, halt.

Q. Who did you witness make payments to Mr. Sturgis?

A. A man by the name of Eduardo.

In this case Hunt had testified that he had used the alias "Eduardo." Lorenz had told me about "Eduardo" many years earlier, long before Hunt's code name had surfaced publicly. In addition, Liddy's testimony had established Hunt's later role as a paymaster in the dirty tricks department of the Nixon White House.

Q. Who is Eduardo?

A. That is his code name; the real name is E. Howard Hunt.

The jurors, who had been studying the Marita Lorenz stand-in as she read the answers from the transcript of the sworn statement, looked suddenly at Hunt when his name was given. He saw that he had become the focal point for the jurors; he had been watching them closely. He quickly looked away and began to confer with his attorneys.

Q. Did you know him and meet him during and prior to November 1963?

A. Yes.

Q. Did you witness payments made by Mr. Hunt to Mr. Sturgis or Mr. Fiorini on more than one occasion prior to November of 1963?

A. Yes.

We then moved directly into the events immediately preceding the assassination of President Kennedy.

In a meeting with me, Lorenz had agreed to reveal the details of the entire episode. She had also been trained over the years to remain silent or to offer little specific information if she were ever to be in a position where she was required to testify. The impulse to disclose the facts was modified by her long-standing intelligence discipline. The confluence of these two concepts resulted in a series of oddly staccato, yet entirely relevant and responsive, answers.

Q. Did you go on a trip with Mr. Sturgis from Miami during November of 1963?

A. Yes.

Q. Was anyone else present with you when you went on that trip?

A. Yes.

Q. What method of transportation did you use?

A. By car.

Q. Was there one or more cars?

A. There was a follow-up car.

Q. Does that mean two cars?

A. Backup; yes.

Q. What was in the follow-up car, if you know?

A. Weapons.

Q. Without asking you any of the details regarding the activity that you and Mr. Sturgis and Mr. Hunt were involved in, may I ask you if some of that activity was related to the transportation of weapons?

A. Yes.

Q. Did Mr. Hunt pay Mr. Sturgis sums of money for activity related to the transportation of weapons?

A. Yes.

The date the witness had fixed for the trip was intriguing: November 1963. Yet thus far she had not been asked about either the destination or the purpose.

Q. Did Mr. Sturgis tell you where you would be going from Miami, Florida, during November of 1963, prior to the time that you traveled with him in the car?

A. Dallas, Texas.

Q. He told you that?

A. Yes.

Q. Did he tell you the purpose of the trip to Dallas, Texas?

A. No; he said it was confidential.

Q. Did you arrive in Dallas during November of 1963?

A. Yes.

Q. After you arrived in Dallas, did you stay at any accommodations there?

A. Motel.

The jurors no doubt wondered if the witness was going to testify that she had seen Hunt in Dallas shortly before the assassination. The suspense ended within the next moment.

Q. While you were at that motel, did you meet anyone other than those who were in the party traveling with you from Miami to Dallas?

A. Yes.

Q. Who did you meet?

A. E. Howard Hunt.

Marita Lorenz then provided details about her stay in Dallas.

Q. Was there anyone else who you saw or met other than Mr. Hunt?

A. Excuse me?

Q. Other than those?

A. Jack Ruby.

Q. Tell me the circumstances regarding your seeing E. Howard Hunt in Dallas in November of 1963?

A. There was a prearranged meeting that E. Howard Hunt deliver us sums of money for the so-called operation that I did not know its nature.

Q. Were you told what your role was to be?

A. Just a decoy at the time.

Thus far the role of Hunt as the control of the CIA operation had been largely hearsay as far as Lorenz was concerned. Sturgis had told her that Hunt had made the arrangements, was the crucial contact, and would provide the operating funds, cover, and plans for exit from the area once the assignment was completed. Now the question turned to what Lorenz had observed of Hunt's behavior that day.

Q. Did you see Mr. Hunt actually deliver money to anyone in the motel room which you were present in?

A. Yes.

Q. To whom did you see him deliver the money?

A. He gave an envelope of cash to Frank Fiorini.

Q. When he gave him the envelope, was the cash visible as he had it in the envelope?

A. Yes.

Q. Did you have a chance to see the cash after the envelope was given to Mr. Fiorini?

A. Frank pulled out the money and flipped it and counted it and said "that is enough" and put it in his jacket.

Q. How long did Mr. Hunt remain in the room?

A. About forty-five minutes.

The implication was apparent; the two-car caravan, the transportation of weapons to Dallas, and the meeting between Sturgis and Hunt all may have been the prelude to the assassination. Yet no direct evidence had yet been offered regarding the purpose of the CIA operation.

Q. Did anyone else enter the room other than you, Mr. Fiorini, Mr. Hunt, and others who may have been there before Mr. Hunt arrived?

A. No.

Q. Where did you see the person you identified as Jack Ruby?

A. After Eduardo left, a fellow came to the door and it was Jack Ruby, about an hour later, forty-five minutes to an hour later.

Q. When you say Eduardo, who are you referring to?

A. E. Howard Hunt.

The presence of Ruby, the man who had been a hit man for organized crime as early as 1939 in Chicago, and who served as an FBI informant in Dallas since 1959, brought the circle closer.

It was now imperative to establish the date in November when Hunt met Sturgis in Dallas and turned the funds over to him so that the operation could go forward.

Q. When did that meeting take place in terms of the hour; was it daytime or nighttime?

A. Early evening.

Q. How soon after that evening meeting took place did you leave Dallas?

A. I left about two hours later; Frank took me to the airport and we went back to Miami.

Q. Now, can you tell us in relationship to the day that President Kennedy was killed, when this meeting took place?

A. The day before.

Q. Is it your testimony that the meeting which you just described with Mr. Hunt making the payment of money to Mr. Sturgis took place on November 21, 1963?

A. Yes.

Q. When was the first time that you met me?

A. In 1977.

Q. On that occasion, did you tell me in words or substance exactly the same thing that you have testified to today?

A. Yes.

The jury had heard the witness testify that Hunt had been in Dallas on November 21, 1963.

The original focus at the first trial by Hunt's lawyer, Ellis Rubin, upon the importance of establishing Hunt's alleged absence from Dallas on November 22 had so skewed the defense that the CIA sought out witnesses and documentary evidence to provide a false alibi for the wrong day. Over the years Hunt, in defending against the charge that he had been involved in the assassination, developed, as we have seen, a never-ending variety of stories and apocryphal witnesses regarding his whereabouts when Kennedy was killed. Unless Hunt was accused of actually firing one of the weapons that day, and I know of no responsible person who has ever made that charge, his presence in Dallas on the day of the assassination was largely irrelevant to the charge that he had been involved in the conspiracy to murder President Kennedy.

Thus Hunt's CIA witnesses, misled as to the implications of the record, focused upon November 22 to the exclusion of the previous day. Kuzmuk, as available and flexible a witness as I have met in a legal proceeding, was asked to testify that he had seen Hunt on the afternoon of the assassination. Being nothing if not an obliging colleague, he obliged. On cross-examination, since he apparently had not been asked to provide Hunt with an alibi for other dates, he frankly stated that he could not recall having seen Hunt between November 18 and some time in December 1963. Kuzmuk testified that he lived just fifty yards from Hunt in Sumner and that at the workplace, his office was just a few doors from Hunt's. Certainly, his testimony implied that Hunt may not have been around during that time.

Hunt himself was misled as to his own objective. When I confronted Hunt with the fact that CIA records disclosed that he had taken eleven hours of sick leave in the two-week period ending on November 23, 1963, he responded that he was quite sure he had not utilized any of those eleven hours on November 22.

Having decided that he had exculpated himself from the relevant potential accusation, he agreed that it was certainly possible that he had been absent from work on November 21.

Having exhausted his special resources in order to prepare a spurious defense for November 22, Hunt was left vulnerable to the truth regarding his presence in Dallas on the previous day. Not a single witness could be found, not a record could be located, to demonstrate that he was anywhere else but in Dallas on that day. Hunt himself had testified, as had his last remaining alibi witnesses, that he may not have been where he should have been that day—at his office in downtown Washington on a weekday.

During the Lorenz deposition I inquired about her identification of the man she described as Jack Ruby.

Q. Two days after President Kennedy was assassinated, that is on November 24, 1963, Lee Harvey Oswald, who was arrested and charged with the assassination of President Kennedy and the murder of police officer J.D. Tippit, was killed in Dallas by a man named Jack Ruby?

A. Yes.

Q. On that occasion and subsequent to that time, did you see pictures of Jack Ruby in the newspaper and did you see Jack Ruby on television?

A. Yes, I did.

Q. Is it your testimony that the man who killed Lee Harvey Oswald is, to the best of your ability to identify him, the person who was in the room in the motel in Dallas the night before the president was killed?

A. Yes.

Q. Had you ever seen Jack Ruby before November 21, 1963?

A. No.

Dunne's cross-examination of Lorenz did not succeed in calling into question a single statement which she had made. Indeed, it provided an opportunity for her to fill in a number of details.

In response to his questions, she stated that she was then working for an intelligence unit of the New York Police Department and the Drug Enforcement Administration. During his deposition, Frank Sturgis confirmed the accuracy of that testimony. Lorenz further testified that she had been recruited by the CIA during 1959.

When asked why she had not appeared before the Warren Commission, she testified that she was instructed by her superiors in the CIA not to do so. Dunne persisted.

Q. Is it your testimony today, that today's testimony is consistent with what you said before the House Select Committee?

A. That's right.

Q. When was the first time you met Howard Hunt?

A. 1960, in Miami, Florida.

Q. How was he identified to you?

A. Introduced. Introduced as Eduardo.

Q. How do you spell that?

A. E-D-U-A-R-D-O, Eduardo, E-D-U-A-R-D-O. He was to finance the operations in Miami.

Q. What language did he speak to you in?

A. English and Spanish.

Q. English and Spanish?

A. Yes.

Q. Do you speak Spanish?

A. Yes.

Q. Any other languages?

A. German.

Q. When is it that you became aware that this person you know as Eduardo was E. Howard Hunt?

A. About the same time. Eduardo was the name we were to refer to him as, when discussing things.

Q. Who did you believe he was working for at that time?

A. CIA.

Q. Why?

A. Because we were all at that time CIA members of Operation 40. We had been given instructions from Eduardo and had certain rights and permissions to do things that the average citizen could not do.

When Dunne asked Lorenz about her early experience for the CIA in Cuba, she answered:

"I will tell you what is on record. I stole secrets from Cuba. I was trained to kill. Anything else?"

During my interview with Marita prior to the deposition, I had asked for the names of the other persons in the two-car caravan from Miami to Dallas. She was very reluctant to answer that question: "They killed Kennedy. I don't want to be the one to give their names; it's too dangerous." I told her that I would neither pursue the matter then nor inquire of her about their identities at the deposition. I told her that it was possible, however, that Hunt's lawyer might ask that question.

At the deposition, Hunt's lawyer demanded that she provide the name of one more person in the automobile with her. She looked at me, stared at Dunne as if to say, "Well, you asked for this," and responded:

A. The other one was Jerry Patrick—

Q. Jerry Patrick?

A. Hemming.

Q. Is that, H-E-M-M-I-N-G?

A. Yes.

She added that two Cuban brothers named Novo and a pilot named Pedro Diaz Lanz were also in the caravan.

After the deposition I discussed that question with her. She said, "If Hunt and his friends in the CIA wanted that question answered, or were too dumb or too lazy to keep their lawyer from asking it, the responsibility is theirs, not mine."

Dunne wanted to know about the weapons.

Q. Did you see the weapons in the second car?

A. Yes.

Q. What kind of weapons were there?

A. Handguns and automatics.

Q. Could you identify for me today what kind of guns they were, specifically?

A. Rifles; there were cases of machine guns, rifles, thirty-eights, forty-fives.

Q. Have you been trained in firearms?

A. Yes.

Q. What were the kind of rifles that were there?

A. M-16s, M-1s, shotguns; several.

Q. There were machine guns?

A. Yes.

Q. In your work for the CIA Operation 40, was that one of the major tasks you undertook was to transport guns?

A. Yes.

Q. Was that for the anti-Cuba activities?

A. Yes, it was.

Q. What happened to those guns when you got to Dallas?

A. They were in the car and I presume they took them to the motel the next day, the next night. A lot of things they carried in.

Dunne then asked about the place in Miami from which they had departed.

Q. Where did you leave from?

A. From the house in Miami.

Q. Is that a CIA house?

A. A safe house. Yes.

Q. Did everyone meet at the same place?

A. Yes.

Q. Who else was at the house, besides the seven people you identified?

A. This fellow is incarcerated; it is not fair to answer. Another fellow is dead.

Q. Incarcerated where?

A. Out of the country, right now, Venezuela somewhere.

Q. Is his name Bosch?

A. Yes.

Q. What is his first name?

A. Orlando.

Q. Was he one of the anti-Castro Cubans involved in Operation 40?

A. Yes.

Q. Isn't that a matter of public record?

A. Yes.

I broke in to address Dunne: "It is not a matter of public record that he was at the house that day. Be fair with the questions. She is not represented by counsel. She may well have violated the law on numerous occasions in response to your questions."

Q. Who was the person at the house that is now deceased?

A. Alexander Rorke, Jr.

Q. Is he a CIA employee?

A. Yes.

When Dunne wanted to know if Lorenz had told anyone about her experience in Dallas, she responded directly to his question:

Q. What did you do after you got to New York and found out that President Kennedy was just assassinated in Dallas?

A. Talked to the FBI.

Q. You talked to the FBI?

A. Yes.

Q. Voluntarily?

A. They wanted to talk to me anyway about certain things with my child's father and they picked me up and took me to the office.

Q. What day would that have been?

A. A few days after I arrived, after everyone got over the initial shock.

Q. It would be some time in the month of November of 1963?

A. Yes.

Q. In your discussions with the FBI, they inquired about your activities which related to Dallas and this group of seven people that took the car trip?

A. Well, they discussed my associates down there and my relationship with my daughter's father, mostly.

Q. Did they know the names of the people you took the car trip with, from Miami to Dallas?

A. Yes.

Q. Did they ask you about each of those people?

A. Yes.

Q. Did you tell them about the guns and money and about Eduardo?

A. Yes.

Q. I will have to start again because the court reporter cannot take nods down.

A. I was nodding, yes, to each.

Q. What was your answer?

A. They asked me about everything, my daughter's father, and I am glad I am back up here away from that.

Q. You told them about Eduardo?

A. Yes.

Q. And the guns?

A. They know about all those associations. They didn't want to go into it. Those were CIA activities, not FBI.

Before the day ended Marita Lorenz explained why she had left Dallas before the assassination:

"I knew that this was different from other jobs. This was not just gunrunning. This was big, very big, and I wanted to get out. I told Sturgis I wanted to leave. He said it was a very big operation but that my part was not dangerous. I was to be a decoy. Before he could go further, I said please let me get out. I want to go back to my baby in Miami. Finally he agreed and drove me to the airport."

She flew to Miami, picked up her child, and then flew to New York so that she could be with her mother in New Jersey.

Dunne had developed a penchant for not leaving bad enough alone. The testimony of the witness had implicated Sturgis and Hunt in the assassination. Dunne decided to put a fine point to the testimony.

Q. Did you ever talk with Frank Sturgis about it, since then?

Lorenz was reluctant to respond directly to the question.

A. We are not on talking terms, Frank and I.

Q. That was not my question. Have you ever talked about it with Frank Sturgis since 1963?

A. Yes.

Q. Did he indicate to you that he was involved in the assassination of the president?

A. Yes.

Dunne continued to ask questions that Marita Lorenz had requested that I avoid. Due to my commitment to her, I did not make the inquiries, but Dunne rushed in, asking questions to which he did not know the answer.

Later Lorenz, prompted by Dunne's questions, explained that when Sturgis sought to recruit her for yet another CIA project, he told her that she had missed "the really big one" in Dallas. He explained, she said, "We killed the president that day. You could have been a part of it—you know, part of history. You should have stayed. It was safe. Everything was covered in advance. No arrests, no real newspaper investigation. It was all covered, very professional." It may have been very professional, but after the testimony of Marita Lorenz was read to a jury in a United States courthouse, it was no longer all covered.

An objective observer, had there been one in the courtroom, might have concluded that Hunt's defamation case had been overwhelmed by the evidence and rendered moot, that no justiciable controversy remained. Hunt and his entourage, no doubt, would have dissented from that conclusion; it is that sort of difference of opinion that brings cases to the courthouse in the first instance.

Earlier in the trial I thought that the jurors had been intrigued by the long-suppressed evidence about the murder of their president. Now, it seemed to me, they had become committed to learn the truth about the assassination and to act upon it. The group had been transformed; no longer did its members comprise an ordinary civil jury. They were now a moment in the conscience of their nation. They had long since forgotten the *Spotlight* article and Marchetti's predictions, none of which had ever been even remotely realized.

The jurors had listened to the Lorenz testimony with an electric intensity rarely found even when a charismatic witness appears. Here, the words were read to them by a proxy. It did not matter. The jurors were focusing on the evidence, not the manner in which it was packaged. They waited with a growing impatience to discover how Hunt and his colleagues in the Central Intelligence Agency would respond to the evidence they had just heard.

They had seen Hunt, an impressive witness during his direct examination, wither away during cross-examination. They had heard the words of Marita Lorenz, an imposing witness during her direct examination, grow stronger, more certain, and more revelatory throughout the cross-examination conducted by Hunt's counsel.

Hunt and his attorneys were concerned. The Lorenz testimony had come as no surprise. The deposition had been conducted two weeks before trial. Perhaps they had misjudged its potential impact. Counsel for Hunt then asked permission of the court to call as a rebuttal witness Newton Scott Miler. Miler was with the CIA from its creation in September 1947, and had become chief of counterintelligence operations until his retirement. He had been a very high-ranking officer, third in the CIA's hierarchy in its elite counterintelligence section, directed for years by Angleton.

Many lawyers, including inexperienced trial counsel, have come to accept as the automatic order of trial the presentation of the plaintiff's case, followed by the defense case, and then rebuttal evidence followed by surrebuttal. Rebuttal testimony, however, offered by the plaintiff to refute portions of the evidence submitted by the defendant, is not always admissible even if relevant.

Only after both parties rest may rebuttal evidence be offered. Since the concept permitting the reopening of the case, thus providing for an extraordinary remedy, is based on equitable consideration, the tendered evidence must be offered to rebut evidence that might not have been reasonably anticipated by counsel for the plaintiff. If, for example, during the defendant's case, a witness makes an accusation about the plaintiff that is totally unexpected and relevant, it is only fair to permit the plaintiff to reopen his case so that he may offer rebuttal evidence to contest the allegation.

It could not be reasonably argued, however, that the testimony of Lorenz contained any surprises for the plaintiff. His lawyers were present when it was offered and it had been taken and completed before the trial commenced. I believe that Hunt's attorneys, who had sought unsuccessfully to exclude the Lorenz deposition for technical reasons related to procedure, had been hopeful that the jury would not hear it. The judge summarily rejected their plea to exclude it.

I could have, had I wished, allowed the case to end without the testimony of Newton Miler, since he had been improperly offered as a rebuttal witness to Lorenz. Judge Kehoe made it clear that the Miler testimony was not admissible unless I waived my right to object to it. The matter was further complicated by the weather. Miler resided in New Mexico. Snyder told the court that a terrible winter storm was due to strike that area within twenty-four hours and that Miler would be unable to return home safely unless he left Miami shortly. It was then the end of the trial day.

Judge Kehoe was not going to permit the jury to hear the evidence at that time. As to the suggestion by Snyder that the judge preview the testimony and then decide, the judge was reluctant to sit through the night listening to testimony that in all probability would never reach the jury.

I sat there while the judge and Hunt's counsel engaged in colloquy. I hardly heard the exchange. My mind was on the jurors, at that point the representatives of the nation.

They wanted to hear the entire truth. They were entitled to hear all of the testimony each side wanted to offer. No federal rule of procedure should be employed, however soundly, to suppress any of the evidence. There had been too much of that for too long.

I stood and addressed the court, stating that I would waive my objection to the evidence and that I would accommodate Mr. Miler by being present that evening if Hunt's counsel wished to take his deposition then. The deposition could then be read to the jury.

Hunt and his attorneys seemed to react in shock. Their excitement seemed to convey their belief that victory had just been achieved. Judge Kehoe did not even seem surprised. He smiled, thanked me, and the court was adjourned.

After the session in court had ended, I called Willis Carto to tell him what I had done. Whatever apprehension I had experienced before talking with him soon dissipated. "It was the right decision," he said. "Let's get all the facts out there."

That evening, Hunt's two attorneys, Miler, and a secretary with a tape recorder arrived in my room in the Everglades Hotel at seven o'clock.

On such short notice they had been unable to secure the services of an official court reporter authorized to administer the oath to the witness and to record the testimony. At the conclusion of a deposition, the court reporter adds a certificate that, in most instances, reads as did the court reporter's statement in the Lorenz deposition:

CERTIFICATE

I, ANGELO IODICE, hereby certify that the deposition of MARITA LORENZ was held before me on the eleventh day of January, 1985.

That said witness was duly sworn, before the commencement of her testimony, that the testimony was taken stenographically by myself, and then transcribed by myself; and that the party was represented by counsel as appears herein.

That the within transcript is a true record of the examination of said witness.

That I am not connected by blood or marriage with any of the parties. I am not interested directly or indirectly in the matter in controversy, nor am I in the employ of any of the counsel.

IN WITNESS WHEREOF, I have hereunto set my hand this 15th day, of January, 1985.

ANGELO IODICE

It was clear that each provision required to create a valid deposition was about to be violated. The witness could not be duly sworn, the testimony would not be taken and transcribed by a disinterested party, and as a result, Miler would be spared the possibility of being prosecuted for perjury. Nevertheless, I agreed to go forward. I began the odd proceedings with a statement:

"This is a 'deposition' which the plaintiff has asked to take. There is no notary public here, there is no court reporter here. I have agreed to waive any formalities that can be waived so long as when it is all finished the person who made the statement is subject to the penalties of perjury for each of the statements which he has made. I do not know if that can happen under the circumstances, but rather than just tell everybody to go home, I'm willing to proceed with the understanding that I will waive all formalities but, of course, not the requirement that the person making the statement be subjected to the penalties of perjury."

Dunne followed with an explanation as to what he planned; he then sought to initiate the formalities:

"This is Kevin Dunne, one of the attorneys for Howard Hunt. I am going to attempt as an officer of the court to swear in the deponent Mr. Miler and administer the following oath."

DUNNE: Mr. Miler, do you swear under the penalties of perjury that the following testimony that you will give shall be the truth, the whole truth, and nothing but the truth?

MILER: I do.

LANE: For the record, could I ask you, Mr. Dunne, are you admitted to practice in the state of Florida?

DUNNE: No, I am not.

LANE: Terrific start. Okay, let's proceed.

And we did proceed. Dunne asked a series of questions for the purpose of establishing that Miler was a CIA founder, high-ranking officer, and veteran of the Agency. Miler testified that he had served under Ray Rocca, who reported only to the legendary James Jesus Angleton, the chief of counterintelligence. Miler had been chief of counterintelligence operations. He had served the interests of the CIA for almost thirty years, he testified.

Counsel for Hunt, satisfied that Miler had qualified as an expert on CIA affairs, sought to show that Marita Lorenz had not been "employed" by the CIA. Sturgis had previously testified in the Third Press case as to how he had been recruited by the CIA and about the covert assignments he had undertaken for the CIA. He had concluded his testimony by stating that he had never been an "employee" of the CIA. To maintain the illusion of independence from the Agency, he and his CIA control had decided that he should not sign a formal contract.

Dunne asked Miler about Lorenz:

Q. In your time with the agency have you ever heard the name—Strike that. Do you have any knowledge of the name Marita Lorenz?

A. I have read the name.

Q. To your knowledge has Marita Lorenz ever been employed by the CIA for any purpose?

A. No, not when I was in the CIA.

The words were designed to give the impression that Lorenz had not carried out CIA assignments. Yet Miler had not made that allegation. He had merely stated, in response to questions carefully calculated to provide a minimum of information and a maximum of deception, that Lorenz, to his "knowledge," had not been "employed" by the CIA and that he had "no knowledge" that she carried out CIA assignments. He may have heard of operations undertaken by her, but unless he was present when she was given the assignment, he felt free to testify that he did not "know" that she had been assigned.

Dunne continued, using the same precisely crafted language.

Q. I take it then that you would have no knowledge about Marita Lorenz participating in any activities for the CIA?

A. No, I have no knowledge.

Q. And for the CIA in any of the Cuban operations?

A. No, I have no knowledge of any of that.

Counsel for Hunt consulted his notes and his colleagues and then made the same inquiries about Sturgis.

Q. Sir, do you know the name Frank Fiorini Sturgis?

A. I have read the name, yes.

Q. And what does that name mean to you?

A. The name means that he has—it has been alleged that he has been involved in certain CIA activities and activities connected with Mr. Howard Hunt.

Q. Has Frank Sturgis to your knowledge ever been an employee of the CIA?

A. No.

Q. Mr. Miler, Marita Lorenz has testified in this case that she was a CIA agent along with, and who worked for, Frank Sturgis, also a CIA agent—is there any truth to that testimony?

A. Not to my knowledge.

In an effort to utilize Miler as an all-purpose witness to isolate Lorenz from any CIA enterprise, Dunne had gone too far. Miler, perhaps unaware of the voluminous deposition record developed over a period of years in this and related cases, had succeeded instead in dissociating himself from the orthodox position on the question.

Sturgis, still a loyal CIA denizen, had testified before Congress and elsewhere of his work for the CIA and of his association with Lorenz in that work. Richard Helms, the former director of the CIA, as we have seen, had previously stated under oath that Sturgis was a CIA contract agent. Miler's entrance, with its implication that neither Lorenz nor Sturgis had worked for the CIA to his "knowledge," was both late and inadequate. Miler and Hunt had prepared the testimony with precision. Yet they had sought to prove too much and, therefore, had proved nothing. To quote an apocryphal British jurist, when Miler implied that Sturgis had never carried out a CIA operation, his testimony "like the thirteenth strike of a crazy clock cast discredit upon all that preceded it and all that followed."

Miller added that "to his knowledge" the CIA had not assassinated President Kennedy. The CIA had so involved itself with euphemism and deception in order to escape responsibility for its actions, many of which were violations of the criminal law, that proof of anything related to the Agency was often elusive. When I began my cross-examination, I explored that area with Miler, much to his consternation.

Q. Mr. Miler, can you prove to me now that you worked for the CIA?

A. What do you mean by proof?

I had not often seen a witness who had exuded such composure, indeed arrogance, a moment before, become so flustered and angry when asked a relatively simple question. Miler flushed, reached into his pockets, patted himself down, and searched himself as assiduously as if he had just placed himself under arrest in an effort to locate some document.

While performing this self-scrutinization, he said, "I have a card that says I'm retired from the CIA." When I asked him if he could locate the card, he replied, with some bombast, "Certainly." Soon afterward he added, in more mild tones, "At least I think so." Finally he found and presented a little document approximately the size of a business card. It merely said he had been an employee of the United States government and was now retired. It was undated and signed only by him. I presume that retired postal employees are issued similar or identical cards. I continued with the line of inquiry.

Q. Is this card signed by anyone other than yourself?

A. No sir.

Q. Have you any proof that you are—were employed by the Central Intelligence Agency?

A. Other than this card that says I was, I don't have any other proof with me.

Q. But that card is a printed form which you yourself signed, is that correct?

A. Yes.

Q. How do we know you ever worked for the CIA?

A. One reason is because I don't want to subject myself to perjury. I'm telling you the truth.

Q. Marita Lorenz testified that she worked for the CIA and made that statement under a real oath.

A. You can check with the CIA. It's in the public record that I worked for the CIA. I have written articles and it has been published that I was with the CIA.

Q. It has been published that Marita Lorenz was with the CIA and it has been published that Frank Sturgis was with the CIA. In fact, under oath the former director of the CIA, Richard Helms, said that he believed that Frank Sturgis was a CIA agent who worked in Florida in the Cuban operations. Do you have a statement by the former director of the CIA which makes such a strong statement about your relationship with the CIA?

A. No sir.

Hunt, his counsel, and Miler had prepared the testimony with fastidious concern to delineate its boundaries and escape the penalties for perjury. A *prima facie* demonstration had been made; a former high-ranking CIA officer had said that neither Hunt nor Sturgis had been employed by the CIA. Or had he? The jurors were entitled to know what Miler claimed to know.

Q. Do you know every contract agent that worked with the CIA while you were working at the CIA?

A. No sir.

Q. You do not?

A. No sir.

Q. If you do not know every contract agent who worked for the CIA from the time you were employed until the time you left, how can you state that Marita Lorenz was not a contract agent for the CIA?

A. I said to my knowledge.

Q. So you cannot state that she was not employed by the CIA, is that correct?

A. That's correct.

Q. You cannot state that Frank Sturgis was not employed by the CIA, can you?

A. No sir.

Miler's contribution had been rendered not just ineffectual but entirely meaningless.

The CIA's penchant for enshrouding its clandestine work, particularly its numerous failures, was legend. It could not be reasonably asserted that Miler was in a position to offer credible testimony about Lorenz and Sturgis unless he was free to speak openly, should the desire to testify truthfully suddenly overwhelm him.

Therefore I inquired as to whether Miler had been given permission to reveal the facts about Lorenz and Sturgis.

Q. If they were in fact both employed by the CIA, would you be at liberty to reveal that, in view of the secrecy agreement that you signed with the CIA?

A. I would have to seek counsel with the CIA before I could answer that question.

Q. Have you sought counsel with the CIA before answering questions about Marita Lorenz or Frank Sturgis?

A. No sir.

Q. So in fact if you knew that they both were employed by the CIA you couldn't now tell us that, could you?

A. I'm not sure what my legal position on that would be.

Since Miler had said that some doubt existed as to his right to tell the truth in this matter, I decided to put that question to an immediate test. I took a yellow pad from my briefcase, held my pen in hand, poised to write down the names he was about to reveal, and then asked the question.

Q. All right then, tell me the name of every contract agent who ever worked for the CIA whose name you know.

A. No, I could not do that under my secrecy agreement.

Miler had quickly resolved any existing ambiguity about his authority.

There was one area of Miler's expertise that Hunt and his counsel had shown no interest in raising. Miler had been in charge of the interrogation of Yuri I. Nosenko. Therefore, Miler was deeply implicated in the effort to cover-up the facts surrounding the assassination of President Kennedy.

He too had played a part in the Mexico City scenario. I asked about that matter.

Q. Oh, one last thing—do you know the name Nosenko?

A. Yes, I do.

Q. Have you ever interrogated Nosenko?

A. No I have not.

Miler may have been technically accurate; his answer was, nevertheless, thoroughly deceptive. For years Miler had controlled that interrogation, preparing questions, analyzing the responses and determining, with others including Angleton, that Nosenko should be illegally arrested, imprisoned without access to the judicial system, and routinely tortured.

Q. Have you ever played any part in the interrogation of Nosenko in terms of reading reports or suggesting questions for him?

A. Yes sir.

Nosenko had held the rank of lieutenant colonel in the KGB's Second Chief Directorate, an organization that had jurisdiction similar to its counterpart in the United States, the FBI. The organization he had served since 1953 was responsible for surveillance of potential enemy agents within the Soviet Union. He also was accountable for actions against such agents. He was deputy-chief of the division which had jurisdiction over visitors from Great Britain and the United States, the American-British Section.

In 1959, Oswald traveled to the Soviet Union. The intelligence unit of the CIA, operating in the Embassy of the United States in Moscow, sent Priscilla Johnson to meet with Oswald, at that time a transient resident at the Metropol Hotel. Plans made within the Embassy were immediately known to the KGB through various means, including transmitting devices and informants, as we have since learned.

The KGB, being alerted to Oswald's presence and the CIA's interest in him and apparent contact with him, referred the matter to the appropriate section. Nosenko examined the KGB file on Oswald beginning in 1959. He supervised the investigation into Oswald's motives for travelling to the Soviet Union; he was, after all, not a casual visitor. Oswald was at that time talking about repudiating his United States citizenship and becoming a permanent resident of the Soviet Union. He had a liaison with Johnson, who met him at the direction of Richard Snyder, a CIA operative in Moscow.

After the assassination of President Kennedy, Nosenko was charged by his superior officers in the KGB with the responsibility of investigating every contact Oswald had made while in the Soviet Union. Snyder, through Johnson, was apparently Oswald's first contact to engage the suspicion of the KGB.

During 1962, the CIA recruited Nosenko as an espionage agent. During the early part of 1964, Nosenko was the chief deputy to the Soviet representative to the disarmament conference then taking place in Geneva.

On January 20, 1964, Nosenko contacted the CIA by sending a coded telegram. Nosenko was an important spy; a senior CIA officer with the Soviet Russia Division flew to Geneva to meet him. The Russian colonel said that he wished to defect to the United States. The CIA wanted him to remain in place. Nosenko said that he had important information to provide to the Warren Commission. Oswald, he said, had never been associated with Soviet intelligence; the KGB suspected instead that Oswald was part of the intelligence apparatus of the United States. Richard Helms, Deputy Director for Plans during the relevant period, ordered that Nosenko remain in Europe and rejected his application to defect to the United States.

At that time the CIA was telling its Mexico City story to Warren in an attempt to prevent an authentic investigation into the assassination.

Nosenko, who knew the truth about Oswald, posed a threat to the fabricated narrative, and thus to the very existence of the CIA.

On February 3, 1964, the matter was resolved. The KGB ordered Nosenko to return to Moscow. He was certain that the Russian secret police had learned that he had been providing information to the CIA and that if he did not defect to the United States he would face imprisonment and torture.

Nosenko escaped to the United States, only to find imprisonment and torture waiting for him there as well. Helms and Angleton had him placed in solitary confinement in the basement of a CIA safe house in Virginia near Washington, D.C. He was subjected to what the CIA euphemistically calls "hostile interrogation." Nosenko's detention and "questioning" lasted more than three years; during the process many of his teeth were knocked out.

Angleton took the position that Nosenko was not a genuine defector; he asserted that the KGB had sent him to the United States for the purpose of telling the Warren Commission that Oswald had not worked for Soviet intelligence. Nosenko was to be confined and compelled to confess. However, unlike Sylvia Duran, who had been placed in solitary confinement in Mexico as a result of similar CIA orders, Nosenko was a trained professional. He refused to sign a false statement, perhaps because he thought it might result in a death sentence for him.

The more persistent Nosenko became in asserting that he wished to testify before the Warren Commission, the more vociferous Angleton became in his denunciations of his former spy. Of course, Angleton knew from the outset that Nosenko was telling the truth. After the Warren Report was issued, Nosenko was released from his prison. The CIA, admitting that he had been truthful from the outset, purchased a home for him in North Carolina, arranged for him to become a citizen of the United States and gave him an annual allowance of $30,000. The one condition upon which that preferred treatment was bestowed was that he remain silent about the entire matter.

During 1967, John L. Hart, a retired upper echelon CIA officer, was assigned to investigate the Nosenko affair for the CIA. His report concluded that Nosenko had been a genuine defector and that the information he had provided, both prior to his defection and while being tortured in the CIA safe house, was truthful and important.

Helms was later convicted after being indicted for making false statements to a committee of the United States Senate. Angleton was fired. Miler, too, was terminated by the CIA. Dulles, having been fired by

President Kennedy, was later appointed to the Warren Commission. There he played a major part in shaping the course of the non-investigation.

Nosenko never testified. His name does not even appear in the index to the Warren Commission Report or in the name index to the Commission's twenty-six volumes of evidence. Yet Nosenko was, following Oswald's death, perhaps the most important witness the Warren Commission members could have heard. The CIA's Mexico City scenario had prevailed, due to the false imprisonment of two witnesses and the utilization of deceit, torture and perjury.

To complete the circle, almost two decades later, Miler was dispatched to Miami in a vain effort to discredit a witness and keep the CIA's Mexico City story intact.

I questioned Miler about Nosenko, not really in the belief that he would provide truthful answers, but rather to permit the jury to hear him discredit himself. The deposition concluded with Miler becoming increasingly uncomfortable. He perspired profusely in the temperature controlled room, continually looked to his attorneys for help and bolted out of the room the moment the deposition was completed.

Q. Was Nosenko held illegally under arrest for more than three years by the Central Intelligence Agency?

A. I would object to the term illegally under arrest. According to the House Assassination Committee, according to the Church Committee and so forth, he was held—incarcerated.

Q. Did the House Select Committee on Assassinations find that the holding of this man for some three years was improper?

A. Was it the House Assassinations Committee that did that? I don't know whether it was that or one of the other Committees. Yes, they did.

Q. And did the Central Intelligence Agency admit that this was an illegal action by the CIA?

A. That I am not certain of what it admitted to.

Q. Did Mr. Nosenko agree to be locked up in a cell for three years?

A. I do not know that from my knowledge of Nosenko.

Q. Was he ever charged with a crime after he came to the United States?

A. Not to my knowledge—not under U.S. law.

Q. Well, he was in the United States after he came here wasn't he? Did any court in the United States order him to be held in a cell?

A. Not to my knowledge.

Q. You were involved then in an illegal operation against the rights of Mr. Nosenko?

A. How do you mean involved in the illegal rights of Mr. Nosenko?

Q. Did you know that he was being held during that period of time?

A. Yes.

Q. Were you not an accessory after the fact in the destruction of the rights of Mr. Nosenko?

A. I can not interpret that in a legal way.

Q. I have no further questions.

Miler's attorneys, unable to think of a single question that might rehabilitate him, declined to ask any questions during their opportunity to conduct redirect examination. I agreed to waive even the provision that Miler's statements must be sworn to before being submitted to the jury. The presentation of his deposition to the jury concluded the evidentiary aspect of the trial.

Years later, when Stansfield Turner wrote a book, *Secrecy and Democracy*, about his time as the director of the CIA, he sought to minimize the misconduct of the CIA, but he conceded:

"Starting in late 1974, the American and foreign press and television were full of stories of intelligence misdeeds. The CIA, though only one of the alleged offenders, took the brunt of the criticism. The complaints were manifold. Some 300,000 Americans considered to be potentially dangerous to our national security were indexed in a CIA computer, and separate files were created on approximately 7,200. Millions of private telegrams were obtained by the National Security Agency between 1947 and 1975. Countless 'dangerous' citizens were placed under surveillance, with bugs on their telephones, microphones in their bedrooms, or warrantless break-ins of their homes. There was extensive use of fellow citizens as informants. Tax returns were obtained from the IRS and scanned for information about citizens. Army intelligence infiltrated domestic dissident groups, collected information on prominent citizens sympathetic with such groups, and created an estimated 100,000 files on Americans between mid 1960s and 1971. Several plots were hatched—but never carried out—to assassinate foreign political leaders who were irritants to the United States Government."

Turner directed his attention to the Nosenko affair. He agreed that Nosenko had been a useful, high-level spy:

"It was also on Nosenko's side that he gave us some valuable information about Soviet intelligence operations. He led us to uncover an audio-surveillance system the Soviets had installed in the U.S. embassy in Moscow (fifty-two microphones in the embassy's most sensitive areas), and he directed us to a very high-level Soviet spy inside a Western European government. However, when Angleton balanced the pros against the cons, he decided that Nosenko was a double agent, and set out to force him to confess."

Turner disclosed the methods used by the CIA, under Angleton's supervision, to force Nosenko to retract his truthful statements, "to break the man psychologically." The CIA program was both illegal and elaborate:

"A small prison was built, expressly for him, on a secret base near Washington. He was kept there in solitary confinement for three and a half years. Ostensibly this was to isolate him so that the interrogation would be more effective. In fact, on only 292 of his 1277 days in that prison was he questioned at all. When he was interrogated, sometimes it was for twenty-four hours without any break. When he wasn't being questioned, he was under twenty-four-hour visual observation by guards, who were forbidden to talk to him. He had no contact with the outside world, no TV, radio, or newspapers during the entire time. For over two years he was given nothing to read. When he constructed a makeshift calendar out of threads, it was taken from him.

"His prison cell was concrete, about eight feet square, with no windows, only an opening with steel bars in the top half of the door. A single steel bed with a mattress but no pillow or sheets and an occasional blanket were the only furnishings. From time to time he was allowed to go outside into a small compound surrounded by walls so high that he could see only the sky. His clothing was inadequate for the Virginia winters. He was denied toothpaste and a toothbrush and was permitted to shave and shower only once a week. During the entire period he was administered one or more of four drugs on seventeen occasions. Doctors periodically also pressured him psychologically."

Turner seemed pleased with how the entire matter was concluded:

"Fortunately, and I suppose surprisingly, the story has a happy ending. Nosenko recovered from his ordeal. He has become a remarkably well-adjusted U.S. citizen and has done nothing to cause us to believe he was not a genuine defector."

Apparently it never occurred to Turner that the criminals on his staff might be prosecuted to make future "happy endings" of this sort unnecessary.

Routine close-of-the-case motions were made and ruled upon and a "charge conference" was held with Judge Kehoe. Just before the jury retires to consider its verdict, the judge is obligated to instruct the jury as to applicable law. His final address as to the rules of law the jurors must observe is referred to as the charge. Cases that are reversed by appellate courts due to judicial error are often remanded for a new trial due to a mistake made during the instructions. For this and other reasons, judges schedule a conference with opposing counsel to consider the proposed charge. Each party may offer arguments as to the propriety of the suggested instructions, take exception to the ruling of the court—thus preparing for a possible appeal if the verdict is unfavorable—and submit proposed special instructions for the court's consideration.

The closing argument to the jury by counsel precedes the judge's charge to the jury. Yet the judge invariably communicates to the lawyers his planned jury instructions before closing statements commence. This procedure enables the lawyers to address the legal issues and seek to assist the jurors in applying the law to the specific fact situation in the case. Accordingly, the lawyer during his closing to the jurors will often assert his "belief" as to how the judge will instruct on a certain point. No prescience is required; he has already been notified.

Snyder's closing argument was impressive. Since he represented the plaintiff and therefore had the burden of proof, or the responsibility or duty of affirmatively proving the facts in dispute, he delivered the first statement to the jury and had the right, after I had made my remarks, to once again address the jurors.

He attacked Marchetti's credibility, pointed out that the article was false on its face, stated that Hunt had reformed, and told the jurors how Hunt had suffered as a result of the publication of the story. He accused Marchetti of having written, and the *Spotlight* of having published, false accusations. He stressed the gross profit of the defendant corporation and its income and assets.

Snyder told the jurors that it was unthinkable to consider that the Federal Bureau of Investigation, Chief Justice Earl Warren, the distinguished members of his commission, and other prominent Americans would have made false statements about the assassination of President Kennedy. It is "absurd," he stated, to believe that the FBI or the CIA would cover up the facts. Oswald had killed Kennedy. All the authorities agreed. He had been the lone assassin.

Since the authorities were correct, obviously Marita Lorenz, who had presented an entirely different version, had lied. Have faith in our American institutions, Snyder pleaded, not in renegades like Marchetti.

Snyder walked over to the rail of the jury box to add emphasis to his last words to the jurors. He told them he had selected them because he was certain that they would be fair; they had said they would be. Now, he said, he was going to hold them to their promise.

The tabloid press is waiting for your verdict, Snyder said, and then implied that these publications would be more responsible in the future if the jury found for Mr. Hunt. "It is time to send them a message and let us take the Hunt family off the cross. Thank you very much."

In my statement to the jury, I marshaled the evidence that demonstrated that the CIA had planned the assassination of the president and then carried it out.

I reminded the jurors that Snyder had told them that they must believe our national leaders—"if you cannot have faith in these men, in who can you have faith?" I answered: "In ourselves, in our ability to analyze the evidence."

I concluded, "We are the people, we have forged a democracy, and no small part of it is our jury system. After two hundred years no group of intelligence officers can be permitted to come out of the shadows and make decisions for us."

I conceded that very important men had rendered their verdict in this matter. There is, however, a more important commission than the Warren or Rockefeller commissions, I suggested.

"It is the people's commission. You. You have not been appointed by the president. You have been chosen in accordance with our traditions. It is your responsibility to render in this historic case a just verdict."

Judge Kehoe delivered his instructions to the jury carefully, reading a prepared statement that had been previously submitted for comment to counsel for each party. The jury retired to a room in order to go over housekeeping details, examine the verdict form the court had prepared, and begin to consider the evidence. It was quite late in the afternoon and the judge recalled the jurors into the courtroom to excuse them for the day. He suggested that they go home, relax, and return the next morning, rested, to begin serious deliberations.

At 9:30 the next morning the jurors met to discuss the case. One hour and five minutes later the clerk informed the court that there was a verdict.

"We have a verdict!"

The federal bailiff spoke the words in an expert and practiced manner; loud enough for all assembled to hear, yet hushed and confidential as if ritualistically imparting some sacred private message to each person present. It was his finest hour. He knew it. His reading was perfect.

For each lawyer, each party, and every interested person present, the long-awaited words were met with a silence created by a dread interwoven with anticipation. The former far outweighed the latter in intensity.

For the lawyers, the final word, soon to be spoken by a group of strangers, would cap several years of work with joy and celebration or despair and depression. Late night research, long briefs, arguments to the court, hundreds of hours of depositions and preparation for depositions, legal analysis, and the development of trial strategy would be rewarded by stunning victory or stultifying defeat. The verdict, just a few words to be uttered by the jury's forewoman, would end the emotionally charged, enervating, and often bitter combat, required, or at least sanctioned, by our adversary system.

For the parties the consequences were far greater than wounded pride. E. Howard Hunt and his present wife expected to prevail, enhancing his reputation and gaining the pair financial independence. A verdict for the defendant, however, would be a crushing blow. After all, the newspaper had been summoned to the dock for asserting that Hunt, while in the employ of the CIA, had apparently been involved in the assassination of President John F. Kennedy.

As we know a few years before this day a jury had rendered a verdict for Hunt in the amount of $650,000. Had the United States court of Appeals, a court second in power and reach only to the Supreme Court, not mandated a new trial due to an erroneous instruction to the jury by the trial judge, the *Spotlight* could not have survived.

Years later the case had been tried again. Now, February 6, 1985, the verdict was at hand.

For Willis A. Carto, the founder and principal officer of Liberty Lobby, Inc., and its newspaper the *Spotlight*, a substantial verdict for Hunt in this second trial would be the end of the newspaper, the signal for an orgy of journalistic celebration among the hostile press, and the public destruction of his reputation. Winning meant survival.

Counsel, the parties, and the representatives of the print media gathered together yet separately in the large foyer just outside of the courtroom to hear the verdict. The large, well-lit room was surrounded by a bank of elevators on one side, the doors to the courtroom on the opposite side, the jury room between the two on the left as one faced the courtroom, and the clerk's office to the right. The architect who planned the building had designed an almost unique self-contained unit on each floor.

Missing was Victor Marchetti, the author of the disputed article, who had already departed for home in Virginia. He had decided not to hear the verdict in person.

The courtroom doors opened wide. All surged forward into the courtroom save three representatives of the electronic media who, like salmon swimming upstream, slipped against the current in a rush to the elevators to alert their television crews that news was about to break.

Judge Kehoe took charge from the bench. The jury was led in. Parties, lawyers, and reporters unable to wait for the official word studied the faces of the jurors for a clue. Did they look at Hunt? How? Was that a smile? Did the forewoman nod toward counsel for the defendants? Reporters scribbled notes. Those most interested, the parties and their lawyers, held their breath.

The judge inquired of Leslie Armstrong, the woman selected to lead the jurors, "Have you reached a verdict?" She rose and answered in a clear voice, "Yes, Your Honor, we have." The bailiff took the written verdict from the forewoman, carried it across the well of the courtroom, and handed it to the judge. The judge read the verdict to himself. Scores of eyes watched his eyes and his face as he scanned the verdict, each hoping his expression would betray some discernible emotion. Judge Kehoe remained as impassive and as impartial at the final moment as he had been throughout the entire trial.

The bailiff took the form from the judge and returned it to the standing leader of the jury.

The judge spoke to her.

"What is your verdict?"

In the courtroom dozens of people waited anxiously. In the street below camera crews and radio reporters prepared to carry the verdict to the American people.

The record reveals how the case ended:

[Thereupon the jury entered the jury box at 10:40 A.M.]

THE COURT: Have you arrived at a verdict in this case?

THE FOREPERSON: Yes.

THE COURT: Would you give it to the clerk? Publish the verdict.

THE CLERK: United States District Court, Southern District of Florida, Miami, Florida, case number 80-1121-Civ-JWK. E. Howard Hunt, plaintiff, versus Liberty Lobby, defendant. Verdict as of February 6, 1985. We, the jury, find for the defendant, Liberty Lobby and against the plaintiff, E. Howard Hunt. So say we, all, signed by the Foreperson.

THE COURT: Ladies and gentlemen, we will now go through a procedure which is referred to as polling the jury. As Mary calls you by name, if the verdict just read was in fact your verdict, respond in the affirmative that it was your verdict. If it was not, let us know. The purpose is to be sure the record reflects we have a unanimous verdict.

[Thereupon, the jurors were polled by the Clerk and upon the question, "was this your verdict," the jurors answered in the affirmative.]

THE COURT: Let this verdict which has been duly published upon which the jury has been polled now be recorded.

[Thereupon, the Jury was excused.]

Lawyers tend to demonstrate their professionalism, which they confuse on occasion with a false sense of detachment, by maintaining an appearance of indifference when the verdict is read. While I consider it ill-mannered to celebrate in the presence of the losing party, I believe that in the best tradition of the bar the lawyer should be an impassioned advocate for his client's cause. Generally the victorious lawyers and their clients shake hands with one another and exchange congratulations. No client or representative was present. Brent Whitmore, Flemming Lee, and I shook hands and packed our briefcases.

An historic moment had been achieved. All that remained was that it be communicated to the American people.

The jurors, after gathering their belongings from the jury room, left the courthouse. They were confronted by a group of print, radio, and television reporters waiting for them on the courthouse steps.

Several jurors walked up to me to shake hands and tell me their thoughts about the case. I have always placed a high value on exchanges of this nature. I have learned more from jurors before whom I have tried cases than at seminars devoted to trial techniques.

Unfortunately, in this instance, I could only accept the congratulations of the jurors, thank them, and quickly excuse myself. In addition to the federal rules governing trials, each district court may draft its own set of procedural regulations, known as the local rules. The United States District Court for the Southern District of Florida had published a local rule specifically precluding trial counsel from talking with jurors after the verdict had been published. Of course, any contact with a juror out of the courtroom prior to verdict is not just a violation of a local rule but grounds for disbarment.

The Florida rule was unfair and probably contrary to the United States Constitution, in that it improperly discriminated against certain counsel, while permitting all other persons to interview the former jurors. I was not inclined to test its validity at that time; I was more concerned to hear what the jurors had to say to the media.

The reporters gathered around Leslie Armstrong. What had caused her to vote for the defendant, she was asked time and time again. Patiently she explained that at the outset she was, as were all of the jurors, absolutely objective. None of them had any fixed opinion about either the case or the facts surrounding the assassination of President Kennedy.

I stood off to the side, out of range of the cameras, but close enough to hear each question and each response.

And why had she found against Hunt, she was asked by impatient reporters shouting questions and jostling against each other for better positions for their microphones or cameras.

The evidence was clear, she said. The CIA had killed President Kennedy, Hunt had been part of it, and that evidence, so painstakingly presented, should now be examined by the relevant institutions of the United States government so that those responsible for the assassination might be brought to justice.

Again and again she was asked the same question, each time with a slightly different spin and by a different reporter so that he or she could later tell the nation that the historic answer was given in response to "your reporter's question." Patiently Leslie Armstrong answered each question, both simply and eloquently.

One reporter for a local Miami television station betrayed his sense of outrage at the verdict. He pressed the juror for answers to irrelevant questions. "What about lack of actual malice? Wasn't that the basis for your decision?" She replied that if the jurors had not believed the truth of the essential allegation, that the CIA and Hunt had been involved in the crime, they would have then considered the question of malice. As for her, she said, it never came to that. The evidence was very impressive. It was not necessary for her to consider malice; she believed the accusations of CIA complicity to be truthful. With an almost virulent intensity, the reporter scoffed, "You mean that actual malice is not a factor in a libel case?" Leslie Armstrong said that actual malice is always an element in a defamation case, that the judge had carefully explained that matter to the jury in his instruction, but that in the fact situation presented in this case, since she believed that the main point in the article was truthful, it was not necessary for her to consider the publisher's motive. He had printed the truth; the evidence disclosed that, as far as she was concerned. The reporter left.

That evening the Miami television station reported that Hunt had lost a libel case and that the "foreman" of the jury explained why. Displayed on the screen for a moment was Armstrong. A fragment of one answer had been excerpted. She was seen stating only that actual malice is always an element in a defamation case. The television station is owned by the *Washington Post* and *Newsweek*.

In Washington, the coverage of the news was even more selective. The *Washington Post*, which had devoted a substantial story to Hunt's victory at the first trial, when no issue of national importance had been adjudicated or even raised, declined to publish even a word about the jury's verdict at the second trial, where the question of the CIA's role in the assassination had been decisive. Almost all of the national news media joined in surrounding the historic verdict with an iron curtain, through which the news of the verdict could not filter. Virtually every book publisher in the United States refused to publish this book.

I recalled November 30, 1978, when Anthony Lewis, perhaps the media's most slavish supporter of the Warren Commission Report, writing in *The New York Times*, directed radio and television talk show hosts to prohibit me from speaking. The column, appearing on the op-ed page of the *New York Times*, suggested that editors refuse to publish my books and urged colleagues to ban me from the campus. I had already, Lewis proclaimed, been permitted to raise too many questions about the assassination of President Kennedy.

The executives who rule the multi-million-dollar news business and their eager agents seem willing enough to embrace the Bill of Rights when a judge or a politician interferes with potential profit. However, they have long demonstrated an inability to understand the majesty of the universal application of the First Amendment. While they may decline to publish unpleasant and unsettling truths, the most recent polls disclose that almost no one in the United States or abroad any longer believes the "lone assassin" notion. Even the House Select Committee on Assassinations has determined that there was a conspiracy in the murder of the president. The Warren Report has been declared void, but for the old and loyal apologists the old myths die hard.

Leslie Armstrong, seeing the violence done to the truth by her local television station, called the station's executives that evening. When she persisted, they finally agreed to interview her again, after claiming that the original videotaped interview had been erased. She agreed to the second interview and watched as a very late television news show presented a truthful moment about the jury's verdict.

Viva Ms. Armstrong!

Viva the jury system!

EPILOGUE:
Operation Zapata

T HE NATIONAL MEDIA COULD HAVE SEIZED ON THE VERDICT IN THE HUNT CASE AS an opportunity to reopen the question of who killed President Kennedy. This they have not done.

During the decade just completed, the establishment media, for the most part, have managed the mystery surrounding the assassination of the president with benign neglect, offering the odd lament about the refusal of the American people to believe what they have been told.

The New York Times devoted several pages of its Sunday magazine on November 20, 1988 to an article by David Belin, one of the most imaginative and accommodating young lawyers to serve the Warren Commission. With Arlen Specter, Belin was the proud author of the commission's single bullet theory. In the Times article, entitled "Why We Still Don't Believe It," Belin asserted that "polls have shown that most Americans believe President Kennedy was assassinated as an outgrowth of a conspiracy." He sought to assure the public that the CIA had clean hands and reminded us of our duty to rely upon Earl Warren, "a man whose integrity was above reproach." The reason why "they" don't believe the lone assassin theory, Belin said, was that the Warren Commission acted "in secret."

The explanation is a trifle ironic and more than a bit inaccurate. At the time I had pleaded with the members of the Commission to hold open and public hearings. They declined; they then sealed the essential documents upon which they claimed to have relied and said that they could not be viewed for seventy-five years. Yet, in spite of this unprecedented secrecy, the well-publicized conclusion of the Commission were uncritically accepted and endorsed by the establishment media with panegyrical excess.

The *Washington Post*, which did more than most to prevent the publication of the facts surrounding the assassination and to inhibit serious inquiry by relying in large degree upon the convoluted writings of George Lardner, Jr. finally published a piece on the front page of its Outlook section (November 20, 1983) asking "Did Oswald Act Alone" and then mournfully deploring the state in which we had inexplicably found ourselves, "We Evaded the Truth Then, And Now It Can't Be Found." The article ended, hopefully obviating the need for any further inquiry: "The full truth would have been difficult to discover even in 1963–64; now it is probably lost to us forever."

Even Walter Cronkite from his retirement, perhaps with a wary eye cocked toward future considerations of his reputation, gathered up the old CBS-TV producer who had helped him attempt to prove the accuracy of the Warren Report in four prime time and very deceptive CBS programs, presented on consecutive evenings beginning Sunday, June 25, 1967. (See A Citizen's Dissent, Holt Rinehart and Winston, 1980, for an analysis of the programs) and tried to enter into a plea bargain with posterity. Cronkite entered the lists with a pathetic effort on NOVA, an otherwise reputable Public Broadcasting System program, in which he appeared to say that we may never know.

The intelligence agencies and their previously truculent tribunes had opted for a no-decision resolution. The fall-back position adopted by the establishment press, the "we'll never know" homily that replaced the lone assassin theory, seems to preclude further investigation of the murder. It does not, however, preclude criticism of those who want to keep the inquiry alive.

It was an exhaustive search to find a publisher for this work, but it was quickly eclipsed by the decision of Oliver Stone, the Oscar-winning, powerful and imaginative producer to announce that he was about to create a major, multi-million dollar, star-studded film to tell the truth about the assassination of President Kennedy.

As soon as principal photography commenced, months before the film could legitimately be reviewed, the *Washington Post*, in a premature attempt to discredit the project, dispatched George Lardner, Jr., to Dallas. Lardner, who covers the CIA for the paper, has rarely seen an agency press release he did not covet.

The headline on the front page of "Outlook" for Sunday, May 19, 1991, read "On the Set: Dallas in Wonderland. How Oliver Stone's Version of the Kennedy Assassination Exploits the Edge of Paranoia." In the piece,

Lardner derides Stone and his source who he describes only as the "former New Orleans District Attorney Jim Garrison, whose zany investigation of the assassination in the later 1960s has almost faded from memory."

Lardner states with his own brand of journalistic objectivity that "Stone is chasing fiction" and that "Garrison's investigation was a fraud." In the long, rambling article, which on occassion strays from mere hyperbole to near hysteria, Lardner provides descriptive background for those upon whom he relies. The reader never learns that the former District Attorney serves as a judge on the second- highest court in Louisiana, having been elected to that position years ago and reelected since.

The piece concludes with a caustic comment about a film he describes as "Mark Lane's muddled stew of fact and fiction about the assassination, *Executive Action*." As the credits reveal, the screenplay was actually written by Dalton Trumbo. Donald Freed and I had collaborated on the first draft of the script, which was intended to be a docudrama about the assassination based upon the evidence. It was my first foray into Hollywood, and I soon learned that entertainment concerns occupy a higher priority than fact when banks, insurance companies, film studios and producers decide what is marketable. Moviemaking is big business; a return on the investment is often the paramount consideration.

When we saw what had happened to our fact-based effort in subsequent drafts, Freed and I protested, both privately to the producer and then publicly at press conferences, pointing out the errors in the work. Consequently, our names did not appear as the screenwriters. Lardner and the *Post* had to be aware of all this when they published their most recent false statement on the subject.

Some time ago I met with Oliver Stone's representative in Los Angeles to discuss his film. Stone was interested in my work; unfortunately, he also reserved the right to alter or modify the events to make the film entertaining. I withdrew from discussions with his company and declined to meet with him further. Since the condition precedent was founded upon his right to utilize the material I had uncovered as he wished.

I have since read the working screenplay for the film JFK. It was a brave attempt to explore a mystery of momentous consequence. While the original script may be flawed in detail, it is accurate in its broad strokes and therefore could have made a historic contribution to the debate. Stone, however, has publicly stated that he has rewritten the script following the attempts in the media to discredit him; JFK will now attempt to reconcile different views, thus serving the interests of the box office and the film critics rather than history.

After the Lardner article was published, Stone wrote a letter to the *Washington Post*. The paper made "major deletions," in its own words, and then published the letter as an article on June 2, 1991. The article was followed on the same page by yet another Lardner attack.

The screenplay had dramatized Lyndon Johnson's decision to reverse Kennedy's policy to withdraw troops from Vietnam. Lardner had called the scene "nonsense." In his second assault upon Stone, Lardner quoted from Johnson's NSAM 273 as follows:

"The objectives of the United States with respect to the withdrawal of U.S. military personnel remain as stated in the White House statement of October 2, 1963 [approving among other things 'plans to withdraw 1,000 military personnel by the end of 1963']."

Lardner referred to the Stone film as "just a sloppy mess," asserted that while the "facts speak for themselves Stone doesn't seem to know them," and concluded, relying upon a person he identified only as "Historian Gibbon" that Kennedy "would have done it just as Johnson did it."

Lardner's source seems to have secured data available only through paranormal psychology. A journalist not relying on clairvoyance would have to conclude that Kennedy had ordered the withdrawal of troops from Vietnam during the last days of his life, and that he had promised that they would all be home by the end of the next year. Contrast Kennedy's words and deeds with those of his successor.

Six months after he assumed office, Johnson, in a May 18, 1964, message to Congress, urged that there by an increased appropriation to prosecute the war. In that message he stated that "sixteen thousand Americans" were then in Vietnam. A year later, at a news conference on July 28, 1965, entitled "We Will Stand in Vietnam," Johnson announced that he had ordered more troops to Vietnam and that "our fighting strength would therefore be increased "from 75,000 to 125,000 men almost immediately."[1]

Lardner was correct—the facts do speak for themselves. When Kennedy was assassinated, there were approximately 16,000 Americans in Vietnam. Before the war ended three times that number had died there.

The effort by the *Washington Post* to impede its progress at so early a stage is an indication, neither of its accuracy nor of the accuracy of Lardner's criticism, but of the intrinsic importance of the project. As in the case of the CIA review of *Rush to Judgment*, it tends to heighten the sense in general and expose the specific concerns of those committed to unbridled discretion.

---

[1] See appendix page 379.

Attacks upon those who raise questions about this aspect of our recent national history are neither unexpected nor unpredictable. Yet as we move inexorably closer to the truth in this affair, the most recent defense of the fateful fabrication is startling.

From the original assertion that it was unthinkable that the CIA may have been involved in the national tragedy of unfathomable dimensions, the defenders now apparently are moving toward the position that the assassination of President Kennedy was, on balance, good for the nation.

Thomas Reeves wrote a book, A *Question of Character*, about John Kennedy's private life. The premier intellectual at the *Washington Post*'s Sunday Book review (Book World, May 26, 1991), Jonathan Yardley, said of it:

> "There are no surprises in this biography of John Fitzgerald Kennedy: no new revelations about East Room policymaking, no unduly original insights into the Kennedy legend, no fresh breaths of scandal. Instead A *Question of Character* performs two modest but valuable services: It brings together in a single volume all the existing information about Kennedy, much of which was first reported in books or articles of widely varying import and intentions; and, as its title suggests, it undertakes to assess Kennedy not merely in political or mythological terms, but in moral ones."

Why then, the featured, Yardley page-three, by-lined treatment? Apparently so that the *Post* could offer an analysis that admittedly is more Yardley's than Reeves'.

> "Though Reeves does not quite come right out and say so, his analysis suggests that the assassination of John F. Kennedy, however cruel and ghastly, may have spared the nation something even worse than the prolonged orgy of grief and hagiography that followed it. He suggests that the gentlemen's agreement by which details of Kennedy's private life were kept secret might well have been violated, for whatever reason, during a second term, and that a vote of impeachment might well have followed.
> "This, had it come to pass, could have been more damaging even than Watergate. The spectacle of a president of the United States on trial for illicit liaisons within and without the White House, for questionable relationships with ranking figures of the underworld—this would have been more than the United States of the mid-1960s could have stomached. The proceedings would have torn us apart in ways we can scarcely imagine, and left us with a cynicism

about politics by contrast with which the residue of Watergate would seem a mild case of disenchantment. Better that the handsome young president died a mythical if not actual hero, and that the true story of his character emerged so tentatively and gradually that we were given time to come to terms with it. Had we been forced to bear in a single blow the full import of the story Thomas Reeves tells, it would have shattered us."

Before exploring the *Washington Post*'s newly developed moral concept that appears to argue that capital punishment is appropriate in those few jurisdictions where adultery is still considered a criminal act, it might be useful to examine the major premise it relies upon.'

Kennedy's personal and sexual liaisons, we are told, had underworld overtones courtesy of Frank Sinatra and Sam Giancana. Sinatra, it will be recalled, was inelegantly, publicly, and permanently barred from the White House by Kennedy. The trauma inflicted on the aging singer resulted in an aggravated abandonment of principle: Sinatra became a Republican. He subsequently supported the Reagan-Bush ticket and found himself in the White House quite regularly, both for public functions and private lunches. The *Post* has not yet called for sanctions against Ronald Reagan, George Bush, or Sinatra's lunch partner, Nancy Reagan.

I believe it is the view of most Americans that it was not better that the handsome young president died a mythical, if not actual, "hero" that day in Dallas. Most of us, I suspect, prefer the electoral process and the ballot box rather than the concealed rifles of snipers, as engines to move our democracy.

Perhaps the cynical assessment that Kennedy's death may have benefitted the nation arises out of our distance from the events of 1963. The case is twenty-eight years old.

That same distance, however, can be used to argue that now more than ever is the time to let the truth be known. It is emerging slowly anyway, in fits and starts. Dulles and Phillips are dead. Helms and Hunt have been disgraced in legal proceedings. Haven't all the important players in the Kennedy drama retired or passed away?

They have not. George Herbert Walker Bush, the former director of the CIA and now President of the United States, remains on the scene. Ongoing revelations about his apparent role in the Reagan team's October Surprise and Iran-Contra scandals make his little-known activities on behalf of the CIA in the early '60s still more worthy of note.

When I sued the government in the mid-1970s to enforce the provisions of the Freedom of Information Act, the reluctant keepers of the records at various federal police institutions were required to disgorge docu- ments that had been stamped "Top Secret" and placed in locked vaults. During 1977 and 1978 the FBI alone released almost 100,000 previously classified pages. I read them assiduously, searching for a meaning that might be comprehensible only in the context of the entire puzzle.

When a name of little or no significance appeared my *modus operandi* was to check the name in a reliable reference work. Thus, if I came across the name George Bush during 1977, I would read his biography in the 39th edition of *Who's Who in America* published during 1976. No remarkable entry there would have caught my attention.[2]

Fortunately, Joseph McBride, obviously a relentless researcher, exam- ined some of the FBI documents many years later when the name George Bush rang on the national scene with a much increased resonance. In two important articles published in *The Nation*, he demonstrated that Bush had been involved with the CIA before the assassination of Presi- dent Kennedy.[3]

This was no mean achievement. As Iran-Contra testimony revealed, Bush routinely keeps a diary of plausible deniability, with the same skill employed by a crooked accountant who maintains two sets of corporate book, one of them cooked. In 1976, when Bush was appointed Director of the CIA, questions were raised about his assignment to so high and secret a post since what was publicly known of his background did not seem to provide experience warranting the position.

McBride disclosed a November 29, 1963 memorandum from J. Edgar Hoover, then the director of the FBI, to the State Department. It was entitled "Assassination of President John F. Kennedy November 22, 1963." It stated that on November 23, 1963, while Oswald was in police custody and available for interrogation about his affiliation with agencies of the United States government, FBI Special Agent W.T. Forsyth and

---

[2]BUSH, GEORGE HERBERT WALKER, govt. rep., former chmn. Republican Nat. Com.; b. Milton, Mass, June 12, 1924; s.Prescott Sheldon and Dorothy (Walker) B.' grad. Philips Acad., Andover, Mass, 1942; B.A. in Econs., Yale, 1948; m. Barbara Pierce, Jan. 6, 1945; children—George W., John E., Neil M., Marvin P., Dorothy W. Co-founder, dir. Zapata Petroleum Corp., 1953-59; pres. Zapata Off Shore Co., Houston, 1956-64, chmn. bd. 1964-66; mem. 90th-91st congresses, 7th dist., Tex., mem. Ways and Means com.; U.S. ambassador to UN, 1971-72; chmn. Rep. Nat. Com., 1973-74; chief U.S. Liaison Office Peking, People's Republic China, 1974—. Tex. chmn. Heart Fund. Chmn. Rep. Party Harris County, Tex., 1963-64; del. Rep. Nat. Conv., 1964, 1968; Rep. candidate U.S. senator from Tex., 1964, 1970. Served lt. (j.g.), pilot, USNR, World War II. Decorated D.F.C., Air medals (3). Home: 5161 Palisade Lane NW, Washington, DC 20016. Office: USLO Peking People's Republic of China.

[3]*The Nation*, July 16/23, 1988 and August 13/20, 1988. Both articles are published as appendix page 371.

Captain William Edwards of the Defense Intelligence Agency briefed "Mr. George Bush of the Central Intelligence Agency" about potential problems related to the assassination. McBride states, "A source with close connections to the intelligence community confirms that Bush started working for the Agency in 1960 or 1961, using his oil business as a cover for clandestine operations."

During 1988, Bush, responding to McBride's charges through a spokesperson, denied that he had been associated with the CIA before he was named its director in 1976. Subsequently the CIA said that the George Bush who had been briefed by the DIA and the FBI the day after the assassination was George William Bush, not George Herbert Walker Bush. There the matter might have ended, a footnote to a complex conundrum, had McBride not persisted. He located George William Bush, a lower level researcher, who denied that he had been briefed by either the FBI or the DIA.

The work assignment of George William Bush, who had been employed by the CIA for only six months during 1963 and 1964, was looking over photographs and documents unrelated to the subject matter of the briefing. He was not the "Mr. George Bush of the Central Intelligence Agency" referred to in Mr. Hoover's memorandum.

If the present president worked for the CIA before 1963, the most obvious inquiry is why he lied about it in 1988 and why he has permitted that false statement to persist to the present time.

The subject matter of the DIA and FBI briefing of Bush on November 23, 1963, focused upon contemplated or possible unauthorized military actions against Cuba. Why would the FBI and the DIA believe that Bush might possess information about the unauthorized actions, which would presuppose a knowledge of authorized actions? An examination of the facts surrounding the movements of George Herbert Walker Bush prior to 1963 might provide an answer.

After Bush left New Haven he moved to Texas where he entered into a business arrangement with John Overbey and then Hugh and Bill Liedtke. In 1953 they formed an oil company, Zapata Petroleum Corp., with Bush starting in the now familiar role of vice president. Hugh Liedtke, the Texan with a knowledge of the oil business and ready access to oil money, was president.

Bush had the responsibility of providing additional funding. It was a tradition among Yalies, Bush explained, that OPM, Other People's Money, was the right way to go. (It now seems possible that the OPM gene may be passed on to the male heirs.) Bush returned to the East, where Uncle "Herbie" Walker was pleased to help Prescott Bush's son and to urge his friends on Wall Street to do the same. Thus Bush-Overbey was formed and later merged with the Liedtke family into Zapata Petroleum. With Hugh Liedtke at the helm, Zapata struck it rich, Bush sold his interest in Zapata then he and his wife Barbara moved to Houston where he founded Zapata Off Shore Co., and served as its Chief Executive Officer from 1956 to 1964. Little is known of Bush's activities during this period. When Lee Harvey Oswald returned to the United States from the Soviet Union, he settled in Texas. He was befriended by a wealthy white Russian oil man, named George de Mohrenschildt, then residing in Texas. There is evidence suggesting that de Mohrenschildt served as a CIA control officer who directed Oswald's actions. De Mohrenschildt died from a gun shot just as he was about to be questioned by the House Select Committee on Assassinations. After his death, his personal telephone book was located. It contained this entry: "Bush, George H.W. (Poppy) 1412 W. Ohio also Zapata Petroleum Midland."

The name Zapata was Bush's good luck charm, symbolic of the two successful operations in his public career as a businessman. While Bush resided in Houston with Barbara and ran Zapata during 1961, the CIA planned the Bay of Pigs invasion. The top secret code name given by the CIA to plan for the invasion of Cuba, known only to a select few, was "Operation Zapata."

Col. Fletcher Prouty was responsible for securing the ordinance for the invasion. He was ordered to find two United States Navy crafts suitable for carrying men, tanks, weapons, and ammunition. His instructions were to provide equipment for 25,000 men although only approximately 1,400 were to make the initial landing. He was told that the CIA was confident that the invasion would succeed within seventy-two hours. "There was no doubt about it in their minds," he told me. "Victory was assured. Cuban political leaders were placed in Miami to form a government in exile and to appeal to the OAS. The OAS had been primed and was ready to act at once."

Prouty said that once the OAS recognized the government in exile, the Marines would land in a lightning stroke, their equipment would be waiting for them at the beachhead, and Castro would be gone.

As a backup, according to Michael R. Beschloss (The Crisis Years, Harper-Collins, 1991), "CIA-equipped confederates of Sam Giancana were stalking Fidel Castro with botulinum-toxin pills." At that moment, March 29, 1961, Bissell, representing the CIA, "came to the Cabinet Room and presented a progress report on Operation Zapata, the top-secret plan to invade Cuba from the Bay of Pigs." (ibid.)

Prouty secured two vessels from the Navy that he had located at a U.S.

Navy storage facility utilized by the military. They were sent to an inactive Naval Base near Elizabeth City, North Carolina where the colors of the U.S. Navy were painted over. Trainloads of military equipment were delivered to dockside while the ships were being made seaworthy. New names were painted on the ships for their historic mission—the launching of "Operation Zapata." The new names were "Barbara" and "Houston."

APPENDIX

LANE'S DEFENSE BRIEF FOR OSWALD

National Guardian, December 19, 1963

In an analysis of the civil liberties aspects of the assassination of Lee Harvey Oswald, the American Civil Liberties Union said the "public interest" would be served if the commission named by President Johnson were to make "a thorough examination of the treatment accorded Oswald, including his right to counsel, the nature of the interrogation, his physical security while under arrest, and the effect of pretrial publicity on Oswald's right to a fair trial."

In the public interest the *Guardian* is devoting one-half of its issue this week to a lawyer's brief in the Oswald case which has been sent by the author to Justice Earl Warren as head of the fact-finding commission inquiring into the circumstances of the assassination of President Kennedy. The author is Mark Lane, a well known New York defense attorney, who has represented almost all the civil rights demonstrators arrested in New York. He has also served as defense counsel in a number of murder cases involving young persons.

In 1959, he helped organize the Reform Democrats in New York, an insurgent movement within the Democratic Party, was the first candidate of the movement to be nominated to the New York State Legislature and was elected in 1960.

In his letter to Justice Warren accompanying the brief, Lane urged that defense counsel be named for Oswald so that all aspects of the case might be vigorously pursued, particularly since Oswald was denied a trial during his lifetime. It is an ironic note, as the ACLU statement says, that "if Oswald had lived to stand trial and were convicted, the courts would very likely have reversed the conviction because of the prejudicial pretrial publicity."

The *Guardian*'s publication of Lane's brief presumes only one thing: a man's innocence, under U.S. law, unless or until proved guilty. It is the right of any accused, whether his name is Oswald, Ruby or Byron de la Beckwith, the man charged with the murder of Medgar Evers in Mississippi. A presumption of innocence is the rock upon which American jurisprudence rests. Surely it ought to apply in the "crime of the century" as in the meanest back-alley felony.

We ask all our readers to study this document, show it to as many persons as you can (extra copies are available on request) and send us your comment. Any information or analysis based on fact that can assist the Warren Commission is in the public interest—an interest which demands that everything possible be done to establish the facts in this case. —*The Guardian*

By Mark Lane

In all likelihood there does not exist a single American community where reside 12 men or women, good and true, who presume that Lee Harvey Oswald did not assassinate President Kennedy. No more savage comment can be made in reference to the breakdown of the Anglo-Saxon system of jurisprudence. At the very foundation of our judicial operation lies a cornerstone which shelters the innocent and guilty alike against group hysteria, manufactured evidence, overzealous law enforcement officials, in short, against those factors which militate for an automated, prejudged, neatly packaged verdict of guilty. It is the sacred right of every citizen accused of committing a crime to the presumption of innocence.

This presumption, it has been written, is a cloak donned by the accused when the initial charge is made. It is worn throughout the entire case presented against him, and not taken from the defendant until after he has had an opportunity to cross-examine hostile witnesses, present his own witnesses and to testify himself.

Oswald did not testify. Indeed, there will be no case, no trial, and Oswald, murdered while in police custody, still has no lawyer. Under such circumstances the development of a possible defense is difficult, almost impossible. Under such circumstances, the development of such a defense is obligatory.

There will be an investigation. No investigation, however soundly motivated, can serve as an adequate substitute for trial. Law enforcement officials investigate every criminal case before it is presented to a jury. The investigation in almost all such cases results in the firm conviction by the investigator that the accused is guilty. A jury often finds the defendant innocent, notwithstanding.

That which intervenes between the zealous investigator and the jury is due process of law, developed at great cost in human life and liberty over the years. It is the right to have irrelevant testimony barred. It is the right to have facts, not hopes or thoughts or wishes or prejudicial opinions, presented. It is the right to test by cross-examination the veracity of every witness and the value of his testimony. It is, perhaps above all, the right to counsel of one's own choice, so that all the other rights may be protected. In this defense, Oswald has forfeited all rights along with his life.

The reader, inundated at the outset with 48 solid television, radio and newspaper hours devoted to proving the guilt of the accused and much additional "evidence" since then, cannot now examine this case without bringing to it certain preconceived ideas. We ask, instead, only for a temporary suspension of certainty.

The Case Against Oswald

Long before Oswald was shot to death in the basement of the Dallas courthouse, the Dallas officials had concluded that Oswald was "without any doubt the killer." On Saturday, the press was informed that "absolute confirmation as to Oswald's guilt" had just arrived but the "startling evidence" could not then be released to the press.

Immediately after Oswald was slain, the Dallas district attorney, Henry Wade, announced that the "Oswald case was closed." Despite the deep belief that prevailed throughout the U.S. as to Oswald's guilt, doubts raised throughout Europe escalated with Oswald's murder into almost absolute rejection of the prosecution case.

The Justice Department then announced that the case was not closed. Wade called a press conference to "reopen" the case. In a radio and television statement publicized throughout the world, Wade presented, "the evidence, piece by piece, for you."

Wade is not new to the ways of law enforcement and prosecution. He has held the post of district attorney in Dallas 13 years. He has a staff of 80, and an annual budget of almost $500,000. For more than four years he was an FBI agent before becoming district attorney.

He boasts of obtaining the death sentence in 23 of the 24 capital cases he has prosecuted. It can be assumed that the Oswald case was by far the most important matter that he ever handled, and that his appearance on Sunday to present the evidence was the high point of his career. This was an appearance for which he had abundantly prepared himself.

In that light, we now examine the "airtight case," the "absolute confirmation of Oswald's guilt." Wade presented 15 assertions, some mere conclusions, some with a source not revealed, some documented.

Here are the 15 assertions:

1—A number of witnesses saw Oswald at the window of the sixth floor of the Texas School Book Depository.

2—Oswald's palm print appeared on the rifle.

3—Oswald's palm print appeared on a cardboard box found at the window.

4—Paraffin tests on both hands showed that Oswald had fired a gun recently.

5—The rifle, an Italian carbine, had been purchased by Oswald, through the mail, under an assumed name.

6—Oswald had in his possession an identification card with the name Hidell.

7—Oswald was seen in the building by a police officer just after the president had been shot.

8—Oswald's wife said that his rifle was missing Friday morning.

9—Oswald had a package under his arm Friday.

10—Oswald, while taking a bus from the scene, laughed loudly as he told a woman passenger that the president had been shot.

11—A taxi driver, Darryl Click, took Oswald home, where he changed his clothes.

12—Oswald shot and killed a police officer.

13—A witness saw Oswald enter the Texas theater.

14—Oswald drew a pistol and attempted to kill the arresting officer.

15—A map was found in Oswald's possession showing the scene of the assassination and the bullet's proposed trajectory.

Perused lightly, the list seems impressive. But in capital cases evidence is not perused lightly. It is subject to probing cross-examination, study analysis. The most effective tool available to any defendant, cross-examination, is not available in this case. We rely instead solely upon press reports of statements made, not by witnesses for the defense, not by the defendant, but by the district attorney, police officers or FBI agents. With this oppressive restriction in mind, we move on to an analysis of the evidence.

Point One

A number of witnesses saw Oswald at the window of the sixth floor of the Texas School Book Depository.

Since it is alleged that Oswald fired through that window, that assertion is important. Wade was unequivocal, stating, "First, there was (sic) a number of witnesses that saw the person with the gun on the sixth floor of the bookstore building, in the widow—detailing the window—where he was looking out." Subsequently, it developed that the "number of witnesses" was in reality one witness, who was quoted as follows: "I can't identify him, but if I see a man who looks like him, I'll point him out." (*Newsweek*—Dec. 9.) Such "identification" is at best speculative and would not be permitted in that form at trial.

Point Two

Oswald's palm print appeared on the rifle.

A palm print, unlike a fingerprint, is not always uniquely identifiable. Nevertheless, palm prints possibly belonging to the suspect and present on a murder weapon must be considered important evidence. If the rifle did belong to Oswald, the presence of palm prints there might be normal and need not lead to the inevitable conclusion that Oswald fired the fatal shots. However, speculation in this area is not now required to rebut Wade's second point. The FBI now states that "no palm prints were found on the rifle."

This conclusion, first carried in the Fort Worth press, was later leaked to reporters by the FBI in off-the-record briefing sessions. The FBI at that time took the position that "we don't have to worry about prints in this case." The FBI indicated anger with Wade for stating that a palm print was present when in fact it was not.

Point Three

Oswald's palm print appeared on a cardboard box found at the window.

Wade stated, "On this box that the defendant was sitting on, his palm print was found and was identified as his." Inasmuch as a palm print is not always uniquely identifiable, depending on the number of characteristics that are readable, the palm print very likely was not definitely "identified as his."

It had been alleged earlier that the defendant ate greasy fried chicken at the window. The presence of a palm print indicates that he wore no gloves and took no precautions to prevent a trail of fingerprints and palm prints. Nevertheless, no prints of the defendant were found of the floors, walls, window ledge, window frame or window. Only a movable cardboard carton, subsequently present at the police station while the defendant was also there, is now alleged to have his print.

An over-zealous investigatory staff might arrange to secure such a print after the fact. Certainly the handling of this case by the Dallas authorities was marked by overzealous desire to convict the defendant. A district attorney who states falsely that a palm print is present on the murder weapon might make a similar statement in reference to a cardboard carton.

Point Four

Paraffin tests on both hands showed that Oswald had fired a gun recently.

Paraffin is applied to that portion of the human body which might come in close contact with the gas (released by a weapon's firing) containing solid particles of burned nitrates in suspension. To determine whether a pistol (i.e. a gun) has been fired, tests are made of both hands. To determine whether a rifle has been fired, tests are made of both hands and the area on both sides of the face near the cheekbone, the cheek remaining in immediate contact with a rifle when the trigger is pulled.

In the service, as any veteran, including Wade, well knows, a rifle is always referred to as a rifle. It is never, under fear of company punishment, called a gun (pistol). At Wade's press conference, this dialogue took place:

> Reporter: What about the paraffin tests?
>
> Wade: Yes, I've got paraffin tests that showed he had recently fired a gun—it was on both hands.
>
> Wade: Both hands.
>
> Reporter: Recently fired a rifle?
>
> Reporter: A gun.
>
> Wade: A gun.

Wade's answers, while truthful, were a study in understatement. The district attorney neglected to state the additional facts that tests had been conducted on Oswald's face and that the tests revealed that there were no traces of gunpowder on Oswald's face (*Washington Star*, Nov. 24). One fact emerges here with clarity. The paraffin test did not prove Oswald fired a rifle recently. The test tended to prove Oswald had not fired a rifle recently. This fact alone raises that reasonable doubt that a jury might utilize in finding the defendant not guilty.

Point Five

The rifle, an Italian carbine, had been purchased by Oswald through the mail and under an assumed name.

340

Wade said, "It (the rifle), as I think you know, has been identified as having been purchased last March by Oswald, from a mail-order house, through an assumed name named Hidell, mailed to a post office box here in Dallas." Wade said this was the weapon that killed the president.

Wade had made a very different statement in reference to the murder weapon just a short while before.

Just after the arrest of Oswald, Dallas law enforcement officials announced that they had found the murder weapon. Wade and his associates studied the rifle. It was shown to the television audience repeatedly as some enforcement official carried it high on the air, with his bare hands on the rifle. After hours of examination Wade said without hesitation, that "the murder weapon was a German Mauser."

The next day it was reported that FBI files showed that Oswald purchased an Italian carbine through the mail. It was sent to a post-office box maintained by Oswald in his own name and also A. Hidell. (Clearly no serious effort to escape detection as the purchaser of the rifle was made by Oswald, if he did purchase it.)

Armed with the knowledge that Oswald could be connected with an Italian carbine (it then not being known that the Italian rifle in question might not be able to fire three times in five seconds), Wade made a new announcement. The murder weapon was not a German Mauser, it was an Italian carbine. The prosecution reversal established a high point in vulnerability for the trial—the trial that was never to take place.

Point Six

Oswald had in his possession an identification card with the name Hidell.

Wade said, "On his (Oswald's) person was a pocketbook. In his pocketbook was an identification card with the same name (Hidell) as the post-office box on it."

Almost immediately after Oswald was arrested the police asserted that he was guilty of assassination, was a Communist, was the head of the New Orleans Fair Play for Cuba Committee, and had used an alias, "Lee," the name under which he had rented his eight-dollar-a-week room. The following day, after the FBI had revealed that Oswald had purchased a rifle under the assumed name Hidell, the Dallas DA announced for the first time that Oswald had carried an identification card under the assumed name Hidell on his person when he was arrested the previous day.

One wonders why the police and the DA, in announcing Oswald's political background, failed to mention another alias readily available to them. Clearly, the suspect was immediately searched when arrested. Clearly, an identification card made out to another person fitting Oswald's description exactly was proof on another assumed name. Why did the Dallas authorities publicly "discover" the ID card for Hidell after the FBI said that Oswald purchased a rifle under the name Hidell?

Point Seven

Oswald was seen in the building by a police officer just after the president had been shot.

Wade said, "A police officer immediately after the assassination, ran into the building and saw this man in a corner and tried to arrest him; but the manager of the building said he was an employee and it was all right. Every other employee was located but this defendant of the company. A description and name of him went out by police to look for him." (At this point it might be in order to state that all of the Wade quotations are reproduced unedited, and in their entirety. The text of the Wade remarks appeared in the New York Times, Nov. 26.)

Unexplained by Wade is why the officer was going to arrest Oswald, who was sipping a soft drink in the lunchroom along with others. If the officer had reason to single out Oswald for arrest for the assassination at that time, it seems unlikely that the mere statement that Oswald was an employee might result in immunity from arrest.

Wade does explain, however, how the almost immediate description of Oswald was radioed to the police and to the citizens of Dallas. The explanation: "Every other employee was located but this defendant of the company." The New York Times (Nov. 23) reported: "About 90 persons were employed in the Texas School Book Depository and most of them were out watching the President's motorcade when the shots were fired." Police Chief Curry, who was riding in a car just 40 feet ahead of the limousine carrying the President, said he could tell from the sound of the three shots that they had come from the book company's building. Moments after the shots were fired, Curry said, he radioed instructions that the building be surrounded and searched (New York Times, Nov. 24). The deployment of 500 officers from his 1,100-man force made fast action possible in the manhunt, he said.

The scene painted for us by Wade and Curry finds officers immediately rushing to the building to seal it off and search it. This is the building from which the fatal shots allegedly were fired.

In these circumstances, is it likely that Oswald was permitted to leave the premises after the police arrived? Is it likely that Oswald, after killing the President, and deciding to leave the premises, decided first to stop off for a soda, and had then—only after the building was surrounded, sealed off and the search begun—made an effort to leave? Is it likely that each of the almost 90 employees, most of whom were outside of the building, engulfed in the panic and confusion attendant upon the assassination, could easily and quickly return to his place of employment through the police line, while still on his lunch hour, so that "every other employee was located but this defendant. . ." and the description of the one missing employee radioed at once?

Point Eight

Oswald's wife said that the rifle was missing Friday morning.

Wade said, "The wife had said he had the gun the night before, and it was missing that morning after he left." All indications are from statements made by other law officials and from FBI private briefings that Mrs. Oswald had never been quoted as saying anything remotely similar to Wade's assertion.

Mrs. Oswald was alleged to have said, at the very most, that she saw something in a blanket that could have been a rifle. However, it soon became plain that the Secret Service "leak" was itself absolutely inaccurate. Later we discovered that Mrs. Oswald stated that she never knew her husband owned a rifle nor did she know he owned a pistol (New York Times, Dec. 8).

Perhaps Wade and the Secret Service felt confident that, just as Oswald never got the opportunity to tell his side of the story, Mrs. Oswald might also have difficulty in being heard. Immediately after the assassination, Marina Oswald, Oswald's wife, was incarcerated by the Secret Service. "The widow and relatives of Lee Harvey Oswald are being sequestered here (Dallas) by the Secret Service. A spokesman for the Secret Service said the family was being kept in a secret place for its own protection. . .A Secret Service spokesman said he did not know when they would be released." (New York Times, Nov. 27.)

Inasmuch as there will be no trial, Marina Oswald clearly is not being held as a material witness. Since the federal government has no jurisdiction in any event, there seems to be no legal basis for her incarceration. Lee Oswald's mother, jeopardized by the existing hysteria as much as his widow, after being released from Secret Service "protective custody," requested that a guard be stationed at the door of her home. The Secret Service rejected that request stating that she was not in danger. One wonders then why Marina Oswald, widely and inaccurately quoted by the

Secret Service and the FBI, has remained in custody and practically incommunicado as well. The same issue of the *New York Times* that correctly stated Marina Oswald's view of the rifle said, "Mrs. Oswald has been moved from the motel where she was taken with Mrs. Marguerite Oswald, her brother-in-law and his wife, after her husband was killed. She is now excluded from Oswald's relatives as well as from the public." Several days after the "protective custody" began a reporter sought an interview with Marina Oswald. She indicated a desire to meet the reporter. The FBI then intervened and prevented the interview.

It would seem that the Secret Service move was dictated by a desire to prevent any truthful leaks from Mrs. Oswald's family or friends or through the press in reference to her views. At about the same time more Secret Service and FBI "leaks" regarding Marina Oswald's recollection of her late husband's "attempt to shoot Gen. Walker with the same assassination rifle" flooded the front pages of every daily in America. Marina Oswald's assertion that she never even knew that her husband owned a rifle, buried in the 14th paragraph of a story appearing on page 63 of the *New York Times*, is a total repudiation of that fabrication.

It may be said that when Marina Oswald is released from "protective custody" she will be able to discuss the truth of the statements attributed to her by the FBI, the Secret Service and Wade. The Secret Service has "suggested to her (Marina Oswald) that it might be safer and easier for her to return to the Soviet Union than to try to live in the United States (*Times*, Dec. 8)." Perhaps the Secret Service intended to indicate that it would be safer and easier for the Secret Service, the FBI and Wade and the case against Oswald if Mrs. Oswald quietly left the country.

Meanwhile, back to Wade's "clinched case." Even if Mrs. Oswald did state that her husband owned a rifle and that it was missing Friday morning, such "evidence" would not be admissible under the laws of Texas. The Dallas law enforcement officials, nevertheless, released that "evidence" to the public and, therefore, to all potential jurors in Dallas, while Oswald was alive and facing the possibility of trial. Such conduct did violence both to the spirit and letter of law and ethics and to the rights of the defendant.

In view of Marina Oswald's lack of knowledge regarding the rifle, and in view of the statement made by Mrs. Paine, at whose home the rifle was alleged to have been stored, one questions whether Oswald ever actually possessed the rifle. "Mrs. Paine, a Quaker, said she had no idea what was in the blanket. She said that because of her personal beliefs she would not allow a weapon of any sort in her home." (New York *World Telegram and Sun*, Nov. 25).

Point Nine

Oswald had a package under his arm Friday.

The Prosecutor said, "This day he went home one day earlier on Thursday night, and came back to—with this fellow—and when he came back he had a package under his arm that he said was window curtains, I believe, or window shades."

If Oswald were alive, we would proceed to ask him whether he carried a package to work Friday morning, and if so, what was in the package and what happened to the contents. If Mrs. Oswald were not locked up in a secret location we might ask her about the package. Wade has not indicated what evidence regarding the package led him to the conclusion that he offered (that it contained the murder weapon).

Point Ten

Oswald, while taking a bus from the scene, laughed loudly as he told a woman passenger that the President had been shot.

Wade said, "The next we hear of him is on a bus where he got on at Lamar Street, told the bus driver the President had been shot, the President. (He) told the lady—all this was verified by statements—told the lady on the bus that the President had been shot. He said, 'How did he know?' He said a man back there told him. The defendant said, 'Yes, he's been shot' and laughed very loud."

Wade, in telling his story, made no attempt to explain how Oswald escaped from the building sealed off by scores of Dallas police. We leave that mystery to enter a new one. Why did Oswald, fleeing the scene of a murder, joke publicly about the murder? Why did he "laugh very loud?" Such behavior is hardly consistent with 48 hours of consistent denial of guilt when in custody of the Dallas authorities. The laughter on the bus story seemed so unlikely that the FBI, in off-the-record briefing sessions for the press, conceded that it was untrue. In considering that the bus laughter story is false, we consider also the statement by Wade in telling of that story. ". . .all this was verified by statements."

Point Eleven

A taxi driver Darryl Click, took Oswald home, where he changed his clothes.

Wade said, "He then—the bus, he asked the bus driver to stop, got off at a stop, caught a taxicab driver, Darryl Click—I don't have his exact place—and went to his home in Oak City, changed his clothes hurriedly and left."

On Nov. 27, it was conceded that "Darryl Click" did not drive a taxicab in which Oswald was a passenger. When "Darryl Click" disappeared from the case, "William Whaley" appeared as the man who drove Oswald, not home, but at least in that general direction.

Oswald, it is alleged, fired the shots that killed Kennedy from the sixth floor of the building. Oswald, it is alleged, then walked down four flights of stairs, purchased a soft drink and was sipping it while a police officer approached him on the second floor.

Oswald, it is alleged, later left the building, slipping through the police cordon and proceeded through the panicked street crowds until he found a bus. Oswald, it is alleged, then boarded the bus, paid his fare, got a transfer (that he never used) and spoke to the driver about the assassination.

The driver referred a woman to Oswald, it is alleged, and Oswald spoke with her about the shooting. Oswald, it is alleged, eventually left the bus after riding about six blocks and was walking "from Commerce Street" when the taxicab driver, now named "William Whaley" saw him. Oswald, it is alleged, hailed the taxi, and entered it. "William Whaley's" log shows that Oswald entered the taxi, after having completed this entire trip, at exactly 12:30 p.m. The shots that killed Kennedy were fired at 12:31 p.m.

Point Twelve

Oswald shot and killed a police officer.

Wade said, "He walked up to the car. Officer Tippit stepped out of the car and started around it. He shot him three times and killed him."

This allegation isn't directly related to the murder of the President but it raised interesting points.

The Dallas authorities first said Tippit was shot in a movie theater. Later, it was reported that he was shot on one street and, still later, on another street. The first charge against Oswald was not for the murder of the President but for the murder of Tippit. That charge was made while the investigation of the Kennedy shooting was still going on. Wade announced that the Tippit case was absolutely set and that all the evidence proved Oswald shot the officer.

In view of the certainty of the prosecutor as to a case that had been entirely locked up two days before, the following dialogue (at the press conference) is rather curious.

> Reporter: Was this (where Oswald shot Tippit) in front of the boarding house?
> Wade: No, it's not in front of the boarding house.
> Reporter: Where was it?
> Wade: I don't have it exact.

Point Thirteen

A witness saw Oswald enter the Texas Theater.

Wade said, "Someone saw him go into the Texas Theater."

There has been little conflict about that assertion. The first statement by Dallas authorities indicated that the theater cashier was so suspicious when she saw Oswald change from seat to seat nervously that she telephoned the police.

It soon became obvious that a cashier at a post outside of the theater might have difficulty watching the customers once they entered. So the authorities then indicated that an usher saw Oswald changing seats. The last version has a person outside the theater noticing Oswald's suspicious action, following him into the theater, sealing off the doors with the assistance of the usher, and then notifying the police through a telephone call made by the cashier.

Some questions peripheral to the arrest in the theater persist. What did Oswald do before entering the theater to attract attention? In what manner were his actions "suspicious?" We have been told by the newly emerging firearm-psychologist experts that although Oswald was not particularly talented with a rifle, his "psychotic condition" may have given him "nerveless coordination" so that he might fire accurately.

Evidently that "nerveless coordination" was not present outside the theater, although it could have appeared to Oswald that he had committed the perfect crime, had escaped the police at the Texas Book Depository and was now far removed from the scene. Frantic actions by Oswald, so obvious as to attract the attention of a passerby, in these circumstances, also seem inconsistent with Oswald's reported demeanor moments after the President had been shot. At this time a policeman charged up the stairs of the book depository, pointed a gun at him and sought to arrest him for shooting the President.

Oswald's employer described Oswald's condition at the time as "cool

as a cucumber—although he seemed a little bothered by the gun."
(*Washington Post*, Dec. 1)

Point Fourteen

Oswald drew a pistol and attempted to kill the arresting officer. The firing
pin struck and marked the bullet but it did not explode.

Wade said, "He (Oswald) struck at the officer, put the gun against his
head and snapped it, but did not—the bullet did not—go off. We have
the snapped bullet there. Officers apprehended him at that time. . .It
misfired being on the—the shell didn't explode. We have where it hit it,
but it didn't explode."

Wade was attempting to indicate that when Oswald was arrested in
the theater he tried to shoot the arresting officer and did in fact pull the
trigger of the pistol. There can be no question that the trigger was pulled
since Wade assured us, in his fashion, that the firing pin struck the bullet
and marked the bullet. He further assured us his officer has the "snapped
bullet" in its possession. The arresting officer, however, policeman Mac-
Donald, told the story differently: "I got my hand on the butt of his gun,"
said MacDonald. "I could feel Oswald's hand on the trigger. I jerked my
hand and was able to slow down the trigger movement. He didn't have
enough force to fire it." (*Washington Post*, Dec. 1.)

> Reporter: There was one officer who said that he pulled the
> trigger, but he managed to put his thumb in the
> part before the firing pin. It didn't strike the—
> the bullet didn't explode. Is that. . .?
> Wade: I don't know whether it's that or not. I know he
> didn't snap the gun is all I know about it. (*New
> York Times*, Nov. 26.)

We leave this incident bearing in mind one remarkable fact. Physical
evidence, introduced by Wade—a bullet marked by a firing pin in an
attempt to kill a police officer—now was repudiated by the officer who
was an eyewitness and by Wade himself.

Point Fifteen

A map was found in Oswald's possession showing the scene of the
assassination and the bullet's trajectory.

The day after Wade's historic press conference, and three days after
the Oswald arrest, a new discovery was made.

"Today Mr. Wade announced that authorities had also found a marked map, showing the course of the President's motorcade, in Oswald's rented room. 'It was a map tracing the location of the parade route,' the district attorney said, 'and this place [the Texas School Book Depository, a warehouse from which the fatal shots were fired] was marked with a straight line.' Mr. Wade said Oswald had marked the map at two other places, 'apparently places which he considered a possibility for an assassination'." (*New York Times*, Nov. 25.)

A document written by the defendant showing his intention to commit a crime is important evidence. It seems incredible, were such a map in the hands of the Dallas authorities on the previous day when Wade presented the evidence, "piece by piece," that he would have neglected to mention it.

Oswald was arrested three days prior to the map announcement. On the day of his arrest police removed all of his belongings from his room, telling the landlady that Oswald "would not return." One wonders where the map came from three days later. The same newspapers that hailed the discovery of the map Nov. 25, without a single question as to its legitimacy, origins, or previous whereabouts, totally ignored or buried the last comment regarding this important document. "Dallas officials yesterday denied that such a map exists." (*Washington Post*, Nov. 27.)

The People vs. Oswald

When a criminal case is brought in federal court against an individual, it is entitled, "The People of the United States against" the named defendant. No federal charge was lodged against Oswald; however, in the most fundamental sense the case became the entire country's accusation against one man. Very likely no prospective defendant in the history of civilization has been tried and condemned through the utilization of the media as thoroughly as was Oswald.

The American Civil Liberties Union commented on Dec. 6:

"It is our opinion that Lee Harvey Oswald, had he lived, would have been deprived of all opportunity to receive a fair trial by the conduct of the police and prosecuting officials in Dallas, under pressure from the public and the news media.

"From the moment of his arrest until his murder two days later, Oswald was tried and convicted many times over in the newspapers, on the radio, and over television by the public statements of the Dallas law enforcement officials. Time and again high-ranking police and prosecution officials state their complete satisfaction that Oswald was the assassin. As their investigation uncovered one piece of evidence after another, the results were broadcast to the public.

"...Oswald's trial would...have been nothing but a hollow formality."

In a section headed "Police Responsibility for Oswald's killing" the ACLU stated that the concessions to the media "resulted in Oswald being deprived not only of his day in court, but of his life as well."

On Dec. 4 the chancellor-elect of the Philadelphia Bar Association stated that Lee Oswald had been "lynched" and that this was an "indictment" of the legal profession for its failure to protect Oswald (*New York Times*, Dec. 5). These two comments, made after the death of Oswald and buried by the news media under the avalanche of news attacks against Oswald (including the FBI leaks of other crimes alleged to have been committed by him), constitute to this date almost the only indication of sanity in the country.

After Oswald's death, the FBI acted to prevent certain information from reaching the public. "Most private citizens who had cooperated with newsmen reporting the crime have refused to give further help after being interviewed by agents of the Federal Bureau of Investigation." (*New York Times*, Dec. 6). The FBI acted, not to protect the rights of a defendant, but, after he was murdered, to protect the inconsistent evidence from further scrutiny. Mrs. Oswald, still in Secret Service custody, hidden in an unknown location, was quoted on the front pages of papers throughout the country Dec. 6 and 7 as implicating Oswald in another crime. Such a quotation could have come only from a Secret Service or FBI leak. No one else had access to her. And so the insanity accelerates until the few remaining vestiges of doubt as to Oswald's guilt are obliterated from the American scene.

However, let it not be said that the lawyers are not aroused by an attorney's giving statements to the public in relation to a pending case. "A Dallas Bar Association grievance committee met three hours last night on charges that Tom Howard, attorney for Jack Ruby, had violated legal ethics by discussing Ruby's case with the press...No charges had been placed against District Attorney Henry Wade." (*New York Post*, Dec. 6)

When an entire society moves in for the kill, logic is a weapon of doubtful value. Were logic to prevail, a number of questions might be raised for rational deliberation. For example, one might inquire why the FBI, having questioned Oswald just a week before the assassination and having discovered that he worked in a building directly on the President's line of march, and knowing that Oswald had purchased a rifle, did not watch him on the day of assassination. Certainly, a small portion of the millions of dollars bestowed upon the FBI each year and utilized for following persons of unorthodox political views and tapping their telephones might have been made available under these circumstances, as part of what the FBI and Secret Service referred to as the "greatest security provisions ever taken to protect an American President."

The Question of Motive

Whether the Dallas police through complicity or complacency permitted the murder of the defendant by a police department friend after two warnings through the FBI that such an attempt would be made should be a matter for press discussion. Whether or not the FBI showed Mrs. Oswald, the defendant's mother, a picture of Ruby before Ruby murdered Oswald would ordinarily demand media debate.

There are two matters not even commented upon by the press to date—Oswald's motive and Oswald's plan for escape. Oswald seemed to respect President Kennedy. If Oswald was a leftist, pro-Soviet and pro-Cuban, did he not know that during the last year, with the assistance of President Kennedy, a better relationship was in the process of developing between the U.S. and the Soviet Union? Even the relations between the U.S. and Cuba, while still extremely unfriendly, have progressed past the stage of military intervention. Fidel Castro himself stated, just before the President's death, "He (Kennedy) has the possibility of becoming the greatest President of the United States. . .He has come to understand many things over the last few months. . .I'm convinced that anyone else would be worse." (*New York Times*, Dec. 11)

The press made much of the fact that Oswald had been seen with a copy of the *Worker*, a Communist publication, and that he had received at least two letters from the Communist Party. A New York newspaper referred to him editorially as a "Communist murderer." Did Oswald know that the U.S. Communist Party supported Kennedy when he ran for the presidency in 1960 and that within the last six months Gus Hall urged the Communist Party, which he leads, to endorse and support Kennedy again?

Why should Oswald wish to assassinate the President; and after firing at the President, how did he plan to escape? Did he wish to flee from the building? If so, why did he remain in the lunchroom sipping a soda? Was he in a hurry? If so, why did he take a ride on a bus? It was a very warm day in Dallas. Mrs. Kennedy, sweltering in the open moving car, later said that she was looking forward to the cool relief of riding through the underpass just ahead. Why then, did Oswald, seeking to escape the police, go home to pick up his jacket? If he was planning to leave the city, why did he then go to a movie just as the city-wide search was gaining intensity?

These are genuine areas for speculation by the press now that the defendant is dead. These are, nevertheless, almost the only areas left unexamined by the media.

Perhaps some day, when America is ready for the sunlight of reason to penetrate the national mind, now frozen to a false and unfair conclusion, this article and others far more comprehensive may be read.

An Affirmative Case

Under our system of justice a defendant need not prove he is innocent. It is the obligation of the prosecutor to attempt to prove the defendant guilty beyond a reasonable doubt. Should the prosecutor fail to sustain that burden, the defendant must be declared not guilty.

In the case of Oswald, hysteria and intolerance have so swept our country that the protections guaranteed by our Constitution and by our traditions have failed to operate. Since irrationality is the implacable foe of justice and due process, we are compelled to depart from ordinary legal procedure. At this point we shall submit an affirmative case. We shall attempt to present facts that tend to prove that Oswald did not shoot President Kennedy.

A denial by a defendant that he committed a crime when supported by testimony as to his good character is sufficient in and of itself to cause a reasonable doubt which, even in the face of evidence to the contrary, may result in acquittal.

Oswald denied he shot anyone. He stated that the charges against him were "ridiculous." He persisted in his denial despite the fact that he was questioned for 48 hours without the benefit of counsel.

Denial of counsel, when coupled with extensive questioning, is improper and contrary to long-established principles of law. The principle was developed out of revulsion against the ancient trial by ordeal or trial by fire which forced a person accused of a crime to cooperate in the prosecution of his own case. Great constitutional protections, including the Fifth Amendment to the U.S. Constitution, were developed. It was found that not only would guilty persons confess when sufficient pressure was placed against them, but innocent persons also were likely to succumb.

Great pressure was placed against Oswald. He stood all alone condemned as the slayer of a popular leader. "Oswald was pummeled by the arresting officers until his face was puffed and battered. 'Kill the President will you?' one officer shouted in a choked voice." (*Washington Post*, Dec. 1.)

In addition "Oswald received a black eye and a cut on his forehead." (*New York Times*, Nov. 24.)

When a reporter asked Oswald in a televised interview how he received the bruises and cuts on his face, he answered calmly, "A policeman hit me."

For 48 hours, Oswald was denied the elementary right to counsel of his choice. The Dallas police falsely told the attorneys for the ACLU that Oswald "did not want counsel." Despite physical abuse and absolute isolation, Oswald continued to state that he was innocent. Each previous assassin of an American president immediately and boastfully declared that the act was his.

Character Witnesses

The press has been glutted with attacks upon Oswald since his death, with each informant issuing self-serving declarations as to his own ability to detect incipient mental problems or character weaknesses, when Oswald was much younger.

A former probation officer in New York City permitted an interview which violated principles of a privileged and protected relationship between himself and a young boy. A justice of the Family Court released records to the FBI, and the information was carried in the press.

Nevertheless, those who knew Oswald a little better had some rather kind things to say about him. At a trial, their testimony could have been decisive. The associate pastor of First Unitarian Church, Dallas, Rev. Byrd Helligas, described Lee Oswald as "erudite." "He had a good vocabulary. No dangling participles or split infinitives. In the dictionary definition of the word 'intellectual' he was an intellectual." Helligas added that he sensed "no frustration through erudition. He was calm." (*Washington Post*, Dec. 1.)

Samuel Ballen, described in the press as a "Republican petroleum economist in Dallas," said he found Lee Oswald to be an independent, thinking, inquiring young man. . .He was a rather frail person physically. At least to me, he was the kind of person I could like. I kind of took a liking to him. I wanted to help him a little bit. . .He had a kind of Gandhi, far-off look about him." (*Washington Post*, Dec. 1.)

Roy Truly, the director of the depository where Oswald was employed, said of Oswald, "He seemed just a normal, quiet young fellow."

Mrs. Paine, with whom his wife and children lived and where he stayed on weekends, said, "Marina (Lee Oswald's wife) felt very favorably toward the President and his family. Most of what she learned of American news was provided by Lee, who translated from newspapers and news magazines. Marina said he never transferred any negative feelings toward President Kennedy." (*Washington Post*, Nov. 28.)

Mrs. Paine also stated that, "As far as I know Oswald had never been critical of Kennedy. He had been critical of General [Edwin] Walker, but I never heard him say anything against the President. In fact, it was my impression that he respected him." (New York *World Telegram and Sun*, Nov. 25.)

In 1959, Oswald was interviewed by Priscilla Johnson, an American correspondent while in Moscow. She reported, "I found him rather likeable. He was quiet and didn't have a vehement manner. He was so very young. He was someone you would try to help."

Mrs. Luella Merrett, principal of West Ridglea Elementary School which Oswald attended, said, "If he had problems, we did not recognize them. . .He was interested in things."

Were the case to be tried, persons ordinarily selected as character witnesses would include his employer, a minister, his landlady, a respected businessman, a correspondent who knew him abroad, the Quaker family with whom his wife resided and his school teachers. Judging by the initial response, one could conclude that character testimony for Lee Oswald would be compelling.

Time, Place and Oswald

In addition to consistent denial of guilt by the defendant and statements of character witnesses that seem to indicate a person different from the disturbed, hostile character usually associated with the particular crime, a defendant may offer testimony indicating that he was somewhere other than at the scene of the crime when it was committed. We, of course, can't get such information from this defendant.

However, a valid defense could result in showing that even if the defendant were at the scene he could not have committed the crime. Such a defense is available. If Oswald was on the sixth floor of the book depository armed with the alleged murder weapon, a 6.5mm Italian carbine, he could not have fired three shots that struck President Kennedy and Gov. Connally.

The official homicide report filed by the Dallas Police Department, attested to by two police officers, states under the section "Place of

Occurrence": "Elm Street (approximately 150 feet west of Houston)." The report also states under the section "Pronounced dead by Physician," the name "Dr. Kemp Clark, 1 p.m., Parkland Hospital."

A motion picture taken of the President just before, during and after the shooting, and demonstrated on television showed that the President was looking directly ahead when the first shot, which entered his throat, was fired. A series of still pictures taken from the motion picture and published in *Life* magazine on Nov. 29 show exactly the same situation. The *Life* estimate in an accompanying caption states that the car with the President was 75 yards past the sixth-floor window when the first shot was fired.

The *New York Times* (Nov. 27) reported: "Dr. Kemp Clark, who pronounced Mr. Kennedy dead, said one [bullet] struck him at about the necktie knot. 'It ranged downward in his chest and did not exit,' the surgeon said. The second he called a 'tangential wound,' caused by a bullet that struck the 'right back of his head.'"

The New York *Herald Tribune* (Nov. 27) said: "On the basis of accumulated data, investigators have concluded that the first shot, fired as the Presidential car was approaching, struck the President in the neck just above the knot of his necktie, then ranged downward into his body."

Surgeons who attended the President at the Parkland Memorial Hospital described the throat wound as "an entrance wound." (St. Louis *Post-Dispatch*, Dec. 1), "They said it was in the center of the front, just below the Adam's apple, at about the necktie knot." (Ibid.) Dr. Malcolm Perry began to cut an air passage in the President's throat in an effort to restore an air passage and start his breathing. The incision was made through the bullet wound, since it was in the normal place for the operation. "Dr. Perry described the bullet hole as an entrance wound." (Ibid.) Dr. Robert N. McClelland, one of three surgeons who participated in the operation, said "It certainly did look like an entrance wound." (Ibid.) Dr. McClelland said he saw bullet wounds every day, "sometimes several a day. This did appear to be an entrance wound." (Ibid.)

On Nov. 27, the Secret Service re-enacted the assassination of the President. "The purpose was 'to test whether it could be done the way we believe it was done' an official source said." (*New York Times*, Nov. 28.) The consensus was "that the shooting began after the President's car had made the turn from Houston Street into Elm Street." (*New York Times*, Nov. 28.)

In an interview broadcast from Dallas Nov. 27, Gov. Connally told Martin Agronsky that the shooting began after the car had turned the corner. (*New York Times*, Nov. 28.)

If the throat wound resulted from a shot fired from the book depository the President would have had to turn around with his throat facing almost directly to the rear. Dr. McClelland stated that the doctors postulated that "he (the President) would have had to be looking almost completely to the rear." (St. Louis *Post-Dispatch*, Dec. 1.) The Washington correspondent for the Post-Dispatch stated that, "The motion pictures, however, showed the President looking forward." (Dec. 1.) "Mrs. John Connally, the wife of the Texas Governor, has said that she had just told Mr. Kennedy, 'You can't say Dallas isn't friendly to you today.' Presumably he was about to reply when he was hit." (Ibid.) Mrs. Connally was seated in front of the President.

Relying, therefore, upon a report filed with the Dallas Police by two officers who where eyewitnesses, the motion pictures taken of the shooting, still shots taken from the motion pictures, the statement of Gov. Connally, the consensus of those who re-enacted the scene under supervision of the Secret Service, and the report of the attending physicians, we may conclude that the shot was fired while the back of the President was to the sixth-floor window and many yards removed from that window and that the bullet entered the front of the President's throat.

If Oswald was at the sixth-floor window, as alleged, when the President was shot it would have been physically impossible for him to have fired the first shot that struck the President. In the words of Richard Dudman, the correspondent for the *Post-Dispatch* (Dec. 1), "The question that suggests itself is: How could the President have been shot in the front from the back?"

The Gun and the Experts

The question now arises as to whether any one man, even a skilled expert, could have fired the three shots within a period of five seconds. An Olympic rifle champion, Hubert Hammerer, said he doubted it could be done with the weapon allegedly used. The Dallas sheriff, Bill Decker, said he believed three shots "could be fired in less than 20 seconds." (*Washington Post*, Nov. 27.) The FBI and the witnesses agree the elapsed period was five, possibly five and one-half seconds.

Life magazine (Dec. 6) hired a skilled marksman, the director of the National Rifle Association, to fire a similar rifle. The best he could do was "three hits in 6.2 seconds." The *New York Times*, Nov. 23 reported: "As marines go, Lee Harvey Oswald was not highly regarded as a rifleman."

Debate will continue whether the rifle in question was capable, in the hands of an expert, of the performance the prosecution insists it gave.

All agree, however, that such a remarkable display of shooting would be beyond the ability of any person less qualified. To maintain the ability to fire a rifle accurately, one must practice continually. Oswald's wife and the Paine family, all of whom lived in the house where the rifle was allegedly stored, did not even know Oswald owned a rifle. This would seem to indicate an extremely limited usage of the rifle at the very most. . Oswald did not have the requisite skill to fire three accurate shots within 5 1/2 seconds at a moving target.

Other Uncertainties

If Oswald was where the FBI and the Dallas District Attorney said he was when the shots were fired and if the President was assassinated by one person as charged—Lee Harvey Oswald is demonstrably not guilty. Oswald was in the wrong place and did not have sufficient time to shoot President Kennedy as charged.

The facts as presented to date by the FBI and the Dallas district attorney (soon to be rewritten no doubt) have overcome the presumption of guilt manufactured when the case was initiated.

Dudman wrote in the St. Louis *Post-Dispatch* (Dec. 1): "Another unexplained circumstance is a small hole in the windshield of the presidential limousine. This correspondent and one other man saw the hole, which resembled a bullet hole, as the automobile stood at the hospital emergency entrance while the President was being treated inside the building.

"The Secret Service kept possession of the automobile and flew it back to Washington. A spokesman for the agency rejected a request to inspect the vehicle here [Washington]. He declined to discuss any hole there might be in the windshield."

Undoubtedly the Secret Service has placed the auto in protective custody, "in a secret place for its own protection."

Dudman continued to present startling information. "Uncertainty surrounds the number of shots fired." (Ibid.) Although most witnesses heard three shots fired within a period of five seconds it seems that five bullets have been discovered.

"The first bullet is said by the doctors to have entered the throat, coursed downward and remained in the President's body. The second was extracted from Gov. Connally's thigh. It had lodged there after entering the right side of his back, passing through his body and through his wrist. A third, which may be the one that struck the back of Mr. Kennedy's head, was recovered from the stretcher on which he was carried into the hospital. A fourth was found in fragments in the car. Still another bullet was found by Dallas police officers after the shooting. It was in the grass opposite the point where the President was hit. They did not know whether it had anything to do with the shooting of the President and the Governor." (Ibid.)

One point does emerge with absolute clarity. The theory held by the Dallas police and supported repeatedly by the FBI that "there is an airtight case against Oswald as the sole killer" is based upon an investigation so poor as to be incredible or an investigation devoted to a particular conclusion at the outset.

The Investigation

The FBI, having completed its investigation, has submitted what amounts to its findings and conclusions as well. The verdict, deftly and covertly divulged to the press, and then blared forth throughout the world, is impressively simple: "Oswald is the assassin. He acted alone." This remarkable law enforcement and investigatory agency, unable to solve a single one of the more than 40 Birmingham bombings, is now able to function as investigator, prosecutor, judge and jury. No other American agency has presumed to occupy so many positions of trust at one time.

The essential problem is that no investigating agency can fairly evaluate the fruits of its own work. Were the FBI certain of its conclusions it seems likely it would not be so reluctant to permit witnesses to talk with the press. It might not feel the need continually to leak information favorable to its verdict to the press. Most disquieting of all, however, is that the FBI, once wedded to a conclusion conceived before investigation, might be motivated to discover evidence which supports that conclusion. Within a few hours after Oswald was arrested the Dallas police, with the FBI at its side, announced the very same verdict now reinforced by the latest FBI discoveries. Under such circumstances, we fear that evidence tending to prove Oswald innocent might be discarded and evidence proving him guilty might be developed out of proportion or even created.

The Justice Department has already privately expressed "disappointment" with the FBI report, fearing that it "has left too many questions unanswered."

The Stakes Are Big

The FBI investment in a Warren Commission finding identical with its own cannot be emphasized too boldly. Should the Warren Commission reach and publish a conclusion substantially different from the one submitted so publicly by the FBI, public confidence in the FBI would be so shaken as, in all likelihood, to render the FBI as it is now constituted, almost absolutely useless. One can assume that the FBI wishes to avoid that result.

It may be argued on many different levels of governmental life that a finding by the commission that an American lynched in a Dallas courthouse might be innocent, would result in the further destruction of the American image abroad.

It will be extremely difficult for any commission, in these circumstances, to bear the responsibility imposed upon it. For the sake of our country let us hope that Justice Earl Warren, a fair and great American, may successfully guide his commission through the sea of hatred and malice surrounding this case in its search for the truth.

An Era of Understanding

There are those who have said much good may come from this assassination, that a new era of understanding and unity may result. I doubt this. From hate comes hate. From murder—as we have already seen—murder. And from hysteria—rejection of the great Anglo-Saxon tradition of justice. But if it is possible to leave behind us the America of violence and malice, our national renaissance must begin with a respect for law and disdain for the hysteria that has thus far made fair consideration of this case impossible.

Our national conscience must reject the massive media conviction of Oswald—presumed to be innocent—and begin to examine and to analyze the evidence. We must recognize that the same reckless disregard for human life and decency that resulted in the death of our President resulted also in the death of Oswald while in police custody. And, before that, it resulted in the destruction of every right belonging to an American accused of a crime. The press, the radio and the television stations share that guilt.

The law enforcement officials, however, beginning with District Attorney Wade, who falsely stated evidence to the entire world repeatedly and who gave leadership to the development of a carnival atmosphere, must bear history's harshest judgment.

You are the jury. You are the only jury that Lee Harvey Oswald will ever have.

A terrible crime has been committed. A young, vital and energetic leader of perhaps the world's most powerful nation has been killed by the cowardly act of a hidden assassin. The murderer or murderers were motivated by diseased minds or by such depths of malice as to approach that state. We will perhaps never know their motives. We must, however, know and approve of our own conduct and our own motives.

We begin with a return to an old American tradition—the presumption of innocence. We begin with you.

Let those who would deny a fair consideration of the evidence to Oswald because of a rage inspired, they say, by their devotion to the late President, ponder this thought: If Oswald is innocent—and that is a possibility that cannot now be denied—then the assassin of President Kennedy remains at large.

A Review of Mark Lane's *Rush to Judgment*, *Book Week*, August 28,
1966

by Norman Mailer

On May 14, 1964, when J. Edgar Hoover testified before the Warren
Commission, he said about Marguerite Oswald: "The first indication of
her emotional instability was the retaining of a lawyer that anyone would
not have retained if they were really serious in trying to get down to the
facts." Well, Bill Terry once asked if the Dodgers were still in the league,
and J. Edgar Hoover revealed this day an even more massive incapacity
to judge certain kinds of underdogs and men, for Mark Lane, the lawyer
retained, has come up with 400 pages of facts on the Warren Commission's inquiry into the murders of President John F. Kennedy, Officer J.
D. Tippit, and Lee Harvey Oswald, and they are somewhat staggering
facts. If one-tenth of them should prove to be significant, then the work
of the Warren Commission will be judged by history to be a scandal
worse than the Teapot Dome.

Rush to Judgment is of course a defense attorney's brief, and it seeks
to make its case as best it can, wherever it can. Those looking for a
comprehensive explanation of the mystery of the assassination will not
find it, not here. There is no single overall explanation of the unspoken
possibilities, nor is one even offered. Lane is attempting to prove that
Oswald most certainly could not have committed the crime alone, and
that the odds are great that he did not commit either murder. Lane's
attempt, therefore, is to disprove the case brought in by prosecution—it
is a small continuing shock to recognize, as Lane fortifies his arguments
in the most interesting detail, that the Warren Commission served as an
agent of gentlemanly prosecution rather than as a commission of inquiry.
That this was not head-on evident when the *Report* came out is due to
the lucidities and sweet reasonable tone of the style in which the *Warren
Commission Report* is written. But the gentlest of men often write in a bad
harsh voice, and many a quiet calculating brute has acquired the best of
good tones in prose. Yes, the *Warren Commission Report* convinced a majority of Americans by the reasonableness and modesty of its style—what
casual study did not show, however, was that when the Commission was
being most reasonable in stating that something could not be proved,
it was neglecting to say that the preponderance of unexplored leads to
new evidence was pointed resolutely in the opposite direction from their
conclusion. The scandal of the Warren Commission was twofold—it did

not look into some of the more interesting and fascinating matters before it, and it distorted its hard findings. As Hugh Trevor-Roper points out in a fine British introduction to *Rush to Judgment*, "A pattern was made to emerge out of the evidence, and having emerged, seem to subordinate the evidence to it." It was not enough to read the *Report*; one was obliged, Trevor-Roper points out, to read the 26 volumes of *Hearings*. "To follow the same question through the three successive levels of *Hearings*, *Report*, and *Summary and Conclusions* is to see sometimes a quiet transformation of evidence."

But one may ask: was the Warren Commission in conspiracy to hide the truth, all those fine, separate, august, and honorable gentlemen? And the answer is: of course not. They were not in conspiracy, they never needed to be, no more than a corporation has to be in conspiracy to push out a product which is grievously inferior to the product they are potentially equipped to make, nor the head of General Motors need hire private detectives to hound Ralph Nader. Products come from processes, and a commission's report is a reflection of a method on inquiry. Edward Jay Epstein's book demonstrated even to Fletcher Knebel's satisfaction that the Warren Commission did not work very hard. Walter Craig, president of the American Bar Association, appointed as "protector" of Oswald's interests, attended two out of 51 sessions of the Commission—he was perhaps not the kind of lawyer Mr. Hoover would have recommended to Mrs. Oswald; the only Commission member to be present much more than 50 percent of the time was Allen Dulles of the CIA—perhaps he had the most to protect.

No, for the large part, the seven members of the Commission were abstracted and often distant: The established lawyers who pursued the investigation as their nominal assistants were busy in private practice, and usually absent. So the work passed on down to junior assistants, bright young lawyers with careers to make. They were forced to contend every day with agents, investigators, and detectives who knew more about criminal investigation than they did and were also presumably possessed of more physical strength, more martial arts, as well as endowed with that dead, muted, fanatical intensity which wins much in negotiation across a table. The investigation seemed to push at every turn against the likelihood of inefficiency, corruption, collusion, or direct involvement in the case by the Dallas police, and, in more complex fashion, the CIA and the FBI. The Secret Service, having done a poor job, had their own reputations to protect. In such a situation, what overworked young lawyer is going to continue to make a personal crusade of his own investigation against the revelatory somnolence of the Committee members, and the resistance of the FBI, especially when a routine performance satisfactory to the Commission gives assurance of a happy and accelerated career?

What becomes oppressively evident is that the Warren Commission from the beginning had no intention of trying to find any other assassin than Oswald. Whether from pure motives or from intentions not so clear (It will be remembered that before the Commission began to sit, the Chief Justice was speaking already of information which could not be divulged for 75 years), whether from honest bias or determined obfuscation, the evidence fitted a bed of Procrustes. Everything was enlisted to satisfy the thesis that Oswald, half-mad, had done the job alone, and Ruby, half-mad, had done his particular job alone. So a witness, Brennan, who had poor eyesight, was credited by the Commission with identifying Oswald in a sixth-story window—his eyes, went the unspoken assumption, could see better at one time than another; whereas a man with excellent eyesight named Rowland who saw two men in the window was considered unreliable because his wife told the Commission her young husband was prone to exaggerate the results of his report cards.

Besides, it was a game of experts. The expert always plays a game in which his side is supposed to win—the expert has a psychic structure which is umbilically opposed to finding the truth until the expert finds out first if the truth is good for his side. We have prosecuting attorneys and defense attorneys because a legal case is first a game—each side looks for its purchase of the truth, even if the search carries them into almost impossible assumptions. It is why a fact-finding commission cannot by its nature make discoveries which are as incisive as the evidence uncovered by the monomaniacal, the Ahab-like search of a dedicated attorney. In contrast to him, the totalitarians look to find their truth in consensus. You and I are more likely to find it beneath a stone.

So Lane's book provides the case for the defense. Like all lawyers' briefs, it is not wholly satisfactory as a book. One wishes that the strongest evidence of Oswald's guilt provided by the Warren Commission were presented at least in summary, if only to be demolished, or that the admission were made by Lane that certain crucial damaging points cannot be refuted, but Lane's intent is to do the best for his dead client, and that is what he does. If *Rush to Judgment* accomplishes nothing else, it will live as a classic for every serious amateur detective in America. Long winter nights in the farmhouse will be spent poring over the contradictions in the 26 volumes of the *Hearings* with Lane's book for a guide, and plans will be made and money saved to make a trip to Dallas, which will become a shrine for all the unborn Baker Street Irregulars of the world. Because Lane's book proves once and forever that the assassination of President Kennedy is more of a mystery today than when it occurred.

Well, then—what finally does Lane produce? He presents a thousand items of clear-cut doubt in 400 pages, material sufficient for five years of real investigation by any fair country commission. He makes it clear that most of the witnesses to the assassination thought the shots came not from the Texas Book Depository Building but from behind a fence on a knoll above and in front of the Presidential limousine. And that autopsy which could clarify whether the President was shot from the front, from behind, or from both separate positions—well, that autopsy was mired in massive confusion which the Commission did not dissolve and in fact interred, for X-rays and photographs taken at the autopsy have not been published. The bullet which shattered the President's skull almost certainly had to be a soft-nosed lead round to explode so large a wound; Oswald's gun fired hard-nosed metal-jacketed rounds. The questions raised by Edward Jay Epstein in Inquest about the bullet which was alleged to strike the President and Governor Connally are explored again and point to the same conclusion—one bullet could not have entered where it did, and come out where it came out.

Nor has any satisfactory explanation ever been offered, Lane shows in detail, as to how the police were able to send out a call to apprehend Oswald 15 minutes after the assassinations, nor why the two officers who discovered the rifle on the sixth floor described it in careful detail as a "7.65 Mauser bolt-action equipped with a 4/18 scope, a thick leather brownish-black sling on it. . .gun metal color. . .blue metal. . .the rear portion of the bolt was visibly worn. . ." But the Mauser turned into a pumpkin and became a 6.5 Mannlicher-Carcano. Of course, Marina Oswald, on hearing of the assassination over the radio, went out to the garage to see if Oswald's Mannlicher-Carcano was in place. It was there. It was there? "Later," she said, "it turned out that the rifle was not there [and] I did not know what to think." The Dallas police came in soon to search the garage and later reported that they found an empty blanket upon a shelf. It was that empty blanket, they declared, which Marina had mistaken for the rifle. So the rifle on the sixth floor altered from a 7.65 Mauser bolt-action to a 6.5 Mannlicher-Carcano carbine, a point for the shade of Sherlock Holmes, for unless the police in Texas are such unnatural Texans as to be innocent of rifles, they would know a 7.65 Mauser is the most beloved and revered of bolt-actions, whereas the 6.5 Mannlicher-Carcano rests among the most despised of shooting irons. It is curious; one repeats: it is curious that the Commission taking testimony from the very same officer who discovered the rifle which he had declared a

Mauser did not choose to show this police officer the Mannlicher-Carcano and ask if he might be in error, or if, horror beyond belief, the guns were switched.

Roll-call of these unexplored details continues. The Mannlicher-Carcano had the same scope as the nonexistent Mauser, but Marina Oswald had never seen a scope on a rifle. (She was a woman, after all.) So the suggestion intrudes itself—was the 4/18 scope on the Mauser switched in a great private frantic hurry to the Mannlicher, installed in fact so quickly that the telescopic sight was unrelated to the line of fire! Certainly we have it on record that the scope had to be reset with shims before the Masters of the National Rifle Association could even aim it. This, the rifle supposed to have killed Kennedy? And when they fired for test, these three Masters, six shots each in groups of two at three fixed targets, 18 shots in total by three Masters, they did not fire nearly so quickly or so well at fixed targets as Oswald had fired at moving targets from a more difficult and certainly more extraordinary position. In fact the Mannlicher dispersed its shot group so widely (an estimated 12 inches at 100 yards) that no one of the experts in all their collective 18 shots succeeded in striking the head or neck of the fixed target. Nonetheless, the Commission decided that the Mannlicher-Carcano had done the job. Oswald, of course, had no great record as a rifleman, but perhaps his bad aim, the moving car, the crazy, banged-up scope, the inaccurate barrel, and the very heavy trigger pull came together in the vertigo of the moment to funnel-in two hits out of three. Perhaps. Perhaps there is one chance in a thousand. But a Zen master, not a rifle expert, must be consulted for this.

Questions arise here and everywhere. The package of curtain rods in which Oswald was supposed to have concealed the Mannlicher-Carcano was too small (on the account of both witnesses who had seen it) to contain the disassembled rifle. But the size of the bag remains moot because it was *ruined* in the FBI labs while being examined for fingerprints. Another bag was put together—38 inches in length. The witnesses seemed to think it was about 10 inches longer than the original. (The Mannlicher disassembled is almost 35 inches). The Commission decided the witnesses "could easily have been mistaken in their estimate." So could the FBI, unless there were affidavits on the dimensions of the original bag before it had been subjected to fingerprint tests.

Move on. The only eyewitness to the murder of Tippit was a woman named Mrs. Markham. She was certain the killing took place at 1:06 p.m. The Commission was not able to get Oswald to the spot before 1:16 p.m. So the Commission decided that Mrs. Markham was correct in her identification of Oswald, but wrong in her placement of the time. Mrs. Markham, however, in an interview with Lane, described Tippit's killer as "a short man, somewhat on the heavy side, with slightly bushy hair." The description she gave the police was "about 30, 5'8, black hair, slender."

Tippit leads to Ruby. Among the many potential witnesses who were not called were a variety of people who had been associated with Ruby for years. They made a general collective estimate that Ruby knew personally more than half the officers on the Dallas police force. Ruby kept begging the Warren Commission to get him out of the Dallas jail and into Washington. "I want to tell the truth," he said, "and I can't tell it here. . .Gentleman, unless you get me to Washington you can't get a fair shake out of me." Of course, many witnesses were intimidated in mysterious ways. Two reporters who visited Ruby's apartment just after he killed Oswald were later murdered, one in his Dallas apartment as the victim of a karate attack (where are you, Charlie Chan?). The Commission did not seem to explore this. Another witness, Warren Reynolds, was shot through the head, but recovered. He had seen a man whom he did not identify as Oswald (until many tribulations and eight months later) fleeing the scene of the Tippit murder, pistol in hand. Two months elapsed before Reynolds was questioned. He then told the FBI that he could not identify the fugitive as Oswald—although he had followed the man on foot for one block. Two days after the interview, Reynolds was shot through the head with a rifle and somehow survived. The prime suspect, Darrel Wayne Garner, was arrested by Dallas police, and later admitted he had made a call to his sister-in-law and "advised her he had shot Reynolds," but the charges were dropped because Garner had an alibi in the form of a filed affidavit by Nancy Jane Mooney, a strip-teaser who had been employed once at Jack Ruby's Carousel. Eight days later, Miss Mooney was arrested by the Dallas police for fighting with her roommate, "disturbing the peace." Alone in her cell— less than two hours after her arrival—Miss Mooney hanged herself to death, stated the police report.

Item: In July, 1964, Reynolds—who now owned a watchdog, took no walks at night and whose house was ringed with floodlights—testified that he now believed the man was Oswald. The Commission, in reporting the changed statements, omitted to mention at that precise point the attempt on Warren Reynolds' life.

Item: Information given by Nancy Perrin Rich to the Warren Commission that Jack Ruby brought money to a meeting between various agents and one U.S. army officer for smuggling guns to Cuba, and refugees out, was stricken from the record by the Warren Commission.

Item: A communication from the CIA in response four months late to a Commission inquiry: "an examination of Central Intelligence files has produced no information on Jack Ruby or his activities." Indeed. Which files? The Balkan files? The Ipcress file?

Item: William Whaley, Oswald's alleged cab driver, was killed in an automobile collision on December 18, 1965.

Item: Albert G. Bogard, an automobile salesman who tried to sell a car to a man calling himself Lee Oswald, was beaten up by some men after testifying and was sent to a hospital. The Warren Commission determined that the man buying the car could not be Oswald, but it did not inquire further. That someone might be impersonating Oswald before the assassination was a matter presumably without interest to the Commission.

Item: On Wednesday, January 22, a call came to J. Lee Rankin, general counsel for the Warren Commission. It was from the Attorney General of Texas who told Rankin he had learned that the FBI had an "undercover agent" and that the agent was none other than Lee Harvey Oswald. After much discussion that evening and much resolution that evening to conduct an independent investigation of this charge, the Commission nonetheless ended months later with this verdict: "nothing to support the speculation that Oswald was an agent, employee, or informant of the FBI," citing as its basis the testimony of Hoover, his assistant, and three FBI agents, plus reference to some affidavits signed by various other FBI agents. That proved to be the limit of the "independent investigation." There is nothing to show that the Attorney General was ever asked to give testimony as to how he heard the rumor.

So there we are left in this extraordinary case, and with this extraordinary Commission which looks into the psychic traumas of Oswald's childhood and Jack Ruby's mother's "fishbone delusion," but does not find out by independent investigation which Dallas cop might have let Jack Ruby into the basement, or whether Oswald could ever have been an undercover agent for the FBI, the CIA, the MVD, MI-5, Fair Play for Cuba, JURE, Mao Tse-tung, the John Birch Society, the Nazi Renaissance Party, or whether indeed an agent for all of them. The word of Mr. Hoover is good enough for the Commission. Mr. Hoover is of course an honorable man, all kneel.

No, what we are left with, after reading this book, is an ineradicable sense of new protagonists—the Dallas police—and behind them, opposed to them, for them, beneath them, on every side of them, another protagonist or protagonists. But first, and foremost, the police.

Criminals fall into two categories—good criminals and bad. A bad criminal is the simplest of people—he cannot be trusted for anything;

a good criminal is not without nobility, and if he is your friend, he is a rare friend. But cops! Ah, the cops are far more complex than criminals. For they contain explosive contradictions within themselves. Supposed to be law-enforcers, they tend to conceive of themselves as the law. They are more responsible than the average man, they are more infantile. They are attached umbilically to the concept of honesty, they are profoundly corrupt. They possess more physical courage than the average man, they are unconscionable bullies; they serve the truth, they are psychopathic liars (no cop's testimony is ever trusted without corroboration); their work is authoritarian, they are cynical; and finally, if something in their heart is deeply idealistic, they are also bloated with greed. There is no human creation so contradictory, so finally enigmatic, as the character of the average cop, and these contradictions form the keel of the great American mystery—who killed President Kennedy?

Yet even that oppressive sense of the Dallas police does not satisfy all the resonance of this mystery. For the question remains: was Oswald some sort of agent? We are getting uncomfortably close to the real heart of the horror. So it is time to offer a new hypothesis (or at least offer the beginnings of a working hypothesis), even to make it out of whole cloth without a "scintilla of evidence." Call it a metaphor. So I will say the odds are indeed that Oswald was an undercover agent. He was too valuable not to be. How many Americans, after all, knew Soviet life in the small intimate ways Oswald had known it? And indeed how was it possible for him to arrange his return? If you, sir, were the head of an espionage service, would you not wish to make Oswald work for you as the price of his return? If you were in Russian intelligence, would you not demand that he serve as some kind of Soviet agent in exchange for his release? A petty undercover agent for two services or three, a man without real importance or any sinister mission, he may still have been in so exposed a position that other services would have been attracted to him. Espionage services tend to collect the same particular agents in common, for most of their operations are only serious as a game, and you need a pocket board on which to play. Oswald may have been such a battered little pocket board.

Worked over and played over until he metamorphosed from playing board to harried rat, he may even have nibbled at the edge of 20 Dallas conspiracies. It was all comedy of the most horrible sort, but when Kennedy was assassinated, the espionage services of half the world may have discovered that one little fellow in Dallas was—all pandemonium to the fore—a secret, useless, little undercover agent who was on their private list; what nightmares must have ensued! What nightmares on the instant! What quiet little mind in some unknown council-of-war room, thinking of the exceptional definition of the game which might soon be given by a rat harried past the point of no return, a rat let loose in a courtroom, cried out in one or another Ivy League voice, "Well, can't something be done, can't we do something about this man?" and a man getting up saying, "See you in a while," and a little later a phone call made and another and finally a voice saying to our friend Ruby, "Jack, I got good news. There's a little job. . ." Is it so unreasonable that the tiny, metaphorical center of a host of espionage games should be killed by that precise intersection of the Mafia, the police, the invisible government, and the strip-tease business which Jack Ruby personified to the point.

No, there may have been no formal master plan to murdering Kennedy, just coincidences beyond repair and beyond tolerance, as if all things came together in a blaze of one huge existential moment, and nothing left but the wreckage, paranoia, and the secret bewildered sense in every cop, criminal, and agent of the Western Hemisphere that something beyond anyone's ken had occurred; now the evidence had to be covered. So Kennedy may have been killed by a conspiracy which was petty to its root; certainly he must have been killed by a very petty conspiracy with a few good Texas marksmen in it, but the power of several master conspiracies may then have been aroused to protect every last one of us against the possibility of discovery, against the truth, for no one in power in America knew what that truth was. Not any longer. So the case was fertilized and refertilized—it grew into a thicket. And the Commission was obliged to cut a tidy path through the thicket and this laid the ground for future scandals and disasters out of measure.

If in the next few years some new kind of commission does not establish in hard and satisfactory fashion the known and unknown boundaries of the case, then the way is open to a series of surrealistic political machinations. On that unhappy—let us hope impossible—day when America becomes a totalitarian government of the Left, Center or Right, the materials are now at hand for a series of trials of high government figures which will make the Moscow Trials of 1936 to 1938, following upon the assassination of Kirov, seem like modest exercises in domination, for the wealth of contradictory evidence now upon us from the rot-pile of Dallas permits any interpretation, any neat little path, to be cut through the thicket. From any direction. The Right may now convict the Left. The Left may now stifle the Right. The center may eat them both. The cannibal's pure totalitarianism is near.

So one would propose one last new commission, one real commission—a literary commission supported by public subscription to spend a few years on the case. There are major intellectuals in this country who are old now and have never been able to serve in American life. Not ever. It is time for that. Time for the best of intellectuals to serve. I would trust a commission headed by Edmund Wilson before I trusted another by Earl Warren. Wouldn't you? Would you not estimate that Dwight MacDonald, working alone, could nose out more facts and real contradictions than could 20 crack FBI investigators working together? Laugh, angels, pass the drinks, make this the game for the week. Pick your members of the new commission. It is very funny. And yet the small persisting national need is for a few men who can induce, from contradictory evidence, a synthesis. The solution to President Kennedy's murder will come not from legal or government commissions, but from minds deeply grounded first and last in the mysteries of hypothesis, uncorrupted logic, and metaphor. In the meanwhile, waiting for such a literary commission, three cheers for Mark Lane. His work is not without a trace of that stature we call heroic. Three cheers. Because the game is not yet over. Nor the echo of muffled drums. Nor the memory of the riderless horse.

THE MAN WHO WASN'T THERE

'GEORGE BUSH,' C.I.A. OPERATIVE

by Joseph McBride

The Nation, July 16/23 1988

Vice President George Bush's resume is his most highly touted asset as a candidate. But a recently discovered F.B.I. memorandum raises the possibility that, like many resumes, it omits some facts the applicant would rather not talk about: specifically, that he worked for the Central Intelligence Agency in 1963, more than a decade before he became its director.

The F.B.I. memorandum, dated November 29, 1963, is from Director J. Edgar Hoover to the State Department and is subject-headed "Assassination of President John F. Kennedy November 22, 1963." In it, Hoover reports that the Bureau had briefed "Mr. George Bush of the Central Intelligence Agency" shortly after the assassination on the reaction of Cuban exiles in Miami. A source with close connections to the intelligence community confirms that Bush started working for the agency in 1960 or 1961, using his oil business as a cover for clandestine activities.

Informed of this memorandum, the Vice President's spokesman, Stephen Hart, asked, "Are you sure it's the same George Bush?" After talking to the Vice President, Hart quoted him as follows: "I was in Houston, Texas, at the time and involved in the independent oil drilling business. And I was running for the Senate in late '63." "Must be another George Bush," added Hart.

Because the Vice President's response seemed something of a non-denial denial (he described what else he was doing rather than specifically denying C.I.A. involvement), I put the following queries to him via Hart:

Did you do any work with or for the C.I.A prior to the time you became its director?

If so, what was the nature of your relationship with the agency, and how long did it last?

Did you receive a briefing by a member of the F.B.I. on anti-Castro Cuban activities in the aftermath of the assassination of President Kennedy?

Half an hour later, Hart called me back to say that he had not spoken again to the Vice President about the matter, but would answer the questions himself. The answer to the first question was no, he said, and so he would skip number two. To the third, he repeated Bush's answer quoted above, but added that Bush had also said, "I don't have any idea of what he's talking about." However, when Bush's denial was read back to him, Hart said he preferred that it not be quoted directly, explaining, "It's a week old now, and I'm going off my notes." When I reminded him that we wanted to quote Bush directly, Hart said, "I am a spokesman. However you want to write it, the answer is no" regarding Bush's alleged 1963 involvement with the C.I.A.

"This is the first time I've ever heard this," C.I.A. spokesman Bill Devine said when confronted with the allegation of the Vice President's involvement with the agency in the early 1960s. "I'll see what I can find out and call you back." The next day Devine called back with the terse official response: "I can neither confirm nor deny." Told what the Vice President's office had said, and asked if he could check whether there had been another George Bush in the C.I.A., Devine seemed to become a bit nonplussed: "Twenty-seven years ago? I doubt that very much. In any event, we just have a standard policy of not confirming that anyone is involved in the C.I.A."

Richard Helms, who was a deputy director for plans at the agency in 1963, said the appearance of Bush's name in the memo "must have been some kind of misprint. I don't recall anyone by that name working for the agency. . . .He certainly never worked for me."

Hoover's memo, which was written to the director of the State Department's Bureau of Intelligence and Research, was buried among the 98,755 pages of F.B.I. documents released to the public in 1977 and 1978 as a result of the Freedom of Information Act suits. It was written to summarize the briefings given to Bush and Capt. William Edwards of the Defense Intelligence Agency by the F.B.I.'s W.T. Forsyth on November 23, the day after the assassination, when Lee Harvey Oswald was still alive to be interrogated about his connections to Cuban exiles and the C.I.A. The briefing was held, according to the F.B.I. director, because the State Department feared that "some misguided anti-Castro group might capitalize on the present situation and undertake an unauthorized raid against Cuba, believing that the assassination of President John F. Kennedy might herald a change in U.S. policy, which is not true." Hoover continues:

> Our sources and informants familiar with Cuban matters in the Miami area advise that the general feeling in the anti-Castro Cuban community is one of stunned disbelief and,

even among those who did not entirely agree with the President's policy concerning Cuba, the feeling that the President's death represents a great loss not only to the U.S. but to all of Latin America. These sources know of no plans for unauthorized action against Cuba.

An informant who has furnished reliable information in the past and who is close to a small pro-Castro group in Miami has advised that these individuals are afraid that the assassination of the President may result in strong repressive measures being taken against them, and although pro-Castro in their feelings, regret the assassination.

The substance of the foregoing information was orally furnished to Mr. George Bush of the Central Intelligence Agency. . .

(We attempted to locate William T. Forsyth, but learned that he is dead. Forsyth worked out of the Washington F.B.I. headquarters and was best known for running the investigation of the Rev. Martin Luther King Jr. in the Bureau's subversive control section. Efforts to locate Captain Edwards by press time were unsuccessful.)

Vice President Bush's autobiography, *Looking Forward*, written with Victor Gold (Doubleday, 1987), is vague to the point of being cryptic about his activities in the early 1960s, when he was running the Houston-based Zapata Off-Shore Company. ("Running an offshore oil company," he writes, "would mean days spent on or over water; not only the Gulf of Mexico but oceans and seas the world over.") But the 1972 profile of Bush in *Current Biography* provides more details of his itinerary in those years: "Bush travelled throughout the world to sell Zapata's oil-drilling services. Under his direction it grew to be a multimillion-dollar concern, with operations in Latin America, the Caribbean, the Middle East, Japan, Australia, and Western Europe." And according to Nicholas King's *George Bush: A Biography*, Zapata was concentrating its business in the Caribbean and off South America in the early 1960s, a piece of information that meshes neatly with the available data on Bush's early C.I.A. responsibilities.

Bush's duties with the C.I.A. in 1963—whether he was an agent, for example, or merely an "asset"—cannot be determined from Hoover's memo. However, the intelligence source (who worked with the agency in the late 1950s and through the 1960s) said of the Vice President: "I know he was involved in the Caribbean. I know he was involved in the suppression of things after the Kennedy assassination: There was a very definite worry that some Cuban groups were going to move against Castro and attempt to blame it on the C.I.A."

The initial reaction of Senator Frank Church, chair of the Senate Select Committee on Intelligence, to the firing of William Colby and the naming of Bush as Director of Central Intelligence in 1975 was to complain that it was part of a pattern of attempts by President Gerald Ford (a former member of the Warren Commission) to impede the Church committee's nearly concluded investigation into C.I.A. assassination plots, with which Colby was cooperating but which Ford was trying vainly to keep secret.

Bush's autobiography skips capriciously over the period of the early 1960s, easing back into coherence only when he makes his official entry into public life as chair of the Harris County, Texas, Republican Party in 1963-64, runs unsuccessfully for the Senate in 1964 against Democratic incumbent Ralph Yarborough, quits the oil business in 1966 and becomes the victorious candidate for Congress from Houston, serving two terms before losing the 1970 Senate race to Lloyd Bentsen, who had defeated Yarborough in the primary. Asked recently about Bush's early C.I.A. connections, Yarborough said, "I never heard anything about it. It doesn't surprise me. What surprised me was that they picked him for Director of Central Intelligence—how in hell he was appointed head of the C.I.A. without any experience or knowledge." Hoover's memo "explains something to me that I've always wondered about. It does make sense to have a trained C.I.A. man, with experience, appointed to the job."

Bush's appointment as the agency's director in 1975 was widely criticized because, as Bush writes, "Bill Colby, a professional in the intelligence field, was being replaced by a nonprofessional outsider—and a politician to boot." Senator Church commented: "It appears as though the White House may be using this important post merely as a grooming room before he is brought on stage next year as a vice-presidential running mate." Speaking against the appointment, Church said he knew of "no particular reason why [Bush] is qualified for the job; Bush himself characterized the appointment as a "real shocker." In his autobiography Bush points out, "I'd come to the CIA with some general knowledge of how it operated." His remark in the book that his "overseas contacts as a businessman" helped qualify him for the controversial appointment by President Nixon to the post of ambassador to the United Nations could also refer to previous C.I.A. experience. Agents often adopt the cover of a businessman. And business people have also served as informants for the agency, passing along information picked up on their travels.

Bush's C.I.A. connections might throw new light on his knowledge of the *contra* funding and supply operation, and his alleged knowledge of *contra* drug smuggling and the activities of General Noriega. It is worth noting in this context that, as Leslie Cockburn writes in *Out of Control*, "The anti-Castro C.I.A. team in Florida were already drawing attention to their drug-smuggling activities by 1963," and that it was Felix Rodriguez, the C.I.A., "alumnus who wore Che Guevara's watch and counted George Bush among his friends," who allegedly coordinated a $10 million payment to the *contras* by the Colombian cocaine cartel.

"Do the American people really want to elect a former director of the C.I.A. as their President?" Tom Wicker asked in *The New York Times* on April 29. "That's hardly been discussed so far; but it seems obvious that a C.I.A. chief might well be privy to the kind of 'black' secrets that could later make him—as a public figure—subject to blackmail. Given the agency's worldwide reputation for covert intervention and political meddling, moreover, one of its former directors in the White House certainly would be the object of suspicion and mistrust in numerous parts of the globe. And well he might be."

It was characteristic of George Bush, when sworn in as Director of Central Intelligence in 1976, to declare: "I am determined to protect those things that must be kept secret, and I am more determined to protect those unselfish and patriotic people who, with total dedication, serve their country, often putting their lives on the line, only to have some people bent on destroying this agency expose their names."

Bush has absorbed the code of the C.I.A. well, and he may feel that he is duty-bound to draw a veil of secrecy over his activities of the early 1960s. But now, as candidate for the presidency, he has a higher duty of honesty to the American people. If the man who would be President has a longstanding history of involvement in covert activities, then the people are entitled to know about it. Thus far Bush has refused to directly deny such involvement. Either he is intentionally misleading us, or he is a victim of mistaken identity. If it's the latter, he or President Reagan should instruct the gnomes of Langley to turn over the personnel records of the other George Bush. The claims of national security pale beside the overriding national interest in the truth.

Joseph McBride is the author of a biography of Frank Capra.

The Nation, August 13/20, 1988

by Joseph McBride

Where *was* George? The saga of Vice President George Bush's alleged involvement with the Central Intelligence Agency in 1963 grows curiouser and curiouser. In an article in *The Nation* of July 16/23 [" 'George Bush,' C.I.A. Operative"], I reported the discovery of a memorandum from J. Edgar Hoover, then director of the F.B.I. saying that "Mr. George Bush of the Central Intelligence Agency" had been briefed by the Bureau on November 23, 1963, about the reaction of anti-Castro Cuban exiles in Miami to the assassination of President John F. Kennedy.

After the article appeared, the C.I.A. put out a story that the George Bush mentioned in the memorandum was not Vice President George Herbert Walker Bush; he was George William Bush, who had worked for the agency in 1963-64. Although the agency claimed that his present whereabouts were unknown, I located George William Bush. He told me he was a coast and landing-beach analyst with the agency in those years, with the rank of GS-5, but that he definitely did *not* receive the F.B.I. briefing in 1963.

As reported in my article, Vice President Bush, through spokesman Stephen Hart, denied that he was the man referred to in the memo: "I was in Houston, Texas, at the time and involved in running the independent oil drilling business. And I was running for the Senate in late '63. I don't have any idea of what he's talking about." Hart added, "Must be another George Bush." When I first asked the C.I.A. about Hart's theory, it invoked its policy of neither confirming nor denying anyone's involvement with the agency.

But after the *Nation* story received wide coverage in the media, the C.I.A. evidently changed its mind. On July 19, agency spokeswoman Sharon Basso told the Associated Press that the Hoover memo "apparently" referred to George William Bush, who had worked in 1963 on the night watch at C.I.A. headquarters, which "would have been the appropriate place to have received such an F.B.I. report." She said this George Bush left the C.I.A. in 1964 to work for the Defense Intelligence Agency.

Why did the agency break with its longstanding policy of "neither confirm nor deny"? Basso said it believed "the record should be clarified." Another C.I.A. official told the A.P., "We put a lot of effort into this."

In fact, the latest C.I.A. release seems less a clarification than a strategic obfuscation. Hart of the Vice President's office put out the same data to Sarah Perl of *The Nation.* Both Perl and I called the Defense Intelligence Agency, and a spokesman confirmed that George William Bush had worked there between February 1964 and July 1965, performing the same duties that he had with the C.I.A., those of a civilian-grade government intelligence research specialist, leaving with the rank of GS-7. His last known address was 401 Cambridge Road, Alexandria, Virginia. A check of old Alexandria city directories showed that a George W. Bush, "emp US govt," did live at the Cambridge Road address in 1964 and subsequent years, and that he shared the house with Chester K. Bush of the U.S. Army. Current city records show that the deed to the house is in the names of Colonel Bush and his wife, Alice, and that a George William Bush at that address paid his automobile decal fee to the city this February.

I called Colonel Bush, who said he was George William Bush's father. He confirmed that his son had worked for the C.I.A. and still lived at the house, but said he could not come to the phone because he was ill; he asked me to call back the following evening. When I did, I spoke to George William Bush, who is 49 and works as a claims representative for the Social Security Administration. He said he had worked for the C.I.A. for about six months in 1963-64. When I read him the Hoover memo about the F.B.I. briefing, his response was, "Is that the other George Bush?"

While in the C.I.A., he had never received interagency briefings because he was "just a lowly researcher and analyst" and worked only with documents and photographs. He said he "knew neither one" of two people the memorandum mentions as also being briefed, William T. Forsyth of the F.B.I. and Capt. William Edwards of the D.I.A. "So it wasn't me," he said.

Bush said he left the C.I.A. because he was offered a job by the D.I.A. at a higher grade and salary. He said he stayed at the D.I.A. until he joined the Social Security Administration in January 1968. He professed he was "a little bit amazed, but not entirely surprised" that the C.I.A. and the D.I.A. had divulged his employment with them. "I didn't know they were at liberty to release all this," he said. "It was certainly without advance notice." Bush said he had not known of the story in *The Nation* about Vice President Bush's alleged 1963 ties with the C.I.A.

There was a minor discrepancy in this George Bush's account of his background: Although he told me that he went directly from the D.I.A. to the Social Security Administration in 1968, the 1967 Alexandria directory lists his occupation as city social worker. When I inquired about this job, Bush said he had held it for "about a year" before going to work for the Social Security Administration. City personnel records show that he joined the Alexandria Department of Public Welfare as a social worker trainee on August 2, 1965, rose to the rank of social worker on August 10, 1966. and left on January 12, 1968.

The Social Security Administration confirmed that Bush is currently employed in its Arlington, Virginia, office, and other points in Bush's story also checked out. He told me that before he joined the C.I.A. he had been living in Honolulu, where his father was stationed in the Army; that he had attended the University of Hawaii; and that he had worked for the Honolulu Department of Social Services and Housing. The Honolulu city directory for 1962-63 lists Chester K. Bush, "emp USARPAC," as residing at 1172 Koloa Street, and City of Honolulu personnel records confirm that George William Bush lived at that address while working as a trainee social worker for several months in 1963. The registrar's office of the University of Hawaii confirmed that he attended classes there from the fall of 1959 through the summer of 1961, graduating with a B.A. in history on September 1, 1961. The age he gave me checked out as well: According to school records, he was born on May 18, 1939, in White Plains, New York.

In the Alice in Wonderland world of intelligence there is always the possibility that people are not who they say they are. And there is that discrepancy about his job as a social worker, for which there could be a perfectly innocent explanation. At my request, Victor Navasky, editor of *The Nation*, called Bush again and had him repeat his story about his work with the C.I.A. in 1963-64 and his statement that he was not the man of the F.B.I. memorandum.

Why did the C.I.A. indicate that George William was the Bush in question without attempting to locate him first? Why did the media report the agency's version without checking further? And where was Vice President George Herbert Walker Bush on November 23, 1963? If he was working for the C.I.A. then, why hasn't he told us?

Joseph McBride's research has been supported by the Fund for Investigative Journalism and Essential Information. He is grateful for the assistance of Ruth O'Hara and Timothy D. McBride

Introduction

President Kennedy had made it clear that every American would be withdrawn from Vietnam before the end of 1964. These major excerpts from three messages by his successor, Lyndon B. Johnson, established the new administration's repudiation of Kennedy's policy of withdrawal. On May 18, 1964, Johnson acknowledged that there were 16,000 Americans in Vietnam. On July 28, 1965, he stated that he had that day increased American forces from 75,000 to 125,000. On February 23, 1966, he asserted that since the previous spring he had added 200,000 additional troops. Before the war ended, more than twice that number had served in Vietnam. These documents have been printed as *Documents on American Foreign Relations*, published for the Council on Foreign Relations by Harper and Row, for the years 1964, 1965, and 1966.

"WE WILL STAND IN VIETNAM":

NEWS CONFERENCE STATEMENT BY THE PRESIDENT,

JULY 28, 1965[1]

My fellow Americans: Not long ago I received a letter from a woman in the Midwest. She wrote,

> Dear Mr. President:
> In my humble way I am writing to you about the crisis in Vietnam. I have a son who is now in Vietnam. My husband served in World War II. Our country was at war, but now, this time, it is just something that I don't understand. Why?

Well, I have tried to answer that question dozens of times and more in practically every state in this Union. I have discussed it fully in Baltimore in April, in Washington in May, in San Francisco in June. Let me again, now, discuss it here in the East Room of the White House.

Why must young Americans, born into a land exultant with hope and with golden promise, toil and suffer and sometimes die in such a remote and distant place?

The answer, like the war itself, is not an easy one, but it echoes clearly from the painful lessons of half a century. Three times in my lifetime, in

---

[1]Text from *Department of State Bulletin*, August 16, 1965, pp 262-265. For Context see *The United States World Affairs*, 1965 pp. 231–232.

two world wars and in Korea, Americans have gone to far lands to fight for freedom. We have learned at a terrible and brutal cost that retreat does not bring safety and weakness does not bring peace.

It is this lesson that has brought us to Vietnam. This is a different kind of war. It is guided by North Vietnam, and it is spurred by Communist China. Its goal is to conquer the South, to defeat American power, and to extend the Asiatic domination of communism.

There are great stakes in the balance.

Most of the non-Communist nations of Asia cannot, by themselves and alone, resist growing might and the grasping ambition of Asian communism.

Our power, therefore, is a very vital shield. If we are driven from the field in Vietnam, then no nation can ever again have the same confidence in American promise or in American protection.

In each land the forces of independence would be considerably weakened and an Asia so threatened by Communist domination would certainly imperil the security of the United States itself.

We did not choose to be the guardians at the gate, but there is no one else.

Nor would surrender in Vietnam bring peace, because we learned from Hitler at Munich that success only feeds the appetite of aggression. The battle would be renewed in one country and then another country, bringing with it perhaps even larger and crueler conflict, as we have learned from the lessons of history.

Increase in U.S. Fighting Strength

What are our goals in that war-stained land?

First: We intend to convince the Communists that we cannot be defeated by force of arms or by superior power. They are not easily convinced. In recent months they have greatly increased their fighting forces and their attacks and the number of incidents. I have asked the Commanding General, General [William C.] Westmoreland, what more he needs to meet this mounting aggression. He has told me. We will meet his needs.

I have today ordered to Vietnam the Air Mobile Division and certain other forces which will raise our fighting strength from 75,000 to 125,000 men almost immediately. Additional forces will be needed later, and they will be sent as requested. This will make it necessary to increase our active fighting forces by raising the monthly draft call from 17,000 over a period of time to 35,000 per month, and for us to step up our campaign for voluntary enlistments.

THE PRESIDENT URGES INCREASED UNITED STATES AID: MESSAGE TO THE CONGRESS, MAY 18, 1964[2]

To the Congress of the United States:

Last January, in my budget message to the Congress, I pointed out that this budget made no provision for any major new requirements that might emerge later for our mutual defense and development program. I stated then that if such requirements should arise I would request prompt action by the Congress to provide additional funds.

That need has emerged in Vietnam. I now request that the Congress provide $125 million in addition to the $3.4 billion already proposed for foreign assistance; $70 million is required for economic and $55 million for military uses in Vietnam.

Since the 1965 budget was prepared, two major changes have occurred in Vietnam:

First, the Viet Cong guerrillas, under orders from their Communist masters in the north, have intensified terrorist actions against the peaceful people of South Vietnam. This increased terrorism requires increased response.

Second, a new government under Prime Minister [Nguyen] Khanh has come to power, bringing new energy and leadership and new hope for effective actions. I share with Ambassador [Henry Cabot] Lodge the conviction that this new government can mount a successful campaign against the Communists.

In March, Prime Minister Khanh declared his intention to mobilize his nation. This intention had now been confirmed by his new and enlarged budget for 1964. It provides for:

> Expanding the Vietnamese Army, Civil Guard, Self-Defense Corps, and police forces, and integrating their operations with political, economic, and social measures in a systematic clear-and-hold campaign.

---

[2]House Document 307, 88th Cong. 2nd ses.; text from *Department of State Bulletin,* June 8, 1964, pp 891-898.

Greatly expanding and upgrading the Vietnamese civil administrative corps to increase the Government's effectiveness and services at the village, district, and Province level. Local government capacity, responsiveness to popular needs, and initiatives are to be strengthened.

Better pay scales for the men and adequate budgets for the organizations engaged in this struggle of many fronts.

Manifold expansion of training programs, to provide teachers, health workers, agricultural, financial, and administrative staffs for the rural areas.

These and other measures, if promptly carried out, will require an increase of about 40 percent in Vietnam's domestic budgetary expenditures over the 1965 level—a far greater expansion of Vietnamese effort than was assumed in the assistance plans submitted in January. Under present circumstances, Vietnam's domestic revenues cannot be increased proportionately. Severe inflation resulting from a budget deficit would endanger political as well as economic stability, unless offsetting financial actions are to be taken. We expect the Vietnamese Government to take all possible self-help measures to deal with this problem internally, but substantial increases in economic assistance also will be required. We must share the increased costs of the greatly intensified Vietnamese effort.

Our more direct support of the expanded Vietnamese military and civil operations also must keep pace with the intensified Vietnamese effort. On the civil side—through AID's [Agency for International Development] counterinsurgency program—this means more fertilizer, medical supplies and services, repair parts and replacements for war-damaged railway rolling stock, school supplies and building materials, well-drilling equipment and teams to bring fresh water to the villagers, and enlarged advisory staffs in the Provinces.

On the military and paramilitary side, additional equipment, ammunition, training, and supplies will be needed as the organization and functioning of the armed forces improves. Additional aircraft, pilot training for the Vietnamese, and airfield improvements are required. Increased activity will require additional ammunition. Additional support equipment is required for all forces.

The vigorous decisions taken by the new Government of Vietnam to mobilize the full resources of the country merit our strongest support. Increased Communist terror requires it.

By our words and deeds in a decade of determined effort, we are pledged before all the world to stand with the free people of Vietnam. Sixteen thousand Americans are serving our country and the people of Vietnam. Daily they face the danger in the cause of freedom. Duty requires, and the American people demand, that we give them the fullest measure of support.

We have reviewed the entire budget for mutual defense and development programs once again to determine whether we can accommodate within it these added requirements. We cannot. In fact, recent events in Brazil and elsewhere may add to the economic programs originally planned. Military programs have already been cut to the bare minimum. We cannot respond to the new situation in Vietnam within the limits of the original budget proposal without unacceptable danger to our other basic security interests.

DEFINING THE AMERICAN COMMITMENT:
ADDRESS BY PRESIDENT JOHNSON ON RECEIVING
THE NATIONAL FREEDOM AWARD
NEW YORK, FEBRUARY 23, 1966[3]

Tonight in Vietnam more than 200,000 of your young Americans stand there fighting for your freedom. Tonight our people are determined that these men shall have whatever help they need, and that their cause, which is our cause, shall be sustained.

But in these last days there have been questions about what we are doing in Vietnam, and these questions have been answered loudly and clearly for every citizen to see and to hear. The strength of America can never be sapped by discussion, and we have no better nor stronger tradition than open debate, free debate, in hours of danger. We believe, with Macaulay, that men are never so likely to settle a question rightly as when they discuss it freely.

We are united in our commitment to free discussion. So also we are united in our determination that no foe anywhere should ever mistake our arguments for indecision, nor our debates for weakness.

So what are the questions that are still being asked?

First, some ask if this is a war for unlimited objectives. The answer is

---

[3]Text from *Weekly Compilation of Presidential Documents*, February 28, 1966, pp. 253-261. For the context, see *The United States in World Affairs*, 1966, pp. 40-41.

plain. The answer is "no." Our purpose in Vietnam is to prevent the success of aggression. It is not conquest; it is not empire; it is not foreign bases; it is not domination.

It is, simply put, just to prevent the forceful conquest of South Vietnam by North Vietnam.

Second, some people ask if we are caught in a blind escalation of force that is pulling us headlong toward a wider war that no one wants. The answer, again, is a simple "no." We are using that force and only that force that is necessary to stop this aggression. Our fighting men are in Vietnam because tens of thousands of invaders came south before them. Our numbers have increased in Vietnam because the aggression of others has increased in Vietnam. The high hopes of the aggressor have been dimmed and the tide of the battle has been turned, and our measured use of force will and must be continued. But this is prudent firmness under what I believe is careful control. There is not, and there will not be, a mindless escalation.

Third, others ask if our fighting men are to be denied the help they need. The answer, again, is and will be a resounding "no." Our great military establishment has moved 200,000 men across 10,000 miles since last spring.

These men have, and will have, all they need to fight the aggressor. They have already performed miracles in combat. The men behind them have worked miracles of supply, building new ports, transporting new equipment, opening new roads.

The American forces of freedom are strong tonight in South Vietnam, and we plan to keep them so. As you know, they are led there by a brilliant and a resourceful commander, Gen. William C. Westmoreland. He knows the needs of war and he supports the works of peace. And when he asks for more Americans to help the men that he has, his requests will be immediately studied, and, as I promised the nation last July, his needs will be immediately met.

INDEX

PETITION

In 1960 Senator John F. Kennedy was elected President of the United States. That election was an example of the continuing national experiment which marks our country as a democracy.

On November 22, 1963, President Kennedy was assassinated. In spite of doubts as to the identity of his killers, expressed through polls and surveys during the past quarter of a century by the vast majority of the American people, the United States government has refused to make available to its citizens files and documents about the murder and has declined to permit a full-scale investigation into the facts. Indeed, the government of the United States has instead authorized official efforts to discredit and demean those who have called for such inquiry. The government has, therefore, acted in a fashion which challenges the very democratic nature of our society.

We are neither "assassination buffs" nor "conspiracy theorists." We are the American people—lawyers, farmers, students, workers, teachers—and knowing that what is past is prologue are determined that our heritage be revealed so that we may better confront the future.

Accordingly, we call upon the leaders of the United States to respond to the will of the majority of the people by immediately releasing full copies of all documents previously sequestered regarding the death of John F. Kennedy and to appoint immediately as a special prosecutor a person of unquestioned integrity and commitment to the truth so that the final inquiry into the facts sought by the American people may be initiated. Let the rule of law be applied at last to this most tragic and important crime committed during our lives.

To this effort we pledge our names, our honor and our irrevocable commitment.

Please return to Citizen's Committee, P.O. Box 67, Prince Street Station, New York, N.Y. 10012